African environments and resources

L. A. Lewis

Clark University, Worcester, Massachusetts

L. Berry

Florida Atlantic University, Boca Raton, Florida

Boston
UNWIN HYMAN
London   Sydney   Wellington

Allen & Unwin, Inc.
8 Winchester Place, Winchester, MA 01890, USA

Published by the Academic Division of
Unwin Hyman Ltd
15-17 Broadwick Street, London W1V 1FP, UK

Allen & Unwin (Australia) Ltd,
8 Napier Street, North Sydney, NSW 2060, Australia

Allen & Unwin (New Zealand) Ltd in association with the
Port Nicholson Press Ltd,
60 Cambridge Terrace, Wellington, New Zealand

First published in 1988

Library of Congress Cataloging-in-Publication Data

Lewis, Laurence, 1939–
    African environments and resources.
Bibliography: p.
Includes index.
1. Natural resources – Africa. 2. Ecology – Africa.
3. Natural resources – Government policy – Africa.
4. Environmental policy – Africa. I. Berry, Leonard, 1930–
I. Title.
HC800.L48 1987   333.7′096   87-16751
ISBN 0–04–916010–9 (alk. paper)
ISBN 0–04–916011–7 (pbk.: alk. paper)

British Library Cataloguing in Publication Data

Lewis, L. A.
    African environments and resources.
1. Natural resources – Africa –
Management
I. Title   II. Berry, L.
333.7′096   HC800
ISBN 0–04–916010–9
ISBN 0–04–916011–7 Pbk

Set in 10 on 11 Bembo by Paston Press, Loddon, Norfolk
and printed in Great Britain by Biddles of Guildford

Preface

For the rest of this century and beyond, most Africans will derive their living from the productivity of the soil, water, and vegetation resources of the continent. Yet this continent, perhaps more than all others, has real physical constraints on the productivity of the environment. These limitations have been compounded by layers of human misuse and mismanagement.

In attempting to analyze the most important features of the African environment we have deliberately focused on those characteristics and issues which we judge to be most important in the current and future management of environmental resources. Issues of management of the environment are, therefore, woven into the fabric of the text.

However, this is not a comprehensive analysis of development problems in Africa. We are well aware of the complex combinations of historical, social, economic, and political factors which interacting upon the physical environment explain individual current African country and regional situations. We have attempted to acknowledge these issues where they are especially relevant to our themes but it is not practical to explore them in any great length in a book of this size. Rather we direct ourselves to the considerable task of analyzing the salient environment issues in this large and important continent and through this introduction present the background for more detailed studies and analysis.

This work is meant to be read by the nonprofessional in the field. It is hoped that it will also serve some of the overview needs of professionals in resource management, environmental conservation and development; and to students in these and other fields interested in Africa. The introductory chapters provide an overview of the environmental characteristics of the continent in an analysis of the geographic and environmental history of Africa. This we judge is important in providing the physical setting of the continent and in exploring some of the distinctiveness of Africa from other continental size areas. Africa does have distinctive characteristics of dryness, widespread plateau or plainlands topography, generally old and somewhat infertile soils, and peculiar river basin patterns. Some background to the evolution of the management of resources over this large continent is provided in Chapter 3 which particularly emphasizes the historical evolution of ethnic and national management systems.

In the next section of the book we take a broadly defined ecosystem approach. Here we identify and address the major environmental and resource issues of the tropical rainforest, the savanna – dry forest, the arid and semi-arid areas, the highlands, and the extratropical zones of northern and southern Africa. Each of these systems has distinctive patterns of natural occurrence and responses to change. The most dramatic changes occur when rainforest and highland ecosystems are inappropriately modified by human actions; the most widespread and in some respect currently most important transformations are those in the savanna and dry areas of the continent. Although these ecosystems are more resilient than the tropical rainforest or highland ecosystems, they are undergoing

iii

a process of desertification over wide areas, and it is difficult to create new management styles which could reverse this trend under current constraints.

The extratropical areas of northern Africa are discussed mostly in the context of coastal and urban problems; in southern Africa the unequal segregation of land along racial lines is taken as the main context in which to look at resource management.

In the last section of the book we take a thematic approach to a number of topics not adequately covered by the ecologic divisions. These include river basin issues, urban resource problems, and environment issues associated with mineral and industrial development. River basin management is a vital component of Africa's development and the physical factors influencing this development are discussed in Chapter 9. Urban growth is a significant factor of African development over the last twenty years and as towns and cities grow new kinds and new dimensions of resource management occur both within the city and in its hinterland. City growth has created a new and important set of environmental problems in Africa.

The general conclusions reached are indeed somewhat pessimistic. There are no quick or easy solutions to the complex of African environmental and resource-management problems. But based on a better understanding of the environment and of the management systems involved in the different parts of Africa, there are clear paths forward. It is vitally important that a beginning is made on addressing the issues raised here. It is timely that the direction be set and the first steps taken in that direction. If this book can help in the process of achieving better resource management in Africa, we will feel truly rewarded.

L. A. Lewis and L. Berry

Acknowledgements

In the preparation and writing of this book, we greatly benefited from the numerous experiences we had during our visits to Africa. Many of the individuals and organizations that helped shape our attitudes are listed in the references and bibliography. However, missing from these sources are the countless Africans living directly on the land. It is our conversations with these people, whose existence and well-being are intimately connected with the African environment, that have influenced us most.

Many individuals have helped us through the various stages of this publication. We were particularly fortunate in that the reviewers of the manuscript for the publisher made numerous constructive comments during the initial phases of writing. In addition, Mary Hartman, Jeanne Kasperson, and Ophelia Mascarenhas helped us locate information that would not otherwise have been found. Finally, enough praise cannot be given to Karen Shepardson, who not only typed the final manuscript from a rough draft but had to contend with both authors' handwriting.

We are grateful to the following individuals and organizations who have kindly given permission for the reproduction of copyright material (figure numbers in parentheses):

Elsevier Science Publishers (1.2, 1.7, 4.5, 4.11, 4.12, 4.14, 7.3(c), Table 6.1); Table 1.2 by permission of McGraw-Hill; Figures 1.3, 3.3, 3.6, 3.10, 4.3, 8.4, 8.10 and 11.1 reproduced from W. A. Hance, *The geography of modern Africa*, © 1964, 1975 Columbia University Press; Figure 1.11 by permission of Pergamon Press; Figure 2.1 reproduced from *Earth* 4th ed., by F. Press & R. Siever, W. H. Freeman and Company, © 1986; Heinemann Educational Books (2.2, 3.12, 6.9, 11.1); A. A. Balkema (2.3, 2.4, 2.10); D. Reidel Publishing Company (Table 2.6); *Journal of Arid Environments* (Table 2.7); Figure 2.14 reproduced from Rodhe & Virji, *Monthly Weather Review* **104**, 306–15, by permission of the American Meteorological Society; Figure 2.15 reproduced with permission from *Food and development in the semi-arid zone of East Africa*, by P. W. Porter, copyright © 1979 the Maxwell School of Citizenship and Public Affairs, Foreign and Comparative Studies Program, Syracuse University; Figure 3.1 adapted from Murdock, *The Geographical Review* **50**, 523–40, by permission of the American Geographical Society; Oxford University Press (3.2, 3.7, 4.15, 4.16, 4.17); University of Michigan Press (3.4); Methuen & Co (3.5); Figures 3.8 & 8.3 reproduced from *The careless technology*, by M. T. Farver & J. P. Milton by permission of Doubleday & Co, copyright © 1969, 1972 The Conservation Foundation and the Center for the Biology of Natural Systems, Washington University; Figures 4.1 & 4.2 from *Tropical forest ecosystems* © UNESCO-UNEP 1978; Figure 4.7 reproduced from *The climate near the ground*, by R. Geiger, by permission of Harvard University Press; Figures 4.13, 6.2, 9.6 & 9.7 reproduced from *The inland waters of tropical Africa*, by L. C. Beadle, by permission of Longman; Table 5.7 reproduced from *Village water supply*, by R. J. Saunders & J. J. Warford, published for the World Bank by Johns Hopkins University Press; *Third World Planning Review* (5.10); Hodder & Stoughton Educational (6.4, 6.7); Table 6.4 reproduced from J. M. Kalms in *Soil conservation and management in the humid tropics*, D. J. Greenland & R. Lal (eds), copyright © 1975 John Wiley & Sons Ltd; Figure 6.5, British Crown

ACKNOWLEDGEMENTS

Copyright, reproduced by permission of the Controller of Her Britannic Majesty's Stationery Office; Figure 6.6 by permission of Elsevier Science Publishers and Hodder & Stoughton Educational; Ministere de la Cooperation de la Republique Française (7.3a, 7.3b, 7.5, 10.6); Figure 8.2 reproduced from Boxer, *Science* **202**, 586, copyright © 1978 the American Association for the Advancement of Science; Regional Studies Association (8.7); *Zimbabwe Agricultural Journal* (8.8, 8.9); *Geografiska Annaler* (9.11); Longman (10.1, 10.8); The Scandinavian Institute of African Studies (Table 10.1); Figure 10.2 from *An atlas of African history*, by J. D. Fage, by permission of Edward Arnold; Figures 10.4 & 10.5 from *Lagos – the development of an African city* by A. B. Aberibigbe, by permission of Longman Nigeria Ltd; Europa Publications Ltd (Table 11.1).

L.A.L. and L.B.

Contents

CONTENTS

CONTENTS

List of tables

1 African environments and resources: an overview

Introduction to the African environment

With over 75 percent of its area between the tropics, Africa has a wide range of environmental settings that all differ strikingly from the environments that predominate in Europe and North America. In addition, a large proportion of the lands beyond the tropics are extremely dry. Because of the different environments, both human and physical, on the continent, Africa often is misunderstood. There are numerous broad generalizations, yet few are valid when examined within the diverse realities of the continent. This situation often arises because a single specific case has been extrapolated to represent the whole of the continent.

General climate and vegetation

Figure 1.1 is a generalized map of Africa which delimits areas having adequate precipitation. The formula used to develop this map separates areas with adequate soil moisture for plant growth for much of the year (less than one), areas with adequate moisture for some of the year (between one and two), and areas which have low levels of water availability throughout the year (greater than two). Only a relatively small part of the continent – less than 20 percent – lies in the first zone (humid). A major part of the landmass of Africa thus has either short-term or long-term water deficiencies. This one fact may be the single most important thing to remember about Africa; for the most part, it is a dry continent.

About 90 percent of Africa is classified as having climates which are tropical in character. Average annual temperatures are relatively high over most of the land, exceptions occurring at the northern and southern edges of the continent and at high elevations. However, important seasonal and diurnal temperature changes occur throughout the continent. But, with most of Africa situated in the tropics, the crucial climatic component that divides one season from another is precipitation. Thus, more often than not, the inhabitants divide one part of the year from another into wet and dry seasons.

As this study is concerned with an area over 30,000,000 km^2, almost 20 percent of the Earth's land surface, it is essential to subdivide the continent into areas of roughly similar environmental characteristics. Using Thornthwaite's classification as a basis, Africa is divided into about 12 generalized climatic

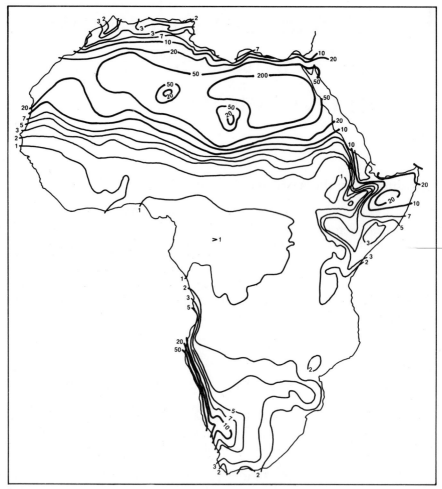

Figure 1.1 Annual moisture characteristics of Africa (from UN Conference on Desertification 1977):

$$\text{dryness ratio} = \frac{\text{mean annual net radiation}}{(\text{mean annual precipitation}) \times (\text{latent heat of vaporization})}.$$

units* (Fig. 1.2). About 37 percent of Africa's total area, according to this classification (Fig. 1.2, category II), is arid; about 13 percent is semi-arid (category IIA, III) and about 23 percent subhumid (category IV, VIII). Once again, moisture is identified as a crucial environmental factor.

*It must be noted that the boundaries that appear on climatic figures, except where topographic features cause sharp breaks, do not represent sharp lines but mark zones where one climatic region grades almost imperceptibly into another.

Vegetation and climate are closely related, except where human activity has significantly altered the plant cover. The basic natural vegetation types found in Africa are characteristic of the tropical, subtropical, and montane conditions. Figure 1.3, a generalized African map of basic natural vegetation types, shows that 8 important categories exist throughout the continent, though they are all subsets of 5 major sets:

(1) the tropical rainforests which are found in areas having rainfall in excess of 1500 mm with no drought period;
(2) the savannas which are found in areas having three to eight months of drought, with heavy rains at other times;
(3) desert vegetation, which is found when rainfall averages less than 200 mm per year;

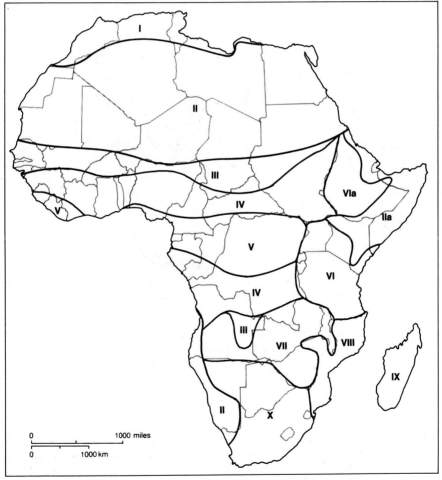

Figure 1.2 Major climatic zones of African climates (from Griffiths 1972).

3

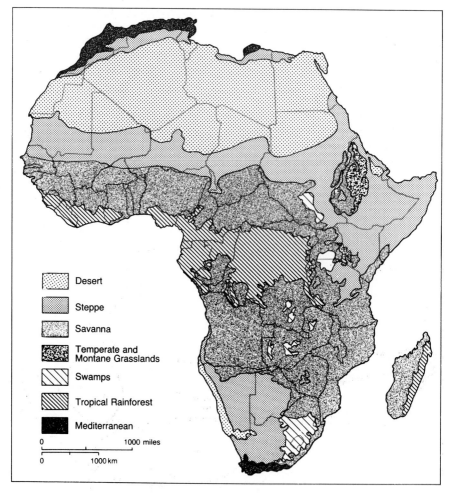

Figure 1.3 Primary African vegetation zones (from Hance 1975).

(4) mountain vegetation, which is found where elevation has lowered temperatures and rainfall is ample – generally in belts between 1500 and 2300 m;

(5) the scrubland categories which exist in zones having nine or ten months of
near drought.

Surface water

Because a large part of Africa has dry climates, only a small percentage of
precipitation that enters into the river systems flows into the ocean. Table 1.1
provides comparative data for the world's major landmasses. Asia, Australia,
Greenland, and Africa all have low levels of runoff per unit area. Europe, North
America, and South America have much higher levels.

4

Table 1.1 World distribution of runoff.

Location	Atlantic slope Area (1000 km²)	Runoff (cm)	Pacific slope Area (1000 km²)	Runoff (cm)	Regions of interior drainage Area (1000 km²)	Runoff (cm)	Total land area Area (1000 km²)	Runoff (cm)
Europe (including Ireland)	7,959	29.0	—	—	1,712	10.9	9,671	26.1
Asia (including Japanese and Philippine islands)	11,981	16.2	16,312	29.1	13,657	1.7	42,271	17.0
Africa (including Madagascar)	13,235	35.6	5,462	21.8	11,113	1.8	29,811	20.3
Australia (including Tasmania and New Zealand)	—	—	4,232	13.9	3,732	0.6	2,964	7.6
South America	15,646	47.5	1,318	44.5	987	6.6	17,977	44.9
North America (including West Indies and Central America)	14,657	27.4	4,862	48.5	834	1.1	20,442	31.5
Greenland and Canadian Archipelago	3,882	18.0	—	—	—	—	3,882	18.0
Malayan Archipelago	—	—	2,621	160.0	—	—	2,621	160.0
Total or average	67,356	31.5	35,250	39.3	32,035	2.1	134,641	26.7

Another indicator of dryness is the percentage of a continent with interior drainage. About 24 percent of the world's land surface has interior drainage – most in Asia, Africa, and Australia. Within Africa, 52 percent of its total area is without permanent streams or has interior drainage. Included in this category is the Sahara, the Lake Chad Basin, portions of the eastern Rift Valley including Lake Turkana, the Kalahari, and the Namib Desert. In spite of the overall dryness, there are a number of large rivers with huge drainage discharges. The biggest, the Zaire (Congo) River, drains the most extensive area of tropical rainforest on the continent. Most other major rivers begin in wetter areas, either mountainous or equatorial moist zones, and flow across drier zones on their way to the sea. Dry season use of these waters is an important potential (Fig. 1.4). The

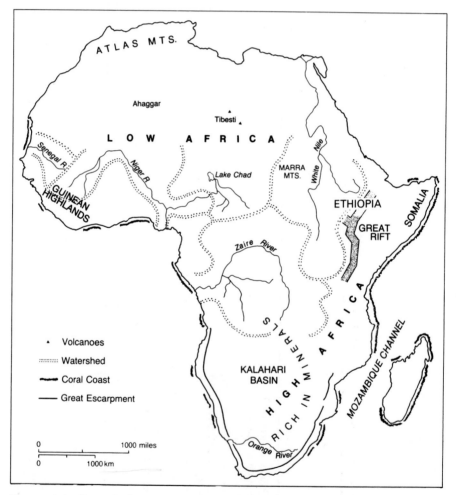

Figure 1.4 General elevation, major river basins, and areas of internal drainage. "High" Africa areas approximately 1000 m above mean sea level (from Grove 1978).

6

Table 1.2 Drainage discharge.

Name	Average annual discharge (cms)	Drainage area (km^2)	Length (km)
Amazon (South America)	203,904	7,180,000	6,250
LaPlata–Parana (South America)	79,296	3,103,000	3,920
Zaire* (Congo, Africa)	56,640	3,690,000	4,600
Yangtze (Asia)	21,806	1,943,000	4,900
Ganges–Brahmaputra (Asia)	20,022	2,055,000	2,880
Mississippi–Missouri (North America)	17,558	3,221,000	6,230
Yenisei (Asia)	17,275	2,590,000	5,680
Mekong (Asia)	16,992	906,000	4,160
Orinoco (South America)	16,992	1,476,000	2,560
Mackenzie (North America)	12,745	1,766,000	4,040
Nile* (Africa)	11,894	3,350,000	6,485
St Lawrence (North America)	11,328	1,463,000	3,440
Volga (Europe)	9,912	1,533,000	3,720
Lena (Asia)	9,204	3,027,000	4,575
Ob (Asia)	—	2,590,000	4,480
Danube (Europe)	8,921	900,000	2,760
Zambesi* (Africa)	7,080	1,330,000	3,520
Indus (Asia)	8,500	965,000	2,720
Amur (Asia)	—	2,040,000	4,640
Niger* (Africa)	—	1,512,000	4,160
Columbia (North America)	6,655	670,000	1,940
Yukon (North America)	4,250	855,000	3,680
Huang (Asia)	3,285	1,015,000	4,320
Limpopo* (Africa)	2,870	1,070,000	1,760
São Francisco (South America)	—	652,000	2,900
Euphrates (Asia)	—	1,114,000	2,720
Senegal* (Africa)	775	235,000	
Murray–Darling (Australia)	370	1,075,000	3,752

Source: Chow (1964).

* African Rivers.

Zaire River, which drains the primary humid zone of Africa (category "1", Fig. 1.1), is clearly the African river with the greatest discharge (Table 1.2). It is also the third largest river in the world in terms of annual discharge. The Nile has the next highest discharge, but its flow is only about 20 percent that of the Zaire, though the Nile is by some measures the world's longest river system. The Niger, Zambezi, Orange, Limpopo, and Senegal are other major rivers on a world scale (Table 1.2). Except for the Zaire, all African rivers show strong seasonal fluctuations in flow, reflecting the basic precipitation patterns. For example, the Nile at Khartoum has a discharge of less than 100 million m^3/per day in June and about 600 million m^3/per day in August and September (Fig. 1.5); the Niger at Lokoja has a May–June average flow of only 3,000 m^3/s and an average October flow of 19,000 m^3/s (Fig. 1.6).

7

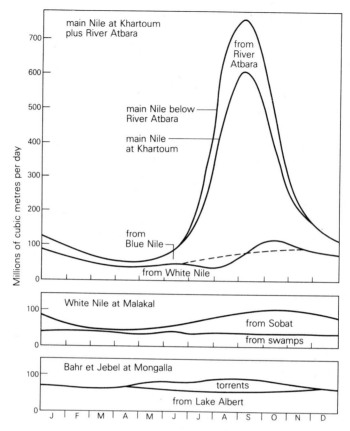

Figure 1.5   The seasonal discharges of the Nile (from Grove 1967).

Interrupting most of the important African rivers are lakes, either natural or man-made. Lakes are an important feature of the African inland water systems. Lake Nasser, which is situated in an extremely arid area, has stopped the flooding rhythms on the lower Nile and actually decreased the river's average discharge because of high evaporation losses. Most of the natural lakes are found in eastern Africa where faulting and warping movements associated with the Rift Valley, along with dams, affect their river flows. The rift floor lakes are usually deep, long, and narrow; for example, Lake Tanganyika is over 1400 m in depth. Some, like Naivasha, Majadi, and Managara, are very shallow. Lake Victoria and Lake Kioga are examples of shallow lakes formed by warping of the land surface. Other lakes, such as Lake Chad and Lake Okavango, are in dry areas of inland drainage.

Because of the nature of the African topography and the seasonal nature of river discharge, in most areas navigable waterways are extremely limited. In North Africa only the Nile is a major water transport route; in West Africa the lower and middle Niger is utilized. The Gambia could be used as a waterway, but, as its lower reach is outside the country where it primarily could be used, Senegal has developed overland transport instead. The remaining rivers are usually navigable for only short distances. In East Africa some of the lakes are important for transportation, especially Lake Victoria.

The African landscape

Africa is an old continent. Since the breakup of Gondwanaland about 200 million years ago, Africa has been relatively stable. This means that only small areas have been affected by major tectonic events, though rift valley formation in the east and localized volcanic activity are important. The continental surface has apparently been warped, resulting in a broad pattern of basins and swells which have helped to form the outline of the river drainage basins, including inland drainage. In the wide diversity of land features, some generalizations are

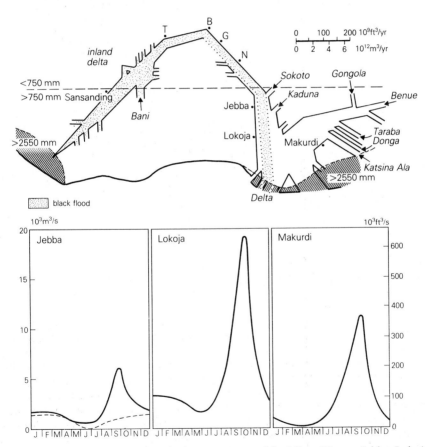

Figure 1.6 The average annual discharge patterns of the Niger River at Jebba, Lokoja, and Makurdi in Nigeria. T, Tombouctou, Timbuktu; B, Bourem; G, Gao; N, Niamey (from Grove 1978).

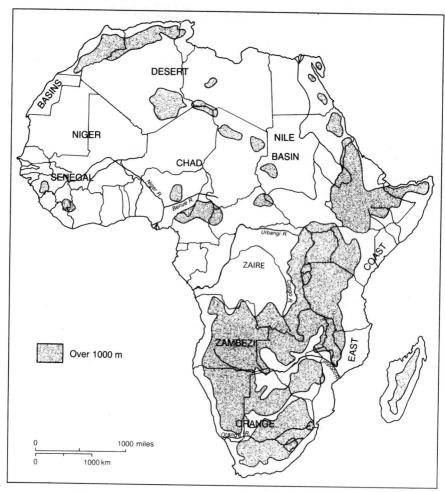

Figure 1.7 Major rivers in Africa (from Griffiths 1972).

possible. Africa is a continent dominated by plateaus and elevated plains (Fig. 1.7). The highest plateau occurs in Ethiopia, an area where major uplifting has occurred; other plateau areas are found in eastern and southern Africa, including Angola, and in the Zaire Basin. West Africa is largely a zone of elevated plains which are broken by isolated plateaus such as the Jos and Bamenda Highlands. The two major rift valleys of East Africa are major world-scale features, that is they are easily detected on globes and other small-scale maps and images. The associated volcanoes are also important landscape features. The highest, Mount Kilimanjaro, reaches over 5500 m above sea level.

The overall landform patterns of Africa present disadvantages to economic development. First, coastal zones are narrow (averaging about 32 km in width), a particularly important factor when it is remembered that about 70 percent of

10

the world's population live on lowlands within 80 km of the sea. Usually the African coastal zones are backed by steep scarps dividing the coast from the uplands (Fig. 1.8). Because of this, African rivers are marked by rapids close to the coast and are difficult transportation routes to the interior. The rift zones also present large local relief barriers. In addition, most plateaus are divided into high basins, with rims that are dissected into rugged, often mountain-like topography. The Ethiopian massif, with high volcanic peaks and deeply dissected plateaus, is one of the most difficult land communication areas in the world. Partly as a result of the topography in Africa, road and railroad construction costs are generally quite high. Africa also has the shortest coastline in relation to area of any continent. The generally straight coasts present few natural harbors,

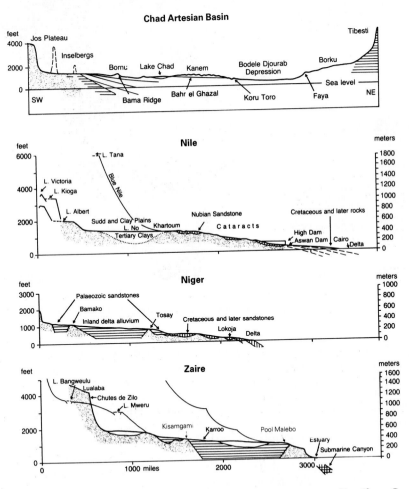

Figure 1.8 Cross-sections and selected African longitudinal river profiles (from Grove 1978).

11

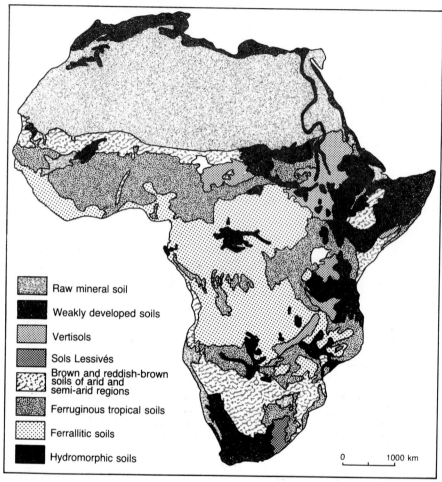

Raw mineral soil

Weakly developed soils

Vertisols

Sols Lessivés

Brown and reddish-brown soils of arid and semi-arid regions

Ferruginous tropical soils

Ferrallitic soils

Hydromorphic soils

0   1000 km

Figure 1.9   The major soils of Africa (from D'Hoove 1964).

and where these exist navigation is often handicapped by offshore bars, shallow water, and shifting channels.

Finally, the tropical location of Africa meant that it was not directly affected by recent glaciation, except in a few mountain areas. Thus most of its soils are generally old and are not rich in soluble minerals. For example, the soils of the savanna do not compare favorably in terms of fertility and structure with the grassland soils of the middle latitudes (Fig. 1.9). There are proportionately fewer young, rich alluvial soils than on any other continent. But good soils do exist on the Nile floodplain and delta, on the volcanic uplands, the Mediterranean lowlands, and the Veldt in South Africa. To a far greater degree than in Europe and North America, the soil resource of Africa requires careful management if it is to be kept productive.

Conceptions and misconceptions about the African environment

For a long period of time, Africa has been viewed by Westerners as a rather uniform, little-known place. Terms such as "The Dark Continent" were common in the 19th century because little was known of its detailed geography. The heroic explorations of Livingstone and Stanley in eastern and central Africa were, after all, little more than 130 years ago. The images of "single place" and "uniformity" in the popular mind have spilled over into this century and, until quite recently, Africa appeared to retain its "unknown" status for many people. Fortunately, scientific understanding of the African environment has increased rapidly, but echoes of the various concepts of Africa still linger, and it is useful to review these perceptions and prejudices to make clear the background to our current patterns of thought. The diversity of simplistic concepts includes the concept of the "limitless" fertile tropics, the notion of Africa as a desert, Africa as a home of exotic wild life, Africa as an unhealthy disease-ridden area, and the more recent perception of Africa as a continent "devastated" by "improper" land use. It would be hard to deny any one of these as applying to a part of the continent at some point in time, but equally absurd to relate any to the whole of the area.

The concept of fertility

Among the earliest general concepts of Africa was the pervasive one of a tropical forested land. The tropical forest with its apparent lush fertility acted as the catalyst for the viewpoint that the African environment was rich, with unlimited agricultural potential. Even the telephone poles were thought to send off roots. As seen in Figure 1.10, fences can sprout in some conditions. This perception evolved in part because the West African coast and the Zaire Basin, both situated in the rainforest zone, were the location of early European links with Africa. These areas are clearly not indicative of the general vegetation characteristics of the continent. However, impressions of the rainforest and explorers' scientific accounts of the richness and diversity of the fauna and flora, similar to those of South America, appeared to initiate the image of great wealth and fertility. The rainforest attracted much early scientific attention at the expense of other areas, reinforcing the early impression of its ubiquity.

Africa as a desert

In sharp contrast to the image just described is another obviously contradictory one: the image of the continent as a desert. This was equally pervasive and seems to be derived from the British, French, and German experiences in the latter 19th century and the early 20th century. The desert image may have come from the reporting of the "River War"* in Sudan or the Boer War in South Africa, because both countries are in arid and semi-arid parts of the continent. This

---

* The war along the Nile in Sudan when the British recaptured Sudan from the Mahdi. Winston Churchill was a war reporter whose newspaper accounts were widely read.

Figure 1.10   Sprouting fences just outside Lagos, Nigeria.

image was maintained through World War II with the African campaign involving British, German, Italian, American, and many other nationalities in the Egyptian, Algerian, Libyan, and Tunisian deserts. The French perception perhaps had been long reinforced by the involvement of the French with Algeria and the dry parts of West Africa. The desert image included the "typical" sand-dune desert with desert storms and no water – surprisingly since the areas mentioned above are not generally characterized by sand-dunes. The most arid parts of North Africa – dry, hot, bare, waterless – are a strong contrast to those images of the tropical rainforest.

Africa as an area of insect and waterborne disease

Another perception of the environment in Africa has been one of the prevalence of disease often associated with insects – river blindness, malaria, yellow fever, and cholera were, to some, "African" diseases. Certainly in the early days of European contact with West Africa there were high death rates associated with tropical diseases and general unsanitary conditions. These two factors were compounded often by the Europeans overdressing for a variety of reasons. This resulted in attacks of heat exhaustion and pneumonia. An early song on the West African coast spoke about "forty men in, and one came out", and the truth was that in the existing unsanitary conditions, hardly helped by the dress of the Europeans of that time, many who arrived did not depart. Environmental disease is still an important problem in Africa, for Africans more than for the generally well-fed and cared for Europeans. Insect-related diseases and malnutrition are a major impediment to human well-being in many areas. Figure 1.11

14

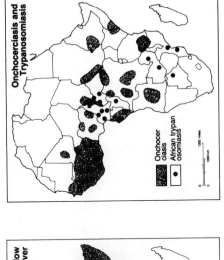

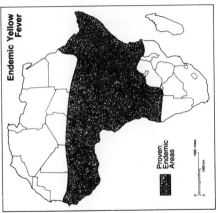

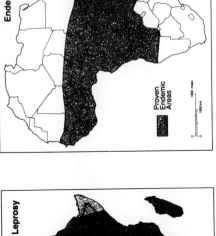

Figure 1.11(a) Distribution within Africa of: onchocerciasis and trypanosomiasis, yellow fever, leprosy (from Environmental Development Action 1981).

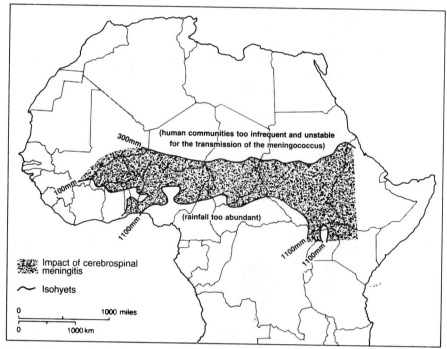

Figure 1.11(b) Distribution within Africa of: cerebrospinal meningitis (from Environmental Development Action 1981).

shows a set of maps illustrating the distribution of some of the most common diseases or health hazards on the continent. It is clear from this and the statistics of disease in Africa that for some areas these issues are much less important. Perhaps because of this, the early impression of an area with high health risks for Europeans has persisted to some extent, though it has been much modified by the settlement of Europeans in central, southern, and eastern Africa and by the spread of modern living conditions. The problems of the poorer people remain.

Africa as a game reserve

Another feature of Africa to catch the imagination of the West was the game-rich areas of East and South Africa. This remains, especially for the tourist, a strong current image. Many visitors arrive at Nairobi or Johannesburg airports and spend much of their time in the magnificent game sanctuaries of those areas. General literature, and schoolbooks with beautiful illustrations, reinforce the image of Africa as an area where wild animals of the savanna dominate the landscape. Herds of wildebeeste, elephant, and antelope move across empty plains. Television features on Africa often devote about 50 minutes of superb photography to wildlife, including fish and frogs, and 3 minutes to the people in the area, who are depicted almost as intruders on an otherwise idyllic natural scene. Yet today vast areas of Africa are almost totally devoid of game animals,

16

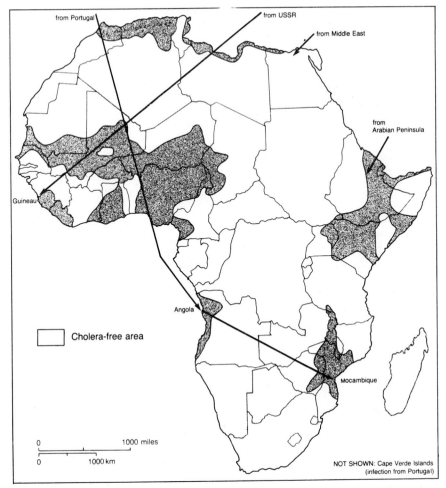

Figure 1.11(c) Distribution within Africa of: cholera (from Environmental Development Action 1981).

and even in existing areas many animals appear to be endangered species. Figure 1.12 shows the actual extent of game parks in East Africa, the area with the largest parks, emphasizing graphically the relatively small proportion of African continent set aside in this way.

Africa as a devastated continent

It is interesting and startling to compare the earlier view of a continent of great fertility with some current assessments of Africa. De Vos (1975) conveys the general message of a devastated continent. Both De Vos and other recent general reviews, such as Eckholm (1976), depict Africa as a place with some diversity, but the overwhelming general impression portrayed is one of ecological devasta-

17

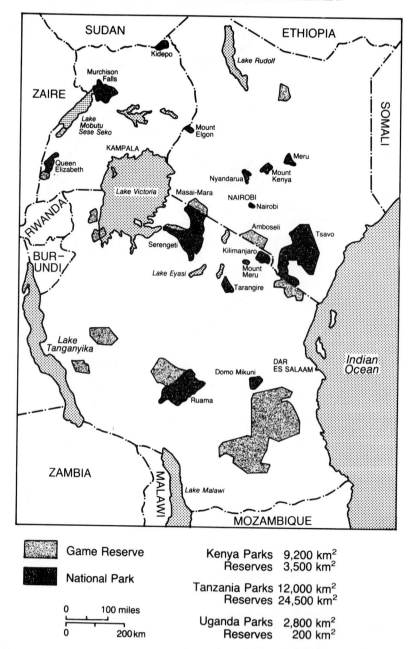

Figure 1.12 Game parks and reserves in East Africa (based on map in Nairobi office of the East African Wildlife Organization).

Kenya parks	9200 km²	Tanzania parks	12,000 km²	Uganda parks	2800 km²
reserves	3500 km²	reserves	24,500 km²	reserves	200 km²

tion. The various authors cite the Sahel, loss of forest land, desertification, decreasing population of some species of wildlife, and ubiquitous soil erosion as all indicating deteriorating environments in Africa. The general picture is that the continent is a place with severe environmental problems, potential productivity becoming lower with each year, and that a generally fragile environment is being undermined.

Is Africa a fertile forest, a barren desert, a devastated landscape, an idyllic game reserve, or a plain of insect and waterborne illnesses and disease? Although the different images have had their vogue, the common factor is that outsiders have tended to see Africa as a continent of uniformity; all too often the actual complexities of Africa are collapsed into a single simplistic image.

In the other chapters in this book we shall demonstrate that the diversity of environments belies a single static viewpoint. 'Parts of Africa may today exemplify each one of those images; many other parts will fit none of them. Africa defies simple definitions and characterization; its environment is complex, dynamic, and worthy of a more sophisticated approach. Common problems are found, but the different environmental and developmental context of the ecologic and geographic regions demands particular approaches to these problems and their solution.

Introduction to development issues in Africa

Historical overview

By the 19th century, Africans had long been organized into a large number of communities. With the possible exception of a few small groups, such as Khoi (Kalahari) and Twa (Zairean rainforest), the economies of true subsistence had largely disappeared. In eastern Sudan and the Nile Valley, state-forming processes began around 3000 BC; in tropical Africa, states began to take shape during the first 500 years AD. Thus states are far from a new phenomena in Africa (Fig. 1.13). However, the state boundaries and nations that exist today have little resemblance to the political development model that was evolving prior to the colonial period (Fig. 1.14). Boundaries were largely delimited by the colonizing European powers and were independent of existing human–political considerations, as well as environmental–economic realities. Historical human groupings are often today separated between two or more nations. For example, the Somali people today are divided among four political units: Ethiopia, Somali, Kenya, Djibouti. The constraints placed on contemporary African nations by these inherited boundaries still have a major impact on the population, economies, and environments of modern Africa.

Although precise data are not available, it is likely that Africa had a steady, albeit slow, population growth until 1900 (Table 1.3). The population of the continent in 1900 is estimated to have been between 115 and 155 million. After the colonial intrusion, population growth appears to have been checked, perhaps through a combination of circumstances, including the impact of rinderpest in East Africa; and around 1900, a population decline occurred, especially in equatorial Africa. Beginning around the 1930s, population growth

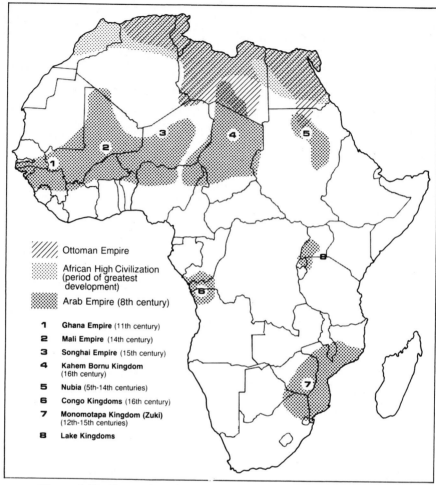

Figure 1.13 Former kingdoms and empires in Africa (from Hoy 1978).

Table 1.3 Growth in population of Africa in millions (estimated).

	1650	1750	1800	1850	1900
Africa	100	106	107	111	133
world	543	791	978	1260	1630

	1930	1950	1971	2000
Africa	164	222	354	865
world	2069	2513	3706	6920[a]

[a]Recent 1982 demographic projections suggest a significantly lower figure for year 2000.

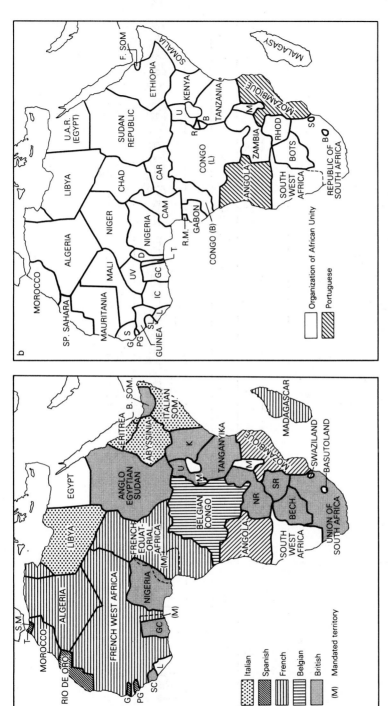

Figure 1.14 Africa political units: (a) 1939, (b) 1966 (from Grove 1978).

Table 1.4 Price of tractor imports and cotton.

Tractor imports (US$ per tractor).

Country	1979	1978	1977	1976	1975	1974	1973	1972	1971	1970	1969
Kenya	15,866	12,395	10,008	8,957	7,644	6,415	6,361	6,825	6,450	4,441	4,350

Cotton (US$ per 100 kg)

Country	1979	1978	1977	1976	1975
Kenya[a]	32	30	28	20	18

Sources: Government of Kenya (1979). *Republic of Kenya Statistical Digest,* vol. 17 (2). Ministry of Economic Planning and Community Affairs.
Note: These values are for seed cotton, AR grade. To obtain values for lint cotton (seeds removed) use a 34 percent conversion rate.

[a] These values are for seed cotton, AR grade. To obtain values for lint cotton (seeds removed) use a 34 percent conversion rate.

again took place, perhaps partly due to changes in colonial policy, as well as to the beginnings of the diffusion of medical care and public health programs. Around 1950, there was a more rapid growth rate, and annual rates of 2–3 percent became established. In specific countries, such as Kenya, the annual growth rate is as high as 4 percent. Today in excess of 500 million people live in Africa. These peoples live within nations whose boundaries were established largely independently of the African situation, with little regard to economic, human, and physical criteria.

Prior to the colonial period, "community economies" existed with complex economic systems dealing with food and other crop production, handicrafts, and trade. Trade was mostly in local or regional frameworks, though some very long distance trading networks were in place. In these indigenous economies, inequalities in wealth, states, and levels of well-being clearly existed within African society. Colonialism to a large degree took advantage of existing structures and altered them to meet the needs of the home economies of the colonizing powers. One fundamental change that was initiated during the colonial period and persists today was the creation of a new trading system through the metropolitan demand for raw materials of plant, animal, and mineral origin. Zones of mineral and cash crop production for export were established, but the larger remaining areas of Africa were placed in the rôle of supplying cheap labor and food to support the existence of this export economy.

Interestingly, the profitable relationships between the export and subsistence economies had to a large degree disappeared around 1950. By the time the African nations became independent, prices of export commodities were at a low level and export earnings were too small to meet the increasing costs of necessary capital goods. The pricing situation has in general continued to move against the African countries. It now takes four times more cotton to pay for a tractor than it did in 1969 (Table 1.4). Since independence almost all countries have been faced with the need to reorient their economies at the same time as facing the demands of a rapidly growing population. Even to stand still economically meant that the national resource base would need to be more heavily taxed, placing ever increasing stresses on the environment. The expansion of population into new areas, the use of new technologies, and the growth of urban areas could only exacerbate these stresses unless the constraints of the environment were understood and accounted for.

Resource utilization

Today every nation needs to utilize its national and human resources in a rational manner if the national goal is to improve the quality of life of its inhabitants for the future as well as the present. For a variety of reasons, in Africa this goal must be met to a very large degree within the constraints of national boundaries. Unfortunately for most African nations, their boundaries do not fit well with ecosystems, sometimes impeding the utilization of resources in a manner that is in harmony with the constraints of the environment. Regional cooperation, let alone integration, has not been highly successful in Africa. Partly this is due to the early stage of nationhood, and partly it is because most African nations are in competition with each other in terms of exports. The majority of African

23

nations are dependent on exports of animal, mineral, and vegetable products
(Table 1.5). Almost all exports are primary products. These export types all
have direct links with the natural environment. With the exception of the Ivory

Table 1.5 Export commodities from African countries.

Algeria	petroleum, wine, fruit and vegetables
Angola	coffee, petroleum, diamonds, iron
Benin	cocoa, coffee, palm products
Botswana	diamonds, copper, meat
Burkina Faso	livestock, cotton
Burundi	coffee
Cameroon	coffee, cocoa, wood alumina, petroleum
Central African Republic	diamonds, cotton, coffee, wood
Chad	cotton
Comoros	perfume plants, vanilla
Djibouti	salt
Egypt	cotton textiles, petroleum, fruits
Equatorial Guinea	cocoa
Ethiopia	coffee, hides and skins
Gabon	petroleum, manganese
Gambia	peanuts
Ghana	cocoa, wood, alumina
Guinea	alumina, coffee
Guinea-Bissau	peanuts, bauxite
Ivory coast	coffee, cocoa, pineapples, wood
Kenya	coffee, tea, refined petroleum
Liberia	iron, rubber
Libya	petroleum
Madagascar	coffee, cloves
Malawi	tobacco, tea, peanuts
Mali	livestock, cotton
Mauritania	iron, fish
Mauritius	sugar
Morocco	carpets, leather goods, grapes
Niger	peanuts, uranium
Nigeria	petroleum, cocoa
Peoples Republic of Congo	wood, palm oil
Rwanda	coffee, tea, wolframite
Sao Tome and Principe	coffee, coconut products
Senegal	peanuts, phosphates
Sierra Leone	diamonds, cocoa, coffee
Somalia	livestock, bananas
South Africa	manufactured goods, gold, other minerals
Sudan	cotton, gum, sesame
Swaziland	sugar, wood, asbestos, fruit, iron
Tanzania	coffee, cotton, sisal, cloves
Togo	phosphates, cocoa, coffee
Tunisia	olive oil, petroleum, phosphates
Uganda	coffee, cotton
Zaire	copper, other minerals, diamonds
Zambia	copper

Table 1.6 Pastoral activities in arid and semi-arid areas.

Pastoral activity dominant or of high growth potential	Pastoral activity significant or possessing moderate growth potential	Pastoral activity of limited importance and growth potential
Chad	Algeria	Angola
Mali	Botswana	Central African Republic
Mauritania	Burkina Faso	Congo
Niger	Burundi	Egypt
Somali Republic	Cameroon	Gabon
Sudan	Ethiopia	Gambia
	Kenya	Ghana
	Lesotho	Guinea
	Libya	Guinea-Bissau
	Morocco	Ivory Coast
	Nigeria	Liberia
	Senegal	Malagasy Republic
	South Africa	Malawi
	Swaziland	Mozambique
	Tanzania	Sierra Leone
	Tunisia	Togo
	Uganda	Zaire
		Zambia
		Zimbabwe

Coast, Cameroon, Kenya, and Zimbabwe, African countries are net importers of foodstuffs. And even these countries must import food in poor harvest years. This seeming paradox of exporting food products though being deficient in food is a result of physical environmental constraints, as well as a complex of human–political factors.

Table 1.6 lists those countries that have large and significant percentages of their land area in arid and semi-arid environments and designates those countries whose exports are mainly animal products. In most of the arid countries in the two left-hand columns there are tremendous land pressures because of their attempts to feed their people at the same time as needing to export agricultural products. Various strategies have been adopted to attempt to improve the abilities of these nations to produce more foodstuffs. Well drilling, dam building, and irrigation all seek to increase water supplies, both in quantity and reliability. Improved animal stock, new hybrid plants, new farm machinery, and the conversion of pastoral peoples to sedentary life styles are also methods of attempting to increase food production to meet the needs of the African nations.

Problems of the states

Fifty-three states make up Africa today; nearly all have achieved independent status only in the last 25 years. There are a few large countries: Algeria, Nigeria, Egypt, Sudan, and Zaire. All these countries have large land areas, but Nigeria

25

and Egypt also have large populations. However, many states are small in area and population, over half having populations of less than 5 million people. Nigeria and Sudan of all African countries have the widest range of ecological conditions. Ethiopia, Kenya, and a few others have a good diversity of ecosystems within their borders, but many others are single-ecosystem countries or countries dominated by one ecosystem. An example is Niger, a relatively large country in area, made up almost completely of arid and semi-arid lands. The small size of population and/or land area, with the common lack of diversity in many states, creates many difficulties in resource development and may be a very significant factor in the widespread problems of natural resource utilization.

The states of Africa can be divided into three main types with respect to level of economic development as depicted by GNP per capita (Table 1.7). The least developed nations, the poorest; the intermediate nations, which generally have a more diversified resource base than the poorest nations; and the higher GNP nations, which as a group have mineral resources that contribute to a larger GNP. Although GNP per capita is not a good measure of development, it is most commonly used to give a general indication of levels of living. With the exception of a few countries such as Libya, the GNP per capita in Africa is quite well correlated with other indicators, such as the Physical Quality of Life Index (PQLI) (Morris 1979). These three groups of nations reflect some important characteristics in the relationship between development and environment within Africa.

The least developed nations: the lowest GNP per capita

Over half of the nations designated by the United Nations as "poor", "least developed", "most affected", or otherwise disadvantaged are found in Africa. The 18 African nations least developed in Table 1.7 all have a per capita GNP lower than $370 per year. All of them depend on agriculture for a major part of the national economy (Zaire is an exception). The agricultural sector has to supply both a large part of the food needed for consumption within the nation and provide exports to earn foreign exchange to purchase needed imports. The least developed have little ecosystem diversity and tend either to be larger nations with arid or semi-arid ecosystems or small countries with small diversity in ecosystems. This group shows stagnant or declining agricultural productivity and is faced with but modest increases in the value of export crops. The least developed nations rely on the natural resource base for their economic well-being. The trend is that the productivity of that resource base is declining and their economies at best stagnating. The devastating droughts of the 1970s and 1980s have hit these countries hardest, emphasizing in cruelly dramatic ways the previous decline in productivity.

The intermediate nations

The group of countries that make up the intermediate category economically also have some important resource attributes. Some, especially those with lower income levels, such as Kenya, Uganda, Sudan, and Mozambique, have a more

Table 1.7   GNP per capita.

	Population (million) mid-1982	Area (1000 km^2)	GNP per capita Dollars 1982	GNP per capita Average annual growth rate (%) 1960–82
Low-income economies	213.5	12,992	249	0.7
Low-income semi-arid	29.3	4,714	218	−0.1
1. Chad	4.6	1,284	80	−2.8
2. Mali	7.1	1,240	180	1.6
3. Burkina Faso	6.5	274	210	1.1
4. Somalia	4.5	638	290	−0.1
5. Niger	5.9	1,267	310	−1.5
6. Gambia, The	0.7	11	360	2.5
Low-income other	184.2	8,278	254	0.9
7. Ethiopia	32.9	1,222	140	1.4
8. Guinea-Bissau	0.8	36	170	−1.7
9. Zaire	30.7	2,345	190	−0.3
10. Malawi	6.5	118	210	2.6
11. Uganda	13.5	236	230	−1.1
12. Rwanda	5.5	26	260	1.7
13. Burundi	4.3	28	280	2.5
14. Tanzania	19.8	945	280	1.9
15. Benin	3.7	113	310	0.6
16. Central African Republic	2.4	623	310	0.6
17. Guinea	5.7	246	310	1.5
18. Madagascar	9.2	587	320	−0.5
19. Togo	2.8	57	340	2.3
20. Ghana	12.2	239	360	−1.3
21. Kenya	18.1	583	390	2.8
22. Sierra Leone	3.2	72	390	0.9
23. Mozambique	12.9	802	—	—
Middle-income oil importers	56.1	5,959	634	0.9
24. Sudan	20.2	2,506	440	−0.4
25. Mauritania	1.6	1,031	470	1.4
26. Liberia	2.0	111	490	0.9
27. Senegal	6.0	196	490	—
28. Lesotho	1.4	30	510	6.5
29. Zambia	6.0	753	640	−0.1
30. Zimbabwe	7.5	391	850	1.5
31. Botswana	0.9	600	900	6.8
32. Swaziland	0.7	17	940	4.2
33. Ivory Coast	8.9	322	950	2.1
34. Mauritius	0.9	2	1,240	2.1
Middle-income oil exporters	110.3	3,256	889	3.2
35. Nigeria	90.6	924	860	3.3
36. Cameroon	9.3	475	890	2.6
37. Congo, People's Republic	1.7	342	1,180	2.7
38. Gabon	0.7	268	4,000	4.4
39. Angola	8.0	1,247	—	—
sub-Saharan Africa	380.0	22,207	491	1.5
all low-income countries	2,226.5	29,097	280	3.0
all lower middle-income countries	669.6	20,952	840	3.2
all upper middle-income countries	488.7	22,079	2,490	4.1
industrialized countries	722.9	30,935	11,070	3.3

Source: World Bank (1982).

diversified resource base than the least developed group but still rely mainly on the agricultural sector for both food and export crops. These countries have modest-to-good prospects of improving total agricultural-sector production. However, per capita and per area production has not increased significantly over the last ten years.

Another set of these countries has a more diversified economy – for example, Egypt – or has a significant mineral base to improve national income levels. Botswana, Swaziland, Morocco, Mauritania, Guinea-Bissau, and Nigeria fall into this latter category. Nigeria and Egypt stand out in this group. Egypt has a diversified economy but like Nigeria has a very large percentage of its population living and working in a not very highly productive rural sector. Nigeria, which has some oil resource revenues, is trying to diversify its economy and has recently begun to try to develop the agricultural sector after years of neglect.

In the intermediate categories also there are environmental and resource-use problems, but here problems of the type found in the least developed countries are combined with another component, difficulties arising from a higher level of agricultural exploitation, including problems of large-scale irrigation development in Egypt and Sudan, intense population pressure in Swaziland, and problems of range management in Kenya, Sudan, and Botswana.

The higher GNP nations

The nations with a higher GNP per capita exhibit a different set of characteristics. All have a strong export sector, with oil (Algeria, Gabon), gold (South Africa), copper (Zambia), and agricultural produce (Ivory Coast) being the main factors. Each of these countries has a somewhat different resource base and pattern of resource use, but there is a tendency in most for the agricultural sector to lag behind the general level of living. Within these countries there is a better level of wealth which might 'be applied to resource management, and there is a good record of this having been done in some sectors of some countries.

The Ivory Coast has well managed agricultural and tourist sectors, and Libya has invested heavily in agriculture and water development. However, countries like Zambia, Gabon, and Angola have the unfortunate distinction of combining the problems of rural stagnation and resource deterioration with the localized problems of air pollution, spoil heaps, and land contamination associated with mining and forest clearing.

Trends in human occupance

Although there are major differences in economic status between countries in the three groups, most parts of the continent experience general trends which are all part of the process of modernization. Rapid population growth, rapid urbanization, growth in industry, and changes in agriculture are all important components of this process.

POPULATION GROWTH

Population growth is generally more rapid than in the early parts of this century, but both the rates and the impact vary widely.

In small countries with dense populations, like Rwanda and Burundi, it is
generally thought that the continued growth in numbers of people is seriously
impeding any significant improvement in the well-being of the population
under current resource-use systems. Even a country like Kenya, which has a
large land area but only small areas of high potential land, is concerned about the
very high growth rates being experienced again in relation to the pattern of
resource availability and use. In these countries, under current use the population
pressures are heavily taxing the resource base. Conversely, in Sudan and Zambia
there have been periods of labor shortage and there is less apparent pressure on
resources. Here population growth is overall considered advantageous. But as
growth rates have been particularly strong in the last decade the full impact on
the economy and the resource base has not yet been felt in any of these countries.

Most demographers judge that, whatever the change in birth and death rates,
there will inevitably be much larger populations in nearly all African countries
by the end of this century. These major changes in numbers will continue to
result in major changes in the pattern of resource use. A further complicating
factor is the large number of refugees in parts of Africa. Somalia and Sudan are
two countries where the difficulties of managing dry areas have been compounded by the influx of refugees from Ethiopia.

URBANIZATION

Growth of towns and cities has accompanied general population growth, with
towns growing faster than the general population (Table 1.8). Towns existed in
Africa long before the arrival of Europeans. But large metropolitan areas in
excess of 500,000 inhabitants are to a large degree a product of the modern
world. The traditional towns or villages were mainly related to the local
economy, not the national or international world, though a few older African
cities were supported by long-distance trade. These traditional towns usually
had a complementary relation with the lands around them.

Table 1.8 shows the increasing growth of urban population relative to rural
population in Africa. If more recent data were available, these trends would be
even greater. Today large cities, instead of being confined to the extreme north
and south of the continent, are now a feature of all areas and most countries.
Even countries such as Tanzania, which were distinguished in 1950 for the low
percentage of urban population, now have cities approaching a million people.
Besides large (500,000 or greater) cities, there has been a considerable growth in
the size of capital cities in the smaller countries. In most countries south of the
Sahara there is normally a primate city dominating the network of small urban
centers. The primate city is usually the location of most trade and industry as
well as government administration. In Africa, urban areas are growing at rates
from 3 to 7 percent a year, reflecting both internal population growth and new
migration from rural and other urban areas. With the rapidly increasing rates of
urbanization occurring today in many parts of Africa, the food and energy
demands of the urban areas place ever-increasing demands on the rural sectors.

To meet the food needs of both the urban areas and the overall increase in
population, either new lands must become part of the food production system
or existing lands must become more intensely farmed. Technology has been one

29

Table 1.8 Growth and cities.

	As percentage of total population		Average annual growth rate (%)	
	1960	1982	1960–70	1970–82
Low-income economies	9	19	5.6	6.4
Low-income semi-arid	9	18	5.9	5.7
1. Chad	7	19	6.8	6.4
2. Mali	11	19	5.4	4.7
3. Burkina Faso	5	11	5.7	6.0
4. Somalia	17	32	5.7	5.4
5. Niger	6	14	7.0	7.2
6. Gambia, The	12	19	4.2	5.7
Low-income other	9	19	5.5	6.5
7. Ethiopia	6	15	6.5	5.6
8. Guinea-Bissau	14	25	2.6	7.3
9. Zaire	16	38	5.2	7.6
10. Malawi	4	10	6.6	6.4
11. Uganda	5	9	7.1	3.4
12. Rwanda	2	5	5.4	6.4
13. Burundi	2	2	1.3	2.5
14. Tanzania	5	13	6.3	8.5
15. Benin	10	15	5.4	4.4
16. Central African Republic	23	37	4.7	3.5
17. Guinea	10	20	4.9	5.2
18. Madagascar	11	20	5.0	5.2
19. Togo	10	21	5.8	6.6
20. Ghana	23	37	4.6	5.0
21. Kenya	7	15	6.4	7.3
22. Sierra Leone	13	23	4.9	3.9
23. Mozambique	4	9	6.5	8.1
Middle-income oil importers	15	30	6.5	6.4
24. Sudan	10	23	6.8	5.8
25. Mauritania	3	26	15.4	8.1
26. Liberia	21	34	5.6	5.7
27. Senegal	23	34	4.9	3.7
28. Lesotho	2	13	7.5	15.4
29. Zambia	23	45	5.2	6.5
30. Zimbabwe	13	24	6.7	6.0
31. Botswana	2	22	21.9	11.8
32. Swaziland	4	15	9.7	10.5
33. Ivory Coast	19	42	7.3	8.2
34. Mauritius	33	54	4.7	3.6
Middle-income oil exporters	13	23	4.9	5.4
35. Nigeria	13	21	4.7	4.9
36. Cameroon	14	37	5.8	8.0
37. Congo, People's Republic	30	46	5.0	4.4
38. Gabon	17	38	4.4	4.7
39. Angola	10	22	5.7	5.8
sub-Saharan Africa	11	22	5.5	6.1
all low-income countries	17	21	4.1	4.4
all lower middle-income countries	24	34	4.4	4.4
all upper middle-income countries	45	63	4.4	3.9
industrialized countries	68	78	1.9	1.3

Table 1.9 Food production.

	Average annual growth rate of volume of production (%)		Average annual growth rate of total production per capita (%)	
	Food 1970–82	Agriculture 1970–82	Food 1970–82	Agriculture 1970–82
Low-income economies	1.0	0.7	−1.2	−1.4
Low-income semi-arid	2.8	2.8	−0.1	−0.1
1. Chad	2.4	2.1	0.4	0.1
2. Mali	2.5	2.7	−0.2	0.0
3. Burkina Faso	2.4	2.5	0.4	0.5
4. Somalia	1.0	1.0	−1.8	−1.8
5. Niger	4.1	4.0	0.8	0.7
6. Gambia, The	−1.0	−1.0	−4.1	−4.1
Low-income other	0.9	0.6	−1.4	−1.6
7. Ethiopia	1.7	1.5	−0.3	−0.5
8. Guinea-Bissau	0.7	0.7	−	−
9. Zaire	1.3	1.2	−1.7	−1.7
10. Malawi	2.9	3.5	−0.1	0.5
11. Uganda	1.7	0.5	−1.0	−2.1
12. Rwanda	3.5	3.7	0.1	0.3
13. Burundi	1.6	1.7	−0.6	−0.5
14. Tanzania	2.1	1.0	−1.3	−2.3
15. Benin	2.6	2.4	−0.1	−0.3
16. Central African Republic	1.9	1.8	−0.2	−0.3
17. Guinea	1.5	1.4	−0.5	−0.6
18. Madagascar	1.7	1.6	−0.9	−1.0
19. Togo	2.3	2.3	−0.3	−0.3
20. Ghana	−0.2	−0.2	−3.1	−3.1
21. Kenya	2.0	2.7	−1.9	−1.2
22. Sierra Leone	1.2	1.2	−0.8	−0.8
23. Mozambique	−1.0	−1.4	−5.1	−5.5
Middle-income oil importers	3.3	2.5	−0.6	−1.2
24. Sudan	2.9	1.6	−0.3	−1.6
25. Mauritania	1.4	1.3	−0.9	−1.0
26. Liberia	3.0	2.1	−0.5	−1.4
27. Senegal	1.5	1.3	−1.2	−1.4
28. Lesotho	0.2	−0.2	−2.1	−2.5
29. Zambia	1.8	1.7	−1.3	−1.4
30. Zimbabwe	1.6	2.2	−1.6	−1.0
31. Botswana	−2.0	−2.0	−6.0	−6.0
32. Swaziland	3.9	4.5	0.7	1.3
33. Ivory Coast	6.0	5.0	1.0	0.1
34. Mauritius	0.8	0.9	−0.6	−0.5
Middle-income oil exporters	2.4	2.3	−0.3	−0.7
35. Nigeria	2.5	2.4	−0.1	−0.2
36. Cameroon	2.1	2.0	−0.9	−1.0
37. Congo, People's Republic	0.9	0.9	−2.0	−2.0
38. Gabon	0.7	0.6	−0.7	−0.8
39. Angola	0.4	−3.0	−2.0	−5.4
sub-Saharan Africa	1.7	1.4	−0.9	−1.1

Table 1.10 Industry as a percentage of gross domestic product in African countries.

Countries	1982
Low-income semi-arid	
Burkina Faso	16
Chad	7
Gambia	9
Mali	10
Mauritania	25
Niger	30
Somalia	10
Low-income other	
Benin	13
Burundi	17
Central African Republic	19
Ethiopia	16
Guinea	23
Guinea-Bissau	9
Lesotho	22
Madagascar	15
Malawi	20
Mozambique	16
Rwanda	22
Sierre Leone	20
Sudan	14
Tanzania	15
Togo	29
Uganda	4
Zaire	24
Middle-income oil importers	
Botswana	30
Cameroon	31
Ghana	8
Ivory Coast	23
Kenya	22
Liberia	28
Mauritius	25
Senegal	25
Swaziland	28
Zambia	36
Zimbabwe	35
Middle-income oil exporters	
Angola	23
Congo	52
Gabon	62
Nigeria	39
Algeria	57[a]
Egypt	35[a]
Libya	72[a]
Morocco	16[a]
Tunisia	35[a]

Sources: World Bank (1978, p. 145, 1981, p. 145, 1982, p. 120, 1984).

Note:
[a] Figure is for 1980.

response to this demand, with irrigation, new hybrid crops, fertilization, and mechanization being introduced. Another response has been to farm lands in the traditional manner but decrease the period of fallow as well as clearing new and marginal areas. As a result, food production has increased but not generally on a per capita basis (Table 1.9).

All of these changes impact on the resource base of the countries. For example, in the attempt to further the process of nation building and the development of national economies, pastoral systems are gradually being altered into various sedentary systems. This change is largely confined to the semi-arid areas. The pastoral system was a traditional adaptation to environments having water deficiencies. To alleviate this water shortage and to implement a policy of change from nomadic to sedentary systems, deep well drilling and dam building have been two main strategies. In the relatively fragile environment of arid lands, this policy has impacted heavily on the resource base of numerous nations, in particular the Sahelian countries, with unexpected negative results. Unfortunately we do not have much specific data on the impact of change in the last two decades on agricultural land, but at least in some areas there are clear danger signals which indicate that there are major problems ahead that must be solved if African food production is to keep pace with continent population and urban growth. These problems will remain even if the drought which has affected food production through the mid-1980s ends.

INDUSTRIAL GROWTH

The industrial sector in most African countries is small by world standards, but, as noted, it is growing substantially and is usually concentrated in a few locations within each country (Table 1.10). Most industries in the countries south of the Sahara are light, though there is a strong petroleum industry in Nigeria, Angola, Gabon, and in the North African countries. In countries with petroleum, industrial growth is often more rapid. Algeria has embarked on a major program of heavy industry, and Egypt has perhaps the widest range of industrial enterprises to serve her 40 million people in Africa, with the exception of South Africa with its wide range of extractive and manufacturing industry.

Much of the industrial development in Africa relies directly on local raw materials as the productive base: coffee or cotton in East Africa and Sudan, lumber in Gabon and Angola, petroleum in several countries, and widespread cement and petroleum and fertilizer plants. But all industry places demands on local resources, the most common being the need for water – lots of it. For the continual growth of industry in Africa, at least two issues will be important:

(a) the competition for the use of water in prime urban locations; and
(b) the control of environmental impacts of industry on the quality of water for the city and its people.

Conclusions

Africa is a continent which depends on the natural resource base for much of its sustenance. Food and other agricultural produce make up the bulk of the production sector in the economy of many countries. Lumber, fish, and animals provide another major part of livelihood for peoples and nations alike. Yet in many parts of the continent the productivity of this resource base is being reduced. The situation is by no means uniform. In areas like Ivory Coast agriculture is thriving, in parts of Zaire and Gabon the rainforest is remote and impenetrable, and in the internal deltas of southern Chad and southern Sudan there are great agricultural potentials. But four interlinked trends are quite pervasive and cause major concern in projecting the pattern of the future.

(a) First, there has been a drop in agricultural production per capita. With a few exceptions, this was a continent-wide trend during the 1970s and early 1980s. In some areas the figures were influenced by the drought which occurred in the early 1970s and 1980s; in others, Nigeria for example, by the diversion of national attention to urban and industrial growth. The pattern suggests general declining soil productivity and lack of attention to the rural areas in services and marketing infrastructure. It is a trend that cannot continue if the region is to achieve better economic and resource-use patterns.

(b) Second, stagnation and/or slow growth in cash-crop agriculture is widespread. In part this reflects changes in ownership and land management; in some countries it is a problem of organizing inputs and marketing, resulting in a drop in the returns to producers and in the efficiency of agricultural projects. In many cases the lag in investment in agriculture has caused a drop in productivity and deterioration in the natural resource base.

(c) Third, major pressure on rangelands is common. Quite apart from the drought, rangelands in Africa have been under steady pressure. Animal numbers have increased fivefold or more in many countries and the addition of new water sources, mostly wells, has produced new areas of land deterioration. Although local studies show wide variations in rangeland conditions, there is a general deterioration continent-wide and some areas of major resource destruction.

(d) Finally, a continuous process of destruction of forests is taking place almost everywhere. This has been important in the high rainfall areas but critical in the moderate-to-low rainfall areas where energy demands for wood are high. In Ethiopia it is hard to find wood for fuel near Addis Ababa; in Burkina Faso firewood and charcoal are chronically short; in Sudan the distance of transport of wood to Khartoum has increased from 5–10 to 100–200 km in the past 20 years. This decrease in woodland has altered crucial water–soil relationships in a way that has generally resulted in the decrease of the productivity of the land.

These four pressures on land are creating a major dilemma for the African governments in their economic and social planning for the 1980s and 1990s. In the continuing reorientation of African economics from tribal to national, demands placed on the human and physical systems are changing. Compared to the slow evolutionary development of modern economies which occurred in most of the highly developed nations, the general situation in the modernization process in Africa is a rapid injection of new technologies that affect only a portion of the nation, are often controlled externally, and cause severe disruptions in the transitional system of resource allocation. Urbanization, rapid population growth, increasing cash-oriented agriculture, high levels of governmental organizational control, and industrialization are some of the major trends existing today in Africa. These result from the importation of higher technologies in the attempt of the countries to improve their standard of living. These trends all result in changes in the utilization of the human and physical resources of Africa.

2 The African environment: an historical overview

Geologic and geomorphologic background

Introduction

This section provides a general introduction to the African landscape, emphasizing those aspects which relate most directly to the origin and dynamics of the present environment. With this emphasis, more attention is paid to the more recent geologic, geomorphologic, and climatic history than to older, less directly influential events.

The African continent is an old one, and many of the general features of the landscape have been evolved over long geologic periods without being submerged under changing sea levels, without being changed dramatically by glaciation, and without major tectonic upheavals. In these respects, Africa contrasts dramatically with North America and Europe, where to a large degree the landscapes have been affected by all these events and are therefore much younger. Because of this relative stability, the geomorphologic history of Africa has much more in common with Australia and India. This historical element of relative geologic stability has allowed many geologic processes to proceed further than in either North America or Europe. For example, the leaching (removal) of many soluble minerals from African soils is clearly as much the result of how long the leaching processes have been working on these soils as it is of the intensity of the processes, despite the fact that tropical temperatures result in more rapid leaching. Thus, compared to most of the best soils in the middle latitudes, which are of recent origin and derived from parent materials related to glacial activities, soils in Africa are older and less fertile with regard to their mineral nutrients.

Most reconstructions of continental locations on the Earth's surface place the six continents close to each other 200 million years ago. This gargantuan earlier landmass is known as Gondwanaland. Since that time, Gondwanaland has broken up into four major blocks, each being carried on a different primary tectonic plate to its current position on the Earth's surface. Most of the attention in this chapter is given to events after the Gondwanaland breakup (Fig. 2.1). Since the breakup, the African portion of Gondwanaland has remained largely in or near its present tropical setting, which has contributed to the lack of interrupting events on its geologic evolution.

36

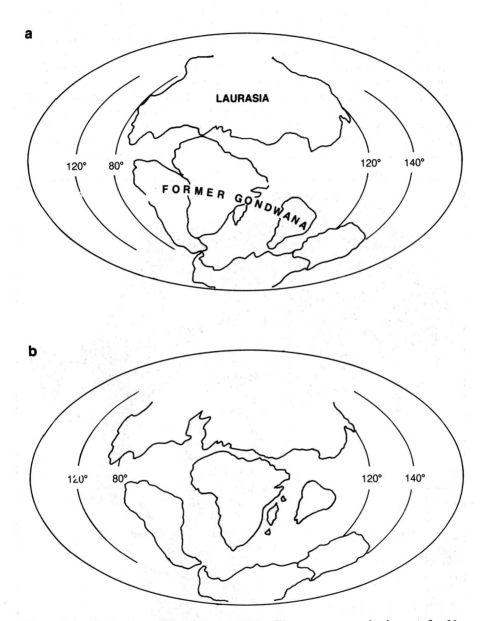

Figure 2.1   The breakup of Gondwana: (a) 180 million years ago – as broken up after 20 million years; (b) 65 million years ago – as it continued to break up after 135 million years. (Modified from Press & Siever 1986.)

Geologic history

Like all continents, the African continent is underlain by crystalline granite rocks of Precambrian age which are often referred to as the Basement Complex. The structure and composition of these rocks is complicated and large parts of the events that produced these rocks remain unknown. The crystalline rocks in Africa are prominent at or near the surface to a far greater degree than in other continents, with the possible exception of Australia. This is especially true in southern and eastern Africa (Fig. 2.2). Overall, Africa has a lower percentage of its area covered by sedimentary rocks than other continents. To the north, the crystalline rocks are partly overlain by sedimentary rocks of the "Continental Intercalcaire" or Nubian Sandstone Series or by alluvial materials deposited by streams in the river basins. Also, sedimentary rocks appear prominently in the

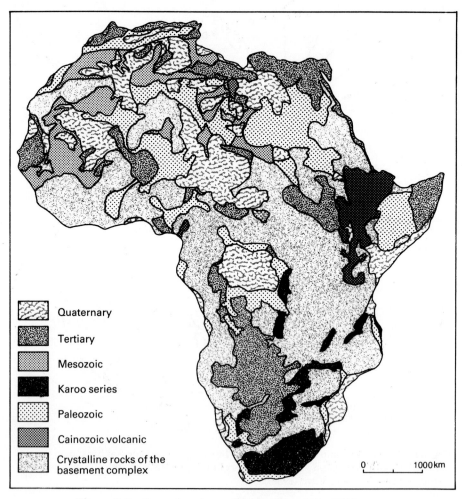

Figure 2.2 General geology of Africa (from Udo 1982).

Cameroon Highlands, the massifs of Ahaggat and Air, the plateau of West Africa and in the lower Niger Basin.

The most important characteristics of the Basement Complex rocks in terms of geomorphology and environment are:

- granite rocks are the predominant rock type in Africa;
- the granites are usually intruded into older schists and gneisses;
- quartzite and other dikes are common throughout the Basement Complex;
- extensive areas of younger volcanic lavas with varied chemical properties exist primarily in East Africa; and
- areas of major basic intrusions of gabbros and other igneous basic rocks are found throughout the Basement Complex.

All of the basement rocks (these do not include the volcanics) are over 750 million years old. They have all been subject to tectonic and exogenic change, but from the environmental perspective it is their weathering and erosional properties which are most important.

The granites and quartzites tend to be the most resistant rocks in the drier climates, but under humid conditions granites weather deeply and the decomposed material is often easily eroded. The deeply weathered crumbly material derived from humid climate weathering of granite covers much of the surface material over wide areas of the African continent. Quartzites are resistant in both humid and semi-arid conditions and thus tend to form topographic highs, such as ridges, in areas where they are located.

Schists and gneisses breakdown relatively fast in both humid and dry areas. Their weathered products are not generally as thick as those derived from granites, but they have many of the same characteristics. Basic igneous rocks weather very rapidly in the humid tropics and, together with the schists and gneisses, generally form low-lying areas; where they are widespread the result is a low-relief landscape. Volcanic lavas and fine-grained igneous rocks are quite resistant to weathering and erosion and are found in many of the highland areas in Africa.

The Cambrian period, more than half a billion years ago, was the last time in geological history that large areas of Africa were covered by water. During this period, thick sandstones and limestones were deposited over the Basement Complex in the basins of this Cambrian Sea that remained for over 200 million years. These sandstones form the Table Mountain, South Africa and the plateaus of the central Sahara.

In Pennsylvanian, Mississippian, and Permian times (Carboniferous) the southern part of the continent was a zone undergoing compression. This resulted in strongly folded rocks locally dated as the Karroo Age. Mountain ranges were built in southern Africa and were immediately subject to weathering and erosion, yielding sediment into surrounding basins. After the Karroo orogeny the southern two-thirds of the continent remained above sea level whereas the northern part was tilted downward and covered by a part of the former Tethys Sea, the ancestor of part of the Mediterranean. The rocks laid down in the north during this period generally covered the basement material in thin sheets, though the Atlas Mountains are highly folded parts of this rock group. The major folded structures of the continent are thus in the extreme north and south.

The effect of other fundamental structural events is highlighted by the African Rift Valley and its associated structures. The Rift Valley system, over 5600 km long, is structurally a fault zone made up of sets of parallel faults about 65 km apart with a zone of multiple small faults and volcanic activity occupying the area between. With the exception of the volcanic features, the rift floor is an area of relatively low to moderate relief. These relief characteristics are further minimized since the deepest areas of the rift are occupied by numerous lakes which mask the greater depressions. The whole feature is very ancient and appears to follow lines of weakness in the basement rocks; it is still an active tectonic zone on the Earth's surface with intermittent faulting and volcanic activity. It remains one of the main features of the Earth's tectonics – one of the few, for example, which are visible from space. It is only partially explained by the current prevailing theory of plate tectonics. The Red Sea, which is part of the rift, is clearly formed at the junction of the two plates. But here the rift is much wider than elsewhere, and in other locations its relationship to plate boundaries is still not understood.

The recent geologic history of the continent is characterized by a general uplift along the continental margin, perhaps a continuing isostatic response to the breakup of Gondwanaland. Inland, the pattern of erosion or deposition has been controlled by the fluvial processes of the great rivers and by the effects of changing climates. These are discussed in a later section.

The main geomorphologic units

Two different perspectives on the geomorphology of Africa are provided by Figures 2.2 and 1.4. Figure 1.4 sets out the major topographic units of the continent. "High" Africa is designated as the southeastern half of the continent and "low" Africa as the northwestern half. Most of the great river basins are located in "low" Africa, although the Zaire and the Nile rise in "high" Africa. The great escarpments and the Rift Valley are important features of "high" Africa.

L. C. King has presented a more complex interpretation of African morphology. King views the African land surface as being made up of a number of denudational (erosional) land surfaces – some of very great age and a number with aggradational surfaces (Table 2.1).

Table 2.1 African surfaces.

Erosional–denudational land surfaces	Geologic age (after King)	Aggradational land surfaces
Gondwana	Jurassic	none recognized
post-Gondwana	Cretaceous	
African	Early Tertiary	African
post-African	Late Tertiary	post-African
Congo (Zaire)	Quaternary (Pleistocene)	modern, also volcanic
	Holocene, Recent	aggradational, various ages

Generally, "high" Africa (Fig. 1.4) is characterized by large areas of denuda-tional land surfaces. The Gondwana surface occurs only in isolated remnants on high ridges and plateaus; the African erosional surface is found over much wider areas and is characterized by smooth rolling skyline topography.

The largest surface area is taken up by the post-African land surface, which is typified by smooth rolling topography and undulating plateaus generally found at lower elevations than the African surface. The post-African denudational surface also occupies large areas of "low" Africa, but here it is almost equalled in extent by depositional surfaces classified at about the same age.

Although King's interpretation is not universally accepted, it is by far the most comprehensive work on the continent, and it does illustrate:

(a)   the great age of much of the African land surface;
(b)   the small portion of the continent classified as "modern" in origin; and
(c)   the broad pattern of erosional and depositional surfaces.

Table 2.2 sets out King's interpretation of the sequence of events of landscape formation and tectonic movements in Africa.

The history of climatic change

No part of lowland Africa was directly affected by Pleistocene glaciation; however, the climatic changes which were so dominant in Europe during this glacial period affected large parts of Africa. The high mountains such as the peaks of the Atlas Mountains, Kilimanjaro, and Mount Kenya were affected by advances of ice and glacier development comparable with the ice ages in Europe. Temperatures were 6.7–9.5°C lower than at present during the glacial episodes on African mountains (Table 2.3).

In addition, large parts of the continent experienced wide fluctuations in rainfall during the Pleistocene. Some periods were considerably wetter than at present, others considerably drier. There appears to be no direct proven correlation between events in Europe and Africa, though the pattern of climatic change was in response to a worldwide dynamic situation.

The Nile Valley has been the location of the most intense studies of long-term climatic history in Africa. Table 2.4 outlines the main events in the evolution of that area in terms of geomorphic evolution and climatic change. The Miocene period (22.5–5.8 million years ago) saw at least four main episodes of climatic and geomorphic changes as detected in Egypt. The climate of this period appears to have fluctuated between arid and semi-arid, with rainfall higher than at present through much of this earlier period. However, by the end of the Miocene, the whole Mediterranean Basin became desiccated and arid.

During the Pliocene (4.5–1.8 million years ago) the Egyptian climate was humid or subhumid in a time of generally higher sea levels. There were probably a number of intervening climatic episodes, but the period ended with a sub-arid climate somewhat akin to the dry savanna–Sahel climates of today.

The Pleistocene (1.8 million to 15,000 years ago) is the geologic period which has had the most direct influence on current conditions. Being relatively recent,

Table 2.2 Cyclic episodes of African geomorphology (southern and central) with tectonic interludes.

Denudational	Depositional		Age
	Continental	Marine	
pre-Karroo landscape of moderate relief, partly glacial	covered by Dwyka, and Beaufort Series	none	Late Carboniferous and Permian
	Mild epeirogenesis		
intra-Karroo landscape, generally of low relief and desert form	Stromerg Series	none	Triassic
	Mild epeirogenesis		
Gondwana landscape of extreme planation	Jurassic deposits known only in Congo Republic (Zaire)	none	Jurassic (and Late Triassic)
	Fragmentation of Gondwanaland		
post-Gondwana dissection, usually in the vicinity of upwarps	Series de Kwango: Cretaceous sediments of Nyasa Rift	Late Jurassic–early Cretaceous Series of east and west coasts	Early Cretaceous
	Mid-Cretaceous disturbances		
African cyclic landscape of extreme planation forming the most perfectly planed surface of Africa much dissected now by later cycles	Late Cretaceous dinosaur bed of Bushmanland; Early Cainozoic Botletle beds, Kalahari marls, Gres polymorphe	littoral Senonian strata of east coast with succeeding Eocene in Mozambique. Late Cretaceous and Eocene strata of Angola	Late Cretaceous

Geomorphic development	Deposits	Earth movements	Epoch
		Widespread epeirogenic uplift of a few hundred feet	
broad valley-floor pediplains widespread into Early Cainozoic; "African" surface	"Plateau sands" of the Kalahari–Congo region, minor laterites and calcretes	Burdigalian Marine Series	Miocene
		Moderate cymatogeny	
second phase of Late Cainozoic valley planation; coastal plains	pipe sandstone of mid-Zambezi Valley	sands unconformably overlying Burdigalian and transected by coastal plain of East Africa	Pliocene
		Strong cymatogeny	
deep gorge-cutting in eastern and western coastal hinterlands; locally multiphase	widespread Kalahari sands (two-phase); cavern deposits	red "Berea" and other coastal sands	Quaternary
		Minor differential movement	
coastal drowning	recent alluvia	recent dune sands	

Source: after King (1967).

Table 2.3 Temperature lowering during glaciations (°C).

Glaciation	Ruwenzori	Kilimanjaro	Mount Kenya
Lake Mahoma	6.7	8.3	7.5
Rwimi Basin	7.3	8.5	—
Katabarus	6.7	—	9.5

it is a period that is known in detail by comparison with the broader outline of older periods. Butzer distinguishes 12 main stages of climatic change and geomorphology in the Egyptian Nile Valley (Table 2.4). During this time the area experienced wide-ranging climates, including humid, subhumid, arid, and semi-arid periods.

The Early Pleistocene appears to have been characterized by semi-arid climates, cloudy and wetter than at present, during which the Nile first aggraded then substantially degraded its bed. The mid–Pleistocene saw a general drying of the climate from a major subhumid period. This subhumid period was long enough for the development of 1–1.5 m thick deep red soils over an even deeper weathering profile. The conditions in this period approximated those found in present-day southern Sudan which has about 800–1000 m of rainfall and a warm climate.

From this point onward, dry climates prevail with semi-arid rather than arid conditions being dominant. There was at least one period when the climate was humid enough for red soil development, but this was relatively brief.

The history of climatic change over this long period in the Nile Valley is not necessarily, or even probably, that of the whole of Africa. But it does provide an indication of the pattern of events in the distant past. Climate in the Nile Valley was very variable. For substantial periods it was much wetter than now, but the dominant climate was semi-arid. It may be that this conclusion is one that does fit Africa as a whole, and that, over much of the latter part of geologic time, climate has been dominantly semi-arid with distinct fluctuations departing substantially from this mean in any particular area.

The record of climatic change over this longer period in the currently humid parts of the continent is less clear. There is considerable evidence to suggest that these areas have been humid or subhumid throughout much of the Late Pleistocene, though here too there is evidence of substantial fluctuation.

In terms of the current environment, the last few thousand and tens of thousands of years are the most important. There is as yet no general synthesis of the detailed pattern of climatic change over the last 20,000–40,000 years in Africa, but in parts of the continent we have clearly articulated sequences of events. The Nile Valley, the Sahara, and East Africa are three such areas.

The Nile Valley

Table 2.5 provides a comprehensive set of important time sequences for the northern part of the Nile Valley in Egypt. This can be seen as an extension and elaboration of Table 2.4, which gave the general Pleistocene chronology for this

Table 2.4 Miocene to mid-Pleistocene geomorphic evolution of the Nile Valley.

Epoch	Phase	Phenomena
Pleistocene		
	18	Nile dissection and wadi downcutting (at least 15 m)
	17	pedogenesis, a red soil (typic haplargid) with 1 m solum; climate sub-arid
	16	Nile and wadi aggradation; Wadi Lorosko substages at 23–25 m and 12–15 m above modern floodplain; includes Dandara Formation silt facies, with first Ethiopian summer-flood heavy minerals; Acheulian *in situ*; climate semi-arid
	15	Nile and wadi dissection (at least 25 m)
Middle (0.13–0.7 × 10⁶ years)	14	Nile and wadi aggradation (locally 120 m thick at Aswan); valley-margin pedimentation (upper Egypt and Nubia); Dakka stage, 30–35 m above floodplain; Acheulian *in situ*; climate semi-arid
	13	major Nile downcutting (by some 135 m) to 10 m above sea level (Aswan)
	12	major pedogenesis, a deep red soil (typic paleargid) with 1–1.5 m B2 horizon and partial decomposition of igneous gravel to 6 m depth; climate subhumid
	11	Nile and wadi gravel aggradation; valley-margin pedimentation; Dihmit stage, 44–48 m above floodplain. After minor dissection, Adindan aggradation in southern Nubia at +40 to +42
	10	Nadi and wadi dissection (at least 30 m)
Lower (0.7–1.8 × 10⁶ years)	9	Nile and wadi gravel aggradation (locally 100 m) and valley-margin pedimentation; Wadi Allaqi stage, 50–55 m above floodplain, with substages; climate semi-arid
	8	major downcutting of Nile (by some 200 m or more) to 55 m below sea level (Aswan)
	7	Nile and Red Sea Hill wadis aggrade gallabe gravels; three substages, 60–74 m above modern floodplain (upper Egypt), or cut fluvial platforms (Nubia); climate semi-arid
Late (1.8–4 × 10⁶ years)	6	marine regression in Nile trench, with sands, gypsum shales, and conglomeratic marls of fluvial, lagoonal, or lacustrine facies (130 m in south), superposed by massive conglomerates, in part gravity breccias (180 m); plateau Tufas (at Kurkur and Kharga); Ostrea–Pecten beds, with Anancus (120 m, in north); climate semi-arid
Pliocene		
Early	5	marine transgression into Nile trench, with glauconitic shales. or estuarine or lagoonal facies as far south as Aswan (−35 m and below); no torrential runoff; climate sub-humid
Late Upper (5–8 × 10⁶ years)	4	desiccation of Mediterranean Basin; uparching of Egyptian stable shelf; cutting of overdeepened Nile Valley (−568 m, Cairo; −172 m, Aswan)
Miocene		
Early Upper (8–10.5 × 10⁶ years)	3	deltaic sedimentation and downfaulting (lower Egypt); block-tilting (Kom Ombo Graben); cutting of Aswan Pediplain (at 180–210 m) in lower Nubia and upper Egypt; climate semi-arid
Middle (10.5–16.5 × 10⁶ years)	2	cutting of Ballana Pediplain (at 230–260 m) (Pediment II at Kurkur Oasis) in lower Nubia; climate semi-arid
Lower (16.5–22.5 × 10⁴ years)	1	cutting of Kurkur Pediplain (at 300–360 m) (Pediment I at Kurkur Oasis) in lower Nubia; fluvial or estuarine El-Khashab Red Beds (west of Cairo); climate semi-arid; local vulcanism; (Red Sea Hills); downfaulting (Kom Ombo)

Sources: Tertiary chronostratigraphy after Berggren (1972); Pleistocene after Butzer (1974a).

Table 2.5 Summary of climatic fluctuations in the Nile Valley.

Period	Climate	Date
14	hyperarid	5,000–13,000 BP
13	arid – some rain	6,000–7,000 BP
12	wadi dissection more humid	6,000 BP
11	arid, sub-arid	8,000 BP
10	hyperarid	11,500 BP
9	arid, wetter	11,500–14,500 BP
8	hyperarid	17,500–18,000 BP
7	hyperarid	18,000–25,000 BP
6	hyperarid	26,000 BP

area. In this dry area the interfacing of Nile deposits as part of the record of flow from the south, and local wadi deposits as the record of climatic and depositional events in a local area, provide an important means of linking these two.

The sequence starts before the Korosko Formation, which is dated over 40,000 years BP and is representative of southern Egyptian conditions. This arid climatic episode was preceded by semi-arid climates. The Korosko Formation is split into two parts by an erosional episode (probably more humid), with the upper part some 10,000–15,000 years later than the lower.

THE NILE IN SUDAN

In the Sudan the Nile shows a somewhat different record over the last 40,000 years. Here much of the record is based on the deposits laid down by the Blue and White Niles. Blue Nile sediments include some carbonates which are dated before 40,000 years BP, but the main record relates to the period of the last 18,000 years. Two schematic models for the Blue Nile in 18,000 and 11,000 BP are illustrated in Figure 2.3. The first illustrates a period when temperatures in the Ethiopian Highlands were substantially lower than at present, the tree-line was lower and the arid and savanna belts were farther south than at present. The 11,000 BP model represents warmer and wetter conditions, both in the uplands and in the Sudan plains. The general validity of these two models in terms of sediment flow is important for the interpretation of the significance of middle Nile sediments.

Figure 2.4 illustrates the wide range of data that we have for high flood and lake levels in central Sudan and the following quotation illustrates a current view of the importance of the climatic changes and flood levels on the central Sudanese environment.

The Late Pleistocene Blue Nile was a highly seasonal river capable of transporting an abundant bed-load of coarse sand and occasional fine gravel (Williams *et al.* 1975). So, too, was the main Nile (Butzer & Hansen 1968, and Chapter 11). Although deprived of runoff from its Ugandan headwaters during 14,500 BP to 12,500 BP and probably also between 40,000 BP and 26,000 BP, or later, the White Nile at least seasonably was competent to transport gravels and sands to the main Nile, until the end of the Pleistocene, when its valley became blocked by dunes from the sandy bed-load. These dunes are usually aligned north–south, so that some water from the White Nile may have continued to flow north through the swales.

The Ethiopian tributaries of the Blue Nile were receiving an abundant supply of coarse sediment from their unstable valley slopes at precisely that stage in Ethiopian Quaternary history when precipitation and ultimately runoff were rapidly declining. The outcome was a seasonally competent Nile–Blue Nile, which became loaded to capacity as time went on.

The higher post-glacial temperatures and the much increased early Holocene rainfall had three effects. Previously unstable slopes became vegetated, soils

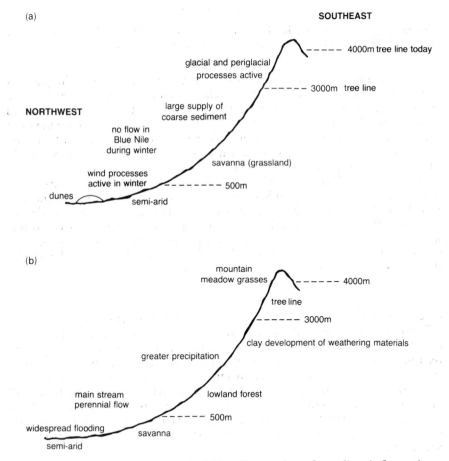

Figure 2.3 Vegetation changes in the Nile valley resulting from climatic fluctuations: (a) 18,000 BP, and cooler period; (b) 11,000 BP, warmer period. (Modified from Williams & Adamson 1980.)

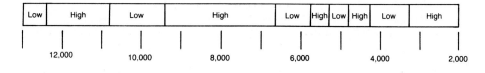

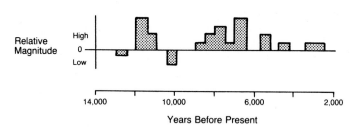

Years Before Present

Figure 2.4 Flood and lake levels of the Blue Nile and White Nile in central Sudan between 12,000 and 2000 BP. (Modified from Williams & Faure 1980.)

developed, and the supply of coarse bedload material from Ethiopia was superseded by an influx of fine silts and clays. Lakes rose and overflowed. The White Nile, its flow now augmented from Lake Turkana in northern Kenya as well as from the Ugandan lakes, breached its aeolian dam, drowning many of the dunes in the process. The Blue Nile flowed in a series of unstable and bifurcating channels across its sandy alluvial fan, leaving a layer of dark clays in the flood basins between the main channels.

Incision by the Blue Nile may have begun in the Early Holocene, but its effects only became noticeable by Middle Holocene times, when former distributaries were beheaded and left deprived of water from all but the most extreme floods. It seems, then, that downcutting coincides with a change from coarse to fine load, with an overall decrease in the volume of flow after about mid-Holocene times, and with a consolidation of flow into one channel as the Gezira distributaries became progressively abandoned.

THE UPPER NILE VALLEY (FIG. 2.5)

In central Africa there exists a rich record indicating climatic change. On Kilimanjaro there is evidence of glaciation up to 500,000 years ago, but, as we need to concentrate on data for more recent times, these data are best supplied in relation to lake levels and sediments. Lake Turkana has an early marked sequence of strand lines which indicate much wetter periods in this currently dry area. At one stage, at least, the lake was linked with the Nile. Its fauna still displays these nilotic links. Low lake levels occurred in Lake Victoria and Lake Mobutu Sese Seko (Albert) before 12,500 BP and Lake Victoria did not overflow northward at this time. The periods when Mobutu Sese Seko was open to the north were:

28,000–25,000 BP
18,000–14,000 BP
12,500 BP to present

48

During the closed periods for Lake Victoria and Lake Mobutu Sese Seko, water levels fell 75 and 56.6 m respectively. Climatic change here is also demonstrated by pollen records. Grass and shrub gave way to trees around 12,500 BP on the margin of Lake Victoria. During the last few thousand years, the relative importance of tree pollen compared with other pollens has declined at many localities. Although the existence of fewer trees in the Late Pleistocene seems to have been due to lower rainfall and lower temperature – the latter most important at higher elevations – the recent decline in forest species appears to be due more to human activity than to climatic change.

THE SAHEL AND WEST AFRICA

A similar record of climatic and environmental fluctuations exists in the Sahel and West Africa. But actual dating of events is more difficult to obtain here than in eastern Africa, largely because of the absence of widespread lake systems. It is quite clear that the Late Pleistocene was more arid than at present, though the causes and exact nature of that aridity are in doubt. In the Holocene more humid spells marked the early and middle part of this period, with a sharply defined period of aridity between them. The details of the other fluctuations that

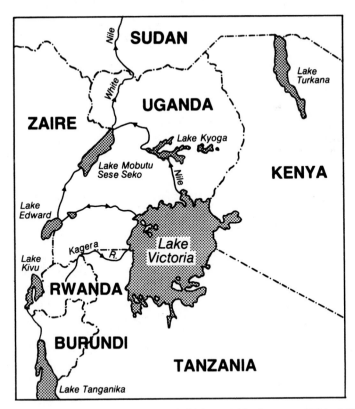

Figure 2.5 The sources, streams, and lakes within the upper White Nile.

49

undoubtedly occurred are not as clearly recorded until the period of the last few thousand years.

In summary, the past 40,000 years have seen quite considerable fluctuations of climate in Africa with consequent changes in other aspects of the environment. During the Neolithic (5000–6000 BP), climates generally throughout the more arid parts of Africa were wetter than at present. About 5000 years BP the climate of these areas changed substantially towards current conditions.

The last 2000 years

Fluctuations in climate appear to have declined in magnitude in the period 4000–2000 BP, and this trend has continued in the last 2000 years, which have been much less variable, though significant changes have occurred. The most important of these variations are:

(a)   between the 16th and early 18th centuries "Neolithic type", wetter climates occurred; and

(b)   in the late 19th century, 20–30 years of more humid conditions existed.

These two episodes are illustrated by several different sets of data. The first is the record of river and lake fluctuation (Figs 2.4 & 2.6) which shows that the high floods and water levels of the 16th, 17th, and early 18th centuries are present in records of the Nile, Lake Turkana, Lake Abhé, Lake Chad, and from a variety of records in Mauritania.

The chronologies of famine and drought correlate well with the record of water systems and the general historical record. All the available information suggests there were prosperous conditions and very infrequent droughts which lasted until at least 1680. For the next 120 years there was a general decline in rainfall which appears to have been initiated by a severe drought in 1681–7 (Nicholson 1976). Despite this trend, conditions in the 18th century remained somewhat wetter than at present. The generality of these conditions appears

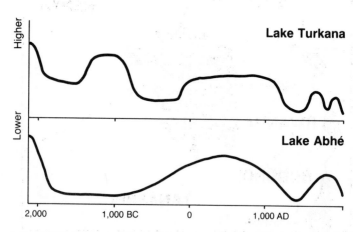

Figure 2.6   Lake level fluctuations of Turkana and Abhe (given to the authors by Sharon E. Nicholson, Florida State University).

Figure 2.7 Major areas of drought and moisture surplus, 1738–56: –, areas of reported drought or famine; +, areas of likely moisture surplus (given to the authors by Sharon E. Nicholson, Florida State University).

well established by observations from Senegal, Guinea Coast, North Africa, Sudan, and elsewhere (Nicholson 1980).

Chambonneau's description, from 1677, further supports the hypothesis of a more humid climate in Senegal and at least Southern Mauritania in the 17th century; he reported thick mangrove strands and palm trees along the banks of the Senegal and in its valley from Saint Louis to Cape Verde (Chamard 1973). Despite the blockage of the mouths of the Senegal and other waterways towards 1700, Adanson's description of Senegal in 1749–55 suggests that the more humid conditions lasted until this time (Adanson 1759). He says, ". . . the island of Sor [near the mouth of the Senegal] was bordered by a very thick wood and thorny bushes". He describes forests on the river's banks near Podor – tamarisks, redgum trees, and thorny acacias – and the thriving organe, lemon, lime, and fig trees which the French planted. Vansina (1976, personal communication) says that several other maps show certain lakes in northern Senegal and southern Mauritania which have since dried up, and a forest in southern Mauritania up to *c.* 18°N, where precipitation today is about 200–250 mm per year.

Figures 2.7 and 2.8 illustrate some of the more recent climatic events drier than normal from 1738 to 1756, and from 1828 to 1839 respectively.

The most dramatic and long-lasting recent climatic change dates to about 100 years ago. For about 20 years in the late 19th century (1875–95) rainfall was well above the current normal average for Africa. This is clearly identified with good data available for the Sahara, eastern Africa, and central Africa.

Lake levels (Fig. 2.9) show a clear sequence, with a sharp drop to a uniform level at the end of the wet period, broken only by a sharp rise in the 1960s. Rainfall records and historical accounts confirm the evidence of the lakes (Fig. 2.10).

The conclusion of this review is that climate is indeed a variable in apparently stable Africa, and in fact the return to dry conditions in the later 19th century had a major impact on environmental conditions in parts of Africa. The drought, combined with the rinderpest epidemic, appears to have resulted in a major reduction in livestock in East Africa and a spread of thorn bush and tsetse fly

Figure 2.8 Major areas and number of years of drought and moisture surplus between 1828 and 1839. Numbers signify the numbers of years for which famine or drought occurred; + signifies an area of precipitation greater than expected (given to the authors by Sharon E. Nicholson, Florida State University).

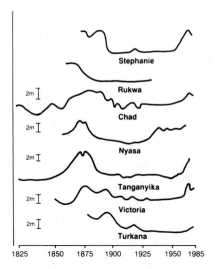

Figure 2.9 Lake level fluctuations for some major lakes between 1825 and 1985.

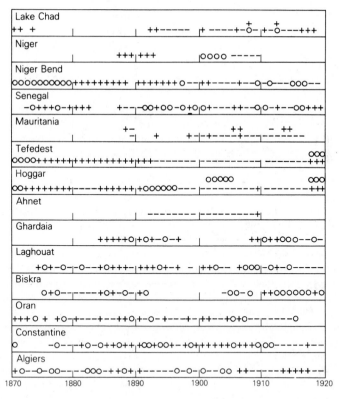

Figure 2.10 Variation of precipitation in western and northern Africa between 1870 and 1920: +, above normal precipitation; 0, near normal precipitation; −, below normal precipitation (from Williams & Faure 1980).

which still remains today. The ecological impact of the change is still in the landscape.

In a subtle way the high rainfall period of the 1960s had important impacts. For many of the countries this decade was the first decade of independence, and the false hopes of agricultural production from that wetter period received a rude setback when the drier conditions of the late 1960s, and early 1970s, and mid-1980s had their impact.

The impacts of climatic change on land–water relationships

This section serves to classify and elucidate the importance of climatic change in current African landscapes. The direct and indirect effects of climatic change are quite complex, and it is not at all clear what the full causal mechanisms are for some of the relationships discussed. The impacts of climatic change are most directly recorded in landforms and water systems, which are indicators of those changes. We shall examine the impact of such changes on lakes, sand-dune formation, and rivers.

Lakes

Lakes are sensitive indicators of changes in the balance between precipitation in the lake basin, water flow into the lake, and evaporation and lake discharges through seepage and drainage. Some of these factors are not directly related to climatic change, but in many lake basins the most important factors influencing lake hydrology are river flow into the lake (and rainfall on large lakes) and evaporation from the surface. The impact of changes in this relationship is greatest in shallow lakes, since a slight change in volume has large areal impacts. The greatest changes in lake form appear to have occurred in arid and semi-arid areas. Lake Chad, Lake Manyara in Tanzania, Lake Naivasha in Kenya, and Lake Tana in Ethiopia are all examples of lakes which have fluctuated considerably in depth and area over the last few thousand years. In addition, there is evidence in several parts of Africa of former lakes that have recently dried up. One such lake used to occupy the valley of the White Nile upstream from Khartoum.

Grove (1981) and others have studied the former magnitude of Lake Chad (Fig. 2.11). At present, Lake Chad is a shallow pond little more than 8 m deep which divides into two shallower marshy depressions during dry years. It seems likely that in extremely dry periods Lake Chad will completely disappear. At the other end of the scale of changes, evidence of lakeshore terraces and overflow channels shows that at one period, possibly 10–20,000 years BP, Lake Chad was a huge lake over 160 m deep, comparable in size to the Caspian Sea. Lake level, now just over 278–282 m, was 320–330 m above sea level. The extra depth was gained because the lake included the now dry Bodele depression. The 320–330 m level was the highest the lake could reach because at this point it overflowed southwestward into the Benue system. This river, discharging overflow from the lake, was also much larger than at present.

In between these two extremes the lake history of the past 20,000 years

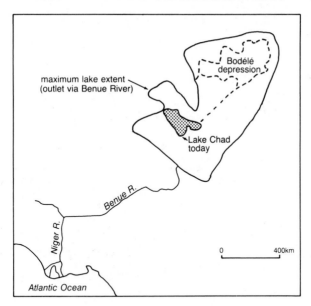

Figure 2.11   The areal extent of Lake Chad, its maximum and present limits.

includes many intervening stages. The topography of the area is such that a relatively small increase in lake level results in an overflow northwards into the Bodele depression, and, for much of this time period, Lake Chad has been two lakes linked by an overflow channel. However, lake terraces show that for long periods there were quite large lakes intermediate in size between the small current lake and the highest lake level (320–330 m).

A similar pattern of change can be traced for the other lakes used as examples (Fig. 2.9). Lake Tana in Ethiopia has been much deeper than at present. It currently overflows at its present level into the Blue Nile. For it to have been deeper the topography would have to have been different. Most probably today's overflow channel had not been cut down to its modern level until late in the Pleistocene.

Lake Naivasha and the other shallow lakes of the Rift Valley floor in Kenya show evidence of much higher levels than at present (Fig. 2.12). Shoreline terraces over 200 m above the present shallow lake surface are clearly indicated, and this deep lake occupied a large area on the floor of the rift. This change of level obviously reflects climatic changes, but the active tectonics in this area also imply that there have been changes in the topography and drainage systems from tectonics as well as climatic changes. Other shallow lakes, such as Manyara and Eyasi, also show evidence of former levels up to 100 m above current watermarks. However, many other lakes do not show similar records. Lake Victoria lies in a shallow downwarp of the crust and overflows to the north. Although there is some evidence of higher levels, the history shows a complicated record of earth movements and water ponding. The deep lakes such as Lake Tanganyika do not appear to have a clear record of higher levels.

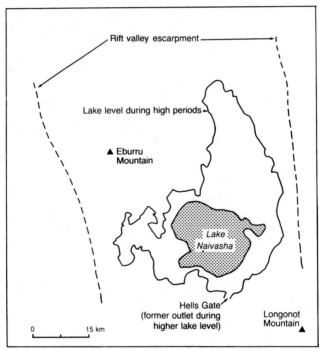

Figure 2.12 Location and areal extent of Lake Naivasha (Kenya), its maximum and present limits.

There is also clear evidence of former lakes where none exist today. One of the most interesting occupied the White Nile Valley south of Khartoum, some 12,000 years ago. For a considerable period the deltaic deposits of the Blue Nile appear to have blocked the channel and lower valley of the White Nile. In this more arid period, the Blue Nile flow northward was reduced, and distributaries helped deposition of a large alluvial cone in the area now known as the Gezira. The result was a long, narrow lake, 300–500 km north–south, located in the White Nile Valley. The margins of this lake are clearly marked by beaches with abundant shell remnants. Presumably the lake eventually overflowed northward, cut a channel across the alluvial deposits and drained.

In reviewing the history of the African environment, the recent past has seen a quite different array of water bodies creating a different mix of ecological systems in the areas concerned. The variety of lakes and their importance is of course related to the basic characteristics of the African landscape. Africa is characterized by large river basins, draining low relief areas, and this means that blockage or ponding of drainage is quite common. Broad warping earth movements have also contributed to low drainage gradients, and these have helped lake formation, especially in central Africa.

These past events have implications also for current and future land use and development in Africa. The Gezira irrigation scheme, "the largest farm in the world", is located on the abandoned inland delta of the Blue Nile where the gently sloping clays are ideal for irrigation. Other lake floors and deltas provide sites of good soils for agriculture and facilitate irrigation. The existence of the former lakes also contributes to current groundwater conditions in those areas. The past is very much the key to the present and the future.

Sand-dunes

Whereas the lakes of Africa illustrated by the record of their former extent show the impacts of wetter periods in the past, the presence of fixed sand–dunes in areas currently too humid to support such dunes illustrates the environmental effect of past dry climates.

Figure 2.13 shows that contemporary dunes are mostly found in areas with less than 150 mm rainfall and appropriate geologic and topological conditions (rocks which supply sand-size debris and generally low or gently undulating topography). However, old dunes are found in a zone well to the south of this 150 mm isohyet line in North Africa and toward the north of the Kalahari in South Africa. These fixed dunes, which occur in a zone up to 300 km wide on

Figure 2.13 The limit of active and inactive sand dunes in northern Africa.

the margin of the current desert, were formed in a drier period or in periods when arid conditions were much more widespread than at present. They became covered with vegetation as the climate became more humid. Today these stabilized dunes are very vulnerable environments, subject to reactivation of dune movement if human activity removes the sustaining vegetation. The current situation is that, if vegetation or soils are altered, the ground environment can become drier. Thus, even if the climate remains constant, the change in the surface vegetation will prevent the dunes from becoming stable.

Besides the fixed sand–dunes, there are considerable areas of sand sheets which bury preexisting topography. In parts of Khordofan in Sudan, subsurface streams flowing on the old topography can be tapped for drinking and irrigation water if their location beneath the sand sheets can be determined. Recent radar images of parts of southern Egypt show the presence of abandoned channels of the Nile now covered by sheet sand (McCauley et al. 1982). Such channels are likely to be preferred sites for subsurface water supply.

Rivers

Obviously the climatic variations which result in greater lakes and a wider extent of sand–dunes and sand sheets also have an influence on stream and river patterns. Some of these have already been alluded to – for example, the different flow pattern of the Benue with a larger Lake Chad, and the White Nile ending in a lake south of Khartoum at one period. Generally, in Africa, the record of the rivers shows a complicated history reflecting both climatic and tectonic changes. Although we know the general pattern, with much higher stream flows during the more humid periods being part of the record, the detailed history is far from clear in most cases.

The pattern of river evolution in Africa is a function of two primary factors: the general geologic nature of the basin, including relief, type of underlying rocks, crustal warping, and volcanic activity; and climatic fluctuations. It is sometimes difficult to separate the effects of climatic change from other factors. For example, the Nile, often cited in this chapter, is a river made up of two major subsystems: the White Nile system and the Blue Nile system. In the modern Nile, the Blue Nile is responsible for most of the floodwater of the lower Nile, and the pattern of climatic change in Ethiopia and central Sudan is probably reflected in the high and low flood levels of the Nile in northern Sudan and upper Egypt. Wetter periods result in high flood levels in a direct way. Conversely it appears that the lake ponding and high water level on the White Nile may be associated with a somewhat drier period, the ponding only occurring when the Blue Nile is depositing material in central Sudan near Khartoum.

The Zaire and the Niger both show high flood levels in response to the wetter periods. Although there have been tectonic changes in their basins, they illustrate the general dominance of climatic change over other factors in river flow.

Case studies

Two case studies are presented in the remainder of this chapter to illustrate some impacts of climatic change. The first, in Mauritania, demonstrates the cumulative impacts of both climatic change and human activity on the environment.

The second, from East Africa, illustrates periodic drought and high rainfall impacts in this area.

MAURITANIA

Mauritania is situated on the northern edge of the Sahel (semi-arid) belt and the southern edge of the Sahara (arid). Thus its location places it in a very delicate environmental situation. As the variation in precipitation from year to year is normally large in this type of transitional climatic area, wide ranges of precipitation are expected even within a consistent climatic period. If either the climate changes or environmental stability is altered by human activities, large-scale changes can occur. The Senegal River, in Mauritania, is located more or less along the boundary between arid and semi-arid climates; it forms an important artery at or near the southern margin of the country. This is the zone where the majority of the population is concentrated; the remaining portions of the country have very low population densities. A long history of environmental change has been described for Mauritania (Gritzner 1981).

The prehistoric pattern of environmental change is related to the climatic history of northwest Africa, as well as to its contact location between the Arabian north and the African south. The first groups that appear to have migrated south through the Mauritanian area appeared during a very dry period (the Ogolian oscillation). This occupation by Aterian people ended with the succeeding humid Chadian (11,000–10,000 BP) climatic period. It is during these two periods that the earliest record of the Mauritania environment is documented. It is important to note that at this period the vegetation was more diversified in both arid and humid times than it is at present. Gritzner (1981) explains that paleolithic hunters may have modified Mauritania ecosystems over many thousands of years. In all cases the ecosystems became less diverse as selective removal of flora and fauna occurred.

The effects of fire and of selective gathering of fruits are clearly major activities that have contributed to the reduction of diversity in Mauritanian ecosystems. In the period 10,000–5000 BP, the climate was humid with the 800 mm isohyet approximately at the Senegal River. Savanna vegetation was dominant in Mauritania and a well developed neolithic civilization evolved during these years.

The first major deterioration in the ecology of the region appears to have occurred in the period 5000–1000 BP when the large savanna animals disappeared from the Adrar and Tisbit regions. This was due in part to increasing aridity and in part to the increased human pressure on resources caused by climatic change. The first report from the historical period is by Hanno (c. 425 BC), who reports of widespread fires in the interior of Africa. This suggests that by medieval times the vegetation of the interior was a greatly degraded fire subclimax.

Comparisons of plant communities reconstructed from medieval sources with the species listed in polynological literature for periods that were comparable climatically do in fact indicate that by the turn of the Middle Ages, the vegetation of Mauritania was already a cultural artifact. (Gritzner 1981, 56)

There are specific details of environmental degradation in the Middle Ages. One example is the oasis of Awdaghart established in the 6th century AD. There are enough records of the oasis to allow the following conclusions to be drawn:

(a) Felling of trees on the desert margin for charcoal production started in the Middle Ages and has continued to exert environmental pressure to the present.

(b) Between the 10th and 11th centuries, dry farming at Awdaghart gave way to irrigated gardens and the need for imported food. Springs appeared to have dried up due to depression of the groundwater table. This could have resulted from either climatic change, soil degradation, or from widespread planting of trees.

(c) In the 11th century the Sonoinke of Ghana dominated the area. They brought with them many sheep and cows, and the grazing of these animals probably caused dramatic changes in the variety of grasses.

Later, Berber and Arab settlements were located for preference on sand-dunes and sandy ridges. This intensive use of sandy areas led to renewed blowing of sand and instability of the topsoil.

In Mauritania, the principle cause of the major environmental degradation before major European contacts in the 15th century were:

(a) brush fires;
(b) charcoal production;
(c) the impact of cattle and sheep;
(d) the impact of Berber and Arab settlements, mostly located on sand-dunes.

The effects of European contacts became distinguishable in the 15th century when Portuguese landings became frequent along the coast. Later the Dutch began to use the gum arabic from the Acacia Senegal forests commercially. Intense European competition for this product was later to result in tapping methods which greatly stressed the trees. This commercial expansion, along with the droughts of the 1700s and 1800s, completed the devastation of the Acacia Senegal forests. In Mauritania, deforestation was thus a major problem long before the 20th century.

The slave trade also had major indirect impacts, as well as the obvious direct effects on the population. The impact of the slave trade was to alter the labor and social relationships within groups, as well as forcing groups and individuals away from the more intensively used areas into more marginal environments. Another effect was the spread of firearms in the area and the consequent major loss of game animals, which clearly left its imprint in the area.

"As the wild herbivores declined in number, their contribution to local diets and to the regenerative dynamics of Mauritania ecosystems (plant stimulation and seed disposal) similarly declined." (Gritzner 1981, 790.) It may also have been that as the wildlife declined, sheep, goats, and cattle became more plentiful and thus in part filled the gap. The destructive impact of cattle and sheep (more than goats) on Mauritania became much more widespread as a result of travel and increased mobility in the 1700s and 1800s. Soil erosion caused by overgrazing was clearly initiated during these early years.

The period of French occupation and pacification which took place over the first third of the 20th century also had its impact on the environment, with severe local land degradation around the military camps and establishments.

Finally, the following quotation illustrates the judgements of Gritzner on the impact of the events of the last 50 years on the Mauritanian environment (Gritzner 1981).

Modern Mauritania

The successful pacification of the country removed several constraints to further environmental degradation. Perhaps most important, the widespread practice of raiding to compensate for shortages of food, for the acquisition of wealth, or for strategic purposes was brought to an end. The cessation of raiding simultaneously initiated a number of environmentally damaging events: agricultural populations that had abandoned Mauritania in order to avoid enslavement and predation reestablished themselves in southern Mauritania. With them came herds of cattle, goats, and sheep. The disfranchised warrior class was left largely with only herding and commerce as acceptable occupations, and economic considerations resulted in a rather abrupt shift in herd composition from camels to cattle, as the latter were more marketable within the context of the new economic order. Furthermore, the French policy of *association*, working through traditional leaders, had strengthened the marabouts at the expense of the warrior class, and the new wealth acquired by the marabouts was characteristically invested in herds of cattle. Finally Tokolor herdsmen interviewed, described recent changes in their herding practices that have emerged from the virtual eradication of wild carnivores in the pastoral zone. In the past, young herders were instructed to avoid forests and thickets in order to maintain herd control and avoid livestock losses to predators. The fear of such losses passed with the elimination of the large carnivores, and herds were permitted to enter wooded areas. The extension of herding into these areas has resulted in the widespread removal of protective understory and seedlings, reduced wildlife habitat, poorer precipitation interception and decreased ground-water recharge, the elimination of many wild plants and animals central to human coping strategies during periods of scarcity, and a general breakdown in critical ecological processes.

Particularly the proliferation of cattle, substantially increased pressure upon the country's environmental systems. The situation was further aggravated by economic incentives and livestock maintenance programs that strongly favored cattle at the expense of better adapted forms of livestock. According to Francis de Chassey, similar economic incentives encouraged agricultural expansion, with emphasis placed upon the production of cash crops. Further environmental degradation has been associated with sedentarization, charcoal production in relation to urbanization, increased vehicular traffic and expanded transportation networks, building construction, and mining activities.

Degradation from all of these causes has increased tremendously since independence. Much of it can be attributed directly to uniformed economic development and opportunism. Cattle populations, for example, continued to increase far in excess of local requirements. In 1959, there were approximately 1,250,000 head of cattle in Mauritania; in 1968, there were an estimated 2,300,000 – an increase of 1,050,000. During the same period, the human population had increased by only some 170,000 individuals. The relative lack of experience of Moors in managing cattle, combined with a progressive loss of herders to sedentarization and other labor alternatives, resulted in poor herd control. Poor management, in turn, can greatly increase the environmental impact of livestock. While herds of cattle were growing rapidly, other forms of livestock such as camels that are better adapted, more easily controlled, and less destructive, registered an aggregate decline of approximately 1 million animals.

It is perhaps somewhat ironic that historical use pressure and the traditional focus of developers upon increased agricultural and pastoral production have largely destroyed the very resources that sustained Mauritanian populations during the period of scarcity. Geographers, anthropologists, and botanists active in the Sahel have long realized that when drought, disease, warfare, or other mishaps result in agricultural failure (requirements in excess of crop yields and storage) or sharply reduced livestock populations, these people were sustained by coping strategies based upon the availability of diverse native plants and animals.

The conclusions of the case study suggest:

(a) that environmental change has occurred over a very long period;
(b) that many influences are important;
(c) that many species have been lost to these ecosystems;
(d) that recent change has been quite rapid and difficult to repair; and
(e) that the impact of cattle and sheep in this particular area is all pervasive and linked with the loss of wild livestock may be the key to many other changes.

EAST AFRICA

The Mauritanian case study reviewed a long series of environmental changes in that country. This East African case study examines some evidence for climatic change as the basis for environmental change during recent periods. The widespread African droughts of the early 1970s raised questions about long-term climatic trends which are addressed here. Three questions are posed:

(1) Is the climate getting drier?
(2) What is the nature of rainfall variability?
(3) What is the nature of drought?

Is the climate of eastern Africa getting drier? In response to the 1970s droughts and rising concern over desertification, many researchers have analyzed climate records for long-term trends that might indicate whether the recent dryness is likely to continue or whether it is within the bounds of the expected range of conditions.

Table 2.6 Climate of eastern Africa, 15,000 to 3000 BP.

Dates	Climate	Theorized global boundary conditions
20,000–12,000 BP	arid and semi-arid climate; advance of sand-dunes in Sudan, dry lakes in Kenya, Blue Nile aggrading its river bed, lower lakes in Djibouti and Ethiopia, Lake Victoria below its outlet for 2000 years	increased temperature gradient between tropics and glaciated northern latitudes, shift of pressure zones toward equator, stronger Hadley cell, suppressed northward movement of ITC
10,000–8000 BP	wet; extensive lake development, lakes formed near Khartoum and Kosti, Lake Victoria outlet to Blue Nile, Lake Turkana 80 m higher than today, East African lakes very high	melting of glaciers in northern latitudes, moderate Hadley cell, weaker than today in S. Hemisphere, stronger in N. Hemisphere, northward displacement of ITC, increased maritime evaporation
7000 BP	brief widespread aridity; lowering lake levels	warmer N. and S. Hemisphere temperatures, temperature gradient less than today, circulation patterns displaced poleward, weaker Hadley cell than today, northward movement of ITC increased
6500–4500 BP	wetter in East Africa, contraction of desert, Nile floods higher (5 m) than today, Lakes Victoria and Naivasha high	

Source: Nicholson and Flohn (1980).

In eastern Africa this is a difficult question to answer. Rainfall is a much more complex phenomenon than in West Africa, partly due to the presence of the East African highlands. Reliable instrument records date, at the earliest, to the late 1800s, with a more extensive network developed in 1920–30, but many of these new stations have gaps in their precipitation data. Records of less than 50 years in length reflect interannual variability that may either mask or overstate longer-term trends. Efforts to extend the instrumented rainfall records rely on correlations with lake and river records and information from journals, geographic surveys, and the like. Of course, even the best of climatic reconstructions without a causal model can only project a continuation of a trend, and not the actual course of events.

On the longest scale, Nicholson and Flohn (1980) have documented wet and dry millennia (Table 2.6). The Late Pleistocene was dry with an expansion of the Saharan and semi-arid climate in East Africa. Based on closed-basin studies, maximum precipitation estimates for East Africa range from 54 percent to about 90 percent of the present normals. Extensive development of lakes occurred in 10,000–5000 BP, followed by a brief dry episode c. 7000 BP. The Neolithic was generally wetter with many lakes larger than at present. Rainfall at the height of the pluvial period, 8000–9000 BP, may have been 165 percent above current averages.

The climate of the last five centuries (Table 2.7) has been reconstructed for

Table 2.7 Climate of eastern Africa, AD 1500 to present.

Years	Probable conditions
AD 1500–1700	generally wetter over much of Africa, but drier in East Africa (lower summer minimum of Nile), wetter in Ethiopia (higher Nile flood)
1681–87	drought in Sudan and Sahel
1738–56	wetter in Sudan, drought in Sahel, dry in Tanzania, wetter in Ethiopia (very high Nile floods)
1750s to 1800	generally more humid
1820s to 1850s	general drought in northern Africa, 7 years of drought in Sudan, much of East Africa dry (lower Nile in general, Lake Tanganyika low)
1870–95	wetter in most areas, wet throughout eastern Africa; precipitation above present normal throughout East Africa (rise in lake levels at Magadi, Nakuru, Jilore, Ngami, Baratuma, Victoria, Rudolf, Tanganyika, Nyasa, Rukwa, Chad, Stefanie); some lake levels fell in 1880s, but were still above present levels
1895–1900	drier (sharp decrease in lake levels)
1900 to 1950s	stable lake levels
1910 to 1920s	severe drought
1960s	rapid rise in lakes, wetter in many parts of East Africa (Lake Victoria rose 2 m in 1961, Lake Tanganyika rose 3 m in 1960–4)
1970s	drier, sharp contrast to 1960s

Source: Nicholson (1978).

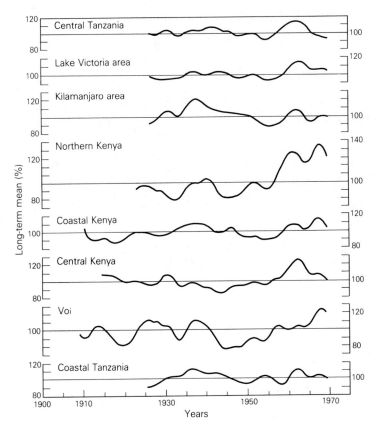

Figure 2.14 General rainfall pattern throughout East Africa between 1900 and 1975 (from Rodhe & Virji 1976, Fig. 4).

northern Africa by Nicholson (1978); she based her conclusions largely on lake and river levels (Fig. 2.6), supplemented with other data. The 1500s to 1700s were generally more humid across most of northern Africa but were probably drier in East Africa. Notable drought occurred in the late 1600s and middle 1700s. There was a more humid climate from the 1750s to about 1800, followed by drought in the 1820s and 1850s. The period 1870–95 saw first a rapid increase, then a decrease in lake levels. A similar humid episode occurred in the 1960s, which appeared to have a brief interruption in the downward trend. Based on lake records, the climate may be returning to the 1900–50 normal, a generally dry period with droughts in 1910–20 and in the 1950s in East Africa. The 1960s, the first decade of independence for many African states, may have been an unusually humid period climatically.

Rodhe and Virji (1976) analyzed annual rainfall for 35 stations in East Africa. The stations were grouped into eight areal average regional series which were then normalized and filtered to remove fluctuations of less than five years (Fig. 2.14). Only northern Kenya demonstrates a long-term (upward) trend, but the data there are suspect due to possible measurement errors (changes in the gauge position). The late 1940s and 1950s appear dry everywhere, followed by the very wet 1960s.

What is the nature of precipitation variability? Precipitation variability has two components – spatial and temporal – both of which are sensitive to scales. Variability decreases (and reliability increases) as the averaging period becomes longer and the geographic region larger. Extreme variability is illustrated in Figure 2.15 for monthly rainfall at one station.

Johnson (1962) found that rainfalls in East Africa occurred in individual storm cells but as part of a larger pattern of general rain. The larger rain systems are not advected, nor can they be described by a simple zonal ITC theory. The progression of rainfall is not uniform, as it appears simultaneously in several places. Sharon (1972) evaluated the spatial correlation of daily rainfall in

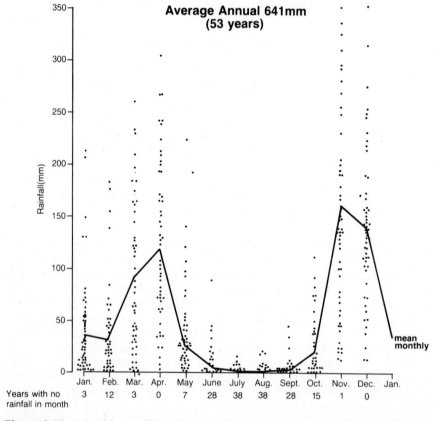

Figure 2.15 Monthly rainfall at Kibwezi, Kenya, for a 53-year period (reprinted with the permission of P. W. Porter, Food and development in the semi-arid zone of East Africa. 1979, Maxwell School of Citizenship and Public Affairs, Foreign and Comparative Studies Program, Syracuse University).

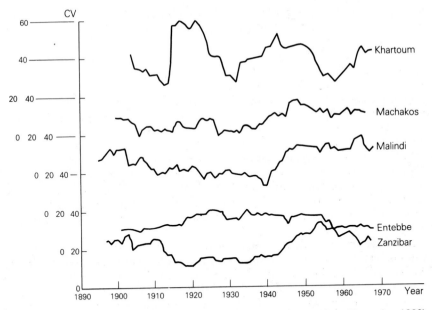

Figure 2.16   Rainfall variability in eastern Africa, 1890–1970 (from Downing 1982).

Sukumaland, Tanzania. Storm cells tended to develop concurrently 40–60 km apart, and also at about a distance of 100 km. A less rigorous study of rain cells in Sudan showed an average distance between cells at 50 km or less (Hammer cited in Sharon 1972).

Due to the distribution of convective cells, the rainfall for a month or longer at one station may be markedly different from the rainfall at stations from less than 1 to 20 km distance, even in areas of uniform relief and similar annual averages (Jackson 1981). Typically 10–15 percent of the rain days contribute 50 percent of the rainfall. This pattern appears to hold true in West Africa too (Lewis 1981). Local relief and aspect may increase the differences and may cause the entire pattern of variability to differ, due to the influence of various rain mechanisms. Thus it may take months for individual localities in a region to receive similar amounts of rain. In years of widespread drought, the spatial pattern is likely to be more homogeneous; dryness probably exists somewhere even in wet years. Regional indicators of rainfall deficiency will be most reliable for areas of similar variability.

Of interest for predicting future rainfall is whether or not precipitation occurs in cycles. Several periodicities have been identified, but so far they have not been useful in forecasting rainfall. Rodhe and Virji (1976) identified periodicities of 2–2.5, 3.5, and 5–5.5 years with a lesser peak at 10 years. The first three periodicities are significantly different from the background noise (at the 95 percent probability level), but, even so, they explain only 25 percent of the variance. We are not optimistic about their predictive value, though this line of research may be useful in establishing the physical basis for the climate and

67

teleconnections, with oscillations recorded elsewhere. At Tanga, Tanzania, the two-year periodicity may be helpful in predicting rainfall from one year to the next. The strong negative correlation indicates that above median rainfall one year will be followed by below median rainfall the next (probability of 62 percent).

To assess climate variability over time, coefficients of variations for 11-year running periods were computed for stations with long records, some of which are illustrated in Figure 2.16. As with the trends in rainfall, no clear pattern was evident throughout eastern Africa, though drier stations predictably showed large precipitation ranges – the effect of single unusually wet years. Stations, particularly those along the East African coast, had large rainfall variabilities in the 1890s to early 1900s and again in the 1960s to 1970s (e.g. Zanzibar). Only three of the 26 stations analyzed throughout East Africa had a decrease in variability in the 1960s to 1970s; twelve evidenced recent increased climatic variability. There appears to be a trend towards generally increased variability.

What is the nature of drought episodes?   Variable precipitation and high evapotranspirative demands result in a pattern of water shortage or drought. The human use of the water cycle determines when the meteorologic dryness becomes a drought of wider concern. Besides simple drought frequencies, of importance are the familiar questions of space and time – for how long will the drought persist and is it likely to be local, regional, national, or transnational?

Johnson (1962) found aridity to be associated with reduced frequency of rainfall, not diminished amounts when it does rain, nor more scattered storms. This is in keeping with the general observation of drought periods as having fewer rain days, and not necessarily a reduction in precipitation. The frequency of droughts follows a pattern similar to that of rainfall variability (Nieuqolt 1978). Roughly from southwest to northwest, drought frequency in East Africa increases from less than 15 to over 25 percent (probability of a month during the growing season receiving less than half its mean rainfall (750 mm), or less than a critical level of 100 mm). The correlation with rainfall variability, while significant, explains only a third of the drought frequencies, implicating other factors in determining drought.

Severe drought in eastern Africa is marked by its duration rather than its intensity. Nieuqolt's (1977) weighted measure of persistence captures the increased severity of longer droughts. The severest droughts in East Africa occur along the coast and to the east of Lake Victoria. An analysis of areally averaged rainfall for the Sahelo-Sudanic zones (including Ethiopia, Sudan, and Somalia, as well as West Africa) found statistically significant persistence (Kraus 1977). But when conditional probabilities were analyzed it became apparent that the relationship had little predictive value – the expected variability is much larger than the expected decrease in rainfall, given a dry preceding year (Katz 1978). This is probably true for East Africa as well.

To document the spatial patterns of drought the annual rainfall for 120 stations was normalized, and dry years were charted and summarized by country (Fig. 2.17). Although this approach gives a broad overview of the drought pattern, using annual values may mask severe seasonal droughts, which are of more importance for agriculture. This is especially likely where the rainy

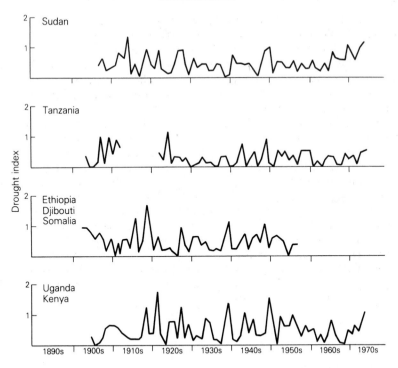

Figure 2.17 Drought patterns in eastern Africa, 1890–1970 (from Downing 1982).

and growing seasons are in December to January. One of the most notable features is that, though the 1960s were wet in the south (East Africa), they (and the 1910s as well) were very dry in Sudan, illustrating the climatic link between Sudan and the West African Sahelo-Sudanic zones. Tanzania appears to have a distinct drought climatology with fewer severe droughts and is less affected by the droughts of the other regions. Major droughts occurred throughout most of eastern Africa in 1918, 1927, 1939, 1949, 1955, 1969, and 1972. The extreme, large-scale droughts rarely extended more than two years; abrupt changes from dry to average or wet conditions are common. Of course local droughts, water supply deficits, and social impacts may extend over several years, linking two meteorologically distinct episodes.

Conclusion

This review of the African environment has emphasized, on the one hand, the age and stability of the continent in terms of its geology and general climatic pattern. Soils and vegetation have been free to evolve on this old land surface for very long periods of geologic time. This has important implications for the pattern of soil formation; generally many of the soils are nutrient poor, though wide areas of fertile younger soils are to be found, especially in the volcanic highlands and along some valley bottoms covered with alluvial soils.

The history of climatic and environmental change in Africa is long and complex. Climatic variability during the Pleistocene and Recent periods has had important impacts on the current environment. There is widespread evidence of both wetter and drier climates. There is also clear evidence of a long history of human interference with the environment. The case study on Mauritania illustrates this with a record of over 2000 years of environmental modification by the various groups of people who have lived in that area. The case study on East Africa deals with the more recent variability of weather and climate in that area and its impact on current conditions. Large areas in Africa have extreme seasonality in precipitation patterns. When the wet season arrives late, or has less than average precipitation, because of the low levels of moisture storage in the soils, crop yields drop. Because of generally low storage capacity, this decrease in food production results in overutilization of many aspects of the resource base. Stress is placed on the soil, vegetation, and water components in large areas of Africa to meet the shortfall in food supply, and environmental problems increase. With increasing population pressures these problems seem to be increasing. These human processes intensify the impact of naturally occurring processes throughout most of Africa.

3 The patterns of political change: relationship to the environment

Precolonial

Political processes acting through the ages resulted in many societies in Africa; Africa was perhaps more fragmented than any other area at the time of European colonial incursions dating variously from the 16th century in West Africa and the 19th century in East Africa. The evolution of African peoples into organized societies from the Neolithic period (7000 BC) to the 16th century took various paths in response to economic endeavors, environmental settings, social and political processes and interactions with people from external areas.

Although the continent was largely populated by hunters and gatherers, sedentary groupings of from 100 to 1000 people had already evolved by the Late Stone Age. Fishermen, especially in the lands of the eastern lake areas near Lake Mobutu Sese Seko (Albert) and Lake Turkana, probably represent the earliest groupings of sedentary people in Africa. By 6000 B.C. the processes of change from hunting and gathering to agriculture and stock-raising were under way in parts of Saharan and sub-Saharan Africa. This change in livelihood systems is preserved in numerous rock paintings and archaeological relics. With this evolution to agricultural and pastoral systems the process of people modifying the environment increases. By altering vegetation and domesticating animals, the inhabitants become less dependent on the natural environment, and a cultural environment gradually grows. Once this break in land use occurs, population growth and increasing cultural diversity are possible, since no longer are community size and occupation necessarily directly linked to the availability of wildlife and wild plants.

Environmental linkages in tribal Africa

For lack of a better word, the term "tribe" will be used to differentiate the diverse groups of people inhabiting Africa prior to the colonial period, but throughout it will be borne in mind that in Africa "tribe" encompasses many group relationships. In some cases it represents an African society based on kinship where a given group traces its descent back to a common ancestral beginning. In many cases it represents a grouping having a common language; though in some cases it is no more than a classification of some people grouped by neighbors into a single caregory, which became formalized by colonial administrators.

71

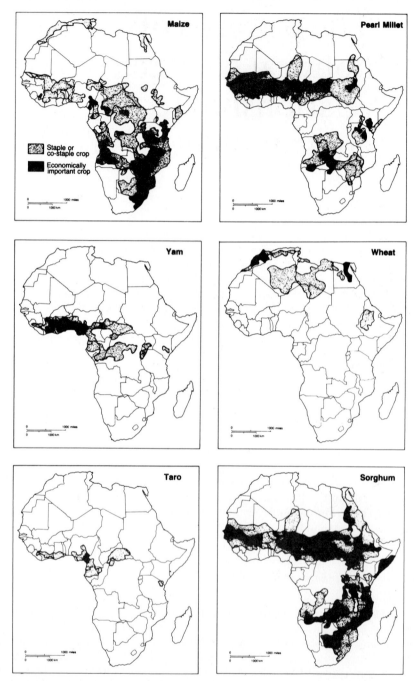

Figure 3.1 Distribution of the major staple crops within Africa: (a) maize; (b) pearl millet; (c) yam; (d) wheat; (e) taro; (f) sorghum; (g) rice and teff; (h) sweet potato;

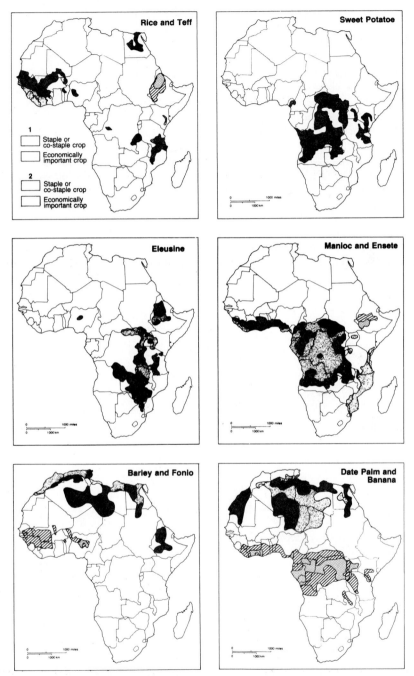

(i) eleusine; (j) manioc and ensete; (k) barley and fonio; (l) date palm and banana. (Adapted by permission of the American Geographical Society from Murdock 1960.)

Before the colonial period, six major types of food staples were utilized throughout the continent (Fig. 3.1). Each of the food types has an environmental context. Treelike crops (banana) predominate in the year-round humid environments of the Zaire Basin; date palms are concentrated in North Africa and the lower Nile Valley; herding predominates in the African dry lands; grains are centered on the wet–dry areas; and root crops are found in both the more humid wet–dry and rainforest areas. Fishing is, of course, found along coasts, lake margins, and waterways.

The grain areas are subdivided into the primarily mid-latitude grains of barley and wheat in northern Africa and tropical grains in the highlands. Barley and wheat were often grown in northern Africa in conjunction with olives and vine crops. In tropical Africa the grain areas grew maize (corn) brought over from America before the colonial conquests, sorghum, millet, rice, and teff. In the Sahalian grazing areas diets were supplemented with dates that were grown in isolated moist areas within this zone. Figure 3.1 delimits the areas where each food type was, and still is, dominant; however, the diversity of food types in any one area of Africa is of greater complexity than illustrated in simplified form in Fig. 3.2. All general climatic areas, such as semi-arid zones, are not homo-

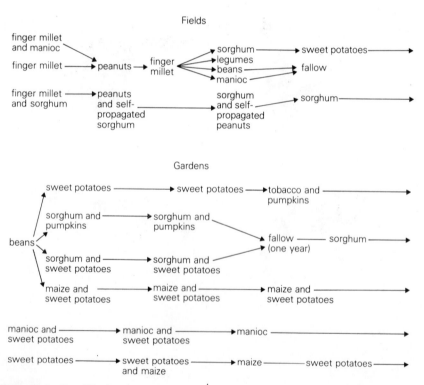

Figure 3.2 Possible diversity of staples in one agricultural farming (rotation) system in Zambia: arrows indicate change in crops from season to season. (Modified from Richards 1961.)

geneous; one adjustment to this diversity is that different peoples often use different methods of food production in their food systems, even if the staple is the same.

Since environments are not static, but change from season to season and over time periods, one characteristic existing prior to the colonial period was the mobility of many Africans. Mobility was an adjustment to environmental fluctuations. Fish supplies move to different areas within river systems; areas of rainfall shift from place to place in semi-arid climates, both seasonally and yearly; and soils in the humid and wet–dry tropics often need to be rested (fallowed) before annual crops can be grown again. All of these environmental factors contributed to the movement of people.

But it must be emphasized that the potential for mobility in response to environmental factors does not mean that shifting cultivation was the prevailing *modus operandi* for farming systems throughout Africa prior to the colonial period. Many husbandry areas were occupied by permanent or semi-permanent settlements where perennial crops could be grown in selected areas, such as along river valley bottoms, year after year.

Smallness of scale is probably the fundamental characteristic of the livelihood systems in existence during the precolonial period in Africa. For farmers both the land under cultivation and the organized production unit were small, whereas for pastoralists the production unit was small, even though large areas were required to satisfy the food needs of the herds. In addition, since the primary economies were either agriculture or herding, there was a very high dependence on the physical environment. In the general case, people acquired farmland or grazing rights at no cost – that is, land-use privileges belonged to the tribes, not to individuals. Tribal lands usually had sufficient areal extent to permit food production for the normal range of environmental situations. Smallness of scale, though presenting difficulties in acquiring surpluses for periods of poor food production, allowed for flexibility in moving to a favorable location within the tribal area. Unlike the perception given by most tribal maps, where divisions between groups appear discrete in many African areas, ter- restrial space was not mutually exclusive; in fact, tribal units were often intermixed, especially in North Africa. In addition, land could be cropped during a portion of the year by one group and grazed during another portion of the year by another group. Neither tribal occupancy nor land use were neces- sarily mutually exclusive in any given environment for many areas in Africa.

In precolonial Africa there was little need to produce agricultural commodities far in excess of the needs of the extended family. This meant that most families in any given year were satisfied with small amounts of land. As the size of the extended family grew, land demands by individual family units remained small, but more tribal or family lands would be used. In very few places in Africa was potential growth restricted by land constraints (one area was in the Nile Valley). Likewise, if local environmental factors such as soil fertility began to affect food production, individual family units usually would just move to a new small parcel of land where they had preemptive rights to utilize it. Thus, given the demands of the inhabitants during the precolonial period, little stress from cultivation was placed on the environment, since when problems occurred sufficient flexibility existed for other lands to be brought into production.

Another generalization about food systems in precolonial Africa and their relationship to the environment is that usually food production systems and their yields were largely determined by the properties of the natural environment. Yet there are exceptions to this general condition. For example, in central and eastern Africa the clearing of land by farmers or agroherders – largely by fire – removed much of the brush in many areas which is critical for tsetse fly infestation. Thus Africans learned to use environments for their livelihood which, without human-induced alterations, would not have been feasible. Indeed, in general pastoralists did use fire as a management strategy for increasing rangeland at the expense of scrub forest.

In northern Africa (Mediterranean) and Ethiopia some drainage and irrigation works, the plow, and other aids were used to make the relationship between society and the natural environment less direct. But in sub-Saharan areas farming and herding operated largely without such aids. For most of these traditional African societies, the response to environmental fluctuations was mutual dependence within family or tribal units and movement to nonutilized lands within the areas where preemptive rights existed. Given this situation, to deviate from traditional practices was risky since, if new crops or techniques were used and failed, hunger was likely. When severe environmental factors, such as drought or locust plagues, cause a given area to no longer be able to satisfy the needs of the people, populations either decreased or moved to other areas. Thus, even under these poor conditions, the physical environment itself was not placed under severe stress and therefore did not undergo irreversible degradation. Before human populations either grew or moved back into the area, the environment had sufficient time to recover from the past environmental fluctuation. This is a critical difference between the past and contemporary Africa. Today, without outside intervention, when physical environments are placed under severe stress (e.g. drought), the inhabitants attempt to keep the areas in production. As a consequence, they sometimes undergo irreversible degradation. However, in some areas, as will be exemplified in later chapters, the early use of the natural environment caused significant changes in the prevailing ecosystems, These changes, though not generally devastating at the time, did set the stage for later severe environmental degradation.

Colonial period

The establishment of colonial boundaries

The multiplicity of environmental impacts resulting from European colonization were due not only to the variety of physical and sociocultural environments found on the continent, but also resulted from the fact that there were various stages of colonization. Prior to the 1880s, Europeans were largely unconcerned with direct annexation of territory. Instead they attempted to establish working agreements with the existing African political systems. In West Africa, this usually took the form of the Europeans providing subsidies to local powers, which in turn provided protection to the commercial activities of the various European trading establishments. During these early European incursions, little change in the activities of Africans occurred, excluding the results of the slave trade. This early stage of colonial activity is largely limited to North and West Africa and, in these areas, European influence was almost entirely restricted to the coastal areas.

This early commercial trading activity helped to start the process of growth in the scale of African economic systems. The general smallness of scale in precolonial livelihood systems was subjected to external influences that began to weaken the generally prevailing subsistence economies. This is not meant to imply that trade was solely in response to outside forces, but rather that European activity encouraged this at the expense of other options. Thus the existing trading systems were altered and new ones grew in response to colonial stimuli. For instance, salt trading centering on Bilma (Niger), Taoudeni (Mali), and Timbuktu (Mali) was in existence long before the interaction with Europeans began. Also trading in cloth between northern Nigeria and the Senegal area and in kola nut from Asante (Ghana) to the savanna areas was underway. But with the arrival of European activity trading patterns changed from a largely interior orientation to the ever-growing importance of an external orientation. This partially is reflected in a comparison of precolonial towns and towns after colonial activity; interior towns such as Timbuktu declined in comparison with coastal towns, some of which – Lagos, for example – were not in existence before the colonial period.

As colonization became ever more formalized, trade patterns between colony and mother country grew at the expense of inter-African movements. Coastal cities grew and trade infrastructures developed along an internal-to-coastal axis (export–import) (Fig. 3.3). For example, in Nigeria a transport system evolved increasing north–south connectivity with little east–west investment in transport systems.

The formalized colonial process began in the 1880s in response to European political events. Beginning with the 1884–5 Berlin Conference, which established the principle that if a country was to make a territorial claim, the land had to be occupied; a series of treaties between European nations divided up the continent (Fig. 3.4). This division, which was almost completely finished by 1900, established boundaries largely in response to an attempt to achieve a competitive balance among the European power brokers. With the complete allocation of lands, colonialization stabilized, except after World War I when former German colonies were redistributed.

Boundaries were now established that had little relation to indigenous processes. These political boundaries established by the colonial powers had little relation to either the physical or socioeconomic environments within Africa. Boundaries often divided tribes, and existing kingdoms,* placed integrated components of a single livelihood system such as wet-season and dry-season grazing lands into two or more political entities, or at times made some political units fall almost completely within a "homogeneous" arid climatic zone. It was within these largely arbitrary boundaries that the colonial

* Exceptions to this were Egypt, Morocco, and Tunisia in the north; Burundi, Rwanda, and Zanzibar in the east; Lesotho and Swaziland in the south.

powers attempted to make these new colonies pay for themselves. Given the rather arbitrary manner in which boundaries between colonial powers were determined, it is clear that European intervention in Africa was not the product of a well developed masterplan of any colonial power. Additionally, with little data existing for most of Africa, the European powers did not know the economic potential of their new lands. Nevertheless, with innovations introduced into the African continent because of colonization, the increasing cultural and economic contacts between Africans and Europeans resulted in both new problems and new opportunities for both parties. To a large degree, colonial policy evolved from a series of ad hoc decisions both in the mother countries and by colonial administrators on site. However, as the Europeans controlled the political and legal systems, it was inevitable that the greatest benefits would accrue to the Europeans during this period.

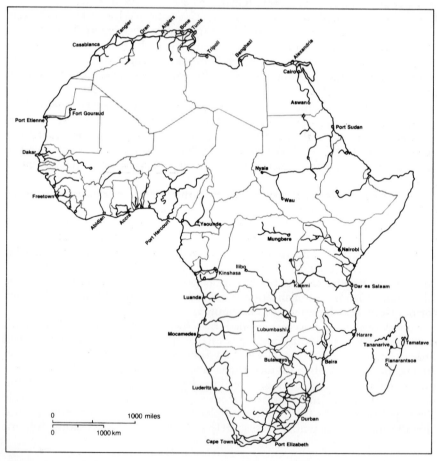

Figure 3.3 Railroads within Africa, illustrating the generally poor connectivity of the networks with the exception of southern Africa. (Modified from Hance 1975.)

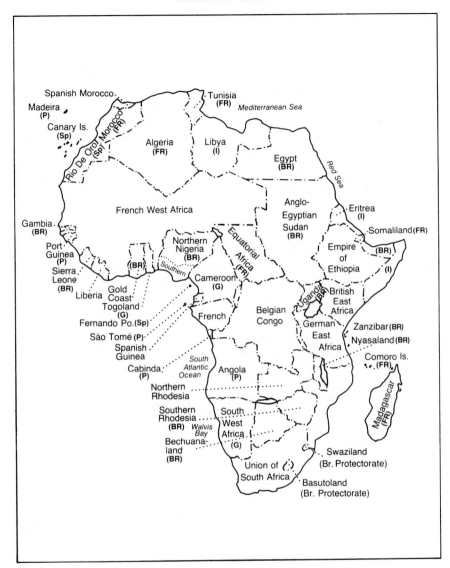

Figure 3.4 Distribution of European colonies within Africa in 1914 (from Hallett 1974).

Colonial impacts on Africa

In Africa, revenue for the colonial power was primarily raised from mineral, foodstuffs, or animal-hide exports. From a colonial perspective, agriculture was the major resource for most of Africa. Thus a major interest of colonial administrators was agricultural development. To develop surplus commodities from each colonial unit was a major priority. This meant increasing yields and introducing new crops for those products that could be exported. No single strategy by any colonial power was universally applied throughout the continent to increase agricultural output. Existing conditions, both in the mother country and in Africa at the advent of colonial occupation, required flexible policies. But three major models for increasing exports evolved. One was largely to take advantage of the peasant farmer already farming the lands. Through market incentives (profit) or tax policy the African farmer was encouraged to grow a percentage of crops that could be exported. A second model was to displace Africans from ownership of their lands, or to use lands not occupied by Africans. On these lands plantations (estates) were established that used European managers and African labor to produce almost solely export crops. In South Africa a variant of this model was used in that, instead of using only African labor, East Indians were encouraged to immigrate into the area and become the source of plantation labor. The third model was again either to displace Africans from land ownership or use nonoccupied areas, and to use settlers (European immigrants) as farmers.

Each of these models with their resulting agricultural change had impacts upon the environment. But in spite of the colonial desire to produce exports from the rural sector it is important to remember that the overwhelming majority of African farming and herding was done by the indigenous people making their own decisions. Only in southern Africa and the Maghrib (the lands north of the high Atlas Mountains in Morocco to southern Tunisia, including northern Algeria) did African farmers produce fewer foodstuffs than the combined outputs of colonial administered developmental schemes, plantation agriculture, and immigrant (settler) farmers.

The environmental impact of colonization was different in the major geographic units (north, south, central, east, west) because of differences in trading patterns, settlement patterns, the timing of the beginning of colonization, the particular colonizing power, and the length of the colonial period. For example, although the colonial period was longer in West Africa than in East Africa, the European impact on the land was greater in East Africa. In West Africa the large European farm was the exception in the prevailing colonial policy, whereas in large areas of the Kenyan Highlands and to a lesser extent in Tanganyika it was the accepted practice. The different colonial impacts in the various geographic units add to the complexity of understanding the diversity in African environments.

WEST AFRICA

Both the French and British tried to introduce plantations in West Africa. By and large, most of these projects failed for two reasons. First, the high mortality of European personnel prevented a large permanent managerial class from becoming established. Second, it was found to be more economical to obtain African products through trade. Although the French were more in favor of plantation development than the British, peasant production was dominant everywhere. In West Africa, as a whole peasant agriculture was the safest way to meet the needs of the colonial powers, both from a political and an economic perspective.

European investment here was largely limited to government, roads, railroads, and ports – all of which were oriented toward export growth. Prior to 1945, little effort was expended on improving the agriculture of the African peasant farmer. Subsistence crops, such as yams and cassava, were of little interest to the colonial powers, with the possible exception of the Germans in Togo and Cameroon. Yet revenues from export crops increased dramatically during this period with minimal technological help and investment from the colonial country.

From an agricultural perspective, the major impact during this period was the change over from subsistence economies oriented toward local areas to cash-crop and subsistence economies where a small percentage of crops were grown for cash or bartered foreign goods. The change to a partial cash economy results from a diverse set of events due to colonial actions. Some of these actions were the reduction of tribal warfare and the introduction of health services. These changes lowered death rates and population growth occurred. With the limited introduction of new agricultural technologies, land shortages began to appear in West Africa. Two responses to this emerging land pressure were: the African farmer began to grow cash crops to help purchase some of his needs, and the beginning of wage labor. Other stimuli resulting in the increase of lands under cash crops were the need of Africans to raise their income to pay colonial taxes and the desire of the people to purchase European goods or services. Dalton describes some effects of these changes in agriculture that in the colonial period resulted in most West African farmers having a cash component or income as "growth without development". As the bulk of the farmers' time and labor was used for their subsistence crops, often they could only cultivate enough cash crops to pay their taxes and to purchase the most basic goods. Nevertheless, in total, West African peasant agriculture produced large quantities of export crops during this period much to the advantage of the colonial powers.

The major export crops of West Africa were peanuts, gum, cocoa, palm oil, and rubber. Other significant exports were timber, hides, and gold. It was the peasant farmer who produced most of these crops, with the exception of rubber. Gum and peanuts were primarily crops of the dry areas, whereas cocoa, palm oil, and rubber were from the humid areas. Gum production was concentrated along the desert fringe, the semi-arid areas in West Africa, such as Mauritania. Peanuts were centered in the drier portions of the savanna areas.

After the introduction of the peanut from America during the colonial period, there was a sudden expansion in peanut production both for domestic consumption and export. From almost zero production in 1830, in Gambia and Senegal production rose to over 40,000 tons between 1875 and 1900. Likewise, the area of peanut production expanded all the way into northern Nigeria from the Gambian and Senegal areas. In French-controlled ports alone over 100,000 tons of peanuts were exported in 1900. The rapid growth of peanut production resulted in people migrating into Gambia, an area previously not heavily populated, from a 700 km wide surrounding area. This migration into peanut-producing areas and consequent population growth was widespread in these areas throughout West Africa. Thus in these dry savanna areas a relatively low, scattered population was replaced by a far larger rural population during the colonial era. Much marginal land was brought under cultivation, and environmental stress resulting from human activities began to become evident. For instance, in Senegal, severe soil degradation began in the 1920s. This lowered the area's overall soil fertility with the result that peanut yields generally decreased. In some specific locations it is now impossible to grow peanuts because of severe soil erosion.

Cocoa, like peanuts, was an American crop in origin. It was first cultivated in West Africa on Fernando Po (Bioko, Equatorial Guinea) on plantations, using much imported labor from the mainland, especially eastern Nigeria. But its major growth occurred as a peasant farmer crop in the more humid portions of the mainland from Nigeria westward. The largest area of cocoa cultivation was in Ghana (Gold Coast), Nigeria, and Ivory Coast. As cocoa requires large labor inputs, population dynamics of growth and seasonal migration were set into motion by this cash crop. The introduction of cocoa into West Africa encouraged population growth – largely through migration – into the forest country. Also, the labor demands during the harvest encouraged seasonal migration between the savanna and semi-arid zones of West Africa. From zero exports in the 1890s, West Africa accounted for about two-thirds of the world's exports by the end of the colonial period.

Rubber production in West Africa was largely concentrated in Liberia and Nigeria. In West Africa, rubber production began to be important during the 1920s after the decline of wild rubber. In Liberia it resulted in an economy almost completely dependent on this plantation crop, whereas in Nigeria the rubber crop was secondary to palm oil in the eastern and southern portions of the country. Growth in the production of palm oil occurred in the early phases of colonization; by the 1880s exports from Nigeria were over 30,000 tons per year. With the introduction of peanuts, palm-oil production stabilized. But palm-oil production remained important throughout the whole colonial period within the humid zones of West Africa. Today it remains a peasant farmer crop in almost all areas.

CENTRAL AFRICA

Within this area the French, Belgians, Spanish, and Portuguese established colonies, but the major colonial powers were France and Belgium. By far the largest area fell within the domain of the Belgians. Unlike other colonies, the Belgian Congo (Zaire) became affiliated with Belgium, not through the initial actions of its government, but by the manipulations of King Leopold. During the early stages of the King's involvement, the areas under his control for all practical purposes were governed as his private empire; for all practical purposes the King's private Congo state was run as a company government with forced labor and labor taxation. The company government was structured as an interlocking conglomerate, with various companies having specific monopolies of production within a given areal sphere. Different companies controlled rubber collection, mineral export, agricultural exports, and transport. The overriding criterion for each individual "corporation" within the King's "conglomerate" was profit. Thus the area comprising the Belgian Congo did not develop as a single entity during this stage. For example, the railway systems developed to export mineral wealth from the Katanga area exited through foreign countries (Fig. 3.3), as this was the least expensive route for export.

Most all other colonial powers attempted to control commerce through the development of transport solely within their areas of territorial control. The major transport in the western Belgian Congo utilized the Congo River, focusing on Stanleyville (Kinshasa) where rapids made overland transport necessary for the movement of goods for export.

Rubber was an early agricultural export, but primarily it was wild rubber collected through the use of forced labor. By 1913 exports dropped to almost zero owing to the competition from plantations outside Africa. In response to the rejection by the British government of the Lever Corporation's request to establish a palm-oil concession in British West Africa (the British favored peasant farmer production), 1.9 million acres (770,000 ha) of land were provided to the Lever Corporation in the Belgian Congo. Here palm oil was grown as a plantation crop and became the Congo's major agricultural export.

The French in central Africa governed three colonies: Gabon, Moyen Congo (People's Republic of Congo), and Ubangi Shari, (Central African Republic). Together these colonies were referred to as French Equatorial Africa. Nowhere was the population large within this area. Gabon became an export center for timber and minerals. Revenues generated in Gabon were used to defer costs in the other two French colonies, a practice that ceased after independence. In Ubangi Shari, the French decided that cotton should become an export crop. Because it was not economical, the colonial government had to resort to forced cultivation. To avoid this coercion, farmers left the countryside for towns; thus the agricultural potential of the countryside was lowered. In addition to cotton, coffee plantations were established in the 1920s to help offset the loss of revenue with the decline of wild rubber. To export crops from the interior of this colony, transport as far as Brazzaville was by river, then by rail to Pointe Noire (Gabon). Nowhere is the impact of colonial policies more evident than in the building of the Pointe Noire–Brazzaville (Congo–Ocean) railroad, since the railroad between Kinshasa and Matadi (Belgian Congo) already built could have been used, but of course this was not on French territory. Thus Moyen Congo was an area of important capital investment for the French, owing to its location between Gabon and the Central African Republic. Although in Moyen Congo investment was primarily in transport, not production, the country relied on river transport, not the railroad. The largest export from this colony was timber but, being the poorest colony of French Equatorial Africa, its primary revenues came from outside its territory, primarily either France or Gabon.

SOUTHERN AFRICA

Beginning in the mid-1600s, the Dutch established a limited number of settlements in South Africa around the Cape Town area, largely to provide supplies and rest for ship crews engaged in trade between Europe and the Dutch East Indies. But by 1700 the Dutch settlers were producing more foodstuffs than required by the passing ships. In addition, the settlers had started to move inland and to become active in both livestock raising and agriculture. By 1795, when the British occupied the Cape peninsula for the first time, over 17,000 Dutch settlers were living in the area. In 1815 a European peace settlement gave British sovereignty to the Cape Colony. In response to a set of complex events resulting from the establishment of British rule in the Cape Colony, between 1835 and 1941 about 6000 Afrikaners, the descendants of the original Dutch settlers, moved inland beyond the Cape Colony area of British control first into Natal and later (1839–40) beyond the Vaal River into what became the Transvaal Republic, Orange Free State (Fig. 3.5). These were humid subtropical areas that were favorable environments for agriculture and grazing. For the Afrikaners it was indeed fortunate that at this date, when they had to find new lands to farm owing to the British abolition of slavery, these areas had become temporarily depopulated through some recent major disturbances among the indigenous groups (the Mfecane). By the 1840s, numerous European settlements had been established in the area between the Orange River and the Soutpansberg Mountains in the north. In this migration the Afrikaners gradually came into conflict with the Sotho Kingdom, which occupied an area where African farmers were producing grain surpluses of wheat, sorghum, and corn. To protect themselves from the Afrikaners, the Sothos asked for and obtained protection from the British government for their homeland. But by the time the British protected this area (1868), Basutoland (Lesotho) had lost a large portion of its productive lands to the Orange Free State. Basutoland was left with mostly mountainous terrain and only a small amount of arable land. This series of events represents a process that occurred in various variant forms throughout southern Africa, namely the best lands became occupied by people of European descent so that the African population was forced to exist on a limited resource base. One result

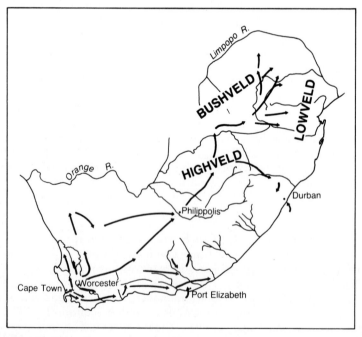

Figure 3.5 Settlement patterns in South Africa moving from Cape Town into the interior (from Cole 1961).

was that the Africans were forced to work for the Europeans to make a livelihood.

Besides the Whites and Africans, East Indians and other immigrants came to South Africa to provide needed labor. The labor was required to help on the farms and to build the railroads, as well as to help extract mineral wealth once it was discovered (1867 diamonds, 1886 gold). Originally, Afrikaner agriculture and pastoral activities were largely self-subsistent, but gradually they became commercially oriented, especially in terms of sugar cane, grapes (wine), maize, and cattle. Yet it was always highly dependent on the use of African labor. Beginning around 1867, the economy started to develop its mineral wealth; it eventually produced an array of mineral products, including gold, coal, and diamonds.

With the best potentially productive lands controlled by the Afrikaner and English population, the Africans became the major providers of labor in South Africa. This is especially true in the mineral sector. It was during the colonial period that the use of African labor throughout all economic sectors became established. This labor gradually evolved from just coming from the local area to draining all of southern Africa. As early as 1900, Nyasa (Malawi) men were migrating into South Africa to work either on farms or in mines.

Like the Dutch, the Portuguese entered southern Africa very early. They first arrived in what is present-day Angola in 1483; and they reached Mozambique during 1498. In the early years of Portuguese contact, the primary interest was not the establishment of colonies but commercial exploitation. To accomplish this end, the Portuguese took advantage of the rivalries that existed among the Africans and made various trade agreements with local people. In Angola, slaves, ivory, gold, and wild rubber were the major commercial interests; in Mozambique the initial interest was to establish coastal defense centers to protect their trade in the Indian Ocean, as well as gold exports from the inland Shona areas (Zimbabwe, northern South Africa). As late as the early 1800s over 80 percent of the revenue derived from these southern Portuguese colonies was from the slave trade. Not until the mid-1800s was there any attempt to encourage European settlements for agricultural activities and to reorient the Angolan economy from slavery to agriculture. Then the initial endeavor was to attempt to grow both cotton and coffee on plantations. With the American Civil War, the cotton plantations eventually became profitable, but coffee's profitability was still greater.

By the 1600s, in Mozambique there were large tracts of land under the ownership of a few families. Many estates were over hundreds of square kilometers; some included over a thousand square kilometers but, as in Angola, slaves were the dominant export through the early 1800s. Despite the large land holdings, Mozambique never became an exporter of significant quantities of foodstuffs, except cashew nuts. The colonial period for these two areas did not end until 1975. By that date, even though over 50 percent of exports from Angola were agricultural, less than 3 percent of the land was cultivated. The dominant export crop, coffee, came both from plantations (15 percent) and small farmers. Sisal, another export, was a plantation crop, but maize was a small-farmer crop. Livestock, coming largely from the drier southern portion of the colony, was produced both on large land holdings and by small herders.

85

Mineral exports, which almost equalled agricultural exports by independence, did not become of major importance until the late 1940s.

Although land concentration was extreme in Mozambique early in the colonial period, the colony never became a major agricultural entity. The greatest source of revenue at the end of the colonial period was derived from the service sector. This was led by the revenue from the use of the rail system and port facilities for mineral exports originating in the surrounding countries.

The British interest in southern Africa, outside of South Africa, Botswana (Bechuanaland), and Swaziland did not begin until the late 1800s. The British arrived in Rhodesia (Zimbabwe and Zambia) in 1889 and 1890, and in Nyasaland (Malawi) in 1891. During the colonial period the attraction of the various southern African lands was not at all equal. This is reflected in the settlement patterns of the Europeans. In Nyasaland as late as 1921, less than 1500 Europeans were in the country, and at independence only about 7000 Whites were living in the country. As a result, a large component of the economy remained in the domain of the small farmers. But primarily because of tax laws, especially the hut tax, the inhabitants in Nyasaland by the turn of the 20th century were forced into entering the cash economy. The lack of capital investment and economic opportunity throughout the country, but especially in the north and central parts, contributed to the initiation of the migration of Nyasa men toward Southern Rhodesia and South Africa in order to raise revenue. From a colonial perspective, the crucial resource of Nyasaland was its labor force. And of major importance was its contribution to the economies of the British colonies of Southern Rhodesia and South Africa. In 1959, just prior to independence, over 163,000 men were estimated to be working outside the country in other areas of southern Africa. The commercial agriculture that did evolve during this period was concentrated solely in the southern portion of the colony. Europeans produced tea and flue-cured tobacco, whereas coffee, cotton, maize, peanuts, and types of Turkish tobacco were largely grown by small farmers.

Northern Rhodesia, like Nyasaland, never attracted many Europeans. But at independence about 75,000 Europeans were living in the country, many of them working in the mining industry. Those that did settle in the country became concentrated along the Lusaka–Livingstone railroad line. It was here that the commercial farmers produced the two major crops of maize and peanuts. To a very large degree the small African farms were subsistence enterprises and, as a result, were not export oriented. The major export and the largest cash employment in the country were related to the copper industry centered around Kitwe. Likewise, it was the copper industry that allowed the railroad to be economically viable. Thus the commercial agriculture that was dependent on the railroad was likewise dependent on the success of the mining sector of the economy. This copperbelt area was the second zone of important expatriate settlement.

Southern Rhodesia was the most attractive country for the British, and it attracted the largest number of European settlers. But even here the White population was always less than 5 percent of the total population. From 1887 until 1923, when it was a colony, the area was administered by the South African Company. The land policy that evolved under this administration resulted in a concentration of the European settlers, including those from South Africa, on

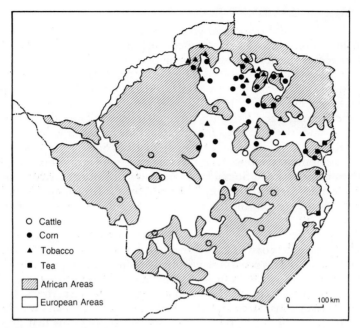

O Cattle
● Corn
▲ Tobacco
■ Tea
▨ African Areas
☐ European Areas

0   100 km

Figure 3.6   European farming areas, major crops, and railroads in Zimbabwe. (Modified from Hance 1975.)

the best potential agricultural lands. In the productive lands of the highveld and highlands, the Europeans displaced the Africans. As a result of this land policy they controlled 76 percent of the high-potential area. For the country as a whole, 40 percent of the European lands have good agricultural potential, but only about 10 percent of African lands are of equal quality. In addition, capital investment, both private and government, was concentrated in the areas of European occupation. The belts of European settlement are roughly parallel to and centered upon the railroad lines (Fig. 3.6). One result of the land policies that evolved during the colonial period was that cash agriculture became almost completely controlled by the White settlers whereas African agriculture became largely subsistence. Given the advantages of controlling the best lands as well as being in the area with the lowest transport costs, the Whites controlled the modern economic sector of the country. Maize was, and still is, by far the largest crop, both for the Africans and the Europeans; however, for the Whites it is a cash crop. Also tobacco, cotton, tea, wattle (used in tannin), and sugar became important cash crops. Besides good agricultural lands, Southern Rhodesia had large mineral wealth, including chrome, copper, gold, and coal. The mining industry evolved in a similar way to commercial farming, with Whites comprising the management and Africans providing the labor. Besides local labor, migrant labor, primarily from either Northern Rhodesia or Nyasaland, was also employed.

EAST AFRICA – THE COLONIAL PERIOD

In contrast to West and Equatorial West Africa where European trading centers evolved into colonial spheres of influence, the European entry into East Africa is both more recent and abrupt. European involvement in East Africa began in the 1870s when Stanley passed through this area. Prior to this date the area was under "Arab" influences, but the Arab contacts had only a modest political character except in Zanzibar. In the late 1880s the major colonial powers in East Africa, the Germans and British became established. The Germans occupied Tanganyika and the Ruanda-Urundi area (Rwanda-Burundi), the British occupied Kenya, Uganda, and Zanzibar and part of Somalia. In East Africa the French were limited to Djibouti and Madagascar while the Italians established themselves in Eritrea and Somaliland, and later in Ethiopia. Kenya and Tanganyika became the areas of dominant interest for the British and Germans, and in both areas they established commercial agricultural products relying on European and imported labor.

The Germans, to open up the interior for commercial agriculture, built railroad lines from the coast of Lake Tanganyika (Dar es Salaam to Kigoma). An important impact of this economic venture was the creation of a labor shortage that required East Indians to be imported for labor. Many remained after the end of the railroad construction to play an important rôle in East African life. With the commercial establishment of sisal plantations, much farmland was displaced from traditional food production. This required the Africans that previously farmed these lands to either enter the cash economy or move to different areas. The Germans were the managers of the plantations, and Africans and Indians supplied labor. During the German period, the dominant export crops became sisal and cotton. To a large degree, Ruanda–Urundi (Rwanda and Burundi) was not of major interest, but even here coffee became a major export crop during the colonial period. However, this crop remained within the domain of the peasant farmer. At the conclusion of World War I, Tanganyika was mandated to the British and Belgium administered Ruanda–Urundi as a separate province of the Congo. Both Tanganyika and Ruanda–Urundi, being protectorates, received less investment than if they had remained as colonies, and their economies stagnated. Ruanda–Urundi's prime rôle was to complement the Belgian economic activities existing in the neighboring Belgian Congo.

Kenya eventually became the major area of interest for the British. But in 1886, when the Anglo-German agreement was signed, East Africa was divided into a German and a British sphere, and it was the Ugandan portion, not the Kenyan lands, that were of paramount importance to the British (Fig. 3.7). The British interest in Uganda was based on the government's desire to deny the control of lands within the entire Nile Valley to any European power (Germany, France) possessing the technical ability to regulate the flow of the Nile waters. This was their strategic policy to protect British rule in Egypt. Between 1888 and 1895 the Imperial British East Africa Company established posts in the main coastal centers and at selected interior locations between Mombasa and Lake Victoria (Fig. 3.7). In 1895 the British government took direct responsibility for its East African lands. The East African Protectorate (EAP) included all lands between the Rift Valley and the coast; the Uganda Protectorate included all lands west of the Rift Valley. In 1902 the EAP acquired the eastern portions of the

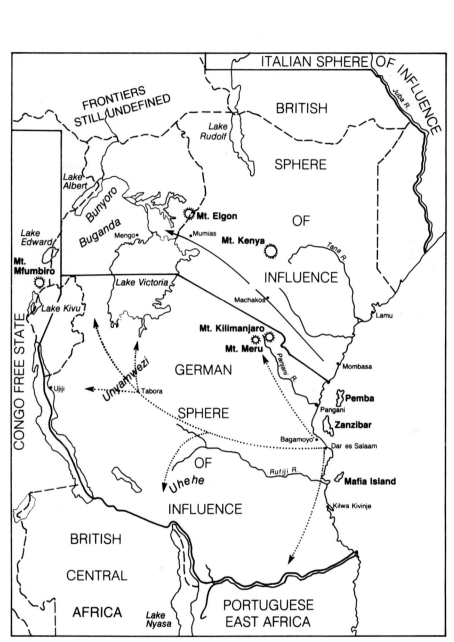

Figure 3.7 The German and British spheres of influence in East Africa, 1884–93 (from Oliver & Mathew 1963).

Uganda Protectorate. The present boundary between Kenya and Uganda reflects this administrative adjustment.

In 1896 the building of the Ugandan railroad from Mombasa to Lake Victoria (Kisumu) was initiated. Its construction and cost (L5.5 million) were justified on the grounds of the strategic need for rapid and easy access to Uganda and the upper Nile. British control of lands within Kenya between 1896 and 1908 was largely restricted to little more than the strip of land along the railroad. While the railroad building was conceptualized as a strategic endeavor, in actuality it was the catalyst for the economic development of the colony and had little military significance for protecting the Nile.

At almost every station on the railroad, commercial centers began to take root. At Nairobi, where the workshops for the railroad were established, Kenya's major urban area began its rapid growth. Prior to the workshop, the lands around Nairobi were largely devoid of any concentrated settlements. It was an area of reliable waters which attracted thousands of wild animals. Thirty-two thousand workers, mostly Asians (East Indians), were recruited to build the railroad as indentured laborers. Many of these individuals remained and became merchants after the building of the railroad. They played a crucial rôle in the development of commercial activity in East Africa, especially in Kenya. Additionally, many British became acquainted with the cool and fertile Kenyan Highlands during the construction of the railroad. A policy of encouraging White settlement seemed the most expedient method of transforming one of the most sparsely populated, high-potential agricultural areas within Africa. By 1914 over 1000 European farmers with holdings averaging between 4000 and 5000 acres (1600–2000 ha) were settled in the Kenyan Highlands. The planters' need to obtain regular supplies of African labor resulted in the colonial government setting up structures that limited the production of profitable cash crops by the Africans.

During the brief 50-year period, large areas of the Kenyan Highlands were transformed into highly commercial landscapes. New varieties of wheat and strains of sheep and cattle were developed for the tropical highland environmental conditions. Coffee, tea, maize, cattle, and dairy production all became established and highly profitable during this period.

In contrast to Kenya, during the colonial period few Europeans settled in Uganda, and less land was removed from potential use by Africans. Whereas sugar cane estates were controlled by either the British or the East Indians, coffee and cotton production was controlled by the indigenous Africans.

NORTHERN AFRICA

European interaction with Mediterranean Africa has a long history, but in a colonial framework it began in 1830 in Algeria and 1912 in Morocco. In terms of European immigration, the maximum number living in this area was reached in the 1950s when about 2 million Europeans were found in Algeria, Tunisia, Morocco, and Libya. There never were many colonialists in Egypt and Sudan, and their numbers had already declined by the 1950s. The vast majority of these Europeans lived in the urban centers and were engaged primarily in government, the service industries, or business. From the mid-1950s to about 1965, massive numbers of Europeans emigrated from these countries, primarily to

France, and consequently the number remaining dropped to about 400,000. There was never a large number of colonial (English) inhabitants in Egypt, but a maximum of about 225,000 "European" resident subjects (including persons born in the Ottoman Empire, such as Syrians, Turks, and Lebanese, who moved to Egypt) were there in the late 1920s. The overwhelming majority of these "European" residents lived in Alexandria; a significantly fewer number resided in Cairo. In the Sudan there never was a significant European component in the population.

Even though the Europeans lived primarily in urban centers, significant numbers became farmers in the Maghreb; and Europeans controlled a large percentage of the agricultural lands. Forty percent of cultivated lands were controlled by colonialists in Algeria, 20 percent in Tunisia, 7 percent in Morocco, and 6 percent in Libya. All of these cultivated lands were in the humid northern Mediterranean areas. The Europeans neither occupied nor developed the drier interior steppes and deserts; they only controlled these areas through military and political devices. Thus, during the colonial period, the interactions between the dry and moist areas in the Maghreb decreased, making the dry areas less productive. Perhaps the greatest impact of this land-holding pattern was the disadvantage it forced on the nomadic peoples. With the removal of the moist areas from the nomadic livelihood system, the quality of life of the nomadic people decreased as the dry areas could not support as many livestock as before when the pastoralists could move their livestock into humid areas during the driest portion of the year. This was the beginning of their loss of political power, and the process of sedentarization began to accelerate in the colonial period, and a decline in importance of the drier area in each country in the Maghreb occurred.

In Egypt, during the colonial period the greatest environmental impact resulted from the start of control of the Nile's waters for irrigation purposes. With the building of the Delta Barrages (1881) and the Aswan Dam (1902), sediment flow into the delta area decreased slightly and erosion began to occur (Fig. 3.8, Table 3.1). But the major decrease in sediment supply to the delta began with the building of the Aswan High Dam in 1968. Now the upstream sediment, much of it originating in the Ethiopian Highlands and transported northward in the Blue Nile, is completely trapped in Lake Nasser, behind the dam. With the erosional forces, such as wave action, remaining constant in the coastal zone, the decrease in the sediment supply brought to the delta in the Nile's waters has upset the balance between the erosional and depositional forces along the Mediterranean/delta interface. The result is that in some places farmland is being lost along the margins of the delta. Thus the loss of some of the best traditional agricultural lands partially offsets the increased agricultural production occurring through the use of Lake Nasser's waters. Concomitantly,

Table 3.1 Delta erosion on the Nile.

Period	1898–1918	1918–26	1926–44	1944–54
retreat (m)	300	620	375	350
average (per year)	15	81	21	35

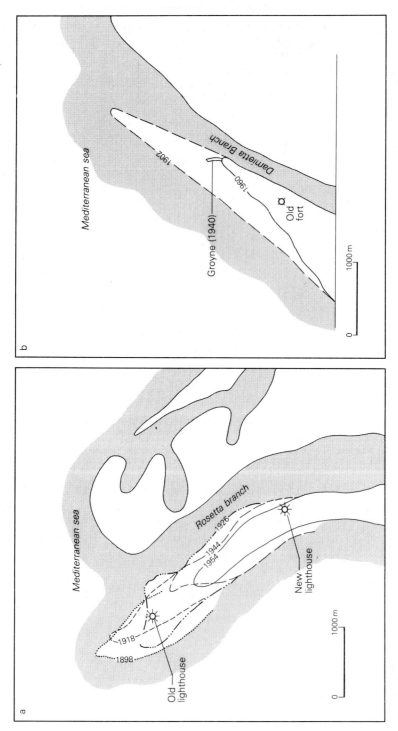

Figure 3.8   Some important areas of erosion on the Nile Delta, 1898–1960: (a) Rosetta mouth of Nile changes from 1898 to 1954; (b) Ras el Bar on the west side of the mouth of Damietta Branch shoreline in 1902 and 1960. (Modified from Farver & Milton 1972.)

with the decrease in river discharge and sediment, a lower nutrient flow into the Mediterranean is blamed for decreasing the numbers of fish in the offshore waters and causing the traditional fishing industry to decline.

In Sudan, in 1923, the British began the Gezira, a major irrigation project between the White Nile and the Blue Nile (Fig. 3.9). This project likewise reduced the flow of sediment in the Nile and increased the problem of soil erosion in the area by increasing bare loose ground during the planting season for cotton when the soil is dry. This makes wind a more effective erosional agent than under natural conditions. But perhaps the most widespread impact of the colonial period in Sudan was the introduction of modern veterinary services. These caused livestock numbers to increase, but there was little effort on the part of the British to improve pasture lands. These two factors, plus the removal of previous pasture for irrigation projects, resulted in the overgrazing of the remaining pasture lands as a normal practice. This initiated major soil erosion in Sudan.

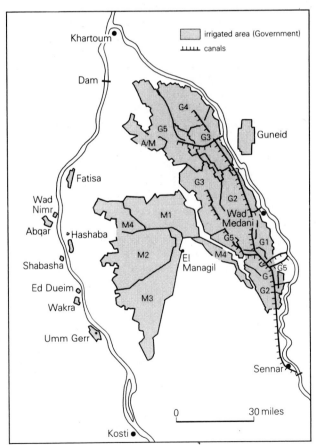

Figure 3.9 Irrigated areas and major canals in the Gezira and Managil areas, Sudan (from Grove 1978).

93

Colonialism: the environment – summary

The environmental impacts resulting from European colonialism are extremely diverse. This diversity results partly from the different reasons for the entry of the colonial powers into the continent, partly from the different natural environments found throughout Africa, partly from the different demographic characteristics of the African continent at the time of colonization, and partly it is due to the time at which the colonial impact took place.

One clear result of colonization throughout all of Africa was the establishment of national entities, usually without regard to either physical or human considerations. Thus, in many places, political units became established that split tribal areas or were situated in environments where production was low. During the colonial period, this latter factor was not as crucial as in the post-colonial period, since the mother country could, through policy decisions, make one colony subsidize another. For example, the relationships between Gabon, Moyen Congo, and Ubangi Shari (French Equatorial Africa) ceased at independence, and Congo-Brazzaville suddenly lost Gabon, one crucial source of income. Thus, with the ending of colonization, the new nations had to utilize, almost solely, their natural resources for their survival. But in many political units the resources were meager and little diversity existed. Along with having lower subsidies and a growing population, in many cases the land resource was overutilized and the stress on the land resulted in environmental deterioration.

Another effect of the colonial period is the introduction of export crops at the expense of foodcrops. A land-use pattern often evolved in which in many areas the best lands were used to grow cash crops, as this is what the colonial powers considered advantageous. Local foodstuffs often had to be grown in more marginal areas, and this resulted in soil loss. In addition, with little investment provided for the growing of foodstuffs, yields remained low and, with rising populations, environmental decay began to occur. This process continues today. Thus most nations in Africa must import food and rely on foreign aid to meet their minimal needs. This food shortage has some of its origins in the policies that developed during the colonial period, when the crucial skills needed for cash-crop production remained under the control of the expatriate population. In West Africa, where crop production remained to a large degree with the indigenous population during the colonial period, the political decisions favoring the urban sector over the rural made after independence have resulted in lower agricultural outputs.

With the end of the colonial period, cash crops decreased and capital available for the importation of foods decreased. In some areas, such as the Maghreb, actual livelihood systems such as nomadic pastoralism, which had evolved in response to the climatic setting of the local area, have declined since the colonial farmers removed access to crucial components of the system from the nomadic peoples. Thus many land-use patterns on the continent result from systems that were created to benefit the mother country and the European immigrants, not the African colony itself, nor its native peoples. Given the political viewpoint that national boundaries must remain fixed, as the former colonies reorient themselves to a national context they must find solutions in an environmental setting that was in most cases placed upon the continent independently of the African situation.

Independence

As former African colonies became independent, each nation began to attempt to restructure its economy into a national framework. A major constraint for many of these new nations was that they were required to attempt to accomplish this end solely within the limitations of the environments inherited from the colonial period. As discussed in the previous section, for many countries this meant they had to attempt to develop their economies within the constraints of a single major ecosystem or environmental zone. Regional cooperation existed in some places during the colonial period. Examples are the arrangements that existed between Gabon, Congo, Central African Republic, between Zimbabwe, Malawi, Zambia, and between Uganda, Tanzania, and Kenya. However, with independence, these regional groupings broke down for a multitude of reasons. Thus the environmental situation for many African countries is less flexible today than it was during the colonial period when options for regional interaction were greater. Of course with time it is possible that regional cooperation will grow among the independent nations.

For some nations, diverse environments do exist within the borders, and there is a potential for the development of complementary land use to meet national goals. An example of such a country is Kenya with its highlands, moist and dry lands, and low coastal areas. The agricultural and pastoral sectors, along with a tourist industry – all of which are directly related to its environmental setting – are the food and revenue producers upon which Kenya is largely dependent for its development.

For some nations, the extreme limitation of their environmental setting greatly restricts the options available to governments for putting practical developmental strategies into operation. One example of such a country is Niger where, despite its large areal extent, the whole country falls within the Sahara or Sahel climatic zones. Despite the best of intentions, with the constraints of national sovereignty such as the limitation of grazing lands for cattle within the national boundaries, where dry years occur, overgrazing and resulting hunger are almost inevitable.

For some nations, the extreme limitation of their environmental setting is greatly offset by their endowment in mineral resources. One example is Libya, where petroleum revenues provide enough capital for the development of the agricultural sector, despite the generally dry environment.

For some nations, both environmental diversity and mineral wealth exist within the country. Examples of such nations are Nigeria, Zimbabwe, and South Africa. For nations of this type, because of their fortuitous inheritance, the greatest number of options exist for the development of their national economies within their environmental setting.

While all African countries are attempting to reorient their economies from a colonial to a national basis, no single strategy is universally practical because of the diverse conditions found throughout the continent. It is the interaction between the environment and the utilization of land that determines the present status of African environments; furthermore, it will determine their future needs.

The policies of many African governments since independence have not in general been conducive to good environmental management. Pricing policies have almost always worked against the rural producer, and the disincentives for crop production have resulted in less effective management of resources. In most countries poor control of vegetational resources have compounded the problem. In a few countries some efforts are now being made to remedy these problems, and major policy statements on resource problems have been a feature of presidential and other senior pronouncements. Unfortunately, these pronouncements have rarely been backed by the monetary support or long-term commitment necessary to reverse environmental deterioration.

Population

Throughout most of Africa today, population growth is a real phenomenon, not just a relative one. Africa has the fastest-growing population and therefore the youngest age distribution of any continent. In many countries, over 40 percent of the national population is under 15 years of age. In 1950, the population of the African continent was estimated at 222 million; with rapid growth the population had more than doubled to 485 million in 1982. Given contemporary trends, by the year 2000 it is estimated that the population will be over 800 million. National growth rates in some countries are among the highest in the world. In Kenya, the 1980 annual growth rate was between 3.5 and 4 percent; in Nigeria the estimated annual rate is 3 percent. Given today's birth:death ratio, it is estimated that Nigeria's population will not stabilize until it reaches 300–400 million unless major changes occur in either its birth rate or its death rate.

The population growth on the continent since World War II is largely the result of investment in the public health sector, including improvements in water supply – both reliability and sanitation – disease eradication, and disease treatment. These public health investments have resulted in the lowering of infant mortality and an increase in the general life expectancy of the population. However, little effort has been directed toward the lowering of the high birth rates that prevail over most of Africa.

A few general population attributes of contemporary Africa resulting from its population dynamics are:

(a) The rapid growth of urban centers. Urbanization is widespread. In countries as diverse as Libya, Tanzania, Nigeria, Egypt, and Zaire the urban component of the population is increasing disproportionately; but the rural population in absolute numbers is also increasing in most countries.

(b) Sedentarization of nomadic peoples is the goal of almost all governments. This, it is hoped, will result in services and investment encouraging the development of fixed rural communities.

(c) In rural areas the population is composed disproportionately of the young, women, and the elderly. The men often migrate to urban areas in search of economic opportunity, or they temporarily migrate to other countries for cash employment. This latter property is particularly important in southern Africa.

(d) A large number of countries have considerable numbers of "permanent" refugees who place severe pressures on the resource base of their host countries. These refugees result from both political and environmental factors.

Urbanization

As populations increase, often rural inhabitants must migrate from their local areas in order to find vacant land to utilize for the production of food to meet their needs. More often than not the migrants are forced to move into areas that are more marginal than the ones they left. In addition, in many places today, even migration into marginal areas is limited. One result of the limited opportunities in the rural areas has been the movement of people to urban centers.

Africa has a long history of urbanization, dating from about 3500 BC in the Nile Valley, 1200 BC along the Mediterranean, AD 500–1000 with the founding of Zimbabwe in the south, AD 1000–1500 with the development of urban centers in West Africa, and between AD 1000–1500 along the East African coast. Despite this long history, through the 1970s Africa was the least urbanized continent; but urban centers having populations of over 100,000 (Table 3.2) are now growing at an average annual rate of around 4 percent. Today Africa is the continent with the fastest urban growth in the world (Fig. 3.10). As an indication of the growth of the larger cities, in 1960 three cities had surpassed the 1 million mark (Cairo, Alexandria, and Johannesburg); in 1984 at least nine additional cities were in this category (Algiers, Addis Ababa, Casablanca, Lagos, Cape Town, Kinshasa, Khartoum, Ibadan, Dar Es Salaam), and other cities, such as Nairobi, were clearly approaching the million mark. Migration is more important than natural increase in accounting for the rapid urban growth in African centers. Almost everywhere, the initial phase of migration involves males between the ages of 15 and 49. Rural population characteristics reflect this. For example, in Kenya one in every five heads of households were absent from rural areas in 1979. Because of the rapid urban growth, the need for the rural areas to increase food production to supply the urban areas is ever becoming larger. But with such a high percentage of young males leaving the rural areas for urban centers, in most countries the ability of the remaining rural labor force to meet these demands is decreasing.

Another attribute of the urban centers having environmental ramifications is that as manufacturing increases in Africa it is concentrated in urban centers. Thus centers that once had primarily one major economic function are becoming multifunctional. Demands on water supplies are expanding even faster than the population growth in most urban areas. Water shortages are becoming a major problem in most large urban areas situated in environments that have a dry season. The rapid increases in water demands, which reflect both growth in population and in industry, usually outstrip the infrastructure required to store and distribute sufficient quantities of water. Also, in many cases the water potential in the local area is limited and new water sources will need to be developed. Water rationing through the shutting down of the water distribution system for a portion of a 24-hour period is a common event in many African urban centers during the dry season. In addition, with the rapid growth of

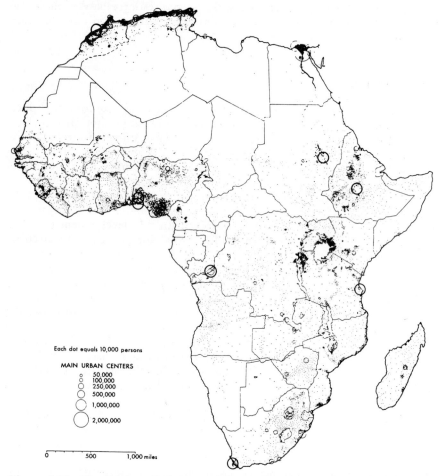

Figure 3.10 Distribution of urban population and major population centers through-out Africa. (Modified from Hance 1975.)

shanty towns, the existing water system – even when water is available in the storage areas – is insufficient to distribute enough water into these areas and can rarely meet the demands of the people.

One result of rapid urban growth, and the fact that many of the new growth areas do not have a sufficient water supply, is the widespread existence of sanitation problems. Estimates for many large urban centers indicate that only in about 10 percent of the total area of most urban centers is water directly available in places of residence. About another 40 to 50 percent of an urban area can have standpipes that bring water into local neighborhoods. Thus, at a minimum, at least 40 percent of most urban areas usually have no piped water available for use. The lack of water, along with the crowded conditions found in many parts of the urban centers, contributes to poor sanitation and an assortment of health problems. Nevertheless, because medical services are usually more

Table 3.2 Percentage of population defined as urban, 1983.

	Urban population (%)	No of cities over 500,000
Algeria	46	1
Angola	23	1
Benin	16	1
Botswana	n.a.	n.a.
Burundi	2	0
Cameroon	39	1
Cape Verde	n.a.	n.a.
Central African Republic	44	0
Chad	20	0
Congo (Brazzaville)	55	0
Egypt	45	2
Ethiopia	15	1
Gabon	n.a.	n.a.
Gambia	n.a.	n.a.
Ghana	38	2
Guinea	26	1
Ivory Coast	44	1
Kenya	17	1
Liberia	38	0
Libya	61	1
Madagascar	20	1
Malawi	11	0
Mali	19	0
Mauritania	25	0
Mauritius	n.a.	n.a.
Morocco	43	4
Mozambique	17	1
Niger	14	0
Nigeria	22	9
Rwanda	5	0
Senegal	34	1
Seychelles	n.a.	n.a.
Sierra Leone	23	0
Somalia	33	0
South Africa	55	7
Sudan	20	1
Swaziland	n.a.	n.a.
Tanzania	14	1
Togo	22	0
Tunisia	54	1
Uganda	7	1
Zimbabwe	24	1
Zaire	38	2
Zambia	47	1

Source: World Bank (1985).

accessible in urban than rural areas, overall health is generally higher in the urban areas.

The destruction of wood resources in surrounding urban areas to satisfy fuel (charcoal) and urban construction needs is another environmental phenomenon associated with rapid urban growth. In the Khartoum area this deforestation is considered to be a critical factor contributing to desertification in Sudan. With the removal of trees and the general degradation of the vegetation cover near urban areas, wind becomes capable of removing the finer soil components. The removal of the finer soil then lowers the capability of the land in terms of vegetation. Thus in many areas irreversible change could be taking place. In the Khartoum area, acacia shrubs which were around the city in the 1950s could only begin to be found 90 km to the south seventeen years later. The removal of the trees has been associated with an increase in dust storms (haboobs) in the area. Because the dust affects the quality of life as well as ruining machinery, drops in worker productivity as well as factory closures have been blamed on this deforestation and desertification – relationship that at least in this area is associated with urbanization.

Another widespread urban–environment relationship in Africa is that the expansion of built-up areas associated with urban growth often occurs at the expense of good agricultural lands, since flat areas are often the most favored areas for construction. Again, around Khartoum this is manifested by the removal of thousands of feddans* of cultivable land for residential and industrial use. Whole rural villages have been absorbed into the urban area. As urban areas grow they require more foodstuffs, but the potential food-producing areas nearby often decrease. Thus new lands have to be developed for agriculture, and improvements to the transportation system are needed to transport the food from more distant areas to urban areas. Development projects of this kind open up new areas to agriculture that are needed to replace former food-producing areas. However, these projects seldom increase overall food production from previous levels. Quite often they merely alter the locations from which food is supplied to the urban areas.

Sedentarization

Sedentarization is a major process occurring among the nomadic peoples of Africa, especially in northern Africa. Yet there is substantial evidence that, as the physical mobility of the population increased, the people's chances of withstanding the 1968–74 Sahelian drought increased. However, in almost every African country containing large semi-arid areas within its territory, it is national policy to encourage the population to become sedentary. This policy is partially a result of the relative ease with which services such as education, health, housing, and agriculture can be delivered to a sedentary population. From a political perspective, especially in terms of developing the concept of nationhood among pastoral people, it is likewise advantageous for most governments to favor sedentarization. However, because the amount of moisture in arid and semi-arid

* 1 feddan equals 1.038 acres or 0.42 ha.

areas varies considerably, both in time and space, creating conditions that are likely to increase the potential for flexibility in the movement of herds and people in such environments is advantageous for pastoral production. This is certainly the case, since in dry areas it is normal for vegetation growth and water supplies to shift from place to place, from season to season, and from year to year. Therefore the policies of most governments which attempt to fix populations in space in these environments are in opposition to the shifting environmental situation found in the dry areas.

Developing African economies are constrained by population growth, which encourages decisions at the governmental level favoring land-use changes from pastoral to agricultural whenever possible. The reason is that increases in food production, at least in the short term, often result from this land-use change. Most contemporary agricultural systems introduce concentrated, intensive, sustained-yield systems into areas that periodically are incapable of sustaining them because of the normal variability in precipitation, or the limitations of water supply for irrigation. During the periods of moisture stress, because of agricultural practices, resources such as vegetation and soil can degrade to a sufficient level to lower the long-term food yields of the impacted area.

One result of desertification is that when dry years occur the ability of the people to cope with water shortages decreases. A contemporary response has been that during dry years people in these arid and semi-arid regions must either become dependent on outside food assistance, become refugees, or move to new areas, usually urban.

Rural populations

General population attributes

According to the 1977 UN *Demographic yearbook*, over 44 percent of Africa's population is under 15 years of age. With over 75 percent of Africa's total population still rural, this youthful population, if it is to remain in food production, will have to bring more lands into the food system by clearing areas not currently utilized, reducing the period of fallow in these new areas, or increasing labor inputs in currently used lands to make food production more labor intensive. However, all too often the response to increased rural populations is urban migration, either temporary or permanent. As a result of economic needs – for instance the need to supplement family income – or the perception of opportunities – for instance rural inhabitants often believe that in urban areas living standards can be raised more easily than in rural areas – a range of migratory movements exists within Africa. Some result in permanent population shifts, whereas others lead only to temporary outmigration from local areas. Yet temporary outmigrations can result in the continuous absence of the most productive individuals from rural livelihood economies. Often it is those individuals who are potentially the most productive who leave rural areas in search of a better life. Because the nature of most temporary population is selective in this way, despite the benefit to the individual who migrates, the process is generally disadvantageous for rural development in that it removes the most able-bodied and ambitious individuals from the area.

In southern Africa employment opportunities for wage earner exist in mining, industries, and farming, but the locales of these activities are generally distant from the African population centers. In 1971 over 90,000 male Malawians were working in South African mines; in addition, there were others working on farms, mainly in Rhodesia (Zimbabwe) and South Africa. Until 1974 it was estimated that about one out of three able-bodied males was working outside Malawi at any one time. Despite the large rural population in Malawi, owing to the temporary outmigration of many of its inhabitants, labor shortages exist during the planting and harvesting periods. This curtails food production and lowers the ability of local peoples to improve their economies through local activities.

External migration is not confined to southern Africa. In Algeria, especially from the 1950s, large numbers moved to Europe – mostly France. This also took place in Tunisia and Morocco, but to a lesser extent. Today, temporary employment of Sudanese laborers in Libya occurs. Also, some Egyptians, Sudanese, Djiboutians, and Somali's are employed in various Gulf States. Although the cash sent back by these temporary migrants is often crucial to the home national economies, there is usually a negative social and economic impact upon the rural countryside, since it is generally the most dynamic and skilled who leave.

However, today the greatest movements in Africa are not external, but internal. And these movements are usually from rural to urban areas. Since independence, many African countries have invested in industrialization that has favored the urban areas. One result of the relative lack of rural investment has been an ever-increasing gap between most nation's food demands and their food supply. One factor contributing to this trend has been the movement of the young to the urban areas in search of a better life.

Refugees

The United Nations estimates that in the mid 1980s over 4 million Africans were refugees. There are two primary reasons for the existence of refugees: one is political, and examples are the situations in the Horn of Africa, Chad, and southern Africa; the other is physical, for instance major droughts (Sahel) during which livelihood systems can no longer support the populations living in the affected areas. In some areas, such as Ethiopia, both factors result in a refugee problem. A problem for rural refugees today is that access to lands that will permit them to engage in food production is becoming ever more restrictive. First, with the continuing rapid population growth in rural Africa, unoccupied lands are rapidly being colonized. Thus availability of land for refugee settlement is becoming more restricted. Second, with land tenure systems generally throughout Africa becoming less communal, and being used ever more for commercial purposes, all forms of shifting populations, including refugees, find less land available. As an example, when droughts occur, traditional lands that had been previously available in more humid settings are now often occupied by agriculturalists and therefore are removed from potential areas of refugee settlement.

Given the financial constraints operating throughout most of Africa, when refugees move into a new area little capital is available, even when lands are available. This results in poor and usually unacceptable levels in general sanitation, water availability, and other critical human needs. In addition, given the need of most refugees to find employment, often wages in the refugees areas are depressed and local food prices increase due to the additional population. Thus the inhabitants living in refugee areas are often adversely affected.

Since external food assistance usually meets only a small percentage of the refugees' needs, the land in the newly settled areas must help support the increased local population. If the better lands are already utilized, marginal lands are brought into food production, and the potential for land degradation increases.

Agricultural crops and change

With the environmental diversity found throughout Africa, wide ranges of crops are grown, both for subsistence and for commercial reasons. An examination of the range of crops found throughout the continent indicates that an overwhelming majority of foodstuffs are not indigenous. In the commercial sphere of agriculture the products that were favored by the colonial powers, with the exception of palm oil, coffee, cotton, sesame, and castor, are almost all from crops introduced into Africa.

Besides the introduction of new crops, agricultural practices encouraged in the past by the colonial governments, or today by most national governments through either investment or land grants, in most cases differ markedly from the traditional practices that evolved throughout the African scene. Although traditional practices usually emphasized crop diversity, those introduced generally encouraged specialization.

Staple crops

According to Murdock (1960), throughout Africa sixteen crops can be classified as staples. Nine of these crops are cereal grains (barley, maize, eleusine, fonio, pearl millet, rice, sorghum, teff, and wheat); five are tubers or root crops (ensete, manioc, sweet potato, taro, and yam); and two are fruits (bananas and dates) (Fig. 3.1). In particular, maize and manioc (cassava) are interesting in terms of their rapid diffusion and acceptance in Africa. Both crops were not introduced into the continent from the Americas until the 16th and 17th centuries. In particular, maize is the most widely distributed food plant in Africa (Fig. 3.1) and is found in diverse environmental settings. From the perspective of conserving soil resources, maize is a particularly destructive crop unless good conservation practices are used. Even as a mature crop, the leaf and root structures of the plant do not protect the soil from erosion. However, when it is intercropped, the erosion potential in areas where it is grown decreases. Manioc's acceptance as a root crop in the hot and humid areas is at least partially explained by the ease with which it grows. Yet a major shortcoming is that it has a relatively low nutritional value. Thus, though it provides food, its heavy utilization contributes to the health (i.e. nutritional) problems of the continent.

Rice is cultivated either as dry or paddy rice, with wet cultivation methods increasing. In the areas where paddy rice is grown, care must constantly be taken to prevent water-related diseases becoming established.

Environmental problems are generally associated more with cereal grains than with either tuber or "tree" fruit staples. The expansion of cereals, particularly into the drier margins of the grasslands along the agriculture/grazing interface, is one important contributing factor in the desertification process. The breaking up of the ground before planting and the presence of bare soil during a portion of the year, both after the harvest and immediately after planting, increase the ability of winds and water to erode the soils in these areas.

Besides the major staple crops just listed, a variety of other food plants, including a multitude of peas and beans, are heavily utilized throughout Africa. A large percentage of the traditional practices associated with food production appear to have been well adapted to their environmental setting. Generally, the practice of intercropping protected the soil from erosion better than monoculture; and the use of the hoe or pole instead of the plow in preparing the soil also minimized erosion. In addition, the intermixture of crops generally kept insect numbers and plant diseases at relatively low levels by preventing the establishment of a habitat favorable for either insects or disease. This thereby lowered the risk of major crop failures. In addition, with intercropping, as various crops mature at different times and respond to various climatic and ground moisture conditions, the risks of major crop failures appear to be lower than in areas where monoculture is practiced.

One traditional practice that is widespread, particularly in wet–dry and semi-arid areas, is that individual families often have their fields dispersed over a wide area, rather than restricting them to a single location. Some fields can be several kilometers away from each other. In the wet–dry and semi-arid areas, where a precipitation event often covers only a small area, the dispersal of fields increases the likelihood that some of the family's fields will receive enough precipitation in any one year to provide sufficient food for the family. Thus the traditional food strategies appear to be well suited to the environmental situation in which they evolved. They seem to minimize the risk of at times not being able to meet their food requirements. But the strategies used by the farmers rarely provide the large surplus which is needed today either to meet the food demands of the growing nonrural population, or the crop exports to meet the national trade needs. In addition, as traditional land use is usually not intensive, but extensive, with the growing population the traditional farming systems continuously require more marginal lands to be used for food production.

Commercial crops

Cash-crop economics began to evolve from the subsistence forms before colonial rule. By the 19th century, Africans were producing for export palm oil, peanuts, and cotton from areas outside European colonial control. With colonization cash-crop production increased in area, variety, and quantity. In particular, coffee and cocoa grew in importance, particularly in the Ivory Coast, Ghana (Gold Coast), and Nigeria. Ever since independence, many African states remained dependent on the production of a single agricultural commodity for 50 percent or more of their foreign exchange. This is true for Benin (palm kernels and palm oil), Ethiopia (coffee), Gambia and Senegal (peanuts), Ghana (cocoa), Somalia (bananas), and Sudan (cotton), to mention a few countries. Today, in addition to the cash crops previously mentioned, sugar, tobacco, tea, olive products, cloves, cashew nuts, and rubber are important crop exports from various parts of the continent. Also, for many countries animal products such as hides are important.

Besides the export cash crops, almost all of the staple crops previously mentioned are also grown as cash crops. In particular, maize is a very important crop, often grown in the context of cash economies. But foreign export crops often tend to be more valuable than crops grown for local markets; in addition, farmers are encouraged by their governments through various mechanisms to grow export crops to help raise the hard currency needed for international trade. Also, through direct government involvement, many large-scale agricultural schemes have been developed to increase, in particular, export crops. With the use of governmental and private monies for the expansion of export commodities, a contemporary trend is often the unnecessary use of foreign exchange to finance the import of foodstuffs. These imported foodstuffs then compete with local products. Because the imported staples often cost less and are of better quality, the local products frequently cannot compete with them. This further encourages investment in export crops.

A high percentage of the large planned governmental agricultural projects in many countries have an irrigational component to ameliorate the water shortages that exist in many areas throughout Africa. Two direct environmental impacts of irrigation associated with these agricultural improvements in many areas are the spread of waterborne diseases and salinization of the soils. The presence of open irrigation canals, along with drainage canals in many irrigated areas, has resulted in the spread of bilharzia (schistosomisis). Similarly, the spread of malaria has occurred in many irrigated areas owing to the presence of standing water resulting from the irrigation schemes. In the case of both diseases, the reservoirs required for irrigation, along with the irrigated waters in the fields, are often likely habitats for either the carriers or the vectors of diseases.

In arid and semi-arid regions soil salinization and related processes are a serious problem threatening land production. The concentration of salts in soils is an ever-present threat to irrigated lands. Based on the UNESCO/FAO 1971 soil map of the world, 70 million hectares of Africa had salt-affected soils. Today this figure must be higher. Salinization of irrigated lands is largely a result of poor management practices. As such it can be prevented. But proper management requires both technical and political skills, as well as a long-term framework of reference.

As only pure water is lost from the evaporation and transpiration of irrigated waters, any soluble minerals present in the irrigated waters will result in a buildup of salts in the root zones of plants, unless management practices are in place to counter the process of accumulation. A basic concept in controlling salts in the soil is that of "salt balance". That is, the inflow of salts on irrigated lands should never be greater than the outflow of salts. The most widespread practice used to maintain this balance is drainage. Enough water must be placed on the soils to ensure that groundwater from the irrigated lands – which will be heavily laden with soluble minerals – flows into a drainage canal. The construction of drainage canals and the disposal of the saline waters is beyond the capability of individual farmers and requires institutional structures. The excess water that must be placed on the land to ensure this groundwater flow does not contribute to the present crop (short-term) yields. As a result, it often happens that not enough water is put on the ground to flush the soluble minerals out of the soil. Gradually the pH level (alkalinity) of the soil rises and if this is not corrected in time salinization occurs.

One other effect not often emphasized in irrigation projects that utilize surface waters is that though the building of dams increases the reliability of water because of the storage capacity of the reservoir, the actual volume of water passing through the system decreases as evaporation losses are usually high from reservoirs. The results of this are that changes in the river discharge, water quality, and river régime occur downstream from the dam. These changes can set in motion a whole series of environmental changes which can have an impact on the inhabitants downstream. When the Kiangi Dam on the Niger River was completed, farmers downstream who utilized the high waters of the river in their agricultural practices had to learn new farming procedures. The régime of the river after the dam was built no longer flooded their lands. These floodwaters had been an important component in their previous system. To give one more example, the traditional Mediterranean fishing grounds along the Nile Delta ceased to be productive after the completion of the Aswan High Dam. This was probably due to the lack of a nutrient supply in the area because the Nile's discharge into the sea had been lowered. This destroyed the economy of the fishing industry in this portion of Egypt.

Of course many cash crops are grown without irrigation mechanisms. This is especially true of crops grown in the humid areas. These include tea, coffee, rubber, cocoa, tobacco, and food crops such as bananas, manioc, and maize. Many of these crops are grown by small farmers utilizing traditional farming practices, by which cash crops as well as subsistence crops are raised. But in recent years there has been an increase in the development of agricultural lands using machinery for clearance and preparation. To be economical, the use of machinery generally requires single crops to be planted in large tracts of land. Also, most farming machinery used for land preparation plows the land. This is in place of the traditional drilling of the soil. In the development of monoculture practices, fertilizers and pest-control methods are often required. Furthermore, the use of heavy machinery can compact the soils; in many places this causes a reduction in their ability to hold water. With plowing, since the soil is normally only broken up to a maximum depth of 15 cm, and the soil below this depth remains compacted, the water-storage capacities of many tropical soils are often lowered. This compaction increases runoff and can shorten the growing season by reducing the water stored in the soil which is necessary for plant growth at the end of the wet season. Also, the exposure of plowed lands with their loose soil can increase erosion potential prior to the establishment of a ground cover by the newly planted crops.

Livestock

In semi-arid and arid lands, with the unreliability of rains from year to year and place to place, agriculture is a risky venture without a reliable water supply, even with the dispersal of fields. In most parts of Africa these drier areas were the home of a multitude of grazing animals such as zebras, impalas, igalas, and wildebeestes. Through the years, camels, cattle, goats, and sheep have been introduced to these lands and domesticated grazing animals are now widespread. In an ideally adjusted land-use system, grazing animals appear to be an effective use of these water-shortage areas. However, animal populations have increased greatly in many locations, and lands that the grazing herds previously used during dry periods are in many cases occupied by farmers; the net result is widespread overgrazing which has set in motion a series of major environmental calamities. In areas of the White Nile Province, Sudan, and along the Senegal River in Mauritania, for instance, overgrazing has destroyed the grass cover in many places. This has allowed previously stable sand-dunes to become activated. The movement of sand-dunes can destroy the little arable land available in these areas because if the sands move they can cover the fields. A large number of the environmental problems associated with the processes of desertification are related to livestock mismanagement.

The development of reliable water supplies – quite often a high development strategy for these grazing areas – has in many cases compounded the environmental problems. In the Sahel, the new reliable water supply attracted large numbers of animals in many areas where wells were dug. But since the pasture supply remained constant, overgrazing in the area of the well occurred and major land degradation resulted. Similarly, the building of dams to improve the water supply for cattle has often created as many problems as the dams were intended to solve. To quote one example, the natural vegetation around Kisongo, Tanzania (Fig. 3.11), was Acacia woodland. In the 1950s the area was settled by pastoral agriculturalists. In this semi-arid area the dry season lasts from May through October. The people in this area continuously ran into economic difficulties because of the water shortages for their cattle during the latter stages of the dry season. An attempt was made to alleviate the shortages by building a dam on the main stream in the area. Upon completion of the dam the reservoir provided enough water to supply the area's cattle throughout the year. But the dam did not, of course, increase the supply of grazing land. The human response to the additional supply of water was to increase the number of cattle. The already sparse grass became overgrazed during the dry season and the soil was laid bare. When the rains did appear, erosion increased, and sedimentation in the reservoir also increased. Table 3.3 shows the rapid infilling of the

Table 3.3 Reduction in Kisongo Reservoir capacity from sedimentation (area upstream from dam, 9.3 km^2).

Year	Reservoir volume (m^3)	% original capacity
1959	121,000	100.0
1969	83,600	69.1
1971	71,700	59.6

Figure 3.11   Erosion in the Kisongo area, Tanzania (photograph provided by Professor A. Rapp, University of Lund, Sweden).

reservoir. With the infilling of the reservoir, in a short number of years water storage was greatly reduced, and the area once again had an unreliable water supply for the cattle.

But, in addition to the water shortage, owing to the few years of overgrazing during the time when the water supply was reliable, the area's carrying capacity for cattle had been reduced by the soil erosion. Thus the area is less productive than if the dam had never been built since the soil is poorer and the water supply is only slightly improved. Similar deleterious cycles of unplanned events are being repeated in the grazing and agricultural areas. They add up to a very serious degradation of the usable environment.

While some negative effects on the environment have been briefly mentioned in relation to the growth of commercial crops and grazing, it must be stressed that it is the cash crops and surplus cattle that represent the food surpluses that feed the growing urban populations as well as providing revenues for many governments. The negative impacts need not occur or at least can be minimized if the environmental constraints of the areas are incorporated into the new food–production systems. With the need to increase food production, including both animal and crop production, the environmental setting of these rural activities should be considered. The relationships between the environment and land use in the diverse settings found in Africa will be explored in subsequent chapters.

Industrial growth

Prior to independence, almost all modern manufacturing industries in Africa (excluding craft industries such as pottery, ironworking, and weaving) concentrated on the production of raw materials to meet the needs of industry in the home country. Usually African industries were only set up to do the initial processing of raw materials to remove waste matter or to convert the raw commodity into a form that could be stored and shipped to factories in Europe and America. Sugar factories, for instance, rarely refined the cane to white sugar. Thus the colony often imported the finished product produced from raw goods exported from it. For example, tobacco, cotton, and wood products would be exported; cigarettes, cloth, paper, and other finished products would be imported. The range of factories found generally in Africa prior to independence included types such as vegetable oil mills, cotton ginneries, leather tanneries, saw mills, canneries, and ore-reduction facilities.

In addition, transportation networks developed during the colonial period were usually built to facilitate the movement of raw goods to the home country. Thus a general transportation characteristic that most African countries inherited at independence was a transportation system that was designed to move goods from various parts of a country to a port, not to move goods within the country. As a result of the nature of industrial development in the colonial period, with independence the countries have all attempted to increase their industrial base and to orient their factories to meet domestic needs. In the process, post-industrial growth in Africa has affected the environment in four major ways. First, through the direct impacts of industrial expansion, such as land disturbances required for site preparation; second, through water and air pollution resulting from the waste by-products of manufacturing processes; third, through the need to develop energy and water sources to run the factories; and fourth, through the need to undertake massive road and some railroad construction to reorient the transportation networks to meet national needs.

Land disturbance

Accelerated sedimentation is found at all construction projects to some degree. The greater the area of land disturbed, usually the greater are the deleterious effects. In tropical areas the ramifications of construction are often exacerbated owing to the high proportion of clays in the soils, as well as the generally high intensity of tropical precipitation. Both of these properties encourage high runoff of surface waters. This increases the potential for erosion. Likewise what is eroded is eventually deposited; hence the sedimentation problems.

Besides the direct alteration of the terrain in construction, when buildings are completed the ground cover in a large area is often changed from a cover of vegetation to a cover of impervious materials, including roof materials, asphalt, and concrete. The rain falling on these new surfaces quickly runs off the buildings and is usually channeled by drains. Some results are that streets flood as sewer intake capacities are surpassed, and previous river-channel geometry undergoes rapid change as the urban channel has to adjust to the new runoff conditions imposed by the construction. Furthermore, the clogging of various drains by sediment can result in the presence of small pools of stagnant water that become new breeding areas for insects. This can result in a range of health problems.

With most industrial development generally being concentrated in the largest urban areas in Africa, the alterations in the erosion–sediment balance of the urban environment is a real problem. Studies in the United States indicate that in areas of new construction at least five times more sediment is produced than in surrounding rural areas. This increase in sediment production increases the turbidity of the water, which increases costs for industries that use it. In extreme cases the sediment can make the water no longer suitable for industrial or urban use. In the tropical and subtropical setting of Africa, with the generally high prevailing rainfall intensity, problems of erosion and sedimentation potentially exist whenever construction occurs. Thus, the alteration of existing construction practices to minimize the negative impacts of excessive runoff could provide long-term savings. Some possible strategies to minimize land disturbances are the scheduling of major land disturbances during the dry season, the use of mulches to cover bare ground, the rapid planting of vegetation, and the designing of building works to meet the constraints of the local site. But in the developing economies of Africa the increased immediate costs of these strategies often prohibit their implementation and their long-term benefits.

Water–air pollution

In addition to the problems associated with land disturbances, the building of an industrial base often results in the lowering of the water and air quality because of the addition of chemical wastes. Throughout most of Africa modern waterworks systems were poorly developed prior to independence. In addition, with rapid population growth and urbanization, governments have not had the resources to build, expand, and maintain the water systems to meet the ever-increasing demands. With the high cost of pollution controls, along with the high costs associated with the establishment of an industrial base, most African governments originally opted for industrial expansion with minimal environmental controls. Therefore, in many African settings today the water and air quality resembles the situation prevalent during the early period of industrialization in Europe and North America. The biggest difference is that in Africa the industrialization is taking place with the importation of high technology, which has greater pollution hazards than those generally associated with industrialization in the late 19th and early 20th centuries.

Water and energy sources

Given the physical setting of the large proportion of Africa, where precipitation is extremely seasonal and groundwater is not available in large quantities, plus the general concentration of industrialization in a few urban areas, in many countries water and energy shortages exist which compound the problems of developing a strong industrial base.

110

Unlike most of the industrial areas in Europe and North America, where the climate is relatively humid throughout the year, in large areas of Africa where industrialization is occurring, precipitation is very seasonal. Waterworks must be built that can collect an ample amount of water during the wet season to carry over through the dry season. As a result, to meet a given water demand in most African settings the reservoirs must be larger than in Europe and North America where water availability is less seasonal and evaporation rates lower. Because of this physical constraint, along with the costs associated with water-system development, many urban areas throughout Africa experience various forms of water rationing. This is especially true during the latter stages of the dry season. The shortage of water also affects energy production in some areas where hydroelectric power is the primary energy source. Water and power are often turned off during the dry season as a rationing device. Of course this involves a tremendous cost for factories, offices, and other infrastructures.

In many African countries, energy generation was intended to be met through oil utilization. But the high cost of petroleum has affected many industrial plans. Countries such as Nigeria, Liberia, Ghana, Algeria, Egypt, South Africa, Gabon, and Zimbabwe which have energy in the form of coal, oil, or water have tremendous advantages over countries such as Chad, Malawi, Mali, Somalia, and Niger which are lacking in these energy sources. In many countries which do have energy sources, these are often far removed from areas which have energy demands. Therefore the infrastructure must be built to move the raw good from the source to the consuming area.

Transport systems

Prior to independence almost all transport systems were built to move commodities from the source areas to coastal areas from which the materials could be exported. Connections for internal distribution of goods were generally poorly developed (Fig. 3.12). In the colonial period, usually railroads were built as the primary means of transport, with roads acting as a feeder system to the railroad. In West Africa, the individual British colonies were separated from each other by French colonies. One result of this separation was that almost no overland transportation links were established between the British colonies, nor were links built to connect with French systems. In French West Africa, due to its continuous areal expression, some international roads existed with independence. But all African countries have to reorient their transport networks because of their desire to develop their own economies.

With the construction of roads – today's favored transport system because of their flexibility – major environmental disruptions often occur. The effects of road construction on the land and water resources are almost identical to those discussed in the section on land disturbances. To minimize the environmental impacts of road construction, many of the construction methods currently employed throughout Africa need to be altered. Guy (1976) lists seven guidelines for minimizing erosion–sediment problems. These include creating sediment-detention basins, limiting each construction site to a small area, and planting vegetation quickly. But, in addition to these guidelines, probably major new

111

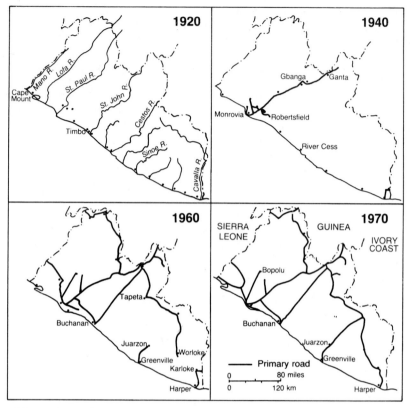

Figure 3.12 Development of roads in Liberia, 1920–70 (from Udo 1978).

road design practices need to be developed for the construction of roads suitable for the heavy short rains and clay situations found in many parts of Africa. Also, the arid areas entail a whole set of other natural problems, such as moving sand, that require other strategies. All too often many roads have been built using engineering practices developed for the middle latitudes. They are thus poorly designed for the African setting. Furthermore, a very large percentage of roads in Africa are surfaced with hard clays which not only become impassable during heavy rains but are a continuous source of sediment.

Summary

During the precolonial and colonial periods population mobility was an important adjustment to both seasonal and annual environmental fluctuations. Some colonial administrative units, such as French Equatorial Africa, developed functional relationships between their various political components. With independence, the integrated components of existing livelihood systems often became separated into two or more independent states. The political fragmentation into over 50 nations, independent of physical and human settings in most cases, is the environmental setting for which development strategies need to evolve.

The growth in the importance of export crops that began during the colonial period remains a crucial element in the economies of a significant number of African countries. Yet most governments make far greater investments in the urban and industrial sectors than in the rural ones. With the continent's growing population and rural-to-rural migration, agricultural and grazing systems need to increase in productivity. However, because of ever-increasing population pressure on the land, along with minimal investment in the countryside, both land degradation and generally stagnant economic conditions are becoming more widespread in rural areas. These trends make it even more difficult to reconcile long-term environmental viability with short-term food and capital needs.

Because of diverse conditions throughout the continent, no single strategy for economic development and environmental maintenance is possible. The costs of protecting the environment, and the resulting benefits to the development process, need to be made clear in order to prevent short-term strategies from destroying the resource base for future African generations.

4   Tropical rainforest environments

Introduction

The tropical rainforest environments are characterized in their natural condition by a continuous growing season. Neither moisture shortages nor temperature extremes exist that require plant dormancy in these environments. Average monthly temperatures almost always exceed 17°C (63°F), and the soils are essentially free of periods of moisture shortages. Although most African rainforest areas experience brief periods of moisture deficit, their intensity is never severe enough to prevent plant growth as sufficient soil moisture storage allows plant growth to continue during these "drier" periods. African rainforests are largely concentrated in Zaire and Gabon, with other areas along the coast and periphery of West Africa as far as Sierra Leone (Table 4.1) (Fig. 4.1). Minor areas of tropical mountain rainforest still exist in the mountainous areas of Kenya, Tanzania, Uganda, Rwanda, and Ethiopia (Ch. 7). The greatest concentration of forested land within Africa occurs within the rainforest environment. The

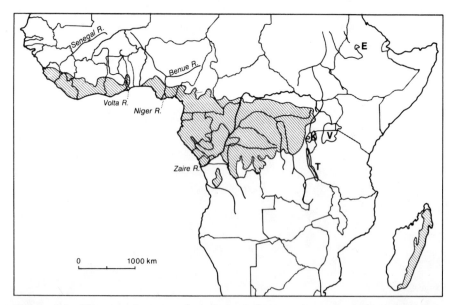

Figure 4.1   The natural extent of tropical rainforests prior to land clearing. E, Lake Tana; K, Lake Kivu; T, Lake Tanganyika; V, Lake Victoria. (Modified from UNESCO 1978.)

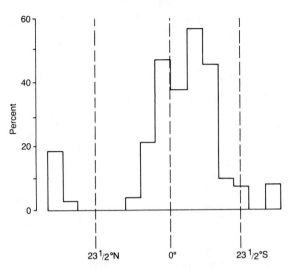

Figure 4.2 Distribution of forested land as a percentage of the total land area in 5° latitudinal zones within Africa. (Modified from UNESCO 1978.)

lower percentage of forest cover north of the equator in part reflects the clearing of rainforests for agriculture in West Africa (Fig. 4.2).

Unlike the other African ecosystems, nutrients in the rainforests are largely stored in the living biomass, especially the vegetation, rather than in the soil. This makes the rainforest system less resilient to change than almost any other African system. If major changes are introduced, such as deforestation, the ability of the ecosystem to return to its previous state is often slight, since the removal of vegetation takes critical nutrients from the area. In addition, microclimatic changes set in motion by the removal of the vegetation alter the climate near the ground to a sufficient degree in many cases to retard germination of many rainforest plant species. Furthermore, the removal of vegetation allows rain to strike the soil directly. This, along with the high erosivity of the tropical

Table 4.1 Approximate area of evergreen rainforests in Africa (in millions of hectares): 1981 estimates.

Cameroon	6.4
Central African Republic	0.75
Equatorial Guinea	2.3
Gabon	16.0
Ivory Coast	4.0
Madagascar	1.4
People's Republic of Congo	3.0
Zaire	50.0

Note: Nigeria, Ghana, Liberia, and Sierra Leone have small areas of forest remaining.

rains, often initiates soil erosion, which further exacerbates the negative processes that together retard natural reforestation.

Within Africa, population growth and the consequent economic and political pressures to utilize the forest areas are increasing. The demand for lumber is an important catalyst in forest clearing, and it is ever increasing. But farmers are generally the major destroyers of African forests. Before the 20th century, shifting agricultural systems allowed the forests to recover to a large extent. Under this low-intensity land use the rainforest was resilient. During the 20th century the forests are being permanently removed for lumber, banana plantations, oil palms, rubber, cocoa, and subsistence agriculture. Slash-and-burn agriculture is the major farming system used to clear the forests. The utilization of the forest lands for food supply is largely an unplanned process by which the peasants attempt to meet their food needs. To a large degree the current agricultural practices of small landholders produce food from a given cleared plot for only a few years. This is partially a result of the need to fertilize the soils for permanent agriculture in order to replace the limited nutrient supply found in the soils. The cost of fertilizer is usually prohibitive for the small farmer so, when yields decrease, he clears new lands and starts the process all over again. Firewood demands are a marginal factor today in contributing to the destruction of rainforests. However, especially in the fuel deficient countries (i.e. Liberia), energy shortages could lead to the forests being cleared directly for fuel and indirectly for the growing of manioc and sugar cane (e.g. Brazil) for fuel production. In some of the mountain rainforest areas (e.g. Kenya), this process has already begun. Because immediate economic demands for the conversion of forests could limit future options, the destruction of these forests must be controlled. Because of the geologic and biologic processes associated with the high annual temperatures and large quantities of precipitation in the rainforests, the soils and water systems are highly vulnerable to degradation where deforestation occurs. Progress, albeit slow, is being made in agroforestry, and this could encourage farmers to plant trees as an economic alternative to the destructive slash-and-burn agriculture. At first glance, this economic activity appears to be one type of viable environmental strategy. But, of course, it requires a variety of infrastructural conditions if it is to have a chance to succeed.

In the Zaire Basin the primary forest still exists as a vast area of continuous cover. But in Africa, and especially in West Africa, the rainforests are clearly in retreat in the face of increasing populations. The once continuous forest in many places is beginning to become patchwork of forests, oil-palm bush, and small farms. In areas where population pressures are high, as in the eastern states of Nigeria, the forest already is replaced by oil-palm bush. In these areas rainforest vegetation is limited solely to forest reserves. In Ivory Coast, the tropical forest is being cut at the annual rate of half a million hectares. The forests that in 1956 covered over 14 million hectares now cover less than 5 million hectares. Tens of thousands of hectares are cut by farmers to plant either food crops, coffee, or cocoa. Timber companies in search of valuable tree species open up hitherto virgin territory to these farmers. The ecological consequences of destroying the forests is far from being completely understood; but the impoverishment of the soil, once tree cover is destroyed, is one usual deleterious effect. Already in parts of West Africa the rainforest as the "potential vegetation" in some areas is quite hypothetical. Because of changes in the floristic composition, seeds for the majority of the rainforest species are no longer available for natural regeneration. Even if seeds were available, microclimatic (climate near the ground) alterations resulting from the removal of the forest make many areas no longer ideal environments for rainforest regeneration. Besides environmental factors, the long–term development ramifications of rainforest destruction for Africa are great. The exploitation of the forests in Ivory Coast is an important factor in the success of the national economy. If this resource were to become exhausted the national economy would clearly be affected.

General population prospectives

Worldwide, over 140 million people live in areas designated as "natural" rainforest. These are areas with high birth rates and rapid population growth.

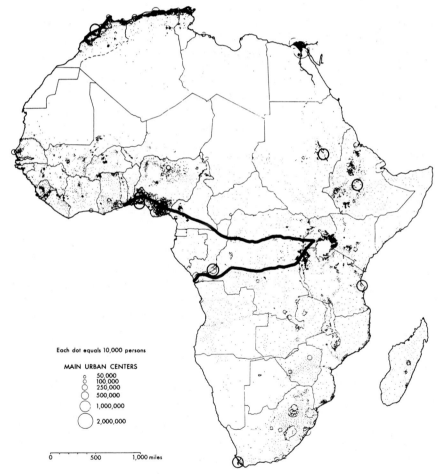

Figure 4.3 Population density of rainforest areas. (Modified from Hance 1975.)

117

To examine the general population attributes of the rainforest areas of Africa it is necessary to divide these "natural" rainforest areas into at least two major areas – areas which are still primarily rainforest, such as the Zaire Basin, and areas cleared or undergoing land clearance, such as large areas in West Africa. Figure 4.3 illustrates the large difference between the population density in areas where the forest has been cleared and areas where the forest is largely intact. In the Zaire Basin, where the largest extent of rainforest remains, population densities are low and large urban centers rare. Where they do exist, they are along the margins of the Zaire River. Mbandaka and Kisangani are the only urban centers of any size, and they are on the fringe of the rainforest. In the rainforest areas the population densities are less than 2 per km^2. Also, this population is young, with over 50 percent under 18 years of age. With the minimal employment opportunities in this area, even with its low population there is an outward migration toward the larger urban areas in the country. The inhabitants living in this area are largely engaged in subsistence agriculture. The estate (plantation) and other forms of commercial agriculture that took place in this area during the colonial period completely collapsed during the 1960s.

In contrast to the Zaire Basin, the population in West Africa occupying areas of cleared rainforest is relatively large. In Nigeria, in the eastern states, there is a high demand for farmland and the forest has been replaced largely by the oil palm. In these areas population densities range between 35 and 300 per km^2. Along the eastern fringes of this oil-palm bush the population decreases to 15–25 per km^2 in Cameroon. West of the oil-palm bush toward Lagos populations range from 55 to 200 per km^2, generally increasing toward the west. From just west of Accra to the vicinity of Freetown the rainforest zone has population densities generally between 20 and 80 per km^2 (Fig. 4.3).

Current trends in areal coverage of rainforest

Prior to modern heavy machinery and powersaws, penetration into the rainforest was difficult. After hunting and gathering, shifting cultivation evolved. This agricultural form is still practiced to a considerable extent in large areas of the Zairian and Cameroonian forests and in other areas of low population densities. The small patches of land clearance cause only a temporary disturbance in the forest microclimate, and natural soil and forest regeneration occur. In wide areas of southeastern Nigeria during the last few centuries, oil-palm bush has largely replaced the rainforest because of population pressures. In addition, the high forest has been substituted by other tree crops in many parts of West Africa to sustain the population. Among the more important tree crops are cocoa, kola nut, coconut, rubber, and raphia palms. In areas of slightly higher elevation, coffee and citrus trees also are found where previously only the high forest existed. Where population pressures were too high even for tree crops, land clearance took place. Because of extreme changes in the microclimate, environmental changes resulted from these major alterations in land use. Large clearances of the land resulted in higher soil temperatures and, in some cases, the formation of hardpans within the soil. The new ground condition, and lower plant transpiration interacting with the high amounts of precipitation, resulted in high groundwater levels; increased runoff and soil erosion also occurred in many areas. In addition, in many parts of West Africa the rainforest cover was critical for protecting the soil moisture during the short dry periods. Once cleared, the soils dried out, especially along the rainforest margins, owing to both high temperatures and solar radiation, as well as to the drying influence of the harmattan winds, which often blow southwestward from the Sahara–Sahel regions during the drier portion of the year. Today, for many areas of West Africa, natural rainforest is only found in atlases. Farming is practiced throughout these former forest areas, and in many areas the land is deserted because of environmental degradation. With modern forest-clearing practices, the forest in West Africa is rapidly being cleared for both agriculture and timber. Although little if any virgin rainforest exists in West Africa, under previous low–density occupancy the forest was generally able to regenerate itself. Now, with the large and growing population and economic demands, the existence of the rainforest in West Africa is precarious. To understand the rainforest and its responses to human occupancy, the physical characteristics of this environmental zone are now presented.

The macroclimatic characteristics: a brief introduction

As with any major ecological unit, there are no universally agreed criteria for delineating the boundaries of the unit. However, distinctive climatic conditions are found within the African rainforest areas. Annual temperature ranges are usually between 3 and 9°C; cloud cover usually prevents excessively high temperatures, and the combination of tropical location, cloud cover, and vegetation canopy result in low diurnal ranges, usually less than 10°C. In particular, cloud cover during the afternoon lowers incoming solar energy, and the forest vegetation lowers counterradiation losses during the night. Dry seasons can exist in rainforest environments, but under natural conditions the length of the dry season is insufficient for vegetation to be under severe moisture stress because sufficient soil-moisture storage exists for plant utilization until the end of the short dry season. Figure 4.4 illustrates the diurnal patterns of temperature for Ilebo, Zaire. Annual temperature ranges within a twenty-four hour period are a maximum of 8°C, with an annual monthly temperature range of only about 2°C. In terms of moisture, the two basic African subtypes within the rainforest are: (1) areas characterized by abundant precipitation throughout the year, such as Yangambi, Zaire (Table 4.2); and (2) areas such as Bitam, Gabon (Table 4.2), which have a brief dry period, but one which is insufficient to dry out the soil moisture stored under the natural vegetation cover. With the major exception of the central basin of Zaire, most African rainforest climates have a short dry season. Climatic data for Douala, Cameroon, illustrate typical temperature ranges. These demonstrate the lack of extreme temperatures in African rainforest areas, along with the presence of a slightly drier season (December–February) (Table 4.2). It is estimated that potential evapotranspiration from tropical rainforests is between 1200 and 1500 mm. On average, about 25 to 30 percent of precipitation in these areas is surplus, and this results in large river discharges per area for these environs.

Table 4.2 Rainfall and temperature: Yangambi, Zaire; Bitam, Gabon; and Douala, Cameroon.

	Jan.	Feb.	Mar.	Apr.	May	June	July	Aug.	Sept.	Oct.	Nov.	Dec.	Annual	Years of record
Yangambi, Zaire														
relative humidity (%)	84	81	84	86	86	87	88	88	87	87	86	88	86	3
precipitation (mm)														
mean	85	99	148	150	177	126	146	170	180	241	180	126	1828	30
max.	229	188	362	264	342	342	266	291	319	381	317	217	2629	30
min.	18	34	58	37	85	25	43	55	79	113	54	0	1220	30
temperature (°C)														
mean														
max.	30	31	31	30	30	30	29	28	29	29	29	29	30	10
min.	20	19	20	20	20	20	19	20	19	20	20	20	20	10
extreme														
max.	36	35	35	35	35	33	32	33	33	34	33	34	36	10
min.	15	14	16	18	17	17	17	17	17	17	18	14	14	10
Bitam, Gabon														
relative humidity (%)	86	84	84	85	87	88	87	85	87	88	87	87	86	10
precipitation (mm)														
mean	49	72	182	191	231	101	26	37	277	297	208	75	1174	12
max.	116	152	336	300	334	153	122	93	440	427	285	134	2159	12
min.	1	7	89	115	99	46	1	3	43	105	90	13	1174	12

	I	II	III	IV	V	VI	VII	VIII	IX	X	XI	XII	year	yrs
temperature (°C)														
mean max.	29	30	30	30	30	30	28	27	27	28	29	29	29	12
mean min.	20	20	20	20	20	20	20	19	19	20	20	20	20	12
extreme max.	33	33	34	35	33	34	33	32	32	32	32	32	35	12
extreme min.	16	17	16	17	18	16	13	14	17	17	17	17	13	12
Douala, Cameroons														
relative humidity (%) max.	98	97	97	98	98	98	98	98	98	98	98	98	98	26
relative humidity (%) min.	64	61	62	63	65	71	77	77	73	68	67	65	68	26
precipitation (mm) mean	57	82	216	243	337	486	725	776	638	388	150	52	4150	30
precipitation (mm) max.	183	185	426	349	599	862	1154	1240	980	602	298	184	5328	30
precipitation (mm) min.	1	5	58	130	141	226	277	248	315	259	36	4	3238	30
temperature (°C) mean max.	31	32	32	32	31	29	27	27	28	29	30	30	30	27
temperature (°C) mean min.	23	23	23	23	23	23	22	22	23	22	23	23	23	27
extreme max.	34	35	34	36	35	33	31	32	33	34	34	35	36	27
extreme min.	19	20	20	20	19	20	20	20	20	19	19	19	19	27

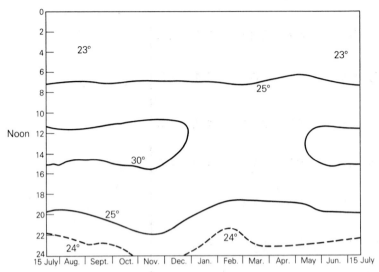

Figure 4.4 The average diurnal temperature pattern during an annual period at Ilebo, Zaire. Temperature range: January, 5°C; March, 5°C; June, 8°C; September, 8°C; December, 6°C (from Birot 1966).

Precipitation characteristics

Although rain events are frequent and most precipitation is of the convective type, the causes of precipitation are exceedingly complex. Along the Atlantic coast, one factor contributing to precipitation is the pertubations of hot humid air moving inland from the Gulf of Guinea. These disturbances result in rains which are both intense and of long duration, particularly during the late night and morning. In the Zaire Basin itself, temperature contrasts between ocean to continent, interacting with the high-pressure conditions in the south Atlantic (around 30°S), result in a flow landward of humid air as far east as the mountains in eastern Zaire and Rwanda (30°E, longitude). Rains resulting from this inland movement of maritime air are convective, but they are discontinuous in areal extent. Thus, even during the heart of the rainy season in central Zaire, only about 50 percent of the weather stations record precipitation on a given day. In the West African areas of the rainforest, precipitation patterns are dominated by the Inter-Tropical Convergence Zone (ITCZ). Warm, moist westerly and southerly flows dominate the year, bringing with them ample moisture for precipitation. During periods when the winds shift in a northeasterly flow, precipitation drops.

On the island of Bioko, Equatorial Guinea, at Ureka the maximum African annual precipitation occurs (over 10,000 mm/yr) (Fig. 4.5). Most annual precipitation in the Zaire Basin is between 1300 and 2000 mm. Along the West African coast, precipitation ranges upward to 4000 mm (Table 4.3). The highest average rainfalls occur along the coast of Guinea where the southwesterly winds interact with the warm Guinea Current. Nevertheless, no matter what the

Table 4.3 Rainfall: Lubumbashi, Zaire; Kinshasa, Zaire; Monrovia, Liberia.

	Lubumbashi, Zaire Precipitation			Kinshasa, Zaire Precipitation			Monrovia, Liberia Precipitation		
	mean (mm)	max. (mm)	min. (mm)	mean (mm)	max. (mm)	min. (mm)	mean (mm)	max. (mm)	min. (mm)
Jan.	256	427	149	128	321	2	51	101	15
Feb.	264	422	130	139	330	49	71	257	1
Mar.	210	378	89	181	429	58	120	304	27
Apr.	53	155	9	209	379	59	154	364	10
May	3	41	0	134	280	22	442	732	232
June	0	4	0	5	38	0	958	–	480
July	0	0	0	1	34	0	797	1460	304
Aug.	0	15	0	4	24	0	354	712	101
Sept.	3	31	0	33	100	2	720	948	546
Oct.	27	72	0	137	282	20	598	866	264
Nov.	166	396	43	236	348	84	237	397	91
Dec.	262	479	113	171	327	47	122	304	28
Annual	1244	1554	868	1378	1824	1124	4624	–	–
Record (years)	30	30	30	30	30	30	10	10	10

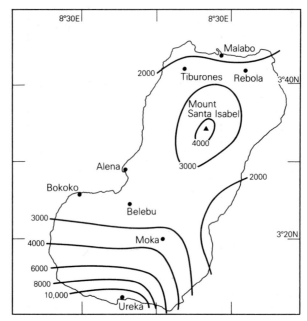

Figure 4.5 The annual precipitation pattern on Bioko (Fernando Po.): mean annual rainfall is in millimeters. (Modified from Griffiths 1972.)

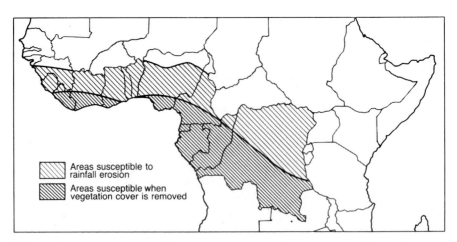

Figure 4.6 Erosion potential due to precipitation patterns in West Africa (from Lal 1976).

Table 4.4 Duration of dry season in some rainforest areas in Zaire.

Region	Start of dry season	Start of wet season	Duration of dry season (days)
Uele (Bambesa)	9 December	8 February	61
Lower Zaire (Kinshasa)	24 May	22 September	121
Kasai (Gandajika)	9 May	28 August	111
Katanga (Lubumbashi)	20 April	22 October	185
Mountain zone (Tshibinda)	17 June	27 August	71

annual amounts are, because the rains are generally of high intensity the erosivity – the potential of the rain to cause soil erosion – is high (Fig. 4.6) in rainforest areas once the land is cleared.

In spite of the high annual precipitation, a relatively high variability is a characteristic of rainforest precipitation in Africa. In the lower Zaire, expected precipitation ranges between 1170 and 1655 mm within 10-year intervals; in the central Zaire Basin, the ranges are between 1535 and 2110 mm. At Harbel, Liberia, annual ranges are between 2321 and 4313 mm. At Lagos, Nigeria, ranges between 1039 and 2934 mm have been recorded. Along with annual variation, the information presented in Tables 4.2 and 4.3 indicates the large variability at the monthly level too. Table 4.4 illustrates the presence of the dry-season phenomenon within most African rainforest climates. The vegetation cover of these areas is a crucial variable contributing to the maintenance of soil moisture during these dry periods. When vegetation is destroyed, soils can dry out during these periods. The direct contact of sunlight with the ground – which does not occur often under a rainforest canopy – dries out the soil during the dry season. In the process the soil temperature increases. These changes can set in motion a series of reactions that can make the area unfavorable for forest regeneration.

In any storm system, rain intensity varies during precipitation. Within the African rainforest, average 10-minute intensities between 30 and 60 mm are not exceptional. Likewise, average 20 to 30 mm intensities for 30-minute periods are noted during afternoon showers. It is the combination of the generally high intensities associated with tropical rain systems, along with the duration of the precipitation, that accounts for the high erosivity (potential for causing erosion) of the rains. Therefore the potential for soil erosion is high whenever vegetation cover is destroyed and the soil is not protected from the direct impact of raindrops.

Cloud cover and solar energy

The absolute humidity does not differ greatly during a 24-hour period. Although relative humidities tend to be high, the relative humidity in this zone does have a diurnal pattern. Generally, with the warmer day temperatures, relative humidity averages between 60 and 70 percent in daytime. In the cooler nights relative humidities increase, often ranging between 90 and 100 percent. These high humidities indicate that the potential for cloudiness in this zone is

Table 4.5 Percentage of sunshine and cloud amounts: Port Harcourt.

	Jan.	Feb.	Mar.	Apr.	May	June	July	Aug.	Sept.	Oct.	Nov.	Dec.
percentage sunshine	45	51	39	40	40	27	20	20	17	29	39	47
mean monthly cloud amounts (OKTAS)												
09h00	6	5	7	7	7	7	7	8	7	7	7	5
15h00	5	6	7	7	7	7	7	7	7	7	7	5

Table 4.6 Frequency of sunshine in Zaire Basin.

Region	Sunshine (%)	Jan.	Feb.	Mar.	Apr.	May	June	July	Aug.	Sept.	Oct.	Nov.	Dec.
central basin (Yangambi) 1956–9	0	3	3	2	4	1	0	5	2	3	3	1	6
	1–30	13	12	29	17	16	21	28	37	32	27	31	25
	31–60	45	28	29	49	36	38	39	37	40	46	37	40
	61–90	39	57	38	39	35	35	28	24	25	24	31	29
	91–100	0	0	2	0	12	0	0	0	0	0	0	0
lower Congo (Kinshasa) 1951–9	0	3	3	3	1	3	3	8	5	4	4	4	3
	1–30	41	41	32	24	35	35	38	31	39	42	35	39
	31–60	40	40	37	46	42	38	30	34	36	38	32	42
	61–90	15	15	28	29	19	24	24	30	21	16	19	16
	91–100	1	1	0	0	1	0	0	0	0	0	0	0
mountain zone (Lwiro) 1956–9	0	0	1	2	0	2	0	2	2	0	0	0	1
	1–30	27	29	21	18	31	23	17	13	11	28	14	26
	31–60	45	35	32	47	43	35	29	35	37	38	55	44
	61–90	26	32	43	34	23	39	46	45	51	34	31	28
	91–100	2	3	2	1	1	3	6	5	1	0	0	1

high. In reality, because of the degree of cloudiness, a general characteristic of African rainforests is that solar radiation reaching the surface is relatively low. Along coastal areas in Nigeria, values for possible sunshine are as low as 35 percent (Table 4.5). Because of the high degree of cloudiness, during maximum precipitation in the rainy season (August) monthly values for sunshine are as low as 18–20 percent. For Yangambi, Kinshasa, and Lwiro Table 4.6 shows another general attribute of rainforest areas; that is, the sky is rarely overcast for the whole day. At the same time, the day is seldom clear for the entire period of sunshine. These general conditions prevail as far west as Liberia where, during the clearest month (March), the maximum hours of sunshine range between 3.2 and 7.1 h (27–58 percent potential sunshine), and during the cloudiest month (August) there are only 0.4 to 2.7 h (3–23 percent) of sunshine each day. Thus, even though the length of day is always around 12 hours in the African rainforest areas, the insolation available for plant growth is significantly lower than at first presumed because of the heavy cloud cover during significant periods of the year. In addition, a small percentage of incoming solar energy is consumed in evaporating moisture from the canopy and is therefore not available for plant growth. This low percentage of solar energy reaching the surface reduces the potential for plant growth in these areas, even though the growing season is the entire year.

Microclimate

For vegetation growth an exchange of energy, nutrients, and matter is required between the soil, the atmosphere, and the plants themselves. In the rainforest large quantities of water are required for plant respiration, transpiration, and transfer of mineral matter from soil to vegetation; at the same time, solar energy is needed for photosynthesis. The intensity of the processes affecting these exchanges is largely a function of temperature, which is itself affected by sunlight intensity. The temperature range for optimal production of plant matter by photosynthesis is between 20 and 30°C. At the higher end of this range, a high proportion of CO_2 in the atmosphere favors photosynthesis. The environmental setting that most affects plant growth is that of the forest, not the open conditions under which official measurements are obtained. It is this microclimatic setting that directly affects plant growth. For example, in undisturbed rainforest the amount of CO_2 present is sometimes twice as much as that in the atmosphere above the forest canopy, but usually it is only slightly more. Yet this slight increase in CO_2 content increases photosynthesis, which in turn encourages plant growth, thus improving the chances of survival for the plants. When forests are cut the microclimates of the area are changed drastically; almost always these changes are of a kind that makes the area less favorable for plant growth.

For rainforest environments the standard meteorological data gathered in clearings at a height of about 1 m above the ground are approximately the same as those for the climate immediately above the forest canopy. The forest canopy alters these standard conditions at the forest floor by offering resistance to air movement, by intercepting a proportion of the precipitation through both reflecting and absorbing a percentage of the incoming solar energy and through being the primary radiating surface of heat loss during the hours of darkness. All these interactions with the canopy cause the climates within the forest (below the canopy) to differ from the standard climatic characteristics used to define the limits and properties of rainforest environments. Thus, even though clearing the forest does not appear to alter the standard climatic conditions of rainforest areas to any great degree, the changes in the climate differ markedly from the conditions that existed under the forest canopy.

Changes in air movement

One indication of the general calm conditions existing within a tropical rain-forest is that in comparison with many other types of plant communities wind pollination and wind dispersal of seeds is not widespread within the plant communities of the rainforest. From a study in Brazil it was noted that during a storm wind gusts of 104 km/h were measured in a clearing, though within the forest, where the trees increase the friction, wind speeds were reduced to less than 4 km/h (Richards 1952). Figure 4.7, though not from a rainforest, illustrates the reduction of wind speeds within forests. Similar relationships must exist within tropical forests as it is often noted that leaves in the forest canopy are in motion, even when the air within the forest is calm. One important effect of the generally calm conditions existing within rainforests is that evaporation is reduced along the forest floor (soil), and the low air movement helps to maintain the moist conditions of the upper portions of the soil.

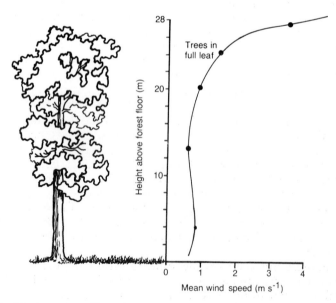

Figure 4.7 The lowering effect of trees on wind speed near the ground (from Geiger 1965).

Interception, stemflow, and throughfall of precipitation

For precipitation to be useful, for most plants the water must both reach the soil and infiltrate into it. Then the roots remove a percentage of the water, as well as the dissolved nutrients needed for growth and transpiration. "Interception" is the quantity of water held by vegetation – on leaves for instance – that never reaches the ground. Thus the net effect of interception is to reduce the water available for plant utilization. Studies on interception of precipitation within Ivory Coast rainforests indicate that between 10 and 22 percent is intercepted. Areas with the higher values reflect a greater forest vegetation density at the intermediate and lower stratas. The highest value documented for a rainforest is 28 percent. From all the data gathered in the world's rainforests, 10–24 percent is found to be the normal range. The broader the leaf and the denser the canopy, the greater the interception; conversely, the greater the rain intensity, the lower the interception. It is the generally greater intensity of tropical rains that probably accounts for the fact that a lower range is found in tropical forests than in some mid-latitude forests where, under gentle rain conditions, up to 50 percent is intercepted. Since the rainforest areas are zones where moisture supply is not a limiting factor for plant growth, the reduction of water loss by interception does not affect growth negatively. However, it reduces the amount of water reaching the surface. Therefore less water is available to enter either the area's surface or groundwater systems, or to cause soil erosion.

The "stemflow" is the quantity of water that enters the ground by flowing down the tree trunk. In contrast to precipitation, stemflow water selectively enters the ground at the same location (the base of the trunk). It concentrates a proportion of the precipitation onto a small area. Measured quantities of stemflow range from less than 1 to 18 percent of the total precipitation reaching the forest surface. Probably the general range is between 1 and 4 percent. The large range in data is largely the result of nonstandardization of data collection. Given that water entering the soil through stemflow has been slowed by the friction on the trunk, its erosivity (potential for causing erosion) has been lowered in comparison to throughfall, though in some situations the concentrated flow down the trunk continues as a small channel flow over the surface. In the tropical rainforest the thick litter usually results in the stemflow soaking directly into the ground.

The "throughflow" is that proportion of the precipitation that reaches the soil either directly from the precipitation or by dripping off the leaves. Estimates and measurements of throughflow indicate that 70–91 percent of annual precipitation in rainforests strikes the ground through throughflow. Table 4.7 shows the values of interception, stemflow, and throughfall for some sites in Ivory Coast. These three variables together determine the way the soil acquires moisture; they also determine the water-balance inputs. In sum total, rainforests tend to ameliorate microclimates in terms of temperature, wind, and moisture conditions. By clearing the forest you increase the water reaching the ground by lowering interception; increase wind speeds by lowering friction; and increase temperature ranges by allowing more energy to reach the ground during the day and by increasing the radiation losses during the night.

Table 4.7   Water balance in a portion of Ivory Coast.

	Banco, plateau 1969–71		Banco, valley 1969–71		Yapo	
	(mm)	(%)	(mm)	(%)	(mm)	(%)
rainfall in the open (P)	1800	100	1800	100	1950	100
throughfall (P_{sol})	1615	90	1555	86	1510	77
stemflow (E_t)	15	1	15	1	15	1
real interception $I = P - (P_{sol} + E_t)$	170	10	230	12	425	22
water evaporated from the soil (ETR − I)	975	54	965	54	1000	51
real evapotranspiration (ETR)	1145	64	1196	66	1425	73
drainage ($D = P -$ ETR)	655	36	605	34	525	27

Vegetation attributes

Despite classification of most of the world's major vegetation types into subsets, there is still no widely accepted classification for the various rainforest eco-systems that exist within Africa. The State-of-the-Knowledge report on tropical forest ecosystems prepared by UNESCO (1978) provides no accepted subsets of tropical rainforests, except lowland and montane.

The lowland rainforests

In terms of vegetation, the most important characteristic of the tropical rain-forest is the diversity of plant species found. Within a single hectare, it is usual to find between 20 and 60 different species of trees. In some Malayan rainforests up to 200 different species of trees are found in 1 ha. As research is undertaken in the largely unstudied Zairian forests, this type of diversity is likely to be found in parts of Africa. Within Ivory Coast, one of the more studied areas of rainforest in Africa, 500 species of trees have been identified. When other types of plant species besides trees are included, the diversity becomes overwhelming. Of a possible 10 million species of plants and animals on Earth, up to 5 million are estimated to be found in tropical rainforests. Yet it is estimated that only 20 percent of plant species in tropical rainforests have been identified. Generally, tropical rainforest plant species have highly specialized ecological requirements, exist at low densities, are often confined to small areas, and, as such, are very vulnerable to extinction.

Although rainforests in Africa and other tropical areas are often lumped together and referred to as if they were a uniform cover of broadleaf evergreen vegetation, this is far from the truth. One ramification of the plant diversity is that, since food for most animals is often limited to a few specific sources and these are scattered widely through the forests owing to the great diversity of flora, the density of fauna is usually low.

130

Although fauna density is relatively low in rainforest areas, to the casual observer it appears even lower. This is because the greatest animal activity is not along the forest floor but above in the tree canopies. It is here that insects are concentrated; thus the birds and mammals that feed on them also live in this above-ground life zone. Similarly, seeds, fruits, leaves, and the other aspects of the trees that are food supplies for animals are concentrated above the ground. Along the surface, fallen fruits, seeds, young trees, and some bushes offer a smaller food supply than up in the tree canopies. This results in a smaller animal population that directly interacts in the same space as humans. It is with the clearing of the forest that insect populations increase at ground level and become a major annoyance.

In mature rainforests, despite the diversity of trees, the vegetation appears quite uniform to the casual observer. Often it is only in detail that tree species differ markedly. It is this uniform appearance that to a large extent accounts for the general perception that all rainforests are the same. The general impression from within the forest is that tree trunks are quite straight with few branches until the top of the tree is reached. Probably as a result of the generally low wind velocities, rainforest trees are generally slender and are prone to damage when high winds occur. A great variety of shapes exist at the base of the tree trunks, but one characteristic not common in most other forests is that numerous trees at their bases have plank buttresses which are flange-like outgrowths. In areas of poor drainage, trees with stilted roots may be found.

Generally, the rainforest canopy (the closed roof of the forest formed by the crowns of the tallest trees) is described as multistorial. Two or three strata is the general rule. The uppermost portion of the canopy is characterized by predominantly dome-shaped emergent crowns. Beneath these emergent trees is the main canopy comprised predominantly of narrow-crowned trees. Despite the general perception of the uniform height of the main canopy, recent studies indicate that it is of variable height and density. This irregularity in the canopy height may increase local air turbulence and thereby increase transpiration, which reduces leaf temperature. In the same way, the dome-shaped emergent crowns shade the main canopy and, because of their shape, are themselves partially in the shade during a portion of the day. When a lower stratum exists, about half of the trees comprising this layer are found to be young ones belonging to species found in the upper stories. Trees within this lower layer generally have crowns that are long, tapering, and conical. Beneath these strata a varied undergrowth exists in the rainforest consisting of shrubs, herbaceous plants, ferns, saplings, climbers, stranglers, epiphytes, and heterotrophic plants. Despite this diversity of flora, except along margins of the forests such as river courses, vegetation along the forest floor in most undisturbed areas is never so dense as to make passage through the forest very difficult.

Most leaves on rainforest trees have high reflectance because their surfaces are generally shiny and waxy. In addition, in Southeast Asia Brunig (1970) found forests where the leaves of the trees are oriented at an angle to the mean direction of solar radiation. Both these properties result in high albedo which tends to moderate high temperatures at the crown–air interface. Another benefit of the high reflectivity of the leaves is that it helps transmit light through the dense canopy, thus allowing saplings to exist until openings in the forest occur, either through death of old trees, lightning destruction, or wind-blown trees. When an opening develops the sapling grows rapidly and becomes a component of the upper strata. Thus the leaf properties permit the vegetation to flourish under conditions of high temperature and at the same time contribute to the regeneration process.

Soil properties of rainforest areas

No real differences exist between the weathering and soil-forming processes in the tropical rainforests and those in soils in humid mid-latitude forests. In well-drained areas the tropical forest soils are generally yellowish or reddish, whereas in the middle latitudes they are usually greyish or brownish. The reddish soils are found to be poorer in silica than the brownish ones. This is interpreted as implying that the tropical soils are older than the soils of the middle latitudes. In Africa this is clearly the case. Despite climatic fluctuations (Ch. 2), the African red soils are almost always found in areas of old surfaces developed during long periods of geologic stability, whereas in many mid-latitude areas the soils are formed on younger parent materials resulting from "new surfaces" formed during the Pleistocene. Although the weathering and soil-forming processes are fairly similar in both areas, in the humid tropics – largely because the processes have operated for longer – the chemical alteration of the parent materials is greater.

Vegetation and rainforest soils

Vegetation has five major impacts on rainforest soils. First, it protects the upper portions of the soil from completely drying out by lowering the amount of solar energy directly reaching the soil, as well as decreasing the length of time that any portion of the soil is in sunlight. Second, it lowers the intensity of precipitation by intercepting a percentage of the precipitation and impedes surface runoff by increasing the friction along the forest floor. Three, it lowers the quantity of water passing completely through the soil due to the high evapotranspiration of the forest vegetation. Four, it helps increase the biological activity in the soil. And five, it produces large quantities of vegetal matter, as well as recycling the organic materials in the soil once they break down.

ORGANIC MATTER AND TEMPERATURE-CHANGE IMPACTS

The accumulation of organic matter in the soil depends upon the difference between the rate at which vegetal debris is deposited in or on the soil and the rate at which it decomposes. A tropical rainforest produces about three to four times as much vegetal matter per hectare as does a mid-latitude forest, but microorganisms decompose this matter at about the same rate as it is produced. Thus, despite high production, little net humus accumulation occurs and organic material within rainforest soils is low. When forests are cleared, the supply of organic matter to the soil decreases, though decomposition rates

Table 4.8 Soil temperatures at different depths and times, dependent on vegetation cover.

Time	Depth (cm)	T (°C) at 8	T (°C) at 11	T (°C) at 14
no vegetation	1	26.8	44.0	53.5
	10	27.5	31.7	36.8
savanna vegetation under grass	1	24.7	41.5	50.4
	10	27.8	32.9	40.1
	20	27.5	33.4	41.1
under shrubs	1	21.6	22.7	26.9
	10	23.0	22.9	24.8
	20	23.8	23.8	25.4
air temperature (°C)		22.2	28.3	36.0

Source: after d'Hoore (1954).

remain high. Because of this imbalance in general a rapid decrease in the organic content of the soils occurs whenever vegetation cover decreases. Also, with the removal of the vegetation, the future supply of nutrients is severely curtailed, since to a large extent they are stored in the living biomass in the rainforest.

Removal of vegetation from rainforest areas also directly affects the temperature properties of soils. Table 4.8 shows that soil temperatures increase once vegetation cover is altered. This change, along with the complex hydrologic changes resulting from forest clearing set into motion by the vegetation alteration, can cause some rainforest soils to develop crusts. The crust formation results from an alteration in the clay components of the soil and the mobilization of the iron in the upper portion of the soil. The mobilized iron moves down through the soil, and at some depth it is deposited within the soil through complex chemical reactions. This results in a cuirassic (crust) deposit (d'Hoore 1954, Maignien 1958, Riquier 1960). As no crusts are observed under forested areas, it is likely that the formation of these extremely hard iron crusts result from a microclimatic change at the soil interface. This change, which can result from vegetation change, triggers soil processes that degrade the soil, and steps must be taken to minimize it when rainforest environments are altered.

Soils within the tropical rainforests usually fall within the oxisol order (ferralsol, FAO), that is, they are mineral soils with a subsurface (oxic) horizon 300 mm or greater comprising 15 percent clay or greater, having little or no weatherable primary minerals. This lack of weatherable primary minerals results to a large extent from the long-term stable geologic environment of the African rainforest areas. The oxic horizon is usually within 300 mm of the surface. Figure 4.8 shows the general distribution of these soils in Africa. The properties of the rainforest soils not only affect the vegetation but are themselves affected by it. It is these aspects of the oxisols that are developed in the following sections since it is the vegetation cover that is usually changed when areas are developed, though the other soil-forming factors, such as parent material and macroclimate, remain the same.

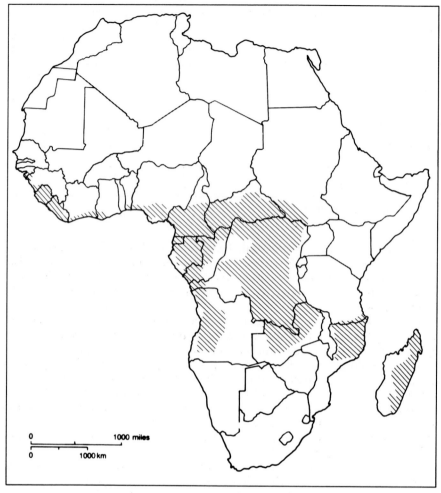

Figure 4.8 The distribution of oxisols in Africa (compiled from data in FAO 1977. *Soil maps of the world - Africa,* vol. VI. Paris: UNESCO).

Hydrology of rainforest areas

Vegetation and hydrology

The relationships between vegetation and hydrology in the tropical rainforests are similar to those in other humid areas. The vegetation intercepts some of the rain and much of this evaporates directly from the leaves. This reduces the total quantity of rain reaching the air–ground interface. Also, vegetation reduces water available for groundwater recharge by removing soil moisture for transpiration; yet it increases groundwater recharge by reducing overland flow

134

and thus permits a larger percentage of the water striking the surface to infiltrate. The major difference between rainforest and other forest areas is not in the relationships between vegetation and hydrology, but in the large quantity of water involved. This reflects the prevailing high precipitation found in tropical rainforest areas.

Rainforests in Africa occupy areas where annual precipitation is greater than the water demands of the plants, and no severe moisture stress on the vegetation ever occurs. As precipitation is not evenly distributed throughout the year, and in some African rainforest areas there are sometimes short periods where potential evaporation is greater than precipitation, during these brief climatic dry periods, ample soil moisture storage must exist to permit plant growth without adjustment. In the rainforest areas, except during these brief dry periods, there is generally a continuous downward movement of water through the soil, as well as a continuous movement of moisture through the vegetal matter. This latter property decreases the water available either for the local groundwater or for runoff. As the quantity of water required for transpiration and maintenance of the biomass is large, the rôle of vegetation is important in the hydrology of these areas. The influence of land-clearing on hydrologic conditions in large areas may differ markedly from that in smaller areas; however, so far data only exist for relatively small land clearings. In the small Sambret and Lagen stream basins in Kenya, it was found that regardless of precipitation intensity, duration, and total amount the heavy vegetation interacting with soil infiltration keeps stream flows at about 10 percent of the quantity of rainfall. Vegetation cover tends to neutralize the importance of intensity and quantity in affecting surface-water flows. The remainder (90 percent) of the precipitation is either lost by evapotranspiration or transferred outside the local basins via groundwater. The consumption of water by the biomass clearly contributes to the soil stability of rainforest areas by reducing the quantity of water passing through and over the ground.

In the general vicinity of the Sambret Basin, land-use alterations were introduced to determine the effects of vegetation cover on water yield (Pereira 1973). Replacing the natural forest vegetation with pine trees increased water yields by over 15 percent. Clearing the lands for food crops (peas, beans, squashes) increased stream flows by over 20 percent; however, the introduction of coffee bushes for tree cover increased water yields from 5 to over 30 percent. Almost all small-area experiments lead to the conclusion that forest cover is the ideal vegetation for protection against surface-water runoff and soil erosion. This is probably true for large areas as well as for the small study areas. Figure 4.9 illustrates the relatively low runoff when a rainforest stream basin's vegetation cover is not modified. When annual precipitation is 1200 mm, less than 10 percent (100 mm) becomes runoff; with an annual precipitation of 1800 mm, runoff only increases to about 14 percent (250 mm). Evidence from eastern Nigeria indicates that, with land-clearing, the excessive erosion that occurs results from the large increase in surface-water flows. The information presented in Figure 4.9 can be considered to represent conditions of minimum water flow for rainforest areas. Any change in vegetation would probably increase the runoff values.

135

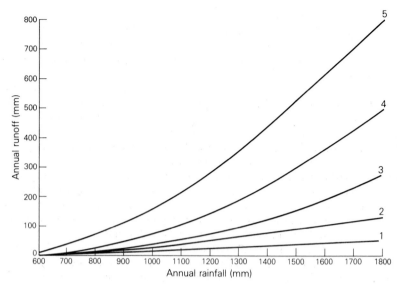

Figure 4.9 Annual rainfall–runoff relationships in some African rainforest environments.

1 Flat catchments covered by deciduous forest and woodland catchments with swamps in lower parts.
2 Undulating woodlands or afforested catchments covered by dry savanna or with a high percentage of bare soils.
3 Rolling catchments with a dense vegetational cover, woodland or forest catchments with swamps in the headwaters and undulating catchments with poor vegetational cover.
4 Undulating to rolling catchments of wet and dry regions, with intermittent streams (erosional processes occasionally seen in the river valleys).
5 Catchments on the slopes of tropical mountains in wet and dry regions and rolling catchments with poor vegetational cover and pronounced erosional processes.

Rivers of the rainforests

Except for some small rivers, no river systems in Africa flow entirely within rainforest environments. For example, a small proportion of the Upper Niger's discharge results from rainforest conditions existing in Ivory Coast. But the river's primary flow characteristics in the upper and middle sections are the result of the moisture conditions existing in semi-arid and savanna areas. It is only at the Niger's mouth (the Delta) that it flows to any large degree in a rainforest climate (Fig. 4.10). The Niger system largely reflects the climatic conditions of the wet–dry areas (Ch. 6) in its flow characteristics. For example, in the middle Niger, during the dry season most of its discharge is lost either by evaporation or groundwater infiltration and its channel diminishes greatly in size. The Rufiji in Tanzania and the Tana in Kenya further exemplify this characteristic in that neither river system flows within a rainforest environment in its middle and lower portions. Yet these two rivers receive a large proportion

136

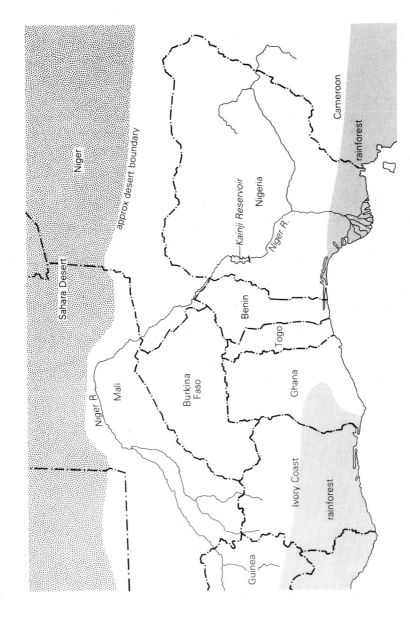

Figure 4.10 The Niger river basin and its location relative to rainforest areas.

of their annual discharge from highland rainforest sources. Without this climate in their source areas, neither river would be a permanent stream in its long course. Both in terms of areal extent and discharge, clearly the most important rainforest river system in Africa is the Zaire, even though again large areas within the basin fall within savanna climates.

Before proceeding with the hydrologic aspects of the rainforest it is important to understand that there is a paucity of long-term data for these areas. Even today, only about half of the Zaire Basin has been explored. For other river systems, too, little long-term hydrologic data usually exist. When more information becomes available, insights into the African rivers will grow. Because of the immense potential for power and exploitable resources in the Zaire and other rainforest basins, a need remains to obtain information for the rational utilization of these waters.

For the river basins that are completely or to a large degree in the rainforest, two major types of rivers, defined according to flow characteristics, are found in Africa. One category includes rivers that have only one major discharge peak in their annual flow régime. The river systems that fall within this category are situated entirely in areas of large rainfall, and no dry season occurs throughout the basin. Precipitation in all parts of the basin is greater than 1700 mm. The Ubangi River at Bangui, Central African Republic illustrates this type of flow régime, with its minimum : maximum mean monthly flow ratio being 0.11 (Fig. 4.11). The second major type of flow régime has two peaks. The Ogoué River in Gabon illustrates this type (Fig. 4.12). Again the basin is in a humid setting and experiences over 1700 mm precipitation. But the precipitation in this basin has a two-period maximum. For the Ogoué, the minimum : maximum discharge ratio is 0.25. Although there are various degrees of complexity in the flow régimes of rainforest streams, most African rivers fall either in the single- or double-peak patterns. As river systems increase in size, their flow régimes increase in complexity owing to the larger potential of different climatic patterns

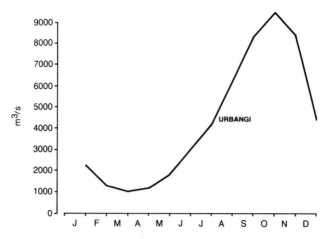

Figure 4.11   Annual hydrograph for Urbangi River. (Modified from Balek 1977.)

138

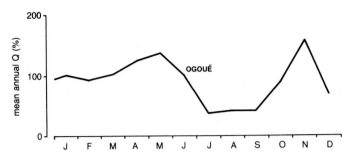

Figure 4.12   The flow regime of the Ogoué River, Gabon. (Modified from Balek 1977.)

occurring within the basins. But the minimum: maximum discharge ratios for rainforest streams are the largest and most steady of all African river systems. This reflects the absence of a severe dry season, as well as relatively constant groundwater supply to rivers in these areas. Finally, rainforest basins produce the greatest discharges per unit area in Africa. This reflects the fact that rainforest areas have the greatest annual moisture surpluses found in Africa.

The River Zaire

The largest river in Africa in terms of discharge is the Zaire. It is the major system draining Africa's largest rainforest area. From a physical perspective the river can be divided into three major sections: the upper, middle, and lower sections (Fig. 4.13).

THE UPPER SECTIONS

Two types of rivers are found in the upper sections (generally above 500 m elevation). In the southwestern portions of the basin the Kwango, Kasai, and Lubefu are the major tributaries. These basins are exceedingly flat in their upper portions. Because of this flatness, during very wet years in the months of greatest precipitation (May, June and October, November) flooding occurs over vast areas (Fig. 4.13). It is possible for some of these waters during these flooded conditions to flow not into the Zaire but into the Zambezi system. This property, namely that the divide between the Zambezi and the Zaire is not discrete, reflects both recent tectonic warping that has prevented either river system from establishing itself by downcutting and the poor drainage resulting from the flatness of the terrain. The critical factor in determining the direction of flow during this high-water condition is not topography, but local winds. In spite of the general flatness in these uplands, rapids do exist in portions of this section. The existence and persistence of rapids in rainforest streams is a common feature and reflects not only the geologic characteristics (resistant rocks) of this area but also the general lack of mechanical denudation found in many rainforest streams (Tricart 1972). Many rainforest rivers are characterized by alterations of stream reaches having very low gradients (a few centimeters per kilometer) with short reaches of rapids or waterfalls. These irregularities persist over long periods, unlike their counterparts in the humid middle latitudes. Reflecting the nonequatorial location of the southwestern portion of the basin, the river régimes in this area have two peaks resulting from the dual maximum of precipitation.

The second type of river found in the upper sections is located in the eastern portion of the basin (Fig. 4.13). Most of the Zaire's major tributaries originate in various lake systems or swamps. The relatively even flows of these tributaries result from the dampening influence of swamps and lakes which minimize flow variability. The Chambeshi's (Fig. 4.14) annual discharge pattern is typical. As in the southwestern portion, despite the generally low gradients of these rivers, rapids and falls mark all the rivers in this area, including the Vele system. The northern portion of the upper section has fewer river systems as its areal extent is quite small. For this reason almost all of the northern portion of the Zaire Basin falls within the middle section.

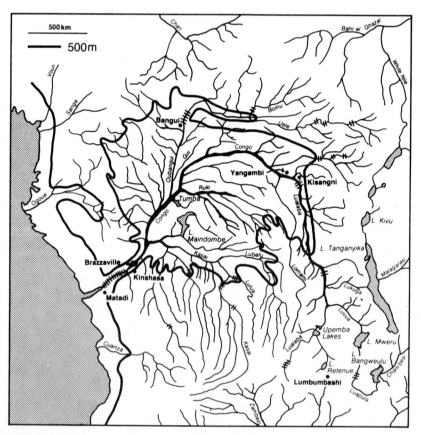

Figure 4.13 The major tributaries of the Zaire river system: the 500 m contour is shown in order to emphasize approximate boundaries of the relatively flat central basin (from Beadle 1974).

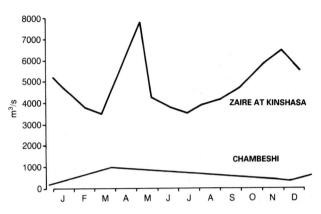

Figure 4.14 The flow régimes of the Zaire at Kinshasa and the Chambeshi. (Modified from Balek 1977.)

THE MIDDLE SECTION

This section (approximately between 300 and 500 m) comprises the largest area of the basin. Unlike the upper and lower sections it is characterized by a lack of longitudinal interruptions (rapids and falls). From Kisangani to Kinshasa, a distance of about 2000 km, the gradient falls only about 100 m. Rivers within this section are wide and generally flow at low velocities. The main channel, along with the primary tributaries (Oubangui, Ruki, and Kasai), is between 3 and 15 km wide. River discharges remain high in this section throughout the year since when the northern portion of the river basin is experiencing rain it is drier in the south and vice versa. Thus tributaries from one part of the basin are always bringing large quantities of water into this section. Because of their width and very low gradients the rivers have flow characteristics resembling lake flows during the periods of maximum discharge (November–December and April, Fig. 4.14). During these months large parts of this section become vast swamp areas. The magnitude of the width of the rivers in this portion, with their seasonal swamps, has resulted in an absence of bridges. To date these flow properties have been a deterrent to development.

THE LOWER SECTION

The Zaire has a discharge near its mouth (Kinshasa) that reflects the wet–dry portions of the basin as well as the properties of the rainforest. The March–April and November–December peaks reflect the interaction of all the tributaries in the basin. This section begins at Stanley Pool and continues to its outlet. Between Malebo Pool and Matadi the river plunges 275 m in a distance of 350 km. It is marked by thirty-two major rapids which cannot be navigated yet probably represent the greatest potential for hydroelectricity in the world. Tributaries entering the river in this section also have rapids.

141

Despite draining a large area and having many navigable sections, the rapids in the upper and lower sections have prevented ease of movement within the basin. This is compounded by the flatness of the interior basin (the middle section), resulting in huge areas being flooded during parts of the year. The middle section is thus relatively inaccessible and a difficult area to integrate into the national economy. This inaccessibility has helped to preserve the largest African rainforest area. Conversely, the physical conditions have made it an area void of much-needed data regarding its environmental attributes. Much remains to be learned, let alone understood, if the Zaire Basin is to be utilized in a rational manner. For example, throughout the river system it is estimated that up to 1000 species of fish exist, with about 550 of them widespread. It appears a large biological wealth is associated with the river. But unless the basin has a data base far in excess of what exists there is a high risk that serious environmental problems will accompany its eventual more intense use.

Human activities: resource use

From an agricultural perspective the rainforest areas would seem to be a very favorable environment for crop utilization. They have ample moisture and temperatures to permit vegetation growth throughout the year without any periods of dormancy. However, continuously high temperatures and precipitation contribute to the difficulty of utilizing the rainforest. These conditions require strategies that differ from those developed in the mid-latitude and savanna areas. For example, mono-agricultural practices usually encourage disease and pest infestations or nutrient shortages in the soil that must be countered with controls such as spraying, dusting, or broadcasting various types of pesticides, fungicides, or fertilizers. These techniques are almost always ineffective in the rainforest areas since either the precipitation washes the substances off the plants and soil too rapidly for them to be effective, or the continuous moisture in the soil does not allow them to be very effective. Many plants of the humid tropics which do well under the "natural" conditions of high plant diversity become susceptible to disease once they are concentrated, and consequently they cease to be economical. For example, in order to control disease, commercially grown bananas are largely cultivated under partial irrigation in wet–dry tropical areas instead of in continuously humid areas.

Another aspect complicating the utilization of rainforest areas is that many food crops in large demand are cereals that need a dry season for harvesting. These crops do not prosper in rainforest environments. One other environmental factor that contributes to the problem of resource use in the rainforests is that it seems that humans generally will not live in forest areas unless they have been forced to do so for their survival. Inhabitants in the rainforest almost always locate their settlements in clearings near rivers. Yet the crops grown in the clearings cannot be grown on a continuous basis because of nutrient shortages in the soil or other constraints, such as soil erosion. The traditional agricultural systems that evolved in the forests in response to these environmental constraints were almost always various forms of shifting agriculture,

142

whereas the modern agricultural systems that have been successful almost always are tree oriented.

Traditional land use in rainforest areas

In Africa as well as in other tropical rainforest areas the general pattern of nutrient utilization by vegetation is that a large portion of the nutrients are stored within the vegetation and only a small amount in forest-floor litter (Table 4.9). Although the majority of the nutrients are in the wood and root components of the vegetation, the largest proportion of annual return of nutrients to the soil is through leaf-fall. Leaf-fall in rainforests is about four times greater than it is in mid–latitude forests. Tropical forests differ from most other ecosystems in three ways: they have a very high vegetation biomass; there is a very high element storage in the biomass (Table 4.9); and there is a rapid rate of cycling from leaf-fall back into the living biomass.

Removal of the forest cover stops leaf-fall; consequently soil nutrient supply rapidly decreases. In addition to the decrease in the accumulation of organic matter, that existing from the previous forest cover rapidly decomposes. This increases both splash erosion and overland flow. The former results from the bare ground being exposed to the direct impact of raindrops, and latter results from the decrease in the absorption of water in the organic matter, which often acts like a sponge. Thus more water flows over the ground once the forest is removed. Given the decrease in nutrients available for plant growth, along with the greater erosion potential once the forest is removed, agricultural productivity usually decreases rapidly. If they are to be viable, agricultural systems using the rainforest areas must either adapt to these changes or offset those conditions that contribute to the rapid decrease in agricultural potential. The traditional agricultural system of shifting cultivation is one type of adaptation widely practiced in Africa.

There are many varieties of shifting agriculture, but as a rule it is characterized by a large diversity in crops. This means that it is basically a form of subsistence agriculture. A large diversity in crops is required to meet the daily needs of the farmer. Shifting cultivation has been called "balanced exploitation". During periods of cultivation, though some of the nutrient supply is consumed by the cultivated plants, part of it is lost through bacterial action and the process of erosion. Since under cultivation the nutrient supply is continuously decreasing, yields decrease with time, and eventually the farmer must clear and cultivate new land to meet his needs. In African rainforest areas the usual period of cultivation is from two to four years. Once the land reverts to fallow, natural regeneration of vegetation begins and gradually soil productivity becomes sufficient for land clearance and fresh cultivation. Depending on the properties of the soil, a fallow period of between 8 to 19 years is usually required to regenerate soil fertility. In Africa, the crops grown by shifting cultivators include bananas, plantains, manioc, beans, peppers, rice, maize, and millet.

The weakness of shifting cultivation in the rainforest is that the productivity of labor and soil are difficult to increase. Thus it is impossible to absorb a growing population or to produce large surpluses that would improve the living standards of the farmers and of the nation. Also, as fields shift, infrastructure

Table 4.9 Storage of material in a rainforest: Kade, Ghana.

Material	Nitrogen (g/m^2)	Phosphorous (g/m^2)	Potassium (g/m^2)	Calcium (g/m^2)	Magnesium (g/m^2)
above-ground vegetation	180	12	81	248	34
below-ground vegetation	21	1.1	9	15	4.4
total vegetation	201	13	80	263	37
litter	3.5	0.1	1	4.5	0.6
soil	460	1.2	65	258	37
total store	665	14	156	525.5	64.6

Note: weight/area = g/m^2.

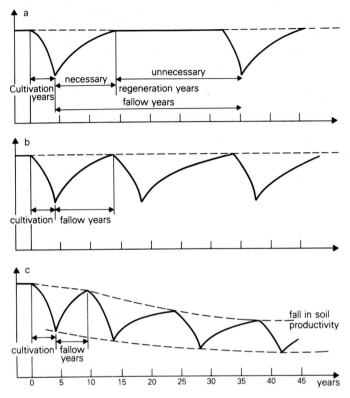

Figure 4.15 The relation between the length of the fallow period and soil productivity (from Ruthenberg 1971).

improvements such as road buildings are difficult. This factor also contributes to the unacceptability of shifting agriculture as a long-term development strategy. Figure 4.15 illustrates the relationship between the length of fallow and soil regeneration. Graph b shows the optimal condition for maximum utilization of the land resource for agriculture. Shifting agriculture requires extensive use of the land. With the increasing demands being placed on the land resource, either by increasing population or the demand for increased production for cash, the land resource often becomes degraded (c) under shifting cultivation. Two modified types of shifting agriculture have been introduced into rainforest areas in response to these demands. At the same time an effort has been made to maintain the soil resources.

The *paysannat (corridor) system*

The corridor system developed in the Belgian Congo (beginning in 1935) attempted to increase agricultural productivity through a systematic rotation of cultivated lands. Rotation in the corridor system did not imply a continuous rotation of food crops, but was a systematic system of food-crop and fallow rotation that attempted to approximate the conditions of optimal land-resource utilization (Fig. 4.15b) while keeping the inhabitants permanently in a given area. The idea was to permit a permanent infrastructure to be established economically. Thus the corridor system was an attempt to establish a commercial agricultural system, using the shifting agriculture attributes of cultivation–fallow, that was clearly environmentally viable in rainforest areas.

In the corridor system a large (1400–2000 ha) area (*paysannat*) was divided into a series of strips. Strips of about 8–12 ha were then allocated to individual families. In any given year, 1–2 ha were cleared or cultivated, with the remainder of a family's strip remaining in fallow. Plots allocated to families were juxtaposed so that, in each year, a cleared corridor ran through the forest. Between each strip cleared (about 100 m wide) alternating strips of forest were preserved (Fig. 4.16) to provide shade and seeds for the regeneration of the cleared lands when they were no longer being cropped. Along with the establishment of a systematic land-use system, there would be a permanent village within the *paysannat* where the farmers could remain while the various strips were utilized from year to year. Approximately 200 families were located within a single *paysannat*. In addition to integrating the agriculture into the economy, the "permanence" of the area made the construction of roads to transport the products to market feasible. Given that the corridor system was meant to be an integrated farming system, coordination between the individual farms was required in terms of crops grown in each strip. Thus, in contrast to the

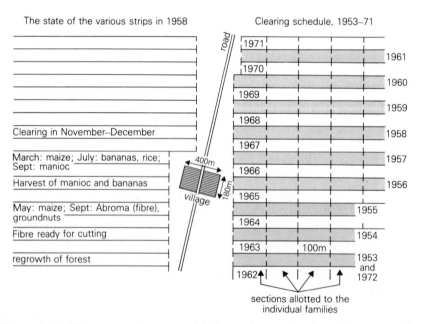

Figure 4.16 The systematic pattern of shifting cultivation in the couloir system (from Ruthenberg 1971).

146

traditional system of shifting agriculture, management for the whole *paysannat* was required.

Ruthenberg (1971) has summarized the advantages of this system as:

(a)   the preservation of the soil resource was achieved by land-use control;
(b)   the systematic cultivation of crops within strips facilitated the introduction of new agricultural practices, such as weed control; and
(c)   the concentration of cultivation reduced transportation costs and marketing could be organized cooperatively.

No matter what the benefits of the corridor system were, it disappeared shortly after independence of the Belgian Congo (Zaire). Besides the security problems that exist in rural areas, its decline was probably due to a combination of other factors including:

(a)   the lack of outside staffing to plan and supervise the *paysannat*, and the lack of credit facilities and market outlets; and
(b)   despite improvements in productivity, like shifting agriculture it remained an extensive land-use system with still relatively low productivity per unit of labor force and unit area of land.

Ley farming and perennial crop systems

In Ley farming grass rotation is incorporated with other arable crops. Unlike most fallow systems, when grasses are used for fallow, the area is still usable for some agronomic activity. When it is to be used for arable crops the land can readily be prepared by plowing. This is in contrast to bush and tree fallow rotations. Unfortunately grasses in rainforest areas have a much lower ability than forest or tree crops to regenerate the soil in rainy tropical climates. Ley systems are only feasible if they are supplemented with heavy fertilization – a costly venture that is not possible in most rainforest areas. The most feasible land-use systems to date in rainforest areas that meet both economic and soil resource demands are farming systems that utilize tree, treelike, or shrub crops.

Palms, bananas, coffee and tea bushes, cocoa, and rubber are examples of crops that have been utilized by small farmers in various humid parts of Africa to satisfy both economic and physical environmental demands. No single sequence for the establishment of these perennial crops exists in Africa, but Groenwald (1968) presents one sequence for coconut palms in Tanzania that probably reflects the general attributes of the conversion of forest areas to perennial crops.

First, after clearing a section of the land the farmer interplants perennial and annual crops. During this stage, weeding of the crops is undertaken and the annual crops are grown. Weeding continues so that the permanent crops can establish themselves and the forest (bush) is prevented from becoming reestablished. Second, the area devoted to perennial crops is extended – again through interplanting pernnial crops with annual ones. At this stage the perennial crops have become established in the original cleared area, but they have not reached maturity and thus have little if any economic value. The farmer maintains himself through harvesting the annual crops. Third, the perennial crops begin to

147

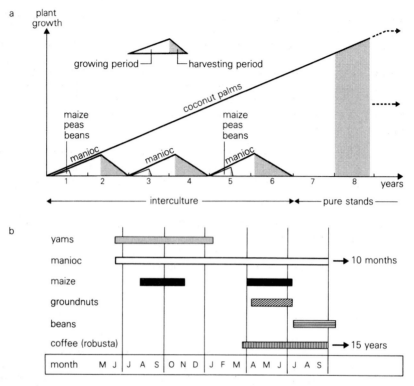

Figure 4.17 Intercropping: (a) at Tanga, Tanzania; (b) in Ivory Coast (from Ruthenberg 1971).

mature. With each additional year they gradually begin to dominate over the annual crops, but a mixed cropping system still exists. Fourth, the perennial crops have largely replaced the original vegetation, providing shade that acts as a weed control as well as protecting the soil through both leaf-fall and canopy protection. Intercropping still exists but is secondary in importance. Figure 4.17 shows two possible sequences for establishing perennial crops, one in Tanzania, the other in Ivory Coast. In both cases the annual crops are vital because they allow the farmer to maintain himself until the permanent tree and shrub crops – which are better from an environmental perspective – become established. Oil palm in Nigeria and cocoa in Ghana have likewise been established by small farmers in areas which were previously forested. The establishment of tree and bush vegetation permits permanent agriculture in areas that traditionally supported shifting agriculture. Yet one critical condition needed for this pattern to become established is land-tenure security, since the perennial crops represent an investment. As the small farmers are also growing annual food crops, they are relatively resilient during the initial stages of this process of land conversion from forest to permanent tree and bush crops. But, as a larger proportion of their effort becomes involved in cash crops, they become less self-sufficient and more dependent on trade.

Modern utilization of rainforest lands

Semi-intensive rainfed crop systems prevail in the African rainforest areas. The corridor, ley, and perennial crop systems, though somewhat more productive than the various forms of shifting agriculture, are not highly productive and produce a relatively low economic return. Yet, at least in the short term, they maintain the soil resource and from a purely physical perspective represent a rational utilization of the rainforest environment. But because of their low productivity most development projects for rainforest environments do not encourage these forms of land use.

With the generally low nutrient supply found in the soils of the African rainforest areas, annual crops require fertilization if yields are to be high enough to justify permanent agriculture. However, because of heavy leaching of soluble minerals in soils, the rapid decay of organic matter, and the high erosion potential, economic costs are almost always too high for the production of commercial annual crops in rainforest areas. Generally, most contemporary development projects for these areas attempt to maximize the use of perennial vegetation. This type of vegetation protects the soil resource from erosion, allows for continuous leaf fall to restore naturally a portion of the minerals and organic matter, and minimizes economic costs. Oil palm, bananas, cocoa, rubber, and timber are the crops that appear to have the highest potential for increasing economic return from African rainforest areas and preventing major environmental problems. Each of these are "tree" crops and thus to a large extent they preserve the microclimatic characteristics of undeveloped rainforest. However, these crops are primarily export oriented, with the exception of bananas in Zaire. Staple crops for local consumption still mainly come from the "traditional" small farm sector. An economically and environmentally feasible solution to the problems of permanent agriculture of annual crops remains elusive in African rainforest areas.

Oil palm, cocoa, rubber, and timber, all being tree crops, require a number of years before they bring any economic return. For timber the case is at its extreme since trees often require 40 or more years before they can be cut. Thus the high investment required excludes most individuals from tree-farming unless a farmer has enough land to grow other crops until the tree crops reach maturity.

OIL PALM

Oil palm is native to West Africa, but usually it is not cultivated. Instead, oil palms growing wild in the bush are carefully preserved and the fruits are collected by the small farmers for sale to an extraction mill. Until around 1940 West Africa was the major exporter of palm oil, but the establishment of plantations in Southeast Asia resulted in a decline in the relative exports of palm oil from Africa. This development, which continues today, illustrates the advantage of plantation systems over small landholders where palm oil is concerned. Since oil palm requires both an agricultural component (the growing and harvesting of the fruits) and an industrial component (milling of the fruits), the systematic organization and capital investment inherent in plantation systems permits a higher yield of oil from each tree. Palm oil is still exported from Nigeria, Senegal, Ivory Coast, Zaire, Benin, Sierra Leone, Guinea, and Liberia.

149

Investment in Ivory Coast has resulted in a marked increase in its production. The particular advantages of oil palm in rainforest environments are:

(a) improved varieties allow the plant to produce fruit in three to four years, a rapid period for tree crops;
(b) high yield of oil per tree, 3–5 tons of oil per hectare, permits high gross return;
(c) oil-palm plantations have almost a complete canopy and thus soil protection is high;
(d) a low labor input relative to other tree crops is required; and
(e) oil palms appear to resist disease better than most other crops grown in the rainforest.

The greatest problem is that capital investment is high for oil palms. It is not any higher than for other tree crops, but it requires the establishment of an oil mill which means a very high start-up cost.

COCOA

Unlike oil palm, which was indigenous to West Africa and rarely cultivated, cocoa is a cultivated crop. The ideal conditions for cocoa are found in the wet tropics. These are heavy precipitation (minimum 1270 mm), high relative humidity, and a shade temperature of about 27°C for young trees. A limiting factor is that the tree also requires well-drained soils. Thus rainforest areas susceptible to flooding, such as large areas in Zaire, are not favorable. Young cocoa trees require shade. In Africa they are usually intercropped with other plants. In particular, the banana plant is often grown with cocoa. Not only does it provide shade, but it protects the soil during the early growth of the cocoa tree and provides income until the tree begins to yield pods (5 years). The cocoa tree yields pods for approximately thirty-five years; thus a single planting provides continuous income over a large proportion of the lifetime of a farmer. At the same time, the mature cocoa trees shade the soil and provide similar ground conditions to an area under rainforest vegetation. Thus they protect the soil for many years. However, if cocoa production is to be maintained, new seedlings should be planted about every 30–35 years. Unfortunately this has not been done and cocoa production has dropped in Ghana and Nigeria, which are the two largest producers of this commodity. However, heavy investment in the agricultural–economic sector has raised production of cocoa in the Ivory Coast.

Cocoa production is carried out both on plantations and on small landholdings in West Africa. But the majority of cocoa comes from the small farm sector. In most of West Africa the farms range between 1 and 6 ha (2–15 acres) in size. Besides cocoa, a variety of crops are intercropped on these small farms, including pumpkins, gourds, calabashes, manioc, maize, beans, peppers, yams, oil palm, kola, as well as bananas. A diversity of plants and ground cover – as found in natural rainforests – are reproduced on these small farms. To help improve yields and reduce disease, agricultural institutes, such as the Cocoa Institute in Nigeria, are trying to improve varieties through breeding as well as instruct the farmer on how to ferment and dry the beans. For example, despite the widespread belief that cocoa requires shade, yields are found to increase when mature trees are not shaded. However, the long-term effects of removing plant diversity need to be evaluated.

RUBBER

Rubber, like cocoa, is grown both on estates and by small landholders; however, as far as crops for export are concerned, estate production clearly dominates. Rubber, like cocoa, is an excellent crop for rainforest areas. The para-rubber tree (*Hevea brasillensis*) produces the greatest yields when precipitation ranges roughly between 1700 and 2000 mm, no dry season exists, there are high annual temperatures (27°C), and days having temperatures not less than 21°C are rare. Like cocoa it requires relatively well drained soils. On estates, rubber groves are kept weed free, yet the rubber tree still protects the soil from excessive erosion (Fig. 4.18). The weeding demands, along with the need to tap, fertilize, and

Figure 4.18 A rubber plantation near Warri, Bendel State, Nigeria.

prune the trees manually, means that once an estate is established labor demand remains constant throughout the year and thus no seasonal unemployment of workers results.

On small landholdings, the rubber tree places few demands on either the land or the farmer as it is intercropped with other plants and is usually tapped only when the farmer needs cash or has time to spare from his other activities. Small landholders, with their diversity of crops, tend not to manage their rubber trees well because they do not tap regularly, do not apply fertilizer, and use unselected seedlings; thus their yields are low. However, because they are low-cost producers their product can compete with that of the larger estates. Moreover, when rubber prices decrease the small landowners are less severely affected than the large rubber producers since the former have other crops and can cultivate them more intensely. In fact, during these low-price periods the small landholders' trees can regenerate themselves, and this helps the trees to survive the stresses that are placed on them by poorer farming practices.

TIMBER

From an ecological perspective, timber would be the ideal crop for rainforests. However, quite a few problems remain to be solved before rainforests can be managed properly instead of merely being destroyed, as happens with current practices of timber extraction. There is widespread evidence in many areas of West Africa that as the forest is removed the soil degrades rapidly as a result of microclimatic changes, removal of nutrient supply, and other factors, so that unless the tropical forest is replanted immediately a resource is destroyed. For a variety of reasons reforestation is minimal in Africa. First, the forests are in countries that need the money from timber to buy critical products, and therefore no surplus capital is generally available for investment in seedlings. Second, because tree growth is slow, timber is a long-term investment. However, for a variety of reasons most investment in Africa is oriented toward short-term returns. Third, only a small number of species in the rainforest are in great demand; thus, if the forests are to be maintained, new uses for many of the trees must be developed. And fourth, the unit cost of bringing logs to points of export is largely determined by the volume of timber removed per area; the greater the quantity of timber removed, the lower the unit costs. Often over 80 tons of timber per hectare are needed in most commercial ventures. This is probably about four times more than what could be removed if the forest were able to regenerate itself without systematic replantings.

Although the West African rainforest is already well along the path to destruction, the vast majority of the African rainforest in Zambia, Gabon, and Cameroon still exists. The destruction of the rainforest is not inevitable. It could be prevented if assistance were provided to help develop strategies in which harvesting and replanting were in phase with each other so as to allow timber to provide a continuous source of wealth for nations with rainforest areas.

BANANA AND PLANTAIN

Unlike the other crops discussed above, the bananas and plantains are not tree crops. The banana and plantain are perennial herbs, that is, they are fast-

152

maturing plants that complete their life cycle within a year. New growth is usually initiated by cutting the old plant after the fruit has been picked. This encourages a new shoot to grow, again reaching maturity in about one year. Although it is not a tree, the banana and plantain's magnitude and leaf cover are sufficient to provide good ground cover during most of the annual cycle; therefore bananas or plantains would seem to be ideal crops for rainforest areas. Yet, except for some parts of Ivory Coast, most bananas and plantains in the rainforest areas are grown solely for home consumption or internal exchange. There are two reasons why the growth of banana production in the immediate future is unlikely. First, bananas are susceptible to diseases which are easily controlled when they are grown under irrigation, but are very difficult to control under the continuous humid conditions of the rainforest. Second, bananas are highly perishable and must be marketed promptly. This requires a well-developed infrastructure lacking in the major African rainforest areas. In Ivory Coast bananas are produced commercially on either large private plantations or government-owned farming cooperatives. Interestingly, in Ivory Coast, in an attempt to diversify export crops, pineapples have been successfully grown with bananas. But the pineapple market is more limited than the banana market. Ivory Coast clearly has shown that agriculture can be successful in the humid tropical areas when government investment and encouragement is given to the rural sector.

Summary

In the African setting it quickly becomes evident that few data are available and that there have been few in-depth studies of rainforest environments. In West Africa, where most research on humid tropical areas is being done, the forest has already largely been altered or destroyed. In Zaire, where the largest areal extent of forest exists, little information is available on many ecologic aspects of the forest.

Most rainforests in Africa are found in areas which have been geologically stable for long periods of time. Thus the soils in these areas have undergone intense weathering and most soluble minerals have been removed from them. Almost all the soils found in African rainforest areas are primarily oxisols or ultisols. Both of these soil types are almost incapable of storing nutrients. In these forest environments the nutrients critical for the support of plant and animal life are largely locked in the living vegetation. The removal of the vegetation therefore lowers the potential for growth. As there is a rapid decay of all dead organic matter because of the warm, moist conditions in these forest environments, the large quantities of leaf-fall and other organics supplied to the forest floor are largely recycled directly from the decaying vegetation to the living plants without first being stored in the soil. It is this thin veneer of partly decaying organic matter resting on the soil – not the soil itself – that must be preserved if the forest is to regenerate. Once cleared of trees, this surface and the upper soil quickly becomes dry and the veneer of partially decayed organics is either destroyed or washed away. Rainforests have been described as deserts covered with trees. But unlike deserts, where often only water is required to

153

initiate vegetation growth, the reclamation of rainforest areas almost always requires a complete replenishment of the nutrient supply. In most areas no sustainable land use is possible once the forest has been destroyed. This is clearly one tropical environment where mid-latitude zone agricultural technologies rarely work.

Besides the constraint of nutrient supply, the rainforest areas often have lower agricultural potentials than would appear from casual observation. The cloudiness in these areas significantly lowers incoming solar energy. Therefore, despite a twelve-month growing season, their potential is less than that of many mid-latitude areas. Additionally, the warm, moist evenings and nights require plants to consume a significant amount of energy in respiration. Also, the continuous moisture and high temperatures facilitate the growth of fungi and plant diseases once commercial agricultural practices are introduced. Under rainforest conditions, most disease-control strategies are either very costly or only partially successful.

Southeast Asia has, over a long period, managed to transform some of its rainforests into successful agricultural areas. Especially important is rice and to a lesser extent rubber. Rubber, being a tree crop, does not radically alter the environment, but rice does. Successful rice cultivation requires a well-organized agricultural system with either a large skilled rural population when labor is primarily by hand, or large capital investment (e.g. California) when it is mechanized. Unfortunately all of these prerequisites are in short supply in most African areas. Thus, in the African context, if the rainforest areas are to be utilized as a long-term resource, a set of new strategies must evolve.

5 The dry areas

Introduction

Locating the dry areas

The dry areas of the African continent are shown in Figure 1.1. They occupy between a third and a half of the entire area. The two largest dry zones in Africa are the Sahara and the Sahel, the former being an extremely dry desert and the latter a semi-arid area experiencing rain for one month in the year in its drier portion and up to three months in the year along its savanna boundary.

In the African continent, areas having less than a three-month rainy season are generally defined as "dry". The boundary of the humid margins in central and southern Africa is with the savanna; and in northern Africa it is with the coastal zone, which has a Mediterranean-type winter rainfall. Although it is useful to define dry zones as those having a rainy season lasting less than three months, they can alternatively be defined as regions with an annual rainfall of less than 500–700 mm. With the temperatures and soil conditions in Africa, these rainfall levels mean that crops cannot be successfully grown year after year in the dry areas unless there is subsidiary watering. However, because of the variability of rainfall in these zones, good crops of grain can be grown in some years and in some locations. But then there come the "lean" years of biblical fame when the crops fail and even animals die owing to lack of pasture.

A wide range of conditions can be found within the dry zones of Africa, partly because the climate, particularly the rainfall, varies widely within the areas, partly because of variations in other physical factors, and partly because of the great variety of human responses to the challenges of living in such environments.

The major dry zones are as follows:

(a)   the Sahara Desert;
(b)   the Sahel;
(c)   the Namibian–Kalahari dry area and its environs;
(d)   the East African dry zones.

THE SAHARA

The Sahara is the largest desert area in the world. It extends east–west over 5000 km from the west coast of Africa in Mauritania to the Red Sea Hills adjoining the Red Sea in Egypt and over 1200 km from north to south. Much of the Sahara is almost rainless, experiencing rainstorms at intervals of between one to five years on average and having a rainfall that averages less than 50 mm per year. There is a wide range of landscape conditions throughout the Sahara, including large areas of sand seas and sand-dunes in the Libyan Desert; huge areas of rocky desert floors; mountainous terrain in the Atlas Mountains, the

Red Sea Hills and in Tibesti; and fertile oases in depressions and along the Nile Valley.

THE SAHEL

The Sahel is a zone extending from coast to coast along the southern margin of the Sahara. In most years rains fall in a single season. They last for one month at the northern boundary and for up to three months in areas above its southern limit. But there is great variability in the amount and distribution of rainfall from month to month and from year to year within the Sahel. It experiences greater climatic fluctuations than the drier Sahara, and this is reflected in its soils. Many soils reflect past climatic conditions, with some showing properties resulting from more humid periods and others having characteristics resulting from drier periods. The Sahel has a much more varied history than that of the true desert of the Sahara. Rainfall in the Sahel is enough to produce scattered grasses, shrubs, and tree growth. The vegetation density generally increases toward the southern margins, and after rains there is extensive grass cover across the areas where precipitation has occurred. This is in contrast to deserts where trees and shrubs grow only along dry stream beds, and the rare grasses flourish only after the infrequent rains.

THE NAMIBIAN–KALAHARI DESERT AND ITS ENVIRONS

Though the Namibian (southwestern) desert is much smaller than the Sahara, it is very dry with wide areas receiving less than 50 mm rainfall per annum. The aridity is emphasized by the flat, sandy nature of much of the zone. The sands allow precipitation, whenever it occurs, to infiltrate rapidly. Thus little water runs off in stream or gully flow, or remains in the soil for long enough to permit plant growth. The Kalahari just inland from the desert is a semi-arid zone in terms of annual rainfall (250–500 mm), but because the surface soil is sandy and permeable the environment is arid. It is the site of several inland deltas, the Okavango being the largest. Extraneous rivers from more humid areas bring wet-season water into large pans and lakes. These contract as the dry season progresses. The margins of the Kalahari, like those along the edge of the Sahara, have a short rainy season with highly variable annual precipitation. Like the Sahel, this zone is used for livestock raising with some grain cultivation in "good" years.

EAST AFRICA

The dry areas of East Africa extend in a belt from central Tanzania to occupy much of northern and eastern Kenya and large areas of lowland Ethiopia and Somalia. This area is not in general as rainless as either the Namibian desert or the Sahara, though localities such as the Danakil are among the driest parts of the world. Generally it is intermediate between the Sahel and the Sahara in rainfall and characterized by scattered scrub vegetation. One difference from the other dry areas is that the East African dry zone is more closely connected with adjacent wetter areas (usually highlands). Rivers from the wetter areas discharge in places into and across the dry zone. The Shebelle, the Juba, the Galana, and the Tana are all major rivers which help to break up the East African dry zone.

INTRODUCTION

The natural distribution of dry areas and man-made desert

There has been much discussion in recent years about the spread of deserts in Africa, a process called "desertification". How far does the current distribution of deserts and dry lands reflect the impact of human activities? How far is it a "natural" distribution?

These are not easy questions to answer. "Nature" is far from constant and it is very difficult to separate patterns of climate and vegetation change from more directly imposed human effects. Some points are quite clear:

(a) that in a general climatic sense there is a series of fluctuations rather than one simple trend;
(b) that some of these fluctuations may be long term (10 to 100s of years), but there is no general consensus about current trends over time periods of this order;
(c) that over large parts of the dry areas there has been a deterioration in levels of vegetation, and this has become emphasized in the last two decades;
(d) that overgrazing around water points, devegetation for firewood, and other human activities are likely to be the major cause of this deterioration.

Because of the changes in vegetation cover, accompanied by changes in the status of soils in some places, the land cover and land-use boundaries between dry areas and wetter ones have changed over the past decades. As a broad generalization, the boundaries between desert and semi-desert and between semi-desert and savanna are some tens of kilometers different today than they would have been under natural conditions. The greatest difference is in the south of the Sahara where 50–150 km would be a very conservative estimate.

PAST EXTENT OF DESERTS

It is hard to draw the line between fact and fancy in our understanding of past desert conditions in Africa. It is clear from archaeological studies that within human experience there have been periods when the climate of the extremely dry desert was more humid. Rock paintings, remains of camp sites and stone tools all show that people and animals lived in areas they could not inhabit today.

Studies of lake deposits, fossils, pollen, and river terraces all suggest the same conclusion: the Sahara has not always been so dry and the Namibia–Kalahari has also seen more moist periods. However, this does not translate into the popular idea that these dry areas were forested, fertile lands in the recent past. Current scientific opinion suggests a quite complex picture, reflecting what we know about the pattern of climatic change all over the world.

Figure 5.1 illustrates the current state of our knowledge. We have a rather more detailed understanding of the climatic change that took place in the north of the African continent than we do of that which occurred in the south. It is clear from the figure that the dry areas of northern Africa have been the scene of fluctuating climates over the last several million years, and that the fluctuations have been around a less dry–more dry norm.

In the moist periods the rainfall in the drier parts of the Sahara, where there is almost no rain now, may have been 100–300 mm a year – about as much as Khartoum gets at present.

157

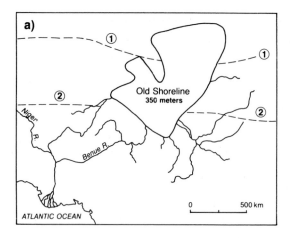

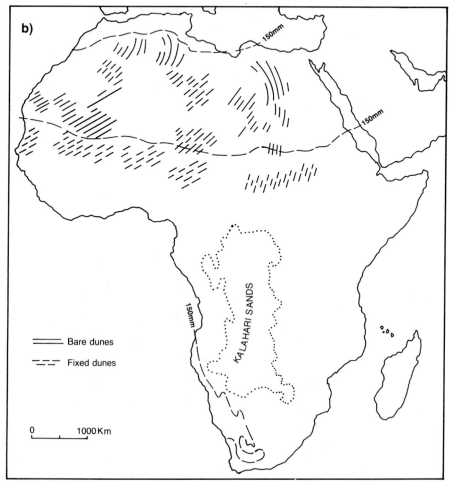

Figure 5.1 Maps illustrating climatic change in Africa: (a) shifting lake shores and desert limits in west central Africa; (b) the location of active and fixed sand dunes (from Grove 1967).

The record of past climatic change is significant for two main reasons. First, it may help us to understand present trends of weather and climate in the dry areas. Second, the deposits and soils formed in the different climatic regions still largely remain. Understanding how to use them and being aware of their vulnerability is partly a function of understanding their origin.

Figure 5.2 shows the soils of the Sahel. They include alluvial soils formed when the lakes in the area (especially Lake Chad) were much larger than at present and some soils, originating from stabilized sand-dunes, which now occur well south of the zone of active dune formation.

Each soil presents opportunities for use, or misuse, under current climatic conditions. If the alluvial soils are well covered and not allowed to remain dry and unvegetated, they are stable and moderately productive. If not, they can be easily degraded and destroyed. Likewise, the stabilized sand-dune soils can be

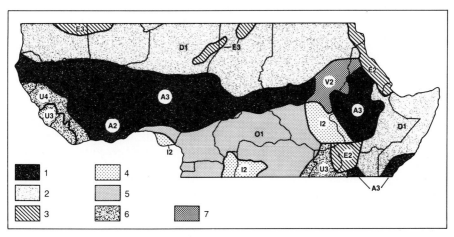

Figure 5.2 The soils of the Sahel (from Man and Biosphere/UNESCO 1975).

1 *Alfisols.* Soils with grey-to-brown surface horizons, subsurface clay accumulation and a medium to high base supply.
   A2 udalfs: Temperate to hot, and usually moist.
   A3 ustaffs: temperate to hot, dry more than 90 cumulative days in the year.
2 *Aridisoils.* Desert or saline soils.
   D1 aridisoils: undifferentiated.
3 *Entisols.* Soils on freshly exposed rock or recent alluvium without pedogenic horizons.
   E2 orthents: loamy or clayey texture, often shallow to bedrock.
   E3 psamments: sand or loamy sand texture.
4 *Inceptisols.* Moderately developed soils.
   I2 aquepts: seasonally or perennially wet.
5 *Oxisols.* Laterites, latosols.
   O1 orthox: hot and nearly always moist.
6 *Ultisols.* Strongly weathered or podsolic soils of low latitudes.
   U3 udults: temperate to hot, usually moist.
   U4 ustults: warm or hot, dry more than 90 cumulative days in the year.
7 *Vertisols.* Soils with a high content of active clays which swell when set and develop deep, wide cracks when dry.
   V2 usterts: dry and cracked more than 90 cumulative days in the year.

moderately productive for some tree crops when care is taken to preserve ground cover. On the other hand, if the trees and grass cover are removed, the dunes can become active and massive soil destruction occurs.

In the drier fluctuations the reverse pattern was in place; dry conditions extended well south of current patterns. The set-up can be thought of as a southward movement of some 200–300 km of the dry conditions. A more detailed discussion of environmental change, including climatic change in the last few hundred years, comes later in this chapter.

DRY COUNTRIES

Many countries in Africa are characterized by a large proportion of dry lands. Among them are:

Algeria	Egypt	Mauritania	Senegal
Botswana	Kenya	Morocco	Somalia
Burkina Faso	Libya	Namibia	Sudan
Chad	Mali	Niger	Tunisia
Djibouti			

These countries all have more than 60 percent of their land area in semi-arid or desert lands. Other countries, including Nigeria, Cameroon, Ethiopia, Uganda, and Tanzania, have smaller but significant proportions of their land in desert or semi-arid conditions.

In general, countries with large proportions of dry areas have large land areas and relatively small populations. They include all of the largest countries of the continent, except Zaire. The "dry" countries with the larger population totals are those bordering the Mediterranean coasts (Algeria, Morocco, Tunisia, Egypt), where most of the people live in the narrow strip of Mediterranean climates, or, in the case of Egypt, along the Nile. The desert countries tend to have strongly contrasting intensities of land use, high population densities in favored locations, high proportions of people in urban areas, contrasting with large areas of little or no current economic use and additional large areas used extensively in pastoral nomadism. The most intensive irrigation and the most extensive animal rearing occur in the dry lands.

The deserts: myth and reality in environmental conditions

The availability of water

Water, by its very rarity, becomes a vital issue in most forms of occupation and utilization of dry lands. Water, though scarce, is far from absent, though it is generally very concentrated both in time and space.

In African arid areas precipitation occurs almost solely as rainfall. Because precipitation usually has a limited areal coverage during any single rain event, the result is "spotty" storm runoff in largely ephemeral streams. In large areas, especially the Sahara, groundwater is in part a relic from previous wetter periods. When permanent river flow occurs it is derived from humid areas beyond the deserts. For large areas, especially in the central regions of the deserts, most of the time there is no water available.

160

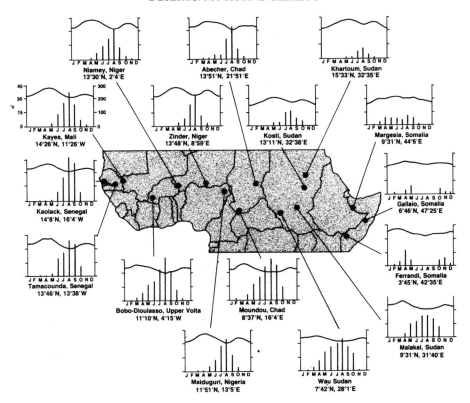

Figure 5.3 Rainfall patterns throughout the Sahel (from Man and Biosphere/ UNESCO 1975).

RAINFALL

No part of a desert is completely rainless, though parts of the interior of the Sahara approach this condition more nearly than most of the rest of the Earth. Figure 5.3 indicates that rainfall averages for the dry areas range from near zero to above 500 mm per year on the southern edge of the Sahel.

Nowhere in this range is rainfall sufficient for regular cropping; however, crops are possible in good years in favored locations, though the risk of crop failure is always high.

The characteristics of the rainfall include:

(a) rain is confined to a short season (1–3 months in duration);
(b) it mostly falls in isolated, somewhat intensive storms;
(c) it is variable from place to place during a given storm;
(d) it is highly variable from year to year.

Table 5.1 illustrates the rainfall in three typical dry-area locations. Table 5.1a represents a set of three Saharan stations. The second (Table 5.1b), a Sahelian

Table 5.1a Rainfall data for Hoggar, Algeria.

Area	Station	Altitude (m)	Yearly number of days with >0.1 mm	Mean annual precipitation (mm)	Minimum annual precipitation (mm)	Maximum annual precipitation (mm)	Maximum amount of rain in 1 day (mm)
Hoggar	Tamanrasset	1376	14	46.1	5.2 (1961)	159.0 (1933)	48.8
	Assekrem	2706	40–45	144.9	37.2 (1961)	267.8 (1957)	130.8
	Assekrem	2706	?	118.7	7.6 (1973)	267.8 (1957)	?

Table 5.1b Climatic table for Moundou, Chad (latitude 8°37'N, longitude 16°04'E, elevation 420 m).

Month	Precipitation			Days >1 mm	Max. 24 h (mm)	Average evaporation (mm)
	Mean	Max.	Min.			
Jan.	0	0	0	0	0	122
Feb.	4	9	0	4	6	132
Mar.	2	52	0	1	26	152
Apr.	40	119	0	4	61	149
May	118	295	19	9	81	142
June	171	293	85	11	107	114
July	244	612	101	15	140	103
Aug.	303	490	134	17	121	97
Sept.	250	441	93	15	79	99
Oct.	96	328	16	8	78	118
Nov.	4	35	6	1	31	121
Dec.	0	2	0	0	2	116
Annual	1228	2186	868	80	140	1464
Rec. (year)	30	30	30	30	30	9

Table 5.1c Climatic table for Maun, Botswana (latitude 19°59'S, longitude 23°25'E, elevation 942 m).

Month	Precipitation			Days >1 mm	Max. 24 h (mm)	Average evaporation (mm)
	Mean	Max.	Min.			
Jan.	110	380	14	10	90	262
Feb.	102	339	8	10	103	208
Mar.	85	275	0	7	120	213
Apr.	26	93	0	3	61	211
May	22	34	0	1	26	188
June	1	10	0	0	10	178
July	0	1	0	0	1	221
Aug.	0	0	0	0	0	277
Sept.	1	12	0	0	8	330
Oct.	15	61	0	3	33	401
Nov.	46	116	1	5	55	312
Dec.	80	233	16	8	71	257
Annual	471	776	285	47	120	3058
Rec. (year)	30	30	30	30	30	3

station, shows a regular rainfall each summer, but there are considerable fluctuations in the total rainfall and in the number of rain days from one year to the next. Data from a similar station, say 50 km away, would show a comparable annual pattern but many differences in the details of rain days and annual totals because of the essentially "spotty" rainfall. A third station (Table 5.1c) from a semi-arid part of Botswana has a regular annual pattern of rainfall, somewhat more regular than the Sahel, but with considerable year-to-year fluctuations.

GROUNDWATER

Africa is largely made up of old basement igneous rocks, usually granite, with complex structures (Fig. 2.2). Thus over much of the continent groundwater is not readily available because the basement rocks are impermeable except in shallow aquifers in alluvial sediments or in strongly localized fault or fracture lines. A large part of the very dry areas of Africa lie in the north, where the basement structure of the continent is tilted down toward the north and is overlain by a series of sedimentary rocks varying in age from 200 million years BP to the Pleistocene. These sedimentary rocks, the dominantly Continental Intercalaire in the west and the Nubian Sandstone Series in the east, overlie the relatively impervious rocks of the basement series and are primarily siltstone and sandstone. These rock types dip generally northward. They have a large proportion of pore spaces and are potentially good aquifers.

Surprisingly for such a dry zone subsurface water is available over quite wide areas, though the water table is very deep in many localities and the water is often brackish. The presence of widespread groundwater has been one reason for the general impression that the Sahara is underlain by "rivers of water" which, if exploited, could turn the deserts green. This is far from the case, though in many Egyptian oases depressions in the land surface have resulted in the aquifer being at or near the surface, allowing some irrigation agriculture on the depression margins.

In the sedimentary series of the Sahara the groundwater appears to be derived from three main sources:

(a) Water soaking literally from the beds of the major rivers that pass through the region, especially the Nile and Niger. It is not known how far away from the rivers this is an important factor, but well logs near the Nile show an elevated "mound" of groundwater extending up to 100 km from the river.
(b) "Fossil" water which ws added to the aquifers in much wetter periods of the Pleistocene and Holocene. These are relic features and, unlike the first source, are not renewable. If it is to be used, this water must be mined.
(c) Current inputs from the occasional heavy rain storms, from seepage from small stream runoff, and possibly by seepage northward from wetter areas to the south.

For a good part of the Saharan aquifers it seems likely that much of the groundwater is fossil. Some C^{14} dates have shown an age of 30,000+ years for samples, though northward migration of water from areas to the south is possible. But this takes a very long time. If the "fossil" find is generalizable, it

164

has important implications for the use of such water. If it is being recharged, it is at an infinitesimally slow rate and the results are practically the same as if it were fossil water. That is, use of the water via wells results in a continuous drawdown of the aquifer, and the danger of salinization of the aquifers is great. In Libya, Egypt, and other areas increasing use is being made of this water.

In other parts of the dry areas of Africa different kinds of aquifers are found. For example, in the area south of the Sahara where arid conditions have previously prevailed there are wide expanses of "fossil" sand sheets and sand-dunes. These cover the previously existing irregular topography in the same way as glacial deposits blanket much of Central Europe and parts of North America. Good supplies of subsurface water can sometimes be found in buried river valleys where water soaking through the sand cover now flows as sizeable subsurface rivers. Seismic surveys can help to locate productive and fresh water supplies in such locations.

Elsewhere in arid areas local aquifers can be found in particular localities, and these form small but important resources for many rural areas. Such localities include:

(a) foothills where subsurface water from the hillslope is concentrated;
(b) stream beds where in the dry season good water supplies can be found in the loose river-channel alluvium;
(c) alluvial fans or inland deltas where flood runoff infiltrates into the sediments;
(d) pockets of weathered rock; and
(e) major fault or shear zones in granite and other rocks.

All of these sources are characterized by low-volume supplies which in some cases run out late in the dry season, but they are all available for local development, and most people who live in arid and semi-arid lands have a clear idea of the availability of sources in their locality. Because these groundwater sources are small and usually shallow, they are highly susceptible to pollution.

RIVER FLOW

A number of rivers, including some of the largest in the world, cross the dry areas of Africa. The most prominent are the Nile, the Niger, the Tana (in Kenya), the Okovango (Botswana), the Senegal, and many smaller streams flowing south from the Atlas ranges.

Table 5.2 illustrates some of the characteristics of these rivers. Typically, most are low in total discharge in relation to drainage area because of the low rainfall and deficit moisture balance in large parts of their drainage basins. All show large variations in flow from wet to dry season, though the variations typically reflect the effect of the wet and dry seasons prevailing in the more humid parts of the drainage basin. Direct tributary flow to the major rivers is not common in the dry areas as most runoff in these zones is absorbed before it reaches the main drainage lines.

A number of major rivers, including the Okovango in Botswana, the Chari and Lagone in Chad, and streams off the Atlas, end in major inland deltas. The Niger north of Bamako has a major inland delta and consequently there is a

Table 5.2 Flow data for large rivers in dry areas of West Africa.

River	Station	Catchment area (km²)	First month of dry season	Mean monthly discharge during stated month after the start of the dry season (m³/s)												Mean annual flow (m³/s)	% of total flow occurring during dry season
				1	2	3	4	5	6	7	8	9	10	11	12		
Sassandra	Guessabo	35,400	Nov.	379	163	83	54	54	73	81	148	309	571	1,101	835	322	21
Bandama	Brimbo	60,300	Nov.	416	152	52	28	20	38	57	118	232	499	1,095	1,149	322	19
N'zi	Zienoa	33,150	Nov.	141	28	9.6	4.2	3.6	16.0	34	93	126	95	185	322	89	19
Come	Anaissue	70,200	Nov.	311	103	32	14.8	14.7	24	39	67	196	409	982	924	261	18
Faleme	Kidira	28,180	Oct.	435	127	44	19.0	11.3	4.7	1.9	1.1	18.0	109	642	892	193	28
Senegal	Galougo	127,000	Oct.	1,495	575	246	131	80	42	20	15	106	539	2,161	2,585	669	30
Senegal	Bakel	232,700	Oct.	1,710	560	230	129	77	46	22	11	122	569	2,351	3,429	774	30
Niger	Koulikoro	120,000	Oct.	4,564	2,089	872	407	197	102	69	98	368	1,250	3,204	5,292	1,549	31
Mayo Kebbi	Cossi	26,000	Oct.	147	93	59	18.6	7.4	2.3	0.6	13.8	54	128	232	327	91	25
Faro	Safai	23,500	Oct.	978	258	82	35	20	18.0	26	99	290	578	798	1,224	369	23
Benue	Riao	31,000	Oct.	689	90	24	11.5	5.0	2.0	0.4	5.6	40	221	745	1,423	272	24

reduced discharge of water downstream of Timbuktu. The Nile passes through a similar inland delta, a very shallow one in the Sudd region of southern Sudan. The Gezira area south of Khartoum is a former deltaic area, but the Blue Nile now maintains an incised channeled flow to the north through the Gezira.

The seasonal pattern of flow and the other physical characteristics of the area create an uneven supply of river water to the dry regions, yet these are areas where water is desperately needed for agriculture and urban living. The rivers, their flood plains, and their deltas have become foci for agriculture and urban settlement. This concentration of activity, coupled with a continued growth of population in rural and urban areas, has, in turn, created new demands on water for irrigation, for industry, and for urban dwellers, as well as new demands for power. As a result there have been widespread efforts to control and use the full flow of the rivers. Such attempts date from early Egyptian dynasties and have continued to the present day.

Indeed in the 1980s the stage has been reached where the water flow of the Nile is stored in a series of dams, finally being halted at the Aswan Dam in southern Egypt and stored in Lake Nasser. Projections suggest that the total flow will be fully allocated by the end of the 1980s.

Ironically the arid and semi-arid zone is one in which modification of water systems can cause major sequential and often unpredicted changes in the environment. Changes in the erosion and deposition patterns of the river, salinity of the land, vegetation, insect and animal life, as well as changes in estuary and delta areas, can all occur in the process of modification of water systems.

The dry areas of Africa have seen concentration of activity in and around rivers, growing demands on river resources, growing control of the rivers, and growing concern about their over-use. The technology of use has in some cases created environmental and other problems.

The character of desert soils

The soils found in dry regions in Africa vary quite widely, and general statements such as "Desert soils are fertile if only there were water" or "Desert soils are infertile" just should not be made. Desert soils vary according to location and a range of other factors. They have some general characteristics based on a range of factors and on the climatic zone in which they are found, but there is no such thing as "a desert soil".

Large parts of the Sahara, the Kalahari, and the dry areas of East Africa do have soils which are loose and sandy, stoney with poor structure, or heavily crusted with salt. All these properties would result in a low agricultural potential, even if water were available. Just as both good and poor soils exist in humid areas, the same is true of soils in arid areas.

Localized areas within the very dry zone do have soils with good structure and composition and a modest-to-good potential for agriculture. These include some soils on the margins of lakes – often deposits of former larger lakes (for example, Lake Chad); soils associated with inland deltas (e.g. the Gash at Kassala, Sudan); soils found in oases; and soils along the margins of major rivers, especially the Nile.

167

Soil types in the dry areas covered in this chapter (Fig. 5.2) include:

Sahel (general)
- aridisols with low organic matter, little nitrogen or phosphorous, and low fertility
- saline soils, especially in depressions
- mollisols with variable fertility, depending on texture, iron content, and whether or not there is an iron-rich pan
- entisols, generally fertile, found along the Niger, the Nile, and other rivers

Sudan
- vertisols, which are clay-rich soils with high swelling characteristics

Southern Somalia
- when wet, the somewhat alkaline soils are good for irrigation if well drained

Northern Somalia
- mollisols

Kenya
- aridisols

Botswana
- aridisols

Namibia
- vertisols

Important environmental processes in dry areas

Environmental processes are the same the world over, but because of the particular vegetation and moisture conditions prevalent in dry areas some environmental processes take on an importance they seldom achieve in other climatic zones. These include wind-blown sand encroachment, forms of wind erosion, dust storms, floods, and accelerated water erosion.

Wind-blown sand encroachment

Wind processes are particularly important in dry areas because, either generally or seasonally, much of the surface material is not well anchored by a continuous vegetation cover. However, the effect of wind depends very much on the nature and cohesion of the materials on the surface. Because wind is not competent in moving large particles, wind can move only dust (clays) and silts in suspension, sand-size materials by saltation, and matter up to pebble size by sliding and rolling. In summary:

Pebbles, rocks, and stones   Wind has little effect.
Sand   Unless consolidated by a cement, sand is very susceptible to movement by wind, but usually this movement is restricted to the lower 2 m of the atmosphere.

Silts Silts are easily picked up by gusty winds, and once airborne the material can be carried great distances.

Clays Although individual clay particles are extremely prone to wind erosion, clay particles usually cohere together and for this reason clay is usually quite resistant to wind erosion unless disrupted by animals, plowing, or other human activities.

Sand is most readily moved by wind. Because it is moved along or near the ground, it is the material which causes the most problems. Wind gusts and variations in pressure near the ground cause the individual sand particles to vibrate and eventually bounce. Even in high winds the bouncing process does not carry sand-size particles above about 3 m. Any material carried above that height is usually silt or matter consisting of finer particles.

Because of the bouncing movement of sand by this process, known as "saltation", it is quite common for sand to move from bare exposed areas until it is halted by changes in slope, by vegetation, or by some other obstacle. Like the sand on the seashore migrating to the tree and shrub-bands of the backshore, sand moves from any exposed area to adjacent areas.

Important source areas for sand are:

(a) bare desert areas with loose sand;
(b) stream or wadi beds;
(c) old sand-dunes which have been devegetated by human activity;
(d) other areas where the vegetation has been removed.

Sand encroachment areas which have caused problems for human occupants include:

(a) margins of oases and lakes in North Africa;
(b) irrigated land in arid areas;
(c) towns, villages, and agricultural land on the banks of the Nile, the Niger, and other rivers;
(d) deltaic areas in clay regions, i.e. Gash, Tokar deltas of Sudan;
(e) agricultural land in somewhat moister regions on margins of degraded land such as in Mauritania near its capital.

Wind erosion

Wind removal of a variety of materials is an important process in many dry regions. The blowing of fine materials (silts and clays) is usually a result of human occupancy and may constitute a severe loss of nutrients from the more fertile soils. Wind erosion is important to people in the following circumstances:

(a) removal of fine topsoil on exposed and dry irrigated land;
(b) removal of fine topsoil from "fixed" dunes in moisture areas;
(c) removal of loose sand from cultivated areas, thus lowering material depths and water-holding capacity;
(d) removal of material from inland deltas.

Dust storms

As explained earlier, sand is moved by saltation, finer particles are moved into suspension in the atmosphere and then may be carried considerable distances. The destinations of this material may be very varied.

Dust storms as phenomena are special and unpleasant features of some dry areas. The dust is carried in swirling clouds often to great heights, visibility is reduced as in a fog, and the fine particles find their way everywhere, onto food, into nostrils, and in every nook and corner of home and office.

Apart from causing such human discomfort the material is preferentially deposited in the following locations and circumstances:

(a) In sandy areas where there is vegetation; some kinds of shrubs are especially efficient in trapping fine material and build up a mound of silts and clays under their branches.
(b) In towns and settlements where the wind velocity is much reduced.
(c) When it rains the fine material is precipitated.
(d) In nearby seas and oceans. During the Sahel drought of the 1970s increased fine particles were recorded as far away as the Caribbean. The Red Sea is thought by some to get its name from the occasional deposition of fine red silt and clay on its waters.

Floods

Floods are a common feature of dry areas. Floods occur in any river basin where the rainfall generates runoff in excess of the channel's capacity. In dry areas the fluvial system receives extremely variable inputs of water and is generally poorly adjusted to the larger storms which occur in any one locality very infrequently.

Some floods are therefore true floods as defined anywhere; the rivers overflow their banks after a heavy precipitation and water surges over the flood plain and nearby areas, maybe damaging fields and dwellings. But floods also occur in the following circumstances:

(a) As streams flow out over inland deltas the direction and pattern of flow may change considerably from one period to another. Floods occur frequently as channels adjust slowly to the changing conditions.
(b) In some dry areas stream channels are blocked by sand movement in the dry season or by the deposits caused by the drying up of the previous flow. New flows then result in temporary ponding and flooding upstream of the barrier.
(c) In some dry areas stream channels are not well defined. Flooding occurs as the water flows overland up to a third of a meter deep over flat terrain.

Patterns of resource use in dry areas

Figure 5.4 sets out a classification of livelihood systems for dry areas.'It was developed as a worldwide classification for the world conference on desertifica-

170

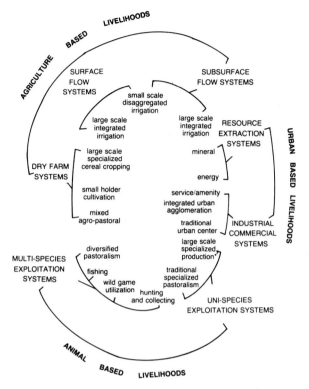

Figure 5.4 Livelihood system in drylands (from UN Conference on Desertification 1977).

tion, but most of the categories are found in Africa. For this chapter, the most important agricultural categories are grazing and irrigation, though urban areas are also an important part of the dry regions.

The dispersed nature of resources in dry areas predisposes two very different kinds of land and resource utilization: a pattern of low intensity use of widely dispersed resources or one of intense use in favored locations where resources can be concentrated. The location of water resources is obviously an important factor, but the location of grazing and good agricultural soils is equally important. In this section, we shall review the patterns of use and change in the use of grazing resources and the patterns of use and change in irrigation.

Grazing economies: a discussion of change in the Sahel, Ethiopia, and Somalia

Figure 5.5 provides an overview of the kinds of livelihood systems in the dry parts of northern Africa. A substantial part of the Sahara has very little use, but both to the north and south of the central dry area nomadic peoples have long fashioned a living even from this dry environment. These are truly nomadic groups, leaning heavily on the camel as a main means of transport and

171

livelihood. The Sahel zone to the south of the Sahara is the zone par excellence of livestock rearing. A variety of livelihood systems are based on combinations of cattle, goats, and sheep. Table 5.3 lists the livestock population for the countries in the Sahel and other dry areas.

Somalia lies almost entirely in the dry zone. The population of Somalia is about 5.0 million, though there are also about 0.5 million refugees in Somalia. Livestock provide a livelihood for 81 percent of the Somali population. The national herd includes 5.3 million camels, 3.7 million cattle, and 24.7 million sheep and goats. Most of the land is used for grazing (Fig. 5.6). Sudan, another

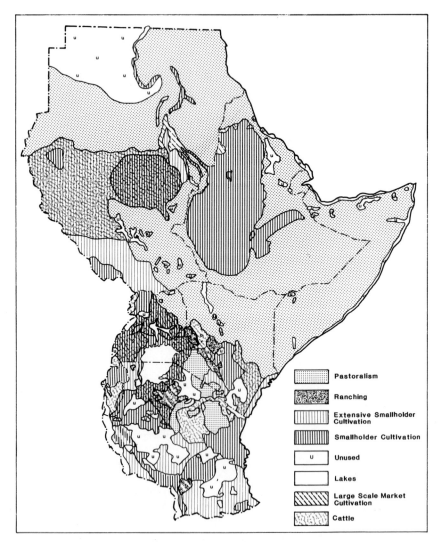

Figure 5.5 Agricultural livelihoods existing in eastern Africa (from Berry *et al.* 1980).

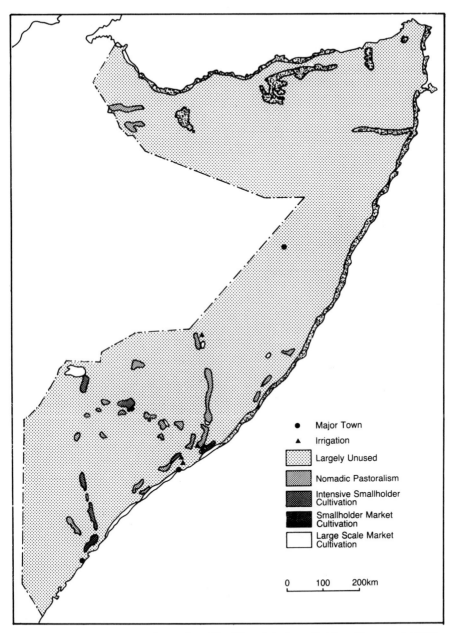

●   Major Town

▲   Irrigation

Largely Unused

Nomadic Pastoralism

Intensive Smallholder
Cultivation

Smallholder Market
Cultivation

Large Scale Market
Cultivation

0   100   200km

Figure 5.6   Distribution of agricultural livelihoods in Somalia (from Berry *et al.* 1980).

Table 5.3 Livestock population in dry areas: sample statistics.

	1969–71	1975	1977	1978	1979	1980	1981	1982	1983	1984
Sheep – 1,000 head										
Benin	551	820†	909	930†	934*	964*	965†	984	999	1,013
Burkina Faso	1,648	1,200	1,700	1,750	1,800	1,855	1,900†	1,952	2,003	2,054
Cameroon	2,000	2,050*	2,100*	2,155†	2,170*	2,160*	2,174†	2,198	2,213	2,228
Cape Verde	2†	2†	2†	2†	2†	2†	2†	2	2	2
Chad	2,200	2,400†	2,230	2,254†	2,300†	2,400†	2,300†	2,383	2,411	2,440
Djibouti	253	96†	290†	300†	310†	320†	330†	340	350	360
Ethiopia	24,077	3,078	23,100†	23,150†	23,200†	23,250†	23,300†	23,350	23,400	23,450
The Gambia	107	99†	95†	90†	152†	158†	165†	194	215	236
Guinea	323	401	420†	425†	430†	437†	400†	445	450	455
Guinea-Bissau	38	69†	71†	72†	45†	50†	55†	42	37	32
Kenya	3,935	3,700†	3,500	3,980	4,000†	4,300†	4,700†	4,920	5,200	5,480
Mali	5,700	4,000†	5,630*	5,849†	6,000	6,250	6,350†	6,568	6,752	6,936
Mauritania	4,300	4,200†	4,700*	4,900*	4,900	5,200†	5,200†	5,370	5,500	5,630
Niger	2,745	2,159	2,550	2,400	2,765*	2,800†	2,850†	2,973	3,073	3,173
Nigeria	8,550	7,650†	8,100†	8,300†	13,350	11,700†	12,000†	14,050	15,170	16,200
Senegal	1,533	1,689	1,760*	1,811†	1,870*	2,070*	2,075*	2,184	2,273	2,362
Somalia	8,967	6,000†	9,800†	9,900†	10,000†	10,100†	10,200†	10,300	10,400	10,500
Sudan	11,419	14,840†	15,248	17,358	17,200	17,800*	18,125†	19,005	19,625	20,244
Uganda	799	1,081	1,072	1,068	1,070†	1,072†	1,075†	1,074	1,075	1,076
	79,147	75,534	83,277	86,694	92,498	92,888	94,206	98,334	101,148	103,871

Cattle—1,000 head

Benin	549	700†	740	770*	756	771	770†	780	786	792
Burkina Faso	2,550	1,700†	2,600	2,650	2,706	2,760	2,800	2,856	2,907	2,958
Cameroon	2,308	2,600*	2,917	2,972†	3,100†	3,200*	3,204†	3,319	3,399	3,399
Cape Verde	13	10†	11†	12†	12†	12†	12†	12	13	24
Chad	4,500	3,600†	3,954	4,012†	3,900†	4,000†	3,800†	3,837	3,805	3,773
Djibouti	21	18†	28†	30†	32†	33†	34†	36	37	39
Ethiopia	26,510	25,879*	25,655*	25,864*	25,900†	26,000†	26,100†	26,212	26,314	26,412
The Gambia	247	300†	290†	275†	312†	321†	333†	346	359	372
Guinea	1,300	1,489	1,600†	1,650†	1,700†	1,760†	1,800†	1,855	1,906	1,957
Guinea-Bissau	190	255†	260†	262†	190†	200†	210†	176	160	143
Kenya	8,433	7,500†	9,400*	9,960*	9,457	11,000	11,500	11,835	12,359	12,883
Mali	5,400	3,886*	4,076*	4,263*	4,765	4,960	5,134	5,483	5,765	6,096
Mauritania	2,003	1,200†	1,192	1,183	1,186	1,200†	1,200†	1,202	1,205	1,209
Niger	4,077	2,508	2,850	2,800	3,122	3,206	3,300†	3,447	3,570	3,709
Nigeria	11,183	11,000†	11,500†	11,800†	12,000†	12,300†	12,500†	12,770	13,020	13,270
Senegal	2,557	2,318	2,440	2,671	2,533	2,238	2,260	2,191	2,111	2,032
Somalia	3,750	2,300†	3,950†	4,000†	3,800†	3,900†	3,950†	3,890	3,880	3,870
Sudan	12,300	14,720	15,892	15,905	17,300	18,354	18,791†	19,723	20,547	21,372
Uganda	3,987	4,765	4,963†	5,321†	5,000	4,800†	5,000†	4,883	4,838	4,800
	91,878	86,748	94,318	96,400	97,771	101,015	102,698	104,853	106,981	109,110

(continued)

Table 5.3 Livestock population in dry areas: sample statistics. (*Continued*).

	1969–71	1975	1977	1978	1979	1980	1981	1982	1983	1984
Goats – 1,000 head										
Benin	578	780†	874	900†	900*	926*	930†	947	961	975
Burkina Faso	2,473	2,100†	2,500	2,600	2,701	2,782	2,900†	2,991	3,089	3,185
Cameroon	1,700	1,550†	1,553*	1,636†	2,400†	2,340*	2,434†	2,740	2,968	3,196
Cape Verde	48	18†	20†	22†	67†	68	68	92	106	120
Chad	2,200	2,400†	2,230	2,254†	2,200†	2,300†	2,300†	2,313	2,331	2,350
Djibouti	527	570†	515†	515†	520†	530†	530†	540	545	550
Ethiopia	17,467	17,232	17,100†	17,120†	17,150†	17,180†	17,200†	17,228	17,254	17,280
The Gambia	115	93†	92†	90†	164†	170†	177†	214	239	266
Guinea	342	374	385†	388†	395†	405†	415†	421	428	436
Guinea-Bissau	103	179†	181†	182†	110†	120†	130†	95	79	63
Kenya	4,237	4,100†	4,390	4,415	4,500†	4,530†	4,580†	4,631	6,681	6,731
Mali	5,483	3,800†	5,500*	5,629†	6,500	6,750	7,000	7,512	7,924	8,336
Mauritania	2,783	2,500†	2,510*	2,610*	2,550†	2,600†	2,600†	2,625	2,642	2,659
Niger	6,122	5,395†	6,540	6,300	6,870	7,000†	7,200†	7,388	7,590	7,792
Nigeria	24,233	22,500†	23,600†	24,000†	24,200†	24,500†	25,000†	25,250	25,580	25,910
Senegal	1,067	844	895*	1,000†	950*	1,100*	1,150*	1,202	1,263	1,324
Somalia	15,167	7,500†	16,000†	16,400†	16,000†	16,300†	16,500†	16,510	16,600	16,690
Sudan	8,736	9,855*	11,592	12,088	12,200	12,570*	12,825†	13,139	13,434	13,729
Uganda	1,822	2,111	2,263	2,144	2,150†	2,155†	2,160†	2,116	2,096	2,077
	95,203	83,901	98,740	100,293	102,527	104,326	106,099	107,954	111,810	113,669

Source: Food and Agriculture Organization of the United Nations (1977, 1980, 1982).

Notes
estimated projections for 1982–4.
* unofficial figure.
† FAO.

country in this zone, has 35 million head of livestock in the dry parts of the country, and Mali, Niger, and Chad show a similar pattern.

Most of the livestock herding is accomplished under one of three types of livelihood systems:

(a) nomadic;
(b) semi-nomadic;
(c) settled (usually as part of a mixed farming system).

NOMADIC AND SEMI-NOMADIC

Nomadic and semi-nomadic peoples mostly occupy areas where grazing resources are scattered thinly over wide areas or where a combination of availability of grazing land and water are hard to find. Nomadic people tend to follow a well-defined general pattern of movement, often related to seasonal availability of resources. Nomadic people have organized their use of resources to take maximum advantage of the seasonal rainfall when it occurs. A variety of different patterns can be observed.

In Sudan the rains come in the summer (July–August) in the dry areas. During these two months, and into September, areas where rainfall is quite small (25–50 mm a year) have a flush of grass; water is found in pools in some stream beds, or is available from shallow-dug wells; and cattle, camels, and sheep can graze and grow fat. By the end of September, the grass is brown, most of the watering holes have dried up, and people and animals need to move south to areas of higher rainfall. In Kordofan and Darfur (Sudan) and in Chad and Niger, this north–south pattern of movement is quite common during an annual cycle. Permanent rivers are another source of dry-season grazing and water supply. In northeastern Africa the Nile has this rôle in some areas, whereas in West Africa the Niger and Senegal Rivers serve this function. For people with access to these water resources the pattern is a movement away from the permanent water bodies in the wet season and a return in the dry season. The margins of the Nile, the banks of the Senegal, and the inland delta of the Niger (in Mali) are the location of huge animal populations in the dry season. In Ethiopia and Somalia a similar pattern exists, though here the movements are often from low ground in the wet season to higher (wetter) land in the dry season.

This pattern of seasonal, flexible, yet regionalized movement is a very effective way of using grazing resources in an inhospitable environment, and the people who achieve this are often rewarded by substantial prosperity in terms of the worth of their herds; on the other hand, they have difficulty in getting educational and health services and of moving beyond basic standards in housing and food.

Nomadic life has always contained a high degree of risk and adaptation to uncertainty. The weather in any particular year is uncertain, the detailed location of storms may not benefit a particular group, and periodic drought may greatly reduce the herds. But in modern times problems appear to have multiplied for nomadic groups. Some of these are:

(a) problems of adjusting to new influences of the modern world, especially veterinary care and new water supplies;

177

(b) problems associated with the desire of governments to sedentarize nomads;
(c) changes in the patterns of land use in neighboring areas so that fewer resources are available to nomads.

Effects of veterinary care and new water supplies In many parts of the dry areas the most pervasive impacts on nomadic livelihood systems have been the provision of improved veterinary services for the animals and the provision of new sources of water. Each of these has had beneficial impacts. Veterinary care has resulted in improved quality of livestock, though camels have gained less than cattle, sheep and goats; new deep wells have reduced the likelihood of animal loss through drought and have helped reduce the concentration of animals around traditional water points. But each of these improvements has also brought significant problems. Veterinary care, especially inoculation programs, has made a major impact on the survival rate of animals. Herds have grown larger. Table 5.4 shows one estimation of the growth in numbers of livestock in Sudan over the past four or five decades. This has resulted in large areas of overgrazed rangeland and some areas of major degradation.

Even the provision of water has created a new set of problems. In the past there was a general balance between water supplies and grazing. Some watering points were deep wells, but most were shallow wells dependent on the seasonal rainfall or rock pools. The availability of water was generally in balance with the pastoral requirement of the herd.

Most improved water supplies are different. They tap the deeper water table which is found in many areas of sedimentary rocks in the Sahel. Depths of 100–200 m are common. This permanent water table, which may in part be fossil water, is generally free from the fluctuations associated with seasonal rainfall. As a result the availability of water provides a new focal point for animals and there is a strong tendency for the herds to remain close to the wells. The result is that the vegetation does not have a chance to regenerate. In the dry years of the Sahel drought (the early 1970s) the new water holes encouraged herders to stay long after the grazing was finished, waiting optimistically in the hope of rain and more grass. For some it was too late and animals were not strong enough to make the journey south.

Even in less traumatic years, air photos of central Sudan have shown circles of bare ground around the major water holes. The concentration of livestock resulted in the eating of palatable grasses, and the herd trampled out the rest.

Table 5.4 Estimates of livestock numbers in Sudan in selected years.

Year	Cattle	Camels	Sheep	Goats
1924	1,500,000	418,000	1,966,800	1,840,000
1970	12,115,000	2,650,000	11,526,000	9,123,000
1977	15,892,000	2,813,000	15,248,000	11,592,000
1982	19,234,000	2,570,000	18,547,000	13,174,000

Sources: for the 1924 annual figures see Consul General (1925); for the 1970 and 1977 figures see Ministry of National Planning (Sudan) (1974–5, 1976–7); for the 1982 figures see FAO (1982).

Provision of new and reliable water sources can be beneficial, but the location of new sources should be determined by the pattern of management and decision making regarding water and grazing, and the system of water use established should be compatible with the grazing and other resources of the area. This is not an easy task either for development pioneers or host governments.

Sedentarization   From a resource manager's point of view nomadism can be viewed as a very effective way of utilizing a set of scattered and dispersed resources. Both the huge Texas ranches and the nomadic herders do this. The sheer number of livestock raised by nomadic or semi-nomadic herding is one testimony to the importance of the livelihood system to regional and even global food production.

However, almost all managers view nomads from a different perspective. They are viewed as creating problems for the normal system of national and local government and for the provision of services. Nomads are hard to tax and difficult to count; furthermore, they move across boundaries and frontiers. It is hard to provide education for nomad children and to deliver health services and the like. Most of all perhaps it is difficult to inculcate such people with a feeling of nationalism, political identity, and the responsibilities of citizenship. Only in a few countries in Africa, Somalia, Mali, Mauritania, and Botswana, are the mobile peoples of the nation politically powerful enough to allow their views and perspectives a good hearing at the national level. In most other countries their numerical and political position is weak.

In these circumstances the dominant national response is to want to settle the nomads. Sedentarization will, it is argued, solve most of the problems. Education and health services can be provided, taxes can be collected, and political responsibilities can be exercised. Sedentarization, however, in the main creates two problems. In most cases, "settling the nomads" means a change in livelihood for them. In some circumstances, irrigation projects are set up as an alternative means of production, in others, there is encouragement to undertake dry farming or work in small towns. Each of these changes obviously makes a major break in the social and cultural pattern of the group, and there are few examples of short-term success, though there are some cases where in the long run a transition is made. In some instances, for example the Shukyria in Sudan, local people tried to make the best of both worlds as individual family groups combined irrigation on the government scheme at Kashm el Girba with continued herding in the traditional way. Some members of the family became tenants and workers on the irrigation scheme growing wheat, maize, and cotton whereas others of the same family group maintained the family herd on the nearby free range. The resources from both activities were utilized by the family economic group as a whole.

This approach solves the other major problem of sedentarization, the problem that settlement eliminates a valuable resource area from utilization. It is clear that considerable numbers of people depend on animals reared in marginal lands for their livelihood and that an important segment of many national economies is based on this resource. Neither can be easily dispensed with – at least in the short run.

179

Changing patterns of land use   The third major impact of nomadic liveli-hood systems is the changing pattern of land utilization on the wetter margins of the dry areas. For a number of reasons the populations of most African countries are increasing rapidly (Ch. 3), and the demand for agricultural land for this expanded population is growing as a consequence. There has, as a result, been a steady push of farming into drier areas and the sharpening of a general zone of conflict in land use between settled agriculture and nomadic dry-season use. Irrigation projects in some cases have deprived or restricted animal herders from access to dry-season water resources, and in some cases *niches* in the landscape reserved for exceptionally dry years have been useful, especially for farming or irrigation. Each of these trends has resulted in the nomad being squeezed in terms of resource availability where it hurts most – dry-season access to grazing land and water. It is this reduced access to resources, as well as the reduced rainfall, which combined to create the extreme problems of the dry years of the 1970s for the nomads in the Sahel.

SETTLED

The transition between nomadic, semi-nomadic, and settled herding systems takes place in several stages. Most nomads have a base area in the dry season, semi-nomadic herders have fixed locations at different seasons, and settled herders have a permanent village settlement with members moving out with the herds for grazing when necessary.

Settled herders, as well as some semi-nomadic groups, usually base their "home" location on a permanent source of water, which is often also a location of some crop agricultural production. Many villages on the Nile in northern Sudan combine cultivation on the banks of the rivers with extensive animal herding in the dry lands away from the river. During the short rainy season herds will move many kilometers away – sometimes for several months – to exploit distant grazing resources, whereas in the dry winter they are fed from crop residue and sparse grazing nearer home. The riverside cultivation often involves some irrigation – typically on a small scale – and some members of the family remain at the field location all year while others tend the animals. Other types of settled herding occurs in the Niger delta area in Mali, along the banks of the Niger River, and in a few favored locations where terrain and local subsurface water allows a permanent location with access to year-round grazing.

Ranching in the western sense is not common in the dry lands of Africa. Some privately owned ranges are found in dry areas of Kenya, and there are a sizeable number of government-sponsored ranching projects in Sudan, Mali, Ethiopia, and other countries. These, in general, attempt to reproduce some features of range management or produce reliable models for more general application. Chief among the problems are those of suitable management styles, adequate economic returns from investment, and transport problems with the produce. Notwithstanding this record, many governments in Africa see some form of centrally managed ranching as the most attractive form of land use.

180

Irrigation

Irrigation has long been a way of life in the dry areas of Africa. Basin or flood irrigation has been the basis of agriculture in Egypt for several thousand years, and the knowledge of irrigation is an important part of the cultural heritage of the Egyptian people.

Opportunities for irrigation using traditional technology were, however, very localized. They were confined to localities such as:

(a)   banks and low terraces of the Nile;
(b)   deltaic or flood basins;
(c)   areas where groundwater is at or near the surface – the typical oasis;
(d)   local zones at the foot of hills where water can be diverted into growing areas.

The simplest forms of irrigation along the Nile included planting on the banks of the river as the flood receded. The water was lifted a few meters onto flat terraces by water wheels or a shaduf (a bucket or a pole). This, together with flood irrigation, served the area well up until the late 19th century. The Niger was much less used by traditional cultivators; however, some irrigation was practiced along the Senegal River. Away from the rivers an intense form of irrigation was practiced in areas where water from shallow wells was carried, often by hand, to tiny fields of vegetables and date trees. Labor input was high, but productivity was high too.

These traditional forms of irrigation had their problems – they were vulnerable to the lack of an adequate flow of water in the rivers each year, and in years when the flow was low little land could be cultivated. They also had – and still have – environmental problems. The environmental problems of traditional irrigation sound surprisingly modern. They include salinization, waterlogging of soils, and the spread of waterborne and water-related diseases.

Salinization appears to have been a problem in parts of Egypt over 2000 years ago, and outside our region it appears as though a combination of salinization and silting up of the canals was instrumental in the decay of the Tigris–Euphrates irrigation system. Silting of canals and drainage channels and erosion and deposition along the Nile banks have been continuing problems for irrigation along the Nile for many hundreds of years.

Waterlogging of soil is a particular problem of basin irrigation. In wetter years, basins may get too much water and if, as is common, drainage is poor, waterlogging results and productivity drops.

Water-associated diseases have long been a problem connected with irrigation. Schistosomiasis has been wisespread in the Nile Delta for many years, malaria expands northward into dry areas where irrigation occurs, and there are many diseases and ailments associated with the small flies (*nimiti*) which multiply along the Nile and Niger.

MODERN IRRIGATION

Modern irrigation in the dry lands of Africa has involved much more comprehensive modification of the environment. Large dams have been built at

181

numerous places on the Nile, Niger, Senegal, and other smaller rivers. In most cases multipurpose dams are designed to provide hydropower and water for irrigation, as well as to control floods and provide a fishing industry. Most include irrigation as one of the priority objectives.

The Nile has been the site of the most comprehensive approach, with Sudan and Egypt assuming the dominant rôle in the management of the river. At present, these two countries have agreements about the use of Nile waters which effectively allocate all of the flow of this great river. It seems likely that in the next few years this allocation will be mostly fully utilized. Additional Nile water is being sought by the cutting of canals (the Jonglei Canal) to drain the Sudd region of southern Sudan, and there is active discussion of further storage dams in Ethiopia and Uganda. Table 5.5 illustrates some of the main irrigation projects resulting from the utilization of the Nile.

In Somalia the Shebelle and Juba Rivers are the major possibility for irrigation in the country, and a number of projects are being developed to utilize most of the waters of these two rivers (Table 5.6), though in this case there is no agreement with Ethiopia, the source area of both rivers.

In West Africa the intensity of river utilization is varied. The Volta, the Niger, and the Senegal are all undergoing comprehensive programs for water development (Fig. 5.7). There is considerable international difference of opinion on the proper pattern of development of these rivers, particularly in view of the history of environmental problems and management problems which have hampered the attainment of economic productivity goals for so many irrigation projects.

Table 5.5 Irrigated crop-production schemes in the Nile system.

Sector	Area (1000 Feddans)	Water consumption (millions m^3)
Blue Nile		
downstream from Sennar	164	976
Gezira-Managil	2,052	7,598
pump schemes upstream from Sennar	452	1,595
Rahad, phase I*	300	1,139
evaporation, Sennar Reservoir	—	669
White Nile		
pump schemes including Melut Asalaya, Kenana*	620	2,840
Main Nile		
pump schemes downstream from Khartoum	420	1,603
Atbara		
Khashm al-Girba	372	1,700
evaporation from Khasm al-Girba Reservoir	—	139
Total	4,380	18,259

Source: Waterbury (1979).

Note
* Projects still partially under execution. Note that no estimates are made for storage losses at Jebel Auliya and Roseires reservoirs.

Table 5.6 Current and prospective irrigation projects in Somalia, August 1976.

Project	Stage of work	Completion date	"Subjective" completion date	Additional area (ha)	Improved areas (ha)
Afgoi-Mordinle	I	1977	1978	3,108	
Jowhar Offstream Storage	I	1977	1979	—	land down stream
Balad (cotton)	I	1978	1979	10,000	
Turda (cotton)	F	1979	1980	2,400	
Fanole I	I	1979–80	1981	8,133	
Juba Sugar (phase I)	T	1980	1981	6,145	
settlement areas to end (phase III)	I	1984	—	—	10,000
Sakow Barrage	F		1979	—	land down
Kalanji	I		1979	800	stream
Northwest Agricultural Development	F		1981		25,000
improvement of existing commercial land	I		1986		18,000
improvement of existing traditional land	I		1982		500,000
Avai	I		1983	500	—
Bardere Dam	F		1984		land down
Golwein	I		1985	1,500	stream
Genale-Bolo Marerta	PF		1985	16,540	11,330
Juba Bardere Youte	PF		1987	10,000	
Fanole II	PF		—	10,000	
Juba Sugar (phase II)	F		—	5,223	

Source: Berry *et al.* (1980).

Notes
About 30,000 ha by 1980 according to completion status. Of this the greater part will already be under some form of traditional production, often by flood irrigation. Thus traditional production could fail by the equivalent of 25,000 tons of maize.
I = implementation; F = feasibility; T = tender; PF = pre-feasibility.

The problems which have resulted from efforts at irrigation in dry lands cannot be easily set off from the important benefits which have been gained. They are set out here not to suggest that irrigation should not be attempted, but rather that it should be approached with full awareness of the risks involved and with the desire to devote as much effort as possible to averting these risks. Given the focus of this book, we shall concentrate on the environmental issues, though we appreciate that there are managerial, economic, social and other issues which need to be addressed elsewhere.

The major environmental problems associated with modern irrigation in the dry areas of Africa are as follows:

(a) salinization;
(b) silting of water reservoirs;
(c) lowering of silt levels in downstream areas;
(d) poor drainage – waterlogging;
(e) spread of water-related diseases;
(f) spread of waterweeds;
(g) water pollution from pesticide or fertilizer use.

Salinization has begun to be a problem in parts of the Gezira irrigation scheme in Sudan. It has been a problem in Egypt and Mali. But salinization problems in Africa have not reached the level of magnitude and occurrence as exists on the Indian Subcontinent (e.g. Pakistan). Yet already in Africa it has resulted in considerable areas either going out of production or suffering reduced productivity. One of the problems is that there is little comprehensive data on the areas affected.

Silting of water reservoirs is a major problem in several places and a significant one in many others. The greatest problem occurs from the debouchment of silt-laden waters from the Ethiopian plateau into reservoirs on the lowlands of Sudan and Egypt. The river Atbara is dammed at Kashm el Girba in Sudan to provide irrigation water for a larger-scale project. In 1980, after some 10 years of operation, the reservoir was estimated to be 40 percent full of sediment, and

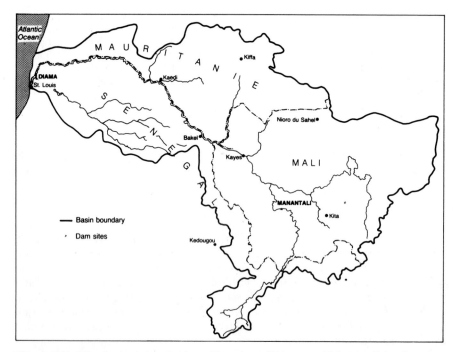

Figure 5.7   The Senegal river basin and location of Diama and Manantali development schemes (from Organisation pour la Mise en Valeur du Fleuve Senegal 1975).

184

without major additional expense water will soon become insufficient for basic irrigation needs. Similar problems occur on the Roseires Dam on the Blue Nile. There is considerable difference of opinion on the rates of sedimentation in the massive Aswan Dam reservoir (Lake Nasser), but most think that this will only be a problem in the distant future.

Lowering of silt levels in downstream areas is, however, a problem which arises from the new Aswan Dam. One facet of this problem is the change in amounts of water and silt reaching the delta. This is part of a sequential process starting with the early dams across the Nile in the late 19th century and continuing until now when the new Aswan Dam has severely reduced flow at all times of the year. Kessa (1972) has shown that, though the delta was previously growing steadily, it stopped early in this century. In recent years it has begun to retreat steadily so that major investments are needed to be made on coastal protection to stop encroachment on the valuable agricultural land which the dam was supposed to help in irrigating.

Poor drainage and waterlogging appear to be a problem with irrigation the world over. Somehow drainage gets a low priority in initial investments, or drainage channels are not well maintained and get silted up. Whatever the reason, a proportion of irrigated land in most dry-land African projects suffers from reduced productivity because of waterlogging. The Office du Niger scheme in Mali, the Gezira in the Sudan, and a few areas in upper Egypt all suffer. As with salinization, it is difficult to get any reasonable measure of the land affected.

Spread of water-related diseases is a very similar process, whether it relates to traditional or modern forms of irrigation, but because of the scale of irrigation and the major changes in the environment which sometimes result the impact is much larger in the latter. Also modern irrigation projects usually involve impoundment of water and this new water body creates a productive environment for insects, some of which carry disease. Bilharzia is clearly one disease which has spread because of irrigation projects. The Gezira project in Sudan has a high rate of incidence of bilharzia, which is hard to control because of widespread infestation of the canals by the host snail. A number of gastro-intestinal diseases, malaria, and cholera have all been related to new patterns of water use (Table 5.7). Irrigation in dry areas provides an especially dramatic change in the environment and is unfortunately too frequently accompanied by an equally drastic change in health hazards.

Spread of waterweeds is another result of irrigation, one which hampers the functioning of the irrigation project. Waterweeds are troublesome in two main locations: in the reservoir behind the dam, and in the canals which distribute water to the fields. Rapidly growing films of floating vegetation can form on water reservoirs; the small "water lettuce" *pistia* and the much larger water hyacinth *Eichorniae crassipies* are two of the most common. The water hyacinth has been an increasing problem on the White Nile for the past 20 years, and at times a mass of vegetation up to 1 km across and 2 km long has blocked the Jebel Aulia Dam just south of Khartoum. The vegetation uses water, blocks transportation, restricts fishing and access to the river. In the canals those plants and a host of others can grow steadily, reducing the flow of water and causing some to be lost by evapotranspiration. Canal-weed clearing may become an important cost in irrigation and if it is neglected substantial inefficiencies in the system may result.

Table 5.7 Diseases for which an aquatic environment is obligatory.

Group	Disease	Route leaving man[a]	Route entering man[b]
waterborne diseases	cholera	F	O
	typhoid	F, U	O
	leptospirosis	U, F	P, O
	giadiasis	F	O
	amoebiasis[b]	F	O
	infectious hepatitis[b]	F	O
water-washed diseases	scabies	C	C
	skin sepsis	C	C
	yaws	C	C
	leprosy	N(?)	?
	lice and typhus	B	B
	trachoma	C	C
	conjunctivitis	C	C
	bacillary dysentery	F	O
	salmonellosis	F	O
	enterovirus diarrheas	F	O
	paratyphoid fever	F	O
	ascariasis	F	O
	trichuriasis	F	O
	whipworm (*Enterobius*)	F	O
	hookworm (*Ankylostoma*)	F	O, P
water-based diseases	urinary schistosomiasis	U	P
	rectal schistosomiasis	F	P
	dracunculosis (guinea worm)	C	O
water-related vectors	yellow fever	B	B mosquito
	dengue plus dengue hemorrhagic fever	B	B mosquito
	west Nile and Rift Valley fever	B	B mosquito
	arbovirus encephalitis	B	B mosquito
	bancroftion filariasis	B	B mosquito
	malaria[c]	B	B mosquito
	onchocerciasis[c]	B	B *Simulium* fly
	sleeping sickness[c]	B	B tsetse

Source: Saunders and Warford (1976).

Notes
[a] F = feces; O = oral; U = urine; P = percutaneous; C = cutaneous; B = bite; N = nose.
[b] Though sometimes waterborne, more often water washed.
[c] Unusual for domestic water to affect these.

Water pollution from pesticide or fertilizer use is a relatively new problem in the dry areas of Africa, but it is fast gaining in importance. With the growing rate of application of pesticides and insecticides on the growing plants in the fields and on waterweeds in canal and reservoir, there is increasing concern about the impact on water quality. This concern is increased in the common circumstances that there are few major waterways and therefore few or no alternatives to the polluted source for other purposes, such as providing water to the urban areas. The scale of the problem can only be guessed at, but preliminary monitoring in both the eastern and western parts of the dry zone suggests that it is a real problem needing better monitoring and appropriate remedial measures.

A case study of environmental problems in dry areas: the northern arid Sudan

Figure 5.8 is part of a national map drawn for Sudan to illustrate the relative importance of various environmental problems in the area. The shading indicates that in this area most districts have, in the opinion of the Sudanese investigators, a moderate-to-severe set of environmental problems. The key to the map sets out in tabular form what the major issues are in each district. From this quite wide range of issues three are selected here for more detailed treatment: overgrazing and the loss of pasture (desertification), the problems of irrigation, and the urban environment problem in dry areas.

DESERTIFICATION IN NORTHERN SUDAN

Desertification is a term coined to express the deterioration of soils and vegetation in arid and semi-arid regions largely as a result of human activities. At a world conference on the topic in 1977, the government of Sudan made a strong plea that a large part of the dry areas of the country were suffering from desertification and a special program was needed to rehabilitate them.

The land and soil environment in northern and central Sudan has been fashioned over a long period of time, and particularly during the last 100,000 years. This period has been a time of fluctuating climate and differing emphases in landscape formation. As discussed in Chapter 3, the last 100,000 years has seen both wetter and drier periods than at present. In north–central Sudan this means that areas that now have 200–400 mm precipitation have experienced periods of near-desert conditions (50–200 mm) and at other times conditions have been quite humid (400–600 mm) (Fig. 2.4).

In the area west of the Nile in the Kordofan and Darfur provinces, the dry periods were characterized by deposits of blown sand from the north. Deposition took the form of widespread sandsheets, often gently undulating, and linear dunes 20–40 m high, but tens or even hundreds of kilometers long. In wetter periods the sand cover became stable through the development of small surface soils which held the particles together and because the soil was protected by the cover of grasses, shrubs, and some trees.

The area east of the Nile is dominated more by soils produced in the wetter periods. Clays, formed in a number of different ways, are the most common soil type. Some are the result of weathering of underlying rocks, others are deltaic-type deposits, and in some areas lacustrine deposits occur. In the current period of low annual rainfall, the clays support a vegetation complex dominated by grasses, some perennial but most annual. Trees and shrubs occur in the south of the area and along the widely spaced drainage channels.

These two areas in north–central Sudan are the areas of most concern to the Sudan government because of the deterioration in productivity of the rangeland and the other resources of the area. Although there are some conditions and trends common to both, it may be helpful to continue to treat them separately.

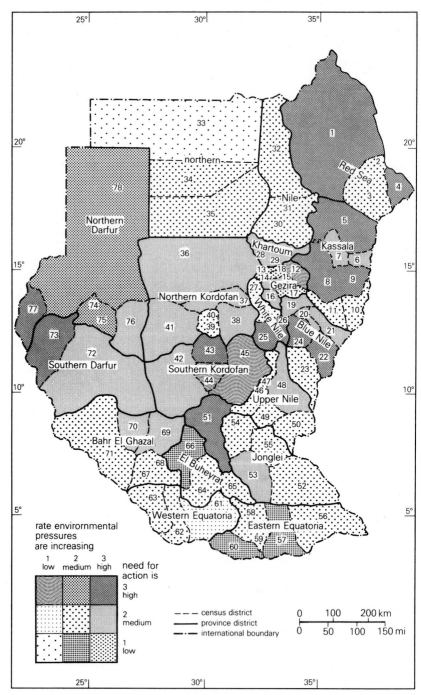

Figure 5.8 Environmental map of Sudan (from Berry 1983).

Key to Fig. 5.8

Province/district	Action	Pressure	Category of problem	Specific problems
Red Sea				
1 Amrar and Bisharin	3	3	development activity/water related/ human disease	isolated, lack of infrastructure, scarcity of water, drought, malnutrition
2 Port Sudan	3	3	development/water related/human diseases	urbanization, industrial development
3 Sinkat	2	2	development activity/water related/ human disease	isolated, lack of infrastructure, scarcity of water, drought, malnutrition
4 Tokar	3	3	development activity/water/human disease	isolated, lack of infrastructure, water scarcity, drought, malnutrition
Kassala				
5 Aroma	3	3	human disease/water/people related	scarcity of water, drought migration dynamics, land tenure, deforestation
6 Kassala	2	3	livestock diseases and plant pests/ development activity/people related	plant pests, impact of modernized agriculture, migration dynamics
7 New Halfa	2	3	livestock diseases and plant pests/ development activity/people related	plant pests, impact of modernized agriculture, migration dynamics
8 Gedaref North	3	3	water/people related	water scarcity, water quality, land-use conflicts; deforestation
9 Gedaref Town	3	3	developmental	urbanization/human diseases/refugees
10 Gedaref South	2	2	people related/water/human disease	land-use conflicts, migration dynamics, water scarcity, water quality, malaria
11 Qala en Nahl	2	2	people related/water/human disease	land-use conflicts, deforestation, water scarcity, water quality, malaria
Gezira				
12 Rufaa	3	2	human disease/water/people related	malaria, schistosomiasis, land-use conflicts, deforestation, soil erosion, water quality, droughts
13 El Mielig	1	3	human disease/development activity	malaria, schistosomiasis, impact of modernized agriculture
14 El Mehiriba	1	3	human disease/development activity	malaria, schistosomiasis, impact of modernized agriculture

Continued

Key to Fig. 5.8 (cont.)

	Province/district	Action	Pressure	Category of problem	Specific problems
15	El Hasaheisa	2	3	human disease/development activity	malaria, schistosomiasis, impact of modernized agriculture
16	El Managil	2	3	human disease/development activity	malaria, schistosomiasis, impact of modernized agriculture
17	El Hosh	1	3	human disease/development activity	malaria, schistosomiasis, impact of modernized agriculture
18	Wad Medani Town	2	3	development activity	urbanization, industrialization
Blue Nile					
19	Sennar	2	3	human disease/people related	malaria, deforestation
20	Singa	2	3	human disease/people related/water	malaria, land-use conflicts, deforestation, water quality
21	Rufaa Shariq	2	3	development activity/human disease/livestock diseases and plant pests	isolation, lack of infrastructure, malaria, animal disease
22	Er Roseires	3	3	human disease/livestock disease and plant pests/development activity	malaria, lack of infrastructure, isolation
23	El Kurmuk	2	2	development activity/human diseases/livestock diseases and plant pests	isolation, lack of infrastructure, malaria
24	Abu Higar	3	3	development activity/human diseases/livestock diseases and plant pests	isolation, lack of infrastructure, malaria
White Nile					
25	Kosti	3	3	livestock diseases and plant pests/people related	land-use conflicts, deforestation
26	Kosti Town	3	3	development activity	urbanization/industrial
27	Ed Dueim	2	2	livestock diseases and plant pests/people related	animal diseases, deforestation
Khartoum					
28	Khartoum	2	3	development activity	urbanization, industrial and mining
29	Three Towns	3	3	development activity	urbanization, industrial development

Nile				
30 Shendi	2	2	people related/development activity/land related	land tenure, migration dynamics, lack of infrastructure, land characteristics preclude cultivation
31 Atbara Town	2	2	development activity	urbanization
32 Berber	2	2	people related/land related	land tenure, migration dynamics, land characteristics preclude cultivation
Northern				
33 Sukkot and Mehas	1	1	development activity	urbanization
34 Dongola	2	2	people related/development activity/land related	land tenure, migration dynamics, isolation, lack of infrastructure, land characteristics preclude cultivation
35 Merowe	2	2	people related/development activity/land related	land tenure, migration dynamics, isolation, lack of infrastructure, land characteristics preclude cultivation
Northern Kordofan				
36 Kababish	2	3	water/development activity/people related	water scarcity, water quality, drought, lack of infrastructure, isolation, deforestation, soil erosion
37 Dar Hamid	2	3	water/development activity/people related	water scarcity, drought, isolation, lack of infrastructure, deforestation, soil erosion
38 Eastern Kordofan	2	3	water/people related	water scarcity, drought deforestation, soil erosion
39 Bedeiriya	2	2	water/development activity/people related	water scarcity, drought, lack of infrastructure, deforestation
40 El Obeid	3	3	water/development activity	water-related diseases, urbanization
41 En Nahud	2	3	water/development activity	water scarcity, water quality, drought, isolation, lack of infrastructure
Southern Kordofan				
42 Mesiriya	2	3	development activity/water/livestock diseases and plant pests	isolation, lack of infrastructure, water scarcity, water quality, livestock diseases
43 Northern Jebels	3	3	human disease/development activities/water	isolation, lack of infrastructure, water scarcity, water quality
44 Southern Jebels	3	2	human disease/development activity/water	isolation, lack of infrastructure, water scarcity, water quality
45 Tegale	3	2	human disease/development activity	isolation, lack of infrastructure

Continued

Key to Fig. 5.8 (cont.)

Province/district	Action	Pressure	Category of problem	Specific problems
Upper Nile				
46 Shulluk	2	2	human disease/animal disease and plant pests/development activity	isolation, lack of infrastructure, malaria
47 Malakal Town	2	2	development activity/human diseases	urbanization, lack of infrastructure
48 Renk	2	3	human disease/livestock diseases and plant pests/development activity	malaria, isolation, lack of infrastructure
49 Sobat	2	2	livestock diseases and plant pests/development activity/human disease	isolation, lack of infrastructure, malaria
50 El Nasir	2	2	livestock diseases and plant pests/development activity/human disease	isolation, lack of infrastructure, malaria
51 Bantiu	3	3	water/development activity/plant pests and animal diseases	water quality, floods, isolation, lack of infrastructure
Jongeli				
52 Bibor	2	2	plant pests and animal diseases/development activity/human disease	lack of infrastructure, isolation, malaria
53 Bor	2	3	development activity/plant pests and animal diseases/human disease	isolation, lack of infrastructure, malaria, venereal disease
54 Zaraf	2	2	water/development activity/plant pests and animal diseases	water quality, floods, isolation, lack of infrastructure
55 Lau Nuer	2	2	livestock diseases and plant pests/development activity/human disease	isolation, lack of infrastructure, malaria
Eastern Equatoria				
56 Eastern Equatoria	2	2	plant pests and animal diseases/development activity	lack of infrastructure, isolation
57 Torit	1	2	human disease/development activity/plant pests and animal diseases	malaria, isolation, lack of infrastructure
58 Juba	2	2	human disease/development activity/plant pests and animal diseases	malaria, isolation, lack of infrastructure, urbanization
59 Juba Town	3	3	development activity	isolation, lack of infrastructure, urbanization
60 Yei	1	2	plant pests and animal disease/develoment activity/human disease	isolation, lack of infrastructure, malaria

Western Equatoria			
61 Maridi	2	plant pests and animal disease/development activity	lack of infrastructure, isolation
62 Zande East	2	plant pests and animal disease/development activity	isolation, lack of infrastructure
63 Zande West	2	animal disease and plant pests/development activity	isolation, lack of infrastructure
El Buheyrat			
64 Rumbek	2	plant pests and animal disease/development activity/human disease	isolation, lack of infrastructure, malaria
65 Yirol	2	plant pests and animal disease/development activity/human disease	isolation, lack of infrastructure, malaria
66 Thiet	1	plant pests and animal disease/development activity/human disease	isolation, lack of infrastructure, malaria
Bahr el Ghazal			
67 Wau	2	human disease/plant pests and animal disease/development activity	malaria; onchocerciases, isolation, lack of infrastructure
68 Wau Town	3	development activity	urbanization, lack of infrastructure, isolation
69 Gogrial	2	plant pests and animal disease/development activity/human disease	isolation, lack of infrastructure, malaria
70 Aweil	2	human disease/plant pests and animal disease/development activity	malaria, onchocerciasis, isolation, lack of infrastructure
71 Raja	2	plant pests and animal disease/development activity/human disease	isolation, lack of infrastructure, malaria
Southern Darfur			
72 Southern Darfur	2	development activity/livestock disease and plant pests/water	isolation, lack of infrastructure, livestock disease, water quality
73 Western Darfur	3	development activity/people related/land related	isolation, lack of infrastructure, land tenure, land-use conflicts, migration dynamics, soil erosion, land characteristics preclude cultivation

(continued)

Key to Fig. 5.8 (cont.)

	Province/district	Action	Pressure	Category of problem	Specific problems
	Northern Darfur				
74	El Fasher	3	2	water/people related/development activity	water scarcity, water quality, drought, deforestation, soil erosion, isolation, lack of infrastructure
75	El Fasher Town	3	3	development activity	urbanization, lack of infrastructure, isolation
76	Eastern Darfur	2	3	water/development activity/people related	water scarcity, drought, isolation, lack of infrastructure, deforestation
77	Dar Masalit	3	3	development activity/human disease/water	isolation, lack of infrastructure, water scarcity
78	Northern Darfur	3	2	water/development activity/people related	water scarcity, water quality, drought, isolation, lack of infrastructure, soil erosion, migration dynamics

Kordofan and Darfur   Several processes discussed in this chapter and in Chapters 1, 2, and 3 have occurred in these areas. They include:

(a)   increasing numbers of livestock;
(b)   changes in the traditional power structure in allocation of land and water;
(c)   encroachment of agriculture on land traditionally used for grazing;
(d)   increasing demand for fuel, in part in response to population increase.

The problems that result have been evident for at least 25 years. Dixey and Aubert (personal communication, 1960) reported in a reconnaisance study that there was great danger of a whole zone going out of production, and extensive follow-up studies by Doxiades Associates (1964) confirmed the diagnosis. A simplified summary highlights the following points:

(a)   There is widespread overgrazing throughout the area.
(b)   There is intense overgrazing within 5 km of most new water yards and boreholes, and very little vegetation is found within 2 km of the water points.
(c)   The acacia arabica trees which produce gum arabic, an important export of Sudan, have decreased in number partly through cutting and partly because of reduced regrowth brought about by grazing and cutting.
(d)   As the soil and vegetation cover is removed by these processes, wind erosion, more characteristic of drier climatic periods, is becoming important. Blowing sand covers cultivated areas, disturbs replanting efforts, and cuts down annual grass cover.

Although concern has long been expressed about these problems, political changes and other factors appear to have resulted in little concentrated action until the drought of the early 1970s once again highlighted the problem. Several years of little rainfall reduced grazing still further, gum arabic production fell to a new low, and whole groups of people emigrated, perhaps permanently, to other areas. For example, it is reported that one group of 50,000 permanently relocated in the Butana, east of the Nile.

The present is distressingly like the past: awareness has been raised, a number of fact-finding efforts are underway, a few projects are being developed, but the efforts of the Sudan government to bring significant new funds to this problem have not yet really borne fruit.

PROBLEMS WITH IRRIGATION

Irrigation is the basis of modernized agriculture in Sudan. Irrigated agriculture is made up of several very large schemes including Gezira and Rahad, a number of medium-sized pump schemes, and a large number of small pump schemes (Table 5.5). Most irrigation is found along the banks of the Nile in northern Sudan and between the Blue and White Niles in central Sudan. Irrigation along the banks of the Nile is very old; the Gezira project was begun in the 1920s, but in the past two decades huge areas have been added to the irrigation inventory through the Rahad, Kennana, Kashm el Girba, and other projects.

195

Environmental problems with irrigation are partly related to the size and age of the project but are also related to the environmental location. To illustrate the impact of these variables we shall examine the Kashm el Girba scheme, the Gezira, and a typical small pump scheme.

Kashm el Girba This irrigation project is located in the Butana area of Sudan on the margins of the Atabara River (Fig. 5.9). The Atabara has wide seasonal variations in flow. It discharges large quantities of water during the flood stage but has completely stopped flowing by the end of the dry season. In some years in the dry season the river bed is marked only by discontinuous pools of water. Flood discharge is in response to the summer rains on the Ethiopian plateau. The basaltic rocks there yield a fine silt which is carried in suspension, and the granitic rocks yield silts and clays and a range of sand–size particles. The floodwater has

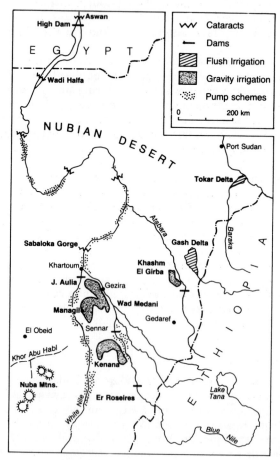

Figure 5.9 The location of dams used for irrigation projects in the upper Nile (from Grove 1978).

a very high suspended load of silt and clay and a bedload of sand which is difficult to measure exactly, given the nature of the river.

All these facts were known before the dam at Kashm el Girba was built, but there was a political as well as a practical urgency for its construction. This was the area to be settled by people displaced from the Wadi Halfa area of northern Sudan by the growth of the lake behind the new Aswan Dam; in fact some of the funds come from compensation for this enforced move.

There have been a number of consequences of this series of events. First, the sediment load was greatly underestimated and the dam, completed in the late 1960s, was over 55 percent full of sediment by 1983. This reduced water availability to the point where irrigation could not be guaranteed for all the cultivated area.

Second, and not nearly as serious, there were areas in the project where salinization was reducing output. Other problems of Kashm el Girba related to management and labor issues as well as relative return for particular crops, but these need not be dealt with here.

Gezira The Gezira has been thought of as an almost ideal irrigation project – at least in its physical setting. It is a huge, 1 million hectare area between the Blue and White Niles. A dam at Sennar and an additional structure at Roseires, both on the Blue Nile (Fig. 5.9), hold up water. The water moves under gravity through a series of canals to the cotton, maize, and other fields of the huge farm. The Sennar Dam, and to a lesser degree the Roseires Dam, were to be operated so that the floodwater with its high silt content could pass through and the dam(s) would later fill on the falling flood with its lower sediment load. Because the Roseires Dam is now also used for power generation, storage needs to be maintained throughout the year, and silting has become a problem in this reservoir.

Therefore, compared with Kashm el Girba, the critical problems appear to be in the distribution and use of the water rather than in its storage. Among the serious environmental issues in the Gezira, three appear to predominate: water pollution by insecticides and pesticides, as well as by disease-bearing organisms; waterweeds and silting combining to block canals; salinization and water-logging. These processes have been mentioned in a general context in this chapter. In Gezira all three combined with management and economic problems to create an emergency situation in 1979–80. The World Bank and its donors concluded that the highest priority in Sudanese agriculture – and perhaps in the economy as a whole – was to rehabilitate the Gezira system. A key component of this assessment was the urgent need to deal with the pervasive environmental issues mentioned above. As that work proceeds it may also turn out that the problem of sedimentation in the Roseires Reservoir may also need attention. Major international funding is now being made available for the rehabilitation of the Gezira project.

Small pump schemes These schemes are usually supplied with water directly from the Nile; the water moves by gravity over a flat or gently sloping terrace. Problems found in these enterprises are of two main types, those affecting the intake and thus the supply of water and those concerning drainage or removal of

197

water. Intake problems are usually the most obvious. The Nile, like most rivers, has a sequential pattern of erosion and deposition along its banks. Intakes become blocked by silt, or erosion removes the bank on which the pump house is located. Either way there are problems! In recent years, floating waterweeds, especially *Eichhornia crassipes*, have blocked up many parts of the bank. They are drawn into the pumping system and either stop water flow or cause havoc with the pump. This is especially true in pump schemes along the White Nile.

Drainage problems are an issue, especially in small pump schemes. Generally, the terrace on which the cultivated land is located is flat or slopes gently away from the river. Farmers are not inclined to invest much in drainage; consequently fields tend to be overwatered and surplus water remains standing on the clay–silt terrace. The result is that frequently less land is cultivated than would otherwise be possible or the productivity of cultivated land is reduced.

In summary, irrigation has indeed been a vital part of modern agriculture for Sudan, which as a country depends on agriculture. But irrigation is at present able to produce much less than it could for both the farmer and for the country as a whole. The possibility of achieving higher levels of productivity will depend very much on the possibility of dealing with the resource, its management, and environmental issues. Other measures are also needed, but resource management and economic management need in this case to go hand in hand.

Urban environments in dry areas

Towns and cities have long been a feature of dry areas, but the last few decades have seen quite rapid changes in the nature and size of many of these urban areas. Those changes have been paralleled by changes in the kinds of problems that need to be faced in the towns. The "three cities" areas of Khartoum, Khartoum North, and Omdurman in Sudan typify the kinds of issues involved; like most things they are a combination of old and new – the examples of

(a) dust storms,
(b) traffic congestion,
(c) disposal of industrial and residential waste,
(d) increase in disease, and
(e) water supply and drainage

may serve to illustrate the point (Fig. 5.10).

DUST STORMS

City dwellers in dry areas in developing countries are faced with two conflicting issues in house and neighborhood design. On the one hand, houses (new or traditional) need to be kept open and airy to keep them cool in hot weather; on the other hand they should ideally also be closed and airtight to keep out the fine dust picked up and carried by the wind – in small amounts at all times and in impressively large quantities during haboobs (either winter or pre-rainy season summer dust storms). The effect of dust is increased in the cities because many of the side roads are not paved and traffic raises new material continuously. For

198

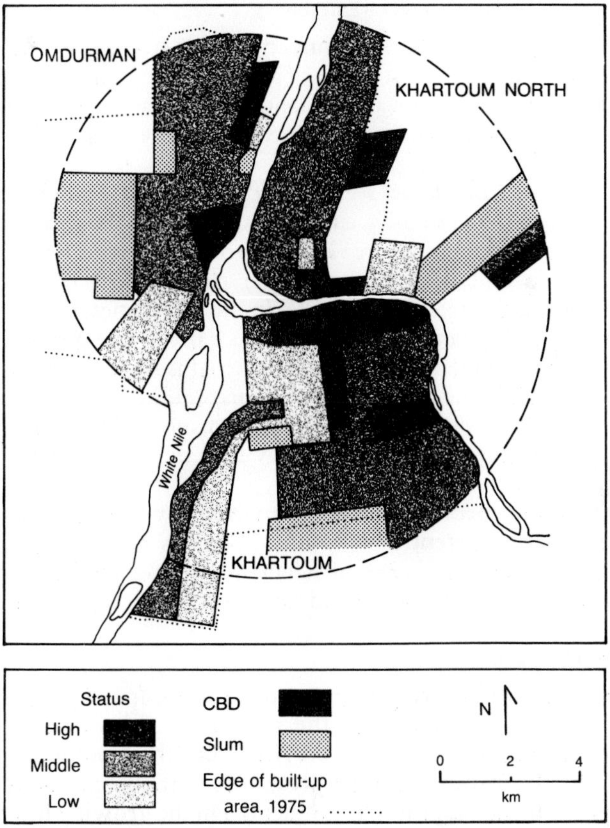
OMDURMAN
KHARTOUM NORTH
White Nile
KHARTOUM
Status
High
Middle
Low
CBD
Slum
Edge of built-up area, 1975
N
0
2
4
km

Figure 5.10 The location and structure of greater Khartoum (from Herbert & Hijazi 1984).

anyone who has experienced a haboob this issue rates very highly. This is a problem which few architects or builders have solved.

TRAFFIC CONGESTION

Dust is an old problem, but traffic congestion is a new one. The dry areas of Africa are also in part areas where people of the Moslem faith live. The preferred type of house in these areas has one story, or at most two, and is surrounded by a compound. Both rich and poor prefer this arrangement. The result is a "Los Angeles" type city spreading far and wide over the countryside. The poor tend to live in the remoter suburbs, the well-to-do in favored areas nearer the core. One result can be a high level of movement of people to work or to market and although only a few own their own cars large numbers of taxis, trucks, buses, and other motor-driven vehicles concentrate along highway circles not designed for such a large flow of traffic or for such an extensive city. Traffic congestion is a way of life, and journeys to and from work occupy a disproportionate part of the day.

DISPOSAL OF INDUSTRIAL AND RESIDENTIAL WASTE

In the past, cities in dry areas, surrounded as they frequently are by little-used areas, have tended to dispose of waste of all sorts by "dumping it in the desert". The dry atmosphere, the low value of land in the areas outside the city, and the relatively small amounts of waste generated allow this to be a somewhat acceptable practice.

The past few decades have seen major growth in both the size and the quantities of waste generated by cities in general and the three cities' areas in particular. A sizeable industrial area has grown up concentrated on the flat lands of Khartoum North, but there are smaller counterparts in Omdurman and Khartoum. There are many more vehicles in the three cities, some of which need to be disposed of each year, and there is the daily waste generated by over 1 million people. Sewerage and industrial disposal is the greatest problem, with alternatives for each being the Nile or the surrounding areas of semi-desert: in both cases the key is adequate treatment before disposal, but the growth in waste material has not been paralleled by a growth in the effectiveness of private or government systems for disposal.

As a result, serious problems arise both with growing water pollution in the Nile – a trend that is currently being monitored by the Institute for Environmental Studies at the University of Khartoum – and with land pollution by waste chemicals and metals, both inside and outside the city boundaries.

INCREASE IN DISEASE

Larger urban populations bring together diverse groups of people in a concentrated area. Unless the increase in the size of the city is accompanied by a complementary increase in health services, health conditions can decrease remarkably. In the national capital area, three circumstances (two of them directly environmental) appear to be influential in the growing health problems. These are:

(a) the creation of environments favorable to mosquitoes and flies;
(b) problems of waste disposal;
(c) the influx of residents bringing disease from other areas.

At one period, Khartoum was not a high malaria-risk area. The dry climate greatly restricted breeding grounds, and malaria was not common among the population, mostly derived from the north. In the last two or three decades several factors have changed. An important step was the setting up of a "green belt" around the southern margin of Khartoum to cut down the impact of dust storms from that direction. This was watered by a canal between the Blue and White Niles, and the resultant irrigated area appears to have been an important factor in linking the Gezira moist environment with Khartoum and allowing malarial mosquitoes to move much more easily between the two areas. This was accompanied by the presence of irrigated gardens in Khartoum and a new resident population, including refugees from Eritrea and Ethiopia and many people from southern Sudan. These people carried the malaria virus to a receptive environment. The result is that Khartoum is now a city where malaria is common.

Similar sets of conditions, together with problems of waste disposal, have kept the levels of gastrointestinal diseases high in parts of the city and have increased the incidence of trachoma and yellow fever.

WATER SUPPLY AND DRAINAGE

Many of the issues concerning water supply and drainage have been touched upon in the preceding paragraphs. The three cities are fortunate in that in the Nile and the underground water table derived from it there is a good supply of water for domestic and industrial purposes. There are problems in distributing this water reliably and problems in drainage. Water for many areas is available through standpipes; in others, wells are the main source. In both cases standing water accumulates around the source, so that it is a potential site for disease transfer and water pollution. Even in house compounds, the water source is often a site for mosquitoes and flies. At all scales, from the industrial enterprise to the home, water disposal is difficult in the flat terrain and, despite the dry climate, semi-permanent wet spots are formed with the health risks which have been discussed.

Other environmental problems also occur in the area of the three cities. For example, despite the dry environment and generally rising air during the day, air pollution can be a problem in certain weather conditions. The rapid growth in numbers of motor vehicles, combined with pollution from small industries, makes this a discernible problem which may grow in the future.

Khartoum and its environs, like other urban areas in tropical dry regions, have to contend with a mixture of environmental problems – some longstanding and deriving from poverty and underdevelopment, others new and accompanying the modern aspects of the urban area. The combination is hard to deal with.

6 The savanna and dry-forest environments

Introduction

The natural savanna and dry-woodland environments are transitions between the more humid environments (rainforest, Ch. 4) and the arid low-latitude environments (dry, Ch. 5) of Africa. Their position between these two major African environments attests to the importance of moisture as the dominant variable in their relative location. It is for this reason that this chapter begins with a brief inquiry into the climatic limits of this environmental zone. However, in many regions the areal extent of contemporary savanna and dry-forest environments largely reflects the major modifications that human activities have induced on the "natural" savannas and dry forests. Thus climatic criteria alone cannot accurately explain the current extent of these environments in Africa today. Clearly, besides the moisture balance as a critical determinant, contemporary savannas and dry forests in many places in Africa reflect generations of human activity, including forest clearing and grass burning.

Savanna is a vegetational term used to describe a range of environments. Savanna suggests a mixture of grassland and trees, and this combination of vegetation types occurs over a range of climates and other environmental conditions. In areas of lower rainfall the trees are very scattered, being located mainly near seasonal water courses. Short seasonal (annual) grasses predominate. In the wetter part of the zone grasses are tall (1–2 m) and woodland occupies a larger portion of the land surface. Terms such as "woodland savanna", "grassland savanna", "parkland", and "scrub" are used to subdivide this category ecologically. These various vegetation descriptors give an indication of the range of varying moisture conditions that exist in savanna areas.

Natural grassland and semi-deciduous forests are primarily a response to seasonal moisture deficiencies when they occur at low and moderate elevations in the tropics. The semi-deciduous forests would be expected to be distributed along the zones bounded by the "1" dryness ratio isoline (Fig. 1.1, p. 2); the savannas would occupy the areas between the 1 and 3 dryness ratio isolines if moisture deficiencies solely determined the distribution of these environments. The number of dry months and their annual distribution are the critical variables for differentiating this major environmental unit into its various subsets. This zone of transition from humid to dry is marked by combinations of grasses, euphorbia, and acacia vegetation.

The savanna changes to the drier Sahelian (semi-arid) zone around the 750 mm (30 in) isohyet in northern Africa. This northern limit of the savanna is approximately the 16th parallel, beginning just north of Cape Verde (Senegal), then extending eastward through Kayes (Mali) to the south of Lake Chad, to Sennar (Sudan), and along the margins of the Ethiopian Highlands. In the other areas of Africa the change from savanna to the drier zones roughly corresponds to an annual rainfall of 750–800 mm (30–32 in). This boundary in southern Africa begins in the west, just inland from the coast of Gabinda (Angola) southward, and then extends northeast to Bukama (Zaire), east to Lake Rukwa (Tanzania), and southward through Lake Malawi to the Mozambique/South Africa border along the coast. In the extreme south the limits of savanna are determined not by moisture but by temperature. In these areas the limit is determined by the occurrence of frost. The savanna is a frost-free environment by definition. The northern and southern savannas are separated from each other by more humid (largely rainforest) zones. This humid margin boundary usually separates areas having more than three dry months (savanna) from areas with a greater moisture surplus (rainforest) (Fig. 6.1).

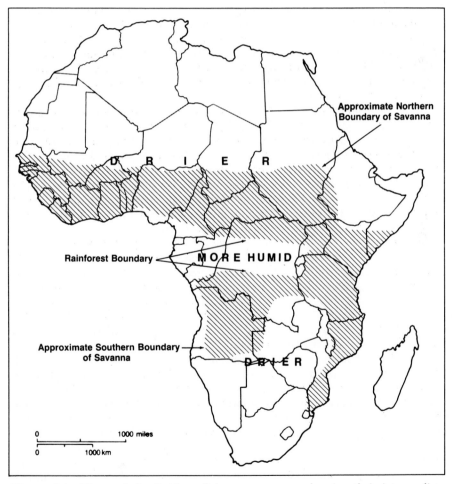

Figure 6.1 The areal distribution of the savanna areas showing their intermediate location between the rainforest and arid areas.

Climate

The critical climatic element in both the dry forests and savannas is water. It affects not only natural vegetation but also agricultural–pastoral and industrial development. In environments with seasonal moisture deficiencies, storage of water is required. Modern industry demands reliable water supplies. In many African urban areas water rationing exists in a variety of forms during the drier periods of the year. For agrarian activities it is important to understand that at the beginning of the growing season soil conditions in the savanna and dry-forest environments are generally the opposite of those in North American and European forests and grasslands. Soil is dry at the beginning of agricultural activity in the African savannas and dry forests. Thus, if after precipitation begins (the start of the growing season) there are significant gaps between later rains, no reserve of soil moisture exists and newly germinated plants become stunted or die. Not only is the amount of moisture critical, but the timing of rain events is crucial for agricultural activities. In middle latitudes, at the beginning of the growing season in the spring, soil moisture from snowmelt provides a significant soil moisture reserve. After germination the young plants are not dependent solely on precipitation to sustain growth. This makes agriculture less risky than in the savannas.

Along the drier margins of the savanna, a precarious moisture balance exists between evapotranspiration and precipitation during the whole growing season since minimal soil-moisture recharge occurs. As a result, any decrease in precipitation or gap in rains in these zones is followed by rapid deterioration in crop yields. Years of moisture surplus and reliability result in bumper crops; years of unreliable rains result in low yields. Because of the nature of the moisture balance of soils in African savanna environments, and the variability of rains both from year to year and within the rainy season, this is an environment that is characterized by fluctuations in food production.

Rainfall–temperature graphs for three locations indicate the wide variety of these two climatic properties for the dry-forest and savanna environments (Fig. 6.2). The distribution and quantity of precipitation in Kumasi places it in the dry-forest category, but the contemporary landscape of its environs clearly indicates a savanna landscape. Kumasi is a "natural" dry-forest environment, but land-use practices have altered the vegetation in the area so severely that it now falls within the savanna classification. Kota Kota and Ndjamena represent "natural" savanna climatic characteristics.

Given that our concern is with African environments as they exist, as opposed to their "natural" state, a wide range of climatic conditions occurs throughout the savannas of Africa. This is the result of human activities that through the years have created a new environmental situation. The three graphs in Figure 6.2 illustrate two important precipitation features of savannas: first, the seasonal fluctuations in rainfall; and second, the general quantity of precipitation. The single-peak rainfall maximum development in the northern and southern extremes of the savannas are shown by Ndjamena and Kota Kota, and the clear wet–dry characteristic is evident. Kumasi illustrates the double rainfall maximum–minimum that savannas in more equatorial regions experience. Besides moisture, the temperature properties of the three areas reflect another

204

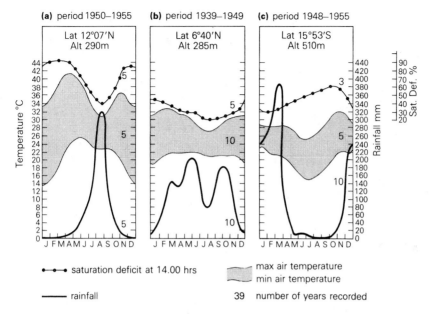

(a) period 1950–1955   **(b)** period 1939–1949   **(c)** period 1948–1955

●–●–● saturation deficit at 14.00 hrs

——— rainfall

max air temperature
min air temperature

39   number of years recorded

Figure 6.2 Average monthly rainfall, temperature, and moisture conditions at (a) Ndjamena, (b) Kumasi, and (c) Kota Kota. (Modified from Beadle 1974.)

critical climatic property affecting agriculture. The lower temperatures during the periods of maximum rainfall are largely the result of the cloud cover these areas experience during the rainy seasons. This cloud cover decreases the potential of vegetation growth owing to the lowering of incoming radiation from sunshine. Kumasi, in spite of having a relatively large rainfall, illustrates one other climatic feature of northern African savannas, namely the importance of the Sahara. In December–February broad areas of northern African savannas are affected by northeasterly winds originating in the desert. The arid harmattan winds that reach the savanna result in extremely large air-moisture saturation deficits. The result is a very high evaporation potential. Surface-water reservoirs therefore lose a lot of water through evaporation, and crops growing under irrigation require large quantities of water during this period.

Table 6.1 permits a more numerical inquiry into the general properties of African savannas. Jos, in central Nigeria, exhibits many general properties of these environments. First, there is a definite dry season (November, December, January, February, March). Second, during a number of months precipitation is less than potential evaporation (October, November, December, January, February, March, April, May); in only a few months is sufficient soil moisture likely to accumulate for agriculture not to be directly dependent on individual rain events (June, July, August, September); there is less sunshine available during the major growing season; there is a risk of crop failure during drier years (precipitation less than evaporation possible for three of the four months with average moisture surplus – see minimum monthly precipitation). The implica-

Table 6.1 Precipitation, evaporation, sunshine, and soil moisture of Jos, Nigeria.

	Possible sunshine (%)	Precipitation (mm) (30 year record) $\bar{x}$	Max.	Min.	Average potential evaporation (mm)
Jan.	85	2	34	0	307 D
Feb.	83	4	68	0	335 D
Mar.	70	24	112	0	368 D
Apr.	58	93	196	21	271 D
May	54	205	351	35	237 D
June	53	229	389	105	200 S
July	39	318	569	185	162 S
Aug.	33	274	500	122	142 S
Sept.	47	219	334	80	182 S
Oct.	66	39	139	0	254 D
Nov.	84	5	46	0	295 D
Dec.	88	2	34	0	305 D
Year	63	1414	1760	1080	3058 D

Source: modified from Griffiths (1972).

Note: D = deficit; S = surplus or recharge.

tion of these moisture properties is that when agriculture in savanna areas relies solely on local precipitation it is continually vulnerable to water deficiencies.

Besides the amount and distribution of precipitation, the nature of rain events in savannas is helpful in understanding the physical setting. Almost all precipitation occurs as rainstorms, that is relatively short periods of rain of varying intensity. The areal extent of most rain systems ranges from 10 to 16 km in diameter. Each storm only affects a small area and persists only for a short time.

This pattern of rainfall is illustrated by the following example. In Nigeria during one rainy season 26 storms occurred, but only 9 of them produced more than a trace of rain locally. However, visual observation of numerous rain clouds clearly indicated significant precipitation in the immediate area (Lewis 1981). This spottiness of rains is a characteristic of savanna areas. For most savannas, it is common for over 50 percent of annual precipitation to occur in 10–20 percent of the rain days. Table 6.2 illustrates rain distribution for three years at Ndjamena, Chad. In the progression from the more humid savannas to the drier savannas, a greater proportion of the annual precipitation takes place during a smaller number of storms.

Besides the spotty nature and short duration of precipitation, those rain events that produce significant quantities of water are usually intense only for brief periods. Values of 500 mm/hr or more for periods of $7\frac{1}{2}$ minutes during these rain events are not exceptional. This type of rainfall results in a significant proportion of the water flowing off the land as surface water runoff. A lower increase in soil-moisture recharge occurs from the local rains because the water does not sink into the ground. Thus, during short dry periods, plants have less

Table 6.2 Precipitation of Ndjamena, Chad, 1963–5.

Day	Jan.	Feb.	Mar.	Apr.	May	June	July	Aug.	Sept.	Oct.	Nov.	Dec.
1963												
1								7.6	1.0	10.3		
2									3.7			
3							11.7	14.8	11.2			
4												
5							2.0		6.0			
6						20.6	1.4					
7												
8												
9												
10						3.1	0.5	57.9				
11												
12							4.1			3.6		
13												
14								17.3				
15					2.9	0.1	0.9					
16						7.2	7.1			2.3		
17							2.4		2.3			
18								18.5	41.7	3.0		
19							8.0		0.5			
20							0.3	16.7				
21				24.3			16.1		15.6			
22						0.5	0.3	7.3				
23						2.5			18.3			
24								0.7				
25						6.5	1.0					
26								35.5				
27									1.0			
28				0.4	4.6		6.9					
29					0.6	0.2	16.5	2.0	34.6			
30								4.5				
31							6.5					
Total				24.7	8.1	40.7	85.7	182.8	135.9	19.2		

continued

Table 6.2 *continued*

Day	Jan.	Feb.	Mar.	Apr.	May	June	July	Aug.	Sept.	Oct.	Nov.	Dec.
1964												
1	•	•	•	•	3.2	•	11.3	23.0	24.4	•	•	•
2	•	•	•	•	•	•	•	7.2	•	•	•	•
3	•	•	•	•	•	•	7.7	22.1	•	•	•	•
4	•	•	•	•	•	3.9	•	13.4	•	•	•	•
5	•	•	•	•	•	•	•	2.9	•	•	•	•
6	•	•	•	•	•	0.6	•	•	0.7	•	•	•
7	•	•	•	•	2.9	•	•	2.3	•	•	•	•
8	•	•	•	•	•	•	•	8.1	4.0	•	•	•
9	•	•	•	•	•	•	•	14.1	3.5	•	•	•
10	•	•	•	•	•	•	1.5	1.0	1.4	•	•	•
11	•	•	•	•	•	1.7	2.3	6.5	5.1	•	•	•
12	•	•	•	•	•	•	•	3.3	•	•	•	•
13	•	•	•	•	•	•	3.2	1.9	0.5	•	•	•
14	•	•	1.9	8.6	•	•	•	0.3	•	•	•	•
15	•	•	•	•	•	•	•	•	•	•	•	•
16	•	•	1.4	•	•	2.5	•	1.6	8.4	•	•	•
17	•	•	•	•	•	4.3	•	7.2	•	8.6	•	•
18	•	•	•	•	•	•	0.9	3.0	•	•	•	•
19	•	•	•	•	•	•	15.1	3.0	•	•	•	•
20	•	•	•	•	•	2.8	•	3.0	•	•	•	•
21	•	•	•	•	•	•	•	36.1	•	•	•	•
22	•	•	•	8.2	•	•	14.2	0.7	6.6	•	•	•
23	•	•	•	•	•	•	•	19.3	0.1	7.2	•	•
24	•	•	•	•	•	•	1.4	•	•	•	•	•
25	•	•	•	•	•	•	•	•	•	•	•	•
26	•	•	•	•	•	•	•	•	•	•	•	•
27	•	•	•	•	•	12.7	32.2	•	1.3	•	•	•
28	•	•	•	•	•	•	0.9	•	•	•	•	•
29	•	•	•	•	•	0.2	9.0	3.9	•	•	•	•
30	•		•	•	8.1	27.4	26.6	1.8	•	•	•	•
31	•		•		•		6.0	•		•		•
Total	•	•	3.3	16.8	14.2	56.1	132.3	182.7	56.0	15.8	•	•

1965												
1	●	●	●	0.8	●	●	0.7	●	●	●	●	●
2	●	●	●	72.8	30.7	●	●	●	●	●	●	●
3	●	●	●	8.8	2.9	1.7	●	3.4	●	●	●	●
4	●	●	●	●	24.2	●	●	●	●	●	●	●
5	●	●	●	29.3	9.8	●	●	●	●	●	●	●
6	●	●	●	0.8	10.8	●	●	●	●	●	●	●
7	●	●	●	●	0.1	45.1	1.6	●	●	●	●	●
8	●	●	●	●	0.3	●	●	●	●	●	●	●
9	●	●	●	●	●	2.7	●	●	●	●	●	●
10	●	●	●	●	●	●	0.3	●	●	●	●	●
11	●	●	●	●	16.5	●	0.4	●	●	●	●	●
12	●	●	●	3.9	●	●	0.6	●	●	●	●	●
13	●	●	●	●	●	2.3	19.6	●	●	●	●	●
14	●	●	●	●	8.7	●	11.1	●	●	●	●	●
15	●	●	●	0.5	●	●	●	●	●	●	●	●
16	●	●	●	●	●	●	●	●	0.8	●	●	●
17	●	●	10.5	0.9	1.5	8.6	7.7	●	●	1.6	●	●
18	●	●	●	●	14.2	●	●	●	●	●	●	●
19	●	●	●	●	●	3.6	●	●	●	●	●	●
20	●	●	●	●	14.7	●	●	●	●	●	●	●
21	●	●	●	–	39.0	2.9	●	●	●	●	●	●
22	●	●	●	0.6	0.7	0.9	●	●	●	●	●	●
23	●	●	●	●	0.6	16.5	●	●	●	●	●	●
24	●	●	●	●	1.9	●	●	●	●	●	●	●
25	●	●	●	●	●	●	33.7	●	0.3	●	●	●
26	●	●	●	●	●	2.2	●	●	●	●	●	●
27	●	●	●	●	38.4	21.7	2.9	●	●	●	●	●
28	●	●	●	18.8	●	5.5	●	●	●	●	●	●
29	●	●	●	●	2.7	●	●	●	●	●	●	●
30	●	●	●	22.4	●	●	●	●	●	●	●	●
31	●	●	●	●	●	1.2	●	●	●	●	●	●
Total	●	●	10.5	159.6	217.7	114.9	78.6	3.4	1.1	1.6	●	●

Note: days without measurable precipitation are indicated by bold points (●).

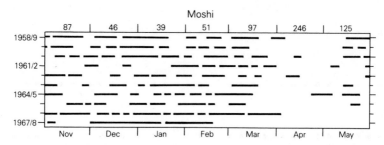

Figure 6.3 Dry spells longer than four days for Moshi, Tanzania. (Modified from Nieuwolt 1973.)

soil moisture to utilize than might be expected from an examination of the rainfall data alone. Because of the spottiness and intensity of rainstorms, even during periods when rainfall occurs, moisture-deficient areas are found in close proximity to areas with sufficient soil moisture. Abrupt as opposed to gradual regional patterns of ground moisture are often the rule in these environments.

One other characteristic of savanna climates is the persistence both of rainfall and dry periods. This is true from year to year, or within a given season. Dry years tend to be followed by dry years and wet years are more likely to be succeeded by wet years. Within a given year, a series of consecutive days with or without rain is the normal meteorological pattern (Fig. 6.3). As a result, even in years which appear moist periods of water deficiency can exist because of the spacing of rains.

Other factors in the savanna and dry-woodland ecology

The climatic factors of moisture and temperature are important variables in determining the distribution of the savanna and dry-forest environments in Africa. But many variables interact in a complex way to create this environment. Rougerie (1961) suggests that two major factors are responsible for the location and differentiation of the savanna and dry-forest environments. One is ecologic, and the other is human. By definition, ecologic factors include climate, geomorphology (landforms and drainage), and soil types. Human activities include the use of fire and other farming techniques, grazing practices, and the following of religious traditions. Because of this complexity, the boundaries of the savanna and dry-woodland areas are often not continuous.

Human activities

Growing numbers of people and shifting cultivation have led to the deforestation of the dry forest over broad areas with concomitant increases in the areal extent of the savanna. The dry forests lend themselves better to clearing than the thick rainforests. Using the traditional African methods, they can be burned

210

during the dry season. These dry woodland areas are usually better agricultural zones than the "natural grassland" areas since rainfall is greater and is usually sufficient to ensure a good crop yield each year. As a result, over large areas of Africa the dry forest has been largely replaced by grasslands. In many savanna areas today, remnants of the dry forest give evidence of their former widespread presence. For example, in certain areas sacred mountains and woods have been preserved, so that isolated islands of dry forest exist surrounded by savannas with identical soil and climatic conditions. However, in many areas, because of the large vegetation changes brought about by prevailing agricultural and pastoral practices, there have been large enough changes in the microclimate in the human-induced grasslands to make it seem to be the "natural" environment. With the countless years in which fire has been used in agricultural and pastoral practices, in many areas the "natural" boundaries between the savanna and the dry forest have been largely effaced.

Desertification is the process that brings about the expansion of desert conditions. Along its drier margins, the savanna (Fig. 6.1) has decreased in areal extent in many places owing to a combination of human and climatic factors. In these areas the savanna has been replaced by semi-arid and arid (Ch. 5) environments. Conversely, along its humid margins, the savanna has grown because of the various land-clearing practices at the expense of the dry forest and rainforest. The "natural" areal extent of the dry forest has been consumed until in many areas the transition from savanna to rainforest occurs only in a very limited zone.

The areal extent of the contemporary savanna implies a continuing process that results in changing environmental conditions along the margins of the dry African lands. Besides the climatic factors of precipitation and temperature already discussed, fire, together with biotic, geomorphic and soil variables need to be examined before the distribution of the contemporary savanna can be understood.

Ecologic factors

FIRE

Some authorities argue that savanna is a fire-climax ecosystem. Over thousands of years, natural and human-induced fire has become a common feature of the tropical grasslands. One of the characteristics of a fire-dominated ecosystem is the elimination of species of grasses and shrubs that cannot survive repeated burnings. The removal of these species results in many savannas having a dominance of woody shrubs which are fire-resistant. Some parts of the savanna are indeed dominated by such plants, but in other areas, despite fires, there is still a broader range of species. One problem appears to be that in the farming and grazing systems now utilized throughout Africa the deliberate burning off of the stubble from the previous year's crops is a common practice. These grass fires can sweep tens of kilometers across the country. Fire incidences have increased and probably the rôle of fire in the savanna ecosystem has increased. Pratt and Gwynne (1977) point out that the nature of the fire is important. If soil temperatures do not rise too much, that is, if the fire is fast moving, seeds are preserved just below the soil and the soil structure is not damaged. Slower fires, with higher temperatures, can destroy seeds and soil structure and thus change the vegetational balance.

PLANT AND ANIMAL LIFE

Despite the apparent general uniformity of the vegetation, there are considerable differences in tree and grass species from one part of Africa to another, partly as a result of regional changes in the physical environment but also because of differences in local climate and soils. Trees of the Acacia and Euphorbia species are common in the drier areas. So are Aristida grasses. The Acacia and Euphorbia species are well adapted to dry conditions. Acacias have hard waxy, sometimes thorny, leaves which reduce evaporation. They also have wide-spreading root systems which can tap water from over a wide area. Euphorbias store water in their fleshy stems and in this way can survive long dry periods. Aristida grasses have a short sequence of germination, flowering, and seeding and are thus also well adapted to conditions of low rainfall. In central Africa Combretum and Commiphora are more common with a mixture of grasses. This may be in part due to botanical processes but is also related to rainfall. In most of central and eastern Africa drought periods are not so prolonged and these species, with their lower levels of drought adaptability, are more common.

Although the savanna is generally thought of as consisting of trees and grassland, the typical savanna ecosystem of course includes much more than these two types of plants. Apart from other forms of plant life, birds, insects, and large and small mammals are important parts of the system. The large mammals are the most dramatic part of savanna wildlife. These include wildebeest, giraffe, deer, buffalo, rhinoceros, zebra, and other "game" animals; but they are now found in large numbers in only a few localities. However, a study of a savanna ecosystem shows that a substantial part of the total biomass consists of insects. Their numbers vary greatly from year to year, and grasshoppers (including the locust), termites, and tsetse fly, among other species, can reach plague proportions at certain times and in certain places. The ecosystem does not have a large number of bird species compared with either the tropical rainforest or the mid-latitudes, but some species occur in large populations. Quelea quelea, for example, at times gather in flocks of several million.

General studies of vegetation productivity show that there is a considerable range within the global savanna zone. In general, the system produces a minimum of 14.1 tons/ha of new vegetation material each year. This contributes to a minimum phytomass of 107.4 tons/ha. Within the African savanna the range includes a phytomass of 20 tons/ha/yr with a productivity of 7 tons/ha/yr, to 150 tons/ha/yr and a productivity of 16 tons/ha/yr. The savanna zone is much less productive of vegetation than the tropical rainforest or the dry woodland, but its grassland component allows ready use of the material by higher parts of the ecosystem. Some scientists believe that there is a quite rapid turnover of energy through the system.

The biologic characteristics of the savanna are important for its human use. The high levels of insect and animal life are a deterrent to the production and storage of food grains, and the slow growth of the woodland places some constraints on the use and replenishment of that resource. On the other hand, vegetation is easily cleared for cultivation and fire is all too easy a tool to use.

GEOMORPHOLOGY AND SOIL TYPES

There is a great variety of soils in the savanna zone, including red loam soils which are very common, black cracking vertisols which dominate certain areas (e.g. central Sudan), some finisols and some salty and clayey soils in the areas of impeded drainage. All of these soil types can occur on the sweeping plateau and basin surfaces typically associated with African savannas. In many areas vegetation associations parallel the soil types. In Zambia, for example, dambos are grassland clearings in generally wooded areas. They occur in areas where poor drainage inhibits tree-root penetration and thus tree growth. In south central Sudan the savanna is dominated by grass species in generally flat areas and trees are found on any small rise in land above the plains, which are better drained. Termite mounds, small abandoned houses, and old village sites – all areas of better drainage – are examples of good tree and shrub sites. In West Africa similar variations of vegetation with ground slope and soil drainage can be found at micro and regional scales.

Cole (1961) points out that the savanna ecosystem itself is in some localities associated with a particular landform, which is, of course, an expression of soil and drainage conditions. In Zambia, Cole shows sharp transitions between grassland–parkland savanna and thick woodland where the broadly sweeping plateau is incised by deep stream valleys. The greater availability of soil nutrients, looser soil structure, and better drainage appear to be important factors in establishing and maintaining the forest. A few tens of meters away on the greatly rolling plateau savanna dominates, due to slight changes in moisture and soil nutrients.

Smith (1953) shows that in Sudan topography has another influence on vegetation by concentrating water flows and providing differential water availability to plants. His study of tree species demonstrates that in run-on-sites particular trees can thrive some hundreds of miles north of their generally more humid provenance; conversely, in runoff sites more arid species dominate. Thus the ground moisture conditions superimposed on the prevailing climate explain a large degree of variability within broad zones. This helps to explain the diversity of tree species in any one zone as many – particularly the acacia species – have well-defined water requirements.

SUMMARY

The savanna ecosystem is an ecosystem with considerable diversity of species and a wide range of characters. Its main characteristic is the combination of grass and trees. Beyond that, biotic factors, soil, drainage, geomorphology, and fire all contribute to the nature of the savanna in any one location.

More recently, different levels of land utilization have resulted in widespread changes. The use of trees for wood and charcoal and the clearing of land for widespread agriculture and irrigation have brought about major changes in the savanna ecosystem. These will be dealt with in the remainder of this chapter.

Farming and grazing in the savanna: an overview

In examining the impact of agriculture and grazing upon dry-forest and savanna environments, the variation of the physical properties in these areas precludes making many generalizations that are valid throughout Africa. To a large degree in the more humid areas (dry forests) the natural vegetation has been or is being cut down. These areas with their shorter and less severe dry season are relatively favorable areas for agricultural activities. The "natural" dry-forest areas are situated on the humid side of the transition from rainforest to arid lands. As such, these areas are less prone to major periods of moisture deficiency and represent relatively low-risk environments for agriculture. Today large areas of former dry forest are areas of derived savanna and agricultural activities. A variety of food products and agricultural export crops have been substituted for the forests. These include pineapples, bananas, cacao, yams, and maize. Because of the more reliable as well as greater precipitation in these areas of derived savanna, there are often different crops grown in the derived savannas than in the "natural" savanna areas.

As the climate becomes drier, maize gives way to various forms of millet, with beans, peanuts, peas, and oilseed crops increasing in importance. On uplands, which are cooler, wheat is often grown. Along the drier margins of the savanna, land-use patterns indicate an increasing importance of grazing and a gradual decline in land under cultivation. Yet these "natural" savannas are areas of recent agricultural expansion. But because of the highly variable moisture balance these new areas of agricultural expansion are highly suscep-tible to crop failure unless irrigation waters are available. During the drier years, yields are very low and can even fail where rainfed agriculture is practiced. Throughout the whole savanna, agricultural and grazing economies are mixed in varying degrees. Sometimes they coexist in harmony and sometimes they are in conflict with each other. With the increasing demand for foodstuffs, an increasing proportion of the savanna is being converted for agricultural use.

In large areas of the savanna the traditional agricultural system was shifting cultivation. Today many African farmers in this environment still use the hoe, farm very small areas, and use slash-and-burn techniques in combination with natural fallowing of the lands after usage. But this type of agricultural system is becoming less universal as population densities increase, since it is a rather non-intensive use of the land and cannot support large populations.

In West Africa the predominant "peasant" form of agriculture is the rota-tional bush fallowing system. In this system fields are permanent. They are cropped systematically and placed in fallow systematically, but mature trees are never allowed to re-establish themselves. The combination of a mix of crops along with an extended period of fallow is the traditional method of maintaining soil fertility. Yet, as population continues to grow, periods of fallow are decreasing with the result that soil fertility is not maintained. Thus in future years this system is likely to decrease in importance as it will no longer be able to meet the demand for food. For a variety of physical (i.e. decreasing soil fertility), demographic (i.e. increasing population), political (i.e. need for population to be permanent for public services), and economic

214

(i.e. need to increase productivity) reasons, the traditional shifting farming systems that evolved in the savanna and dry-forest environments are being replaced by permanent agricultural systems – some mechanized and some still using the traditional farming implements.

What are some of the impacts on the environment as farming systems evolve from traditional shifting to permanent farms? Are crop yields increasing? As agriculture becomes more intense will soils undergo erosion to the degree that future agriculture will be in jeopardy?

Farming and soil erosion

LAND PREPARATION AND SOIL EROSION IN THE SAVANNAS

Agricultural research clearly indicates that there are five crucial factors that affect soil erosion. These are: (1) the intensity and quantity of precipitation; (2) the structural resistance of the soil to erosion; (3) the morphology of the land; (4) the types of crops grown; and (5) the management of the land. How do these five factors operate within the African savanna and dry-forest environment?

Vegetation cover has three important consequences for agriculture. First, it provides protection for the soil by limiting the direct impact of raindrops (lowers rain intensity at ground level). This, by itself, has a major soil conservation effect because it inhibits soil erosion. Second, vegetation provides a supply of litter that builds up organic matter in the soil (structure of soil). In grasslands, roots also make a major contribution to the buildup of organic soil matter. And third, plant growth accumulates minerals which, when plants are burned or die, are largely recycled into new plant growth. When lands are cleared and cultivated (management), the soil maintenance and recycling processes are interrupted. First, unless conservation practices such as mulching are used during the early part of the growing season, the soil is exposed to the direct impact of rain until crops grow to a sufficient size. This increases the possibility of soil erosion. Second, organic and mineral matter in the soil decrease as crops are sent to market and consumed at distant points. The net result of this process, if left alone, is a continuing decrease in crop yields until a farmer must place land in fallow. The sequence of crop followed by fallow is the characteristic response to the decline of soil fertility whenever lands are cleared and soils become less productive. But the increasing food demands which are widespread in Africa require new ways of responding to the maintenance of the environment besides the use of fallow.

Two strategies for offsetting the decline of the soil resource are the use of fertilizers and the development of a proper crop mix. Fertilizers to a large degree only replace the minerals lost. On the other hand, interplanting and various crop mixes can protect the soil from rainsplash erosion by providing a degree of ground cover during the growing season. In a recent study at the International Institute of Tropical Agriculture (at Ibadan, Nigeria, a derived savanna environment), yields of maize, soil erosion, and runoff were related to various widespread farming practices. The traditional method of clearing the land and preparing it for cultivation resulted in the lowest soil erosion,

Table 6.3 Effect of land clearing on yields and soil erosion.

Land clearing and soil management method	Soil erosion (ton/ha)	Runoff (mm)	Grain yield (ton/ha)
traditional clearing	0.01	2.6	0.5
manual clearing, no tillage	0.4	15.5	1.6
manual clearing, conventional tillage	4.6	54.3	1.6
shear blade, no tillage	3.8	85.7	2.0
tree pusher or root rake, no tillage	15.4	153.1	1.4
tree pusher or root rake, conventional tillage	19.6	250.3	1.8

the greatest soil moisture infiltration (low runoff), but the lowest yields (Table 6.3). This system disturbs the soils the least, and trees are left standing among the cleared plots. The shade of the trees is probably a contributing factor in the low grain yield as well as the low density of plantings. On the other hand, because the trees intercept rain more water infiltrates into the ground so that a larger amount of soil moisture is available for plant growth and the water supply in the area becomes more reliable.

In all cases, mechanical clearing of the land resulted in greater runoff and increases in soil erosion. One probable cause of this larger runoff is the compaction of soils caused by the machinery. This lowers the infiltration capacity of the soils. In addition, compaction can result in the death of large numbers of worms, which also lowers the infiltration properties of the soils. The worm castings as well as the boring of the worms into the soil add pore spaces that increase both the soil moisture holding and the infiltration properties of the soil.

Soil erosion in this area is reduced whenever "no tillage" strategies are utilized. The lack of tillage means that only a minimal area of the soil is loosened during planting. Only where seeds are planted are the soils disturbed. Also, in most cases no heavy machinery is used. It would appear that, for long-term benefits, manual clearing (using hand or power saws) and "no tillage" methods would increase production most as yields are dramatically better than with the traditional method and yet erosion is low (Table 6.3). Runoff and erosion could probably be reduced even more if mulching was incorporated into the farming practices.

The importance of utilizing strategies appropriate for an area's precipitation, morphology, and soil properties was emphasized in a study conducted at Bouaké, Ivory Coast. Although similar to the Ibadan area in that it is in an area of derived savanna, the inherent properties of the soils in this savanna zone differ in a few critical attributes so that here "no tillage" management encourages erosion. Table 6.4 shows that "no tillage" methods in this area produce greater soil loss than the practice of plowing and harrowing the soil. In this area's ferriferous gravelly soils, plowing brings gravels from the subsoil to the surface, lowering the erosional effect of rain splash. In addition, plowing helps to lower erosion by increasing infiltration. Because of the gravelly nature of the soil at Bouaké, as opposed to the medium-textured soils found at the Ibadan site, the introduction of plowing as a tool for

Table 6.4 Soil loss, Bouaké, Ivory Coast.

Plots	Plow	Plow and rotovation	Rotovation	No plow
1971	11.5	14.9	12.9	—
1972	19.7	11.0	25.0	17.9
1973	17.6	9.3	48.6	41.1
1974	12.2	11.2	43.8	51.9

Note: soil loss in tons per hectare.

intensifying land use in central Ivory Coast could be favorable since it appears to minimize soil loss. In contrast, plowing at Ibadan produced the highest erosion. This section further illuminates the problem of generalization of farm strategies when dealing with real people who must directly live off the land. Three types of farming systems found in the savannas are now explored and their impact on the environment expanded. These are the traditional, mechanized, and irrigational.

Traditional agriculture In the savanna areas, crop yields tend to be low not only because of the uncertain (highly variable) rainfall found throughout the savannas but also because of the generally low fertility of the soils. The traditional patterns of land use in these environments evolved as sensible responses to these existing physical conditions.

Most individuals in Africa still depend on some kind of traditional agriculture for their livelihood. The impact of this activity on the environment is important because of the magnitude of the areas affected and the vast numbers of people involved. A widespread perception is that traditional agriculture is subsistence. But, for many African nations, its products result in significant quantities of exports that are a critical portion of the national economy. For example, in Sudan at least 13 million people are involved with traditional agriculture (75 percent of the total population) and large quantities of peanuts, gum arabic, meat, and sesame for export come from this sector. Traditional agriculture is to a large degree location specific and therefore it takes many forms throughout Africa.

Generally cultivation is done with hand tools; shifting cultivation is practiced and relatively hardy but low-yielding crop varieties are employed. There is little or no use of pesticides, herbicides, or fertilizers. When they are used, the common case is that they are used incorrectly and thus the advantages provided are minimal. Often fertilizers and bug and weed killers require mixing with water. Because of the limited water supply and a lack of understanding, the mixes tend not to be accurately measured and the results are less satisfactory than expected. Further, the maximum utilization of these aids requires narrow time limits for application. Because of numerous demands on the farmers, as well as a lack of appreciation of the narrow time constraints, a haphazard application often occurs.

Soils in this setting usually have a low cation-exchange capacity and base saturation. Therefore soil fertility and productivity depend to a large degree on the organic matter and physical structure of the soil. These are two important considerations in savanna soil management and improvement. The nutrient status varies largely because of the level of humus accumulation. A strong, stable soil structure contributes to high porosity and permeability – both critical attributes in areas of limited moisture supply. Cultivation generally reduces soil structure and lowers the potential for soil-moisture utilization; organic matter also rapidly decreases. In response to this, yields drop, the land is temporarily abandoned, and lands that had been fallowed are recultivated. During periods of fallow, the soils regain their nutrient status through the buildup of humus, and the physical properties of the soil are regenerated. This is presumed to be directly linked with humus accumulation. Thus the fallow period is a crucial aspect of environmental maintenance in traditional agriculture. From an ecologic viewpoint, it is unfortunate that this balance between land use and the land resource is being seriously disturbed as traditional patterns are disrupted. Increases in human and animal populations, in part due to public health and veterinary programs, are increasing the competition for land, water, and vegetation. As land pressures increase, fallow periods are reduced, and soil fertility begins to decline. In Sierra Leone, 8–10 years of fallow are generally necessary to restore soil fertility after a few years of cultivation; in central and southern Sudan, a 10–15 year fallow between cropping is the normal interval required; in parts of Malawi and southern Tanzania, after 3–5 years of cultivation the land should revert back to fallow for a minimum of 8 years. In large parts of Africa, besides the decrease in fallow length, inhabitants expand into less favorable areas as land pressures increase. These "marginal" lands generally degrade faster and require longer periods of fallow than the better areas. Expansion into these more marginal areas is a continuing process in Africa. In Malawi, according to UN criteria, more land is under cultivation than is classified as theoretically arable. This over-cultivation in fragile areas almost always results in land degradation. This is substantiated by the fact that the Malawi government identifies soil erosion as perhaps its greatest environmental problem.

Under traditional farming systems, not only is the ratio of years of cultivation to years of fallow critical for maintenance of the soil, but also a sequencing of crops is necessary to maximize yields. On the relatively poor sandy soils found in parts of Zambia, millet is usually the first crop, followed in the second year by peanuts and beans, followed in the third year by sorghum and/or cassava. In the more humid savanna areas of Nigeria and Ghana, yams are planted first, followed by maize, beans, and other vegetables. In the second year, maize and sorghum are often grown on the old yam mounds and other smaller crops are interplanted. In the third year, peanuts, millet, and cassava are the usual crop. Afterwards the land goes into fallow.

Experiments have indicated that specific rotations of crops relative to soil type can improve yield without the need for additional periods of fallow. This is one method of maintaining soil fertility and still meeting the increasing demands for food and cash. The alternation of legumes and non-legumes is usually advantageous. Also rotating crops that have different root habits is

Table 6.5 Monocropping versus rotation of crops: yields, Bida, Nigeria.

	1st cycle 1950–2			2nd cycle 1952–5		
	Sorghum	Peanut	Cassava	Sorghum	Peanut	Cassava
monocropping	315	272	4544	354	128	2790
rotation	624	346	5405	668	162	4724

Note: yields in pounds per acre.

useful since this means that the crops make varying demands at different soil depths. At Bida in Nigeria (Table 6.5) where sorghum, peanuts, and cassava were rotated, all crops gave higher yields than when cultivated under monocropping. Except for the sorghum, however, all yields decreased during the second cycle indicating a need for future fallow.

In order to meet the crop mix needed by the people as well as to provide an ample fallow period to restore soil fertility, the traditional pattern requires a large area of land resource per inhabitant. In the drier savanna, more land per inhabitant is necessary than in the more humid savanna areas.

Under traditional nonintensive farming methods, the buildup of pests and diseases is seldom an important cause of low yields. But when population pressure causes a greater proportion of the land to be under cultivation, or when large areas of cash crops are grown, an increase in pests or diseases often occurs. Today the traditional farming system includes a larger proportion of cash crops than before as farmers universally require more currency to purchase such needs as radios, cloth, sugar, and other foodstuffs.

In some areas of Africa traditional agriculture coexists with a transhumance livestock system. One such area is in West Africa between southern Niger and Nigeria. During the wet portion of the year, cattle graze in the Sahel part of Niger, and crops are grown in the savanna areas of Nigeria. With the advent of the dry season, cattle begin to migrate toward the more humid savanna zones. By the time of their arrival the crops are harvested. The remaining stubble in the fields is grazed and manure is deposited by the cattle. This acts as a fertilizer for the next year's crops. If the cattle population is not excessive, this migration increases food supply through maximizing grazing lands and can actually improve the soil fertility. But if cattle populations increase excessive stubble is removed. Also, the excessive pounding of the soil under the hooves of the cattle will break up the soil clods, and this too increases soil erosion potential.

Mechanization and agriculture in savanna lands The substitution of machinery for manual labor in agriculture is a widespread trend in most agriculturally advanced countries. Mechanization has many advantages which have favored its use. Among the most important is the speed with which most operations can be carried out. This is especially emphasized when agricultural yields are compared on a per capita basis. Because of its greater tractive power, machinery can handle heavy soils and break heavy grassland that are beyond the capacity of most traditional African farming implements.

As it allows for increases in labor efficiency, machinery can improve the living standards of the rural population and release surplus labor for other tasks needed in the national economy without any drop in production from the agricultural sector. But in the densely populated areas of Africa (such as in the eastern states of Nigeria) and in most other areas of rural Africa where there is hidden unemployment, the need to economize on human labor is probably not critical. In fact mechanization could even increase rural-to-urban migration and exacerbate the urban unemployment problem. In addition, machinery requires fuel. This often means that hard currency must be sold to purchase fuel and is therefore not available to meet other needs such as fertilizers. Maintaining a reliable supply of fuel at reasonable cost is difficult or impossible in some areas.

Tractors and plows are at their most efficient when the ground is reasonably dry. Because of compaction, heavy machinery can cause damage to the soil structure if it is used when soils are too wet. In the middle latitudes, each year frost helps to minimize this damage. However, in the tropics, where there are no frosts, structural damage from machinery can accumulate from year to year. This factor alone means that in many areas in Africa great care must be exercised when substituting machinery for hand labor.

The use of machinery instead of hand labor for land preparation often produces unexpected results for planners. Mechanization in savannas has actually contributed to poorer farming conditions where land preparation has not been integrated into the complete agriculture picture. It is estimated that for a tractor to break even it must be utilized on 100 ha or more of land. In most traditional agriculture, plots per farmer are much smaller; therefore either cooperatives must be established or land consolidation must occur if mechanization is to be economical. It would appear that mechanization is most beneficial when it is introduced into those areas of the savanna where farming is not currently widespread and rural populations are low.

Because the rainfall is seasonal and variable, early plowing with machines can make the land susceptible to increased wind erosion prior to the start of the rains. It must be remembered that very little if any soil moisture exists before the growing season in the savannas. Thus, once the very dry soil is broken up, it is prone to wind erosion.

One other negative aspect of early plowing is that it can encourage the growth of weeds. Yet, if wind erosion can be prevented and weeds controlled, early plowing can improve the retention of moisture in the soil from the early rains by decreasing surface runoff through the breakup of the soil crust and the increase in soil roughness. Also, with proper safeguards, soil erosion can be minimized, but usually these conservation practices represent abrupt changes from traditional practices and must be introduced at the same time as the machinery. Contour plowing, the maintenance of fallow strips, planting of grass strips, and limiting the field size are some possible methods of reducing erosion. But erosion control must be site specific, and this means environmental data must be obtained before the land is farmed.

In the savannas of Sudan, mechanization as a strategy for utilizing central grasslands has been underway since 1944. The results from Sudan emphasize the need for careful planning when mechanization is introduced. Yet most of these results are tentative since there has not been a systematic study of the impact of mechanization on agriculture and the environment. Thus, how different rainfall patterns, soil conditions, crop selection, and farm practices interact is still not clear. In Sudan's savanna areas land expansion has been impressive since machinery was introduced. Large areas of little-used clay soils have been brought under cultivation. Nearly 2 million hectares of land have been farmed that would be very difficult to cultivate without machinery. In 1976 about 920,000 tons of sorghum, 50,000 tons of sesame, and 5000 tons of cotton came from these lands. Even though these figures indicate the diversity of crops grown on these lands, on individual farms, the general practice is not rotation of crops, but toward a monoculture. In addition, a "suitcase-farming" system seems to have evolved in large areas. The manager and workers are only on the land during planting and harvesting periods. Fertilizers and pesticides are not used. Because of all of these factors soil fertility declines, and after some years the land reverts back to fallow as new lands are cleared. This "ephemeral" mechanized farming system involving the use of extensive lands to obtain relatively low yields over a number of years is a mechanized form of shifting agriculture. It cannot have widespread application in Africa since the Sudanese conditions of large tracts of available and cultivable land with low populations are rare.

Because of lack of actual data, it is difficult to state categorically the environmental impacts of mechanization on the environment. In Sudan, soil fertility appears to be declining, but this could be the result of monocropping. Unfortunately agronomic research has not yet developed reliable rotations for these areas to meet the needs of the soil, the economic constraints, or the limitations of mechanization. The use of mechanization for the large tracts of land under the marginal rainfall conditions of the Sudanese savanna requires new strategies of cultivation, that is practices that can cope with the variable nature of annual rainfall. In drier years a definite increase in dust storms is observed and this is one manifestation of soil erosion. Without mechanization these soils would be preserved for future generations. In some ways the "suitcase" farming system that has evolved in southern Butana and South Kordofan represents a mining operation. The soils have degraded after farming to such a degree in many areas that they cannot be placed under cultivation in the immediate future.

Irrigation In savanna areas, moisture deficiencies are a critical constraint limiting plant growth. Irrigation is one strategy used to ameliorate the water shortage and extend the growing seasons. Four major sources of water exist for irrigation: permanent rivers, seasonal rivers, lakes, and groundwater. Lakes and groundwater supplies are generally limited in the African savanna. To take advantage of rivers, usually dams must be constructed to regulate river flows and to provide ample storage for a reliable supply of water because of wide seasonal variations in flows.

In savanna areas, man-made lakes can lead to environmental changes. The possible nature of such changes should be carefully studied before plans for the construction of such lakes are implemented. Problems associated with these lakes may offset many of the advantages of a proposed irrigation project.

Additionally, irrigation procedures in savanna areas involve risks that do not exist to the same degree in more arid climates. The slow flowing waters of lakes may create conditions favorable for the introduction or increase in intensity of some waterborne-vector illnesses. In East Africa, irrigation projects at elevations below 1500 m increased the transmission of schistosomiasis. The increase in the disease is due to the areal increase in conditions that are favorable for the spread of the vector snail population. The greatest increases in areal extent are along the margins of the man-made lakes and along the irrigation canals (Odingo 1975). The importance of the irrigation canals cannot be underestimated since at the Kainji Project (Nigeria) and Volta Project (Ghana), where irrigation is of minor importance, no significant increases in the disease occurred when the projects were completed. However, even in these areas, the disease has become established, although a greater time interval was involved.

The increase in the length of the malarial season is another negative environmental impact often associated with irrigation in savanna areas. In the Tana River Basin in eastern Kenya, the malarial season used to last from 3 to 6 months before the dams were built. Now that the dams have been constructed in the basin, the season lasts for 12 months. Another negative side-effect is that the increase in soil moisture associated with irrigation can encourage a spread in the growth of bushes. If land is not kept cleared of these bushes the population of tsetse flies can increase. The spread of the tsetse prevents or disrupts the use of an area for cattle grazing. In semi-arid or arid areas, such as in Sudan, where the fly does not occur, this is not a problem when irrigation is introduced. However, it is a potential problem in the savanna areas since this is the habitat of the tsetse.

While other health problems can arise through irrigation, such as growth of the rodent population with increases in leptospiral infection, it is important to remember that especially in the drier savanna areas the uncertainty and unreliability of adequate precipitation for agriculture means that these are often areas of intermittent famine. Thus without irrigation and the increase in food supply associated with it a different array of health problems associated with poor nutrition exists.

Often the best traditional farmlands in savanna areas are close to rivers and within the flood plains themselves. These areas under natural conditions have the highest soil moisture, and the crops are thus less susceptible to natural fluctuations in rainfall. It is these "best" agricultural areas that are normally the lands partially lost through dam construction, as they are flooded by the impoundment of waters.

In the savanna areas a reliable weather forecasting service is a greater need than in semi-arid areas when irrigation is to be utilized. It is crucial not to put too much water on lands, especially on clay soils, which are very common. Too much water leads to waterlogging and serious damage to many crops occurs under these conditions. This is especially true if irrigation is applied to lands before the start of the rainy season as young plants are especially prone to waterlogging damage. If irrigation is applied, and rains coincide with this, waterlogging can result. In savanna areas the likelihood of rainfall is greater than in the drier areas; thus there is a need for better daily weather forecasting to minimize water application to the land when precipitation is likely to occur.

There is no doubt that irrigation, if applied with care, is a viable method for improving agriculture in the savanna areas. There is a strong likelihood that agricultural production could be increased considerably if greater efforts were spent on irrigation in savanna areas rather than in the drier zones. First, because the savanna areas are more humid greater water resources exist than in drier regions, and therefore more land could be irrigated. Second, a smaller volume of water per crop is required in savanna areas to maximize yields as irrigation in these areas is a supplement to, not a requisite for, agriculture. By using irrigation properly plant growth can be maintained during periods of low rainfall within the rainy season. In addition, by adding small quantities of water at the beginning or end of the rainy season the growing season can be extended, permitting the introduction of crops that could not thrive under natural conditions. In Malawi, by supplementing natural rains with irrigation, sugar cane has become a reliable source of hard currency. In many countries, such as Kenya, irrigation efforts have largely been concentrated in the drier portions of the country. If equal efforts had been devoted to the wet–dry lands, results per unit of investment would probaby be greater. However, the need for careful monitoring of soil moisture and precipitation in savanna areas to prevent waterlogging requires a higher level of management skills than is needed for the more arid areas. But, as the savanna lands are in many places already cultivated, the increase in yields associated with irrigation is not as impressive an achieve-ment as the opening up of new lands in the drier portions of the country. Perhaps this is a major reason why water projects have been focused on the more arid regions, not on the savanna areas.

However, we should emphasize that irrigation projects both in savanna and arid areas of Africa have often failed to achieve their potential; sometimes they have failed dismally. Some of the reasons are the environmental ones discussed here. Even when these are properly taken into account, problems of manage-ment and operation arise. When pricing of products, marketing arrangements, and technical know-how are not coordinated difficulties can ensue. Two of the more successful projects are judged to be the Mwea irrigation project in Kenya, in a savanna area, and the Gezira in Sudan, in an arid–semi-arid area (Gaitskill 1959, Chambers 1973).

East Africa: a case study of the savanna

The East African savanna is perhaps the best known in the world, as large areas have been the focus of much scientific and tourist attention. This attention has concentrated largely on the lands designated as sanctuary areas for wild game. However, the game parks are only a small part of the total savanna in East Africa. If we define East Africa for these purposes as Uganda, Kenya, and Tanzania, the total land area of the three states is $1,663,430 \text{ km}^2$ (642,250 square miles). The area designated as savanna is over 35 percent ($624,000 \text{ km}^2$) and the area of the savanna used for game parks is approximately $50,000 \text{ km}^2$ (20,000 square miles), of which the major part is to be found in Tanzania.

As in other parts of Africa there is a considerable difference between the savanna zone as it might be defined by climatic criteria and the savanna as defined

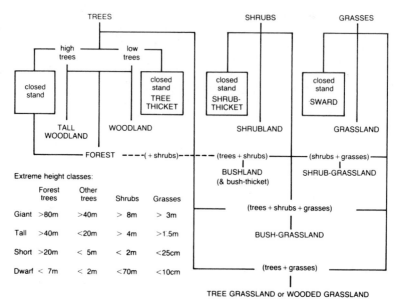

Figure 6.4 Physiognomic vegetation types of East Africa. (a) Vegetation is assumed to be deciduous and perennial on free-draining soil, unless prefixed by evergreen, succulent, annual, saline, alkaline, waterlogged, or seasonally flooded (from Pratt & Gwynne 1977). (*Continued*)

by vegetation and other criteria. Under some climatic criteria as much as 75–80 percent of the whole area could be classified as a savanna zone. But, particularly in Tanzania, there is a huge area of this climatically defined savanna in the western central part of the country, which is Miombo woodland. There is some evidence that in the past this Miombo woodland was a typical wooded savanna. Figure 6.4 shows a vegetational classification of the region and Figure 6.5 a division of the region into six ecological zones based on climatic soil and vegetational characteristics, but clearly climatic factors are emphasized. The area treated in this chapter is indicated on Figure 6.5. It includes some parts of eco-zone III, all of zone IV, and much of zone V.

In land-use terms, zone III is considered to be of good agriculture potential with precipitation annually between 750 and 1000 mm (30–40 in). A large part of zone III is occupied by farming and pastoral peoples. This zone is not typical of Africa because near the equator the two rainy seasons with their modest annual totals give a lower level of biomass than could be obtained from the same total in one rainy season. Zone IV, which has a rainfall of between 625 and 875 mm (25–35 in), has a typical "savanna" climate, except that here also the effect of split rainy seasons is evident. Zone IV is considered to be mostly rangeland, though there is arable agriculture near waterways, as well as areas where the water table is close to the surface. It is in this zone that many of the big game animals naturally live, and there is strong competition between grazing, agriculture, and game for the use of this land.

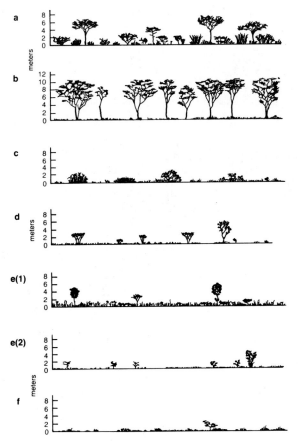

Figure 6.4 (*continued*) (b) Examples: 1, *Lannea–Combreton–Commiphora* bushland thicket; 2, *Brachystegia* woodland; 3, *Euphorbia–Sansevieria* succulent shrubland; 4, short annual *Eriochloa – Acacia reficiens – Boscia* bush grassland; 5i, tall *Hyperthelia–Combreton* wooded grassland; 5ii, *Pennisetum mezianum – Acacia drepanolobium* seasonally waterlogged dwarf tree grassland; 6, short *Enneapogon–Duosperma* dwarf shrub grassland.

Zone V includes areas of savanna vegetation, though the drier parts are mainly grassland and shrub. A few areas which are grassland mainly because of soil factors that encourage excessive drainage, such as the Serengeti, are included in this area. Because the topography of the Serengeti is flat and its soils are rich in volcanic ash, there is rapid infiltration and groundwater conditions are too poor for trees to exist in most places. In this zone there is competition between game parks and agriculture. Also, there is conflict between traditional agriculture and modern ranges and estates. Where annual rainfall is between 500 and 750 mm (20–30 in) game parks predominate; sometimes due to their remoteness or the existence of tsetse fly, vast areas in this zone are underutilized. Large parts of Tanzania and Kenya fall into this category.

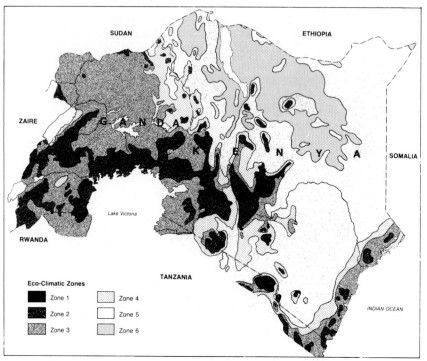

Figure 6.5 (a) Ecology map of Kenya and Uganda. (Dos 3143A–B Ordnance Survey.) (*Continued*)

Key to Fig. 6.5

Climatic zone		Vegetation and land use
Afro-alpine climate (climate governed by altitude, not moisture)	I	Afro-alpine moorland and grassland, or barren land, at high altitude above the forest line; of limited use and potential, except as water catchment and for tourism
Tropical climate humid to dry sub-humid (moisture index not less than −10)	II	Forests and derived grasslands and bushlands, with or without natural glades. The potential is for forestry (sometimes with wildlife and tourism) or intensive agriculture, including pyrethrum, coffee, and tea at higher elevations. The natural grassland requires intensive management for optimum production: one hectare or less, up to 2.5 ha, is required per stock unit, dependent on whether the grassland is productive *Pennisetum clandestinum*, a *Themeda* association, or coarse *Pennisetum schimperi*—*Eleusine jaegeri*. (Ground-water forests occur under climates drier than dry sub-humid)

226

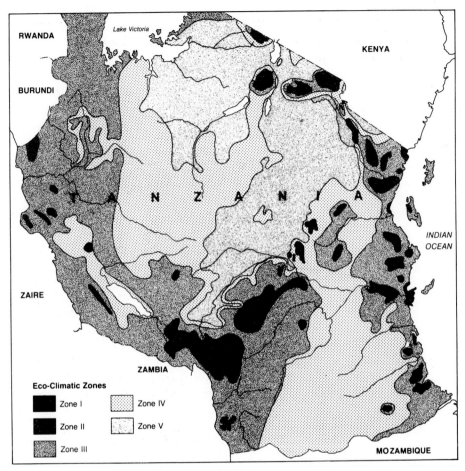

Figure 6.5 (*continued*) (b) Ecology map of Tanzania. (Dos 3143A–B Ordnance Survey.)

| dry sub-humid to semi-arid (moisture index −10 to −30) | III | Land not of forest potential, carrying a variable vegetation cover (moist woodland, bushland or "savanna"), the trees mostly *Brachystegia* or *Combretum* (and their associates) and the larger shrubs mostly evergreen. The agricultural potential is high, soil and topography permitting, with emphasis on ley farming. Large areas are still under range use; with intensive management their stock-carrying capacity can be high – less than 2 ha per stock unit – though it is lower where dry seasons are long (as in southern Tanzania), and full realization of the climatic potential may require bush control and fertilizers. Regular burning may be necessary, particularly where tall *Hyparrhenia* dominates |

continued

227

Key to Fig. 6.5 (cont.)

Climatic zone		Vegetation and land use
semi-arid (moisture index −30 to −42)	IV	Land of marginal agricultural potential (limited mainly to sisal or quick-maturing grains) carrying as natural vegetation dry forms of woodland and "savanna," often an *Acacia–Themeda* association but including dry *Brachystegia* woodland and equivalent deciduous or semi-evergreen bushland. This is potentially productive rangeland – with less than 4 ha required per stock unit, except where dry seasons exceed six months – limited mainly by the encroachment of woody plants and sometimes by leached soils. The more open country with a high density of wildlife is a valuable tourist asset
arid (moisture index −42 to −51)	V	Land suited to agriculture only where fertile soils coincide with very favorable distribution of rainfall or receive run-on; typically rangeland dominated by *Commiphora, Acacia,* and allied genera, mostly of shrubby habit. Perennial grasses such as *Cenchrus ciliaris* and *Chloris roxburghiana* can dominate, but succumb readily to harsh management: more than 4 ha is required per stock unit (though sown *Cenchrus* may support heavier use). Wildlife is important, particularly where dry thorn–bushland predominates. Burning requires great caution, but can be highly effective in bush control
very arid[a] (moisture index −51 to −57)	VI	Rangeland of low potential, the vegetation being dwarf shrub grassland or shrub grassland with *Acacia reficiens* subsp. *misera,* often confined to water courses and depressions with barren land between. Perennial grasses (e.g. *Chrysopogon aucheri*) are localized within a predominately annual grassland; growth is confined largely to unreliable seasonal flushes, and grazing systems must be based on nomadism. Populations of both wild and domestic animals are restricted severely by the environment

[a]The moisture index of zone VI was originally (Pratt *et al.* 1966) extended to −60, but as this figure equates to no rainfall, a revision of zone boundaries now curtails zone VI (the semi-desert) at −57, and recognizes indices −57 to −60 as representing true desert, zone VII, which is not found in East Africa.

This key revised from Pratt *et al.* (1966).

The designated case study area in East Africa typifies the development problems of the savanna. These include:

(a) land use conflict between game, agriculture, and livestock;
(b) pressure on grazing resources;
(c) high levels of tree cutting for wood and charcoal;
(d) low levels of agricultural production in the face of rising populations;
(e) incompatibility of development activities with the environmental system of the area; and
(f) constraints of the natural environment.

This case study will briefly set out the particular characteristics of the East Africa savanna and then discuss these problems in their ecological context.

The savanna

The East African savanna is generally typical of other African savannas, although much of this ecosystem is found at altitudes around 1000 m. As elsewhere, fire is a common annual occurrence. Usually the fires start just before the rainy reason begins. Most of the remaining woody species have become tolerant to fire. As elsewhere in Africa, savanna grasses have increased in areal extent at the expense of woods and forest; however, unlike in most other regions, especially West Africa, there are signs that former large areas of savanna are now being taken over by woodland and thicket.

There are several different vegetation associations. The most common is a savanna woodland with *Combretum* species (including *zeheri, molle, binderanum,* and *ghasalense*) dominating; other trees include *Terminalia* species with species of *Vitex, Maytenus,* and many others. In drier areas, *Albizia amara, Acacia,* and *Commiphora* species becomes more important. The tall grasses are dominated by *Hyparrhenia* species.

Acacia savannas are common in East Africa, but many areas appear to have special soil or drainage conditions. In South Kenya, *Acacia, A. senegal, A. seyal, A. gerrardii,* and *A. nilotica* are the main types, along with *Themeda* grasses. An *A. tortilis* savanna occurs most frequently in drier areas on the margins of the savanna area.

The climatic variation within East Africa largely reflects altitude and latitudinal factors. The latter are important in the pattern of rainfall, the former in temperature distribution. Ecological zones III, IV, and V in which savannas are found have moisture indices of −10 to −30 (III), and −30 to −40 (V). The savanna mostly falls in zones with indices of −20 to −40 (for explanation of index see Fig. 6.5). The map of rainfall regions (Fig. 6.6) shows that much of the savanna lies within zones II (a & b) and III (c & d).

In zones II and III there is a single rainy season starting in March north of the equator (zone II) and in November south of the equator (zone III). In zone II the dry season varies from December to February in the wetter area to September to March in the drier area. In zone III (c & d) the dry season varies from 5 to 7 months. In zone IV, near the equator there is a double rainfall peak from November to December and from April to May with dry periods in between.

229

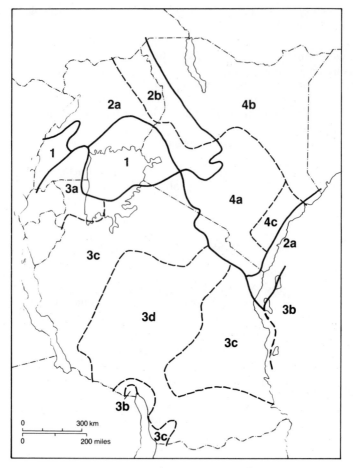

Figure 6.6 Rainfall regions of East Africa (from Griffiths 1962 and Pratt & Gwynne 1977).

1 Year-long rainfall (or dry during January only).
2 Single season rainfall (starting March):
  (a) with short dry season during December–February (2–4 months);
  (b) with long dry season during September–March (5–7 months).
3 Single season rainfall (starting about November):
  (a) with extended rains, starting September–October and short dry season June–August;
  (b) with extended rains, continuing to July, and short dry season August–October;
  (c) with standard rains (November–May) and long dry season June–October (5 months);
  (d) with shortened rains, December–April, and very long dry season May–November (7 months).
4 Double season rainfall (peaks about April and November):
  (a) with good to moderate rainfall November–December and April–May;
  (b) with very low rainfall and short seasons, sometimes mainly April;
  (c) with low rainfall, mostly November–December.

The climate characteristics of some eight typical East Africa savanna stations are found in Table 6.6. Maralal, Mbarara, and Sumbawanga are in zone III, Nakuru, Rumuruti, and Tabora are in zone IV, and Voi and Dodoma are in zone V. These statistics hide the variability of conditions both from place to place and from year to year. Rainfall varies from place to place because much of it comes in heavy localized storms; and from year to year macro-level East African conditions vary owing to the fluctuating character of the equatorial air masses.

The savanna areas of East Africa are nearly all over 800 m above sea level, and savanna is typical of the 1000–1500 m altitudinal zone. Soils are quite varied, though much of the area is underlain by granite rocks producing red/yellow tropical soils and their derivatives. This pattern is diversified locally by volcanic rocks, some of geologically recent origin. There is a general tendency toward low levels of nutrients in most savanna-area soils on gently sloping land. The soils with the highest nutrient supply are usually in isolated alluvial areas. Sloping lands, where drainage is better and production of newly weathered material somewhat faster, tend to be preferred for cultivation, though high levels of soil loss are also experienced from such lands. Thus a delicate balance between erosion and soil production must be maintained when these lands are used.

The soils in the area (Fig. 6.7) suggest a catena-type variation for many savanna areas. This variation is a factor in the detailed pattern of vegetation distribution and in many areas the pattern of land use. The term "catena" was coined in East Africa for a repetitive sequence of soils, correlated mostly with topography. In parts of the savanna area of East Africa, gently rolling country includes scattered small hills or ridges, gently sloping footslopes, and low-to-flat base slopes and valley floors. The steepest hillslopes are often covered with scrub and bush, the lower hillslopes are naturally savanna, and the valley bottoms are often grassland (Fig. 6.8). In Sukumaland, for example, the pattern of land use emphasizes maize and cotton sequentially on the slopes and grazing and rice in the valley bottoms, though the hilltops remain bush covered. Termites are an important soil-forming factor in many areas, helping in soil turnover and creating small zones of better aerated and more fertile soils.

Water is a scarce resource for natural and human systems alike in the savanna zone, though floods may also be a periodic problem. Rain comes in heavy storms. A good part of it flows overland into ephemeral streams and does not infiltrate into the soil to any great extent. In addition, the short and intense rainfall, combined with the generally low porosity of the underlying strata, means that in most areas there are but localized and limited supplies of groundwater for irrigation and other water supply demands. Thus a reliable water supply can usually only be provided when dams are built. Exceptions occur in the layered basaltic rocks and in a few basins of deeply weathered material which, being relatively porous, allow groundwater reservoirs to accumulate.

The savanna region of East Africa is not so densely populated that animals have lost their hold. Although the large game animals are mainly restricted within or near the game reserves (with a strong tendency to be increasingly so localized), smaller animals are found everywhere and insects and birds are all

Table 6.6 Climatic data for eight East African savanna stations.

Climate parameter	Number of recorded years	Mean monthly value												Annual values
		J	F	M	A	M	J	J	A	S	O	N	D	
Station: Maralal; Lat: 01°43′N, Long: 33°37′E, Alt: 3697 ft (1127 m)														
Rainfall (mm)	28	11	19	38	85	69	54	109	92	30	39	52	22	986 (max.) 620 460 (min.)
Air temperature (°C) max.	9	25.0	26.1	25.4	24.1	23.7	22.9	21.6	21.2	23.1	23.8	22.9	23.1	23.6
min.		7.2	7.4	9.3	11.1	10.3	8.6	9.1	8.8	7.5	8.2	9.2	8.1	8.7
Potential evaporation (E_0) (mm)	9	161	159	173	151	151	132	130	132	151	157	139	150	1786
Station: Rumuruti; Lat: 00°16′N, Long: 36°32′E, Alt: 6090 ft (1860 m)														
Rainfall (mm)	56	20	24	47	93	66	48	92	90	38	44	78	33	1006 (max.) 673 339 (min.)
Air temperature (°C) max.	14	26.9	27.8	27.6	26.4	26.0	25.5	24.2	24.0	26.1	26.6	25.1	25.1	25.9
min.		6.8	7.1	8.9	10.7	9.9	9.4	9.4	9.2	8.4	8.6	9.7	8.8	8.9
Potential evaporation (E_0) (mm)	14	181	177	196	171	168	149	150	158	178	186	167	178	2059
Station: * Mbarara; Lat: 00°37′S, Long: 30°39′E, Alt: 4734 ft (1443 m)														
Rainfall (mm)	60	44	62	97	122	81	26	21	61	97	106	113	77	1520 (max.) 907 532 (min.)
Air temperature (°C) max.	31	27.1	27.3	26.8	26.0	25.6	26.1	26.6	26.8	26.3	26.0	25.7	25.8	26.3
min.		14.5	14.8	15.0	15.0	14.8	14.0	13.5	14.6	14.7	14.8	14.7	14.3	14.6
Open water evaporation (mm) (10 in pan)	3	116	112	126	110	118	118	127	129	120	118	104	115	1413
Station: Tabora; Lat: 05°02′S, Long: 32°49′E, Alt: 4151 ft (1265 m)														
Rainfall (mm)	69	132	129	166	134	27	2	0	1	7	17	103	174	1390 (max.) 892 505 (min.)
Air temperature (°C) max.	25	27.6	28.1	28.0	27.7	27.8	27.9	28.2	29.4	31.0	32.1	30.7	28.0	25.4
min.		17.4	17.5	17.4	17.3	16.3	14.8	14.6	15.8	17.6	18.9	18.8	17.7	12.8
Potential evaporation (E_0) (mm)	24	166	158	177	171	179	175	200	220	231	244	200	173	1505

Station: Sumbawanga; Lat: 07°47'S, Long: 35°42'E, Alt: 5650 ft (1710 m)

Rainfall (mm)	34	156	138	164	90	21	2	0	2	5	9	77	154
													1149 (max.)
													818
													620 (min.)
Air temperature (°C) max.		23.0	23.8	24.0	24.1	23.4	23.3	24.1	24.5	26.1	26.8	25.4	24.1
min.		13.0	13.1	13.1	12.7	9.8	7.2	6.3	7.8	9.6	12.2	12.7	13.0
Potential evaporation (E_0) (mm)		161	151	160	147	139	124	143	162	176	208	188	164

Annual: Air temperature max. 24.4, min. 10.9; Potential evaporation (E_0) 1923

Station: Voi; Lat: 03°24'E, Long: 38°34'E, Alt: 1837 ft (560 m)

Rainfall (mm)	59	32	30	73	92	29	7	3	8	15	27	96	126
													1201 (max.)
													538
													184 (min.)
Air temperature (°C) max.		31.8	33.3	33.4	31.7	28.7	29.0	27.9	27.9	29.0	30.8	31.3	30.7
min.		20.4	20.4	21.0	20.2	20.2	18.4	17.5	17.4	17.8	18.9	20.2	20.7
Potential evaporation (E_0) (mm)		183	187	198	176	166	158	156	162	174	189	182	175

Annual: Air temperature max. 30.5, min. 19.4; Potential evaporation (E_0) 2106

Station: Dodoma; Lat: 06°05'S, Long: 37°43'E, Alt: 2860 ft (872 m)

Rainfall (mm)	52	151	115	123	51	5	1	0	1	5	20	106	
													965 (max.)
													578
													221 (min.)
Air temperature (°C) max.		29.3	29.3	29.1	28.7	28.0	27.3	26.6	27.3	29.2	30.6	31.7	30.6
min.		18.3	18.1	18.0	17.6	16.1	13.8	13.0	13.8	14.9	16.4	17.9	18.6
Potential evaporation (E_0) (mm)		167	153	160	149	160	150	160	188	210	229	209	188

Annual: Air temperature max. 29.0, min. 16.4; Potential evaporation (E_0) 2123

Station: Kongwa; Lat: 06°10'S, Long: 36°25'E, Alt: 3350 ft (1021 m)

Rainfall (mm)	11	131	112	93	62	6	0	1	1	1	18	118	
													752 (max.)
													544
													348 (min.)
Air temperature (°C) max.		30.5	29.9	30.5	29.3	28.7	28.2	27.5	28.5	30.1	31.6	32.8	31.5
min.		16.3	15.9	15.9	15.5	13.7	11.5	10.7	11.5	13.0	14.4	16.1	17.2
Potential evaporation (E_0) (mm)		163	150	155	132	133	131	140	159	191	223	210	180

Annual: Air temperature max. 29.9, min. 14.3; Potential evaporation (E_0) 1967

* E_0 data are not readily available for stations in Uganda; wherever possible open water pan evaporation values are given instead.

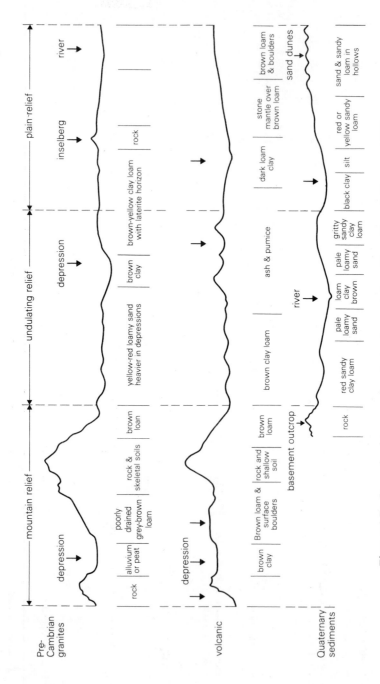

Figure 6.7 Range landscapes and typical soil associations (from Pratt & Gwynne 1977).

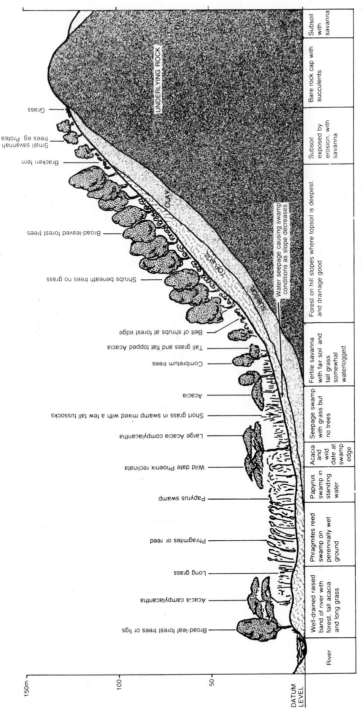

Figure 6.8 Cross-section through a ridge having a constant 1250 mm rainfall showing the variation of vegetation according to the site and soil (from Brown & Cocheme 1973).

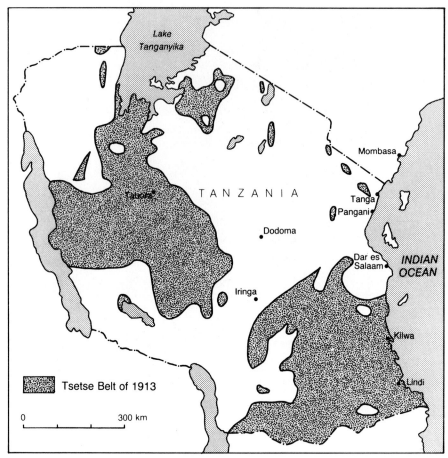

Figure 6.9 (a) The tsetse belts in Tanzania (Tanganika), 1913 (from Kjekshus 1977). (*Continued*)

part of the scene. It is no small coincidence that farmers in the area see pests and animals – especially birds, wild pigs, and monkeys – as the major scourge in their efforts to produce crops.

The East African savanna appears to be still largely in its virgin state, but it has for the most part undergone major changes in the past 100 years and probably many other changes in the years before. Kjekshus (1977) shows that until the 1880s much of the savanna zone of East Africa was a grazing area with very large herds of domestic stock. Then, in the last part of the 19th century, the combination of the colonial intervention and the devastating widespread rinderpest epidemic resulted in many human deaths and the death of a very large proportion of the livestock. Consequently the intensity of land use in the area greatly declined and the focus of population and livestock retreated to the valleys. More woody vegetation gained hold, fire became less frequent, and

236

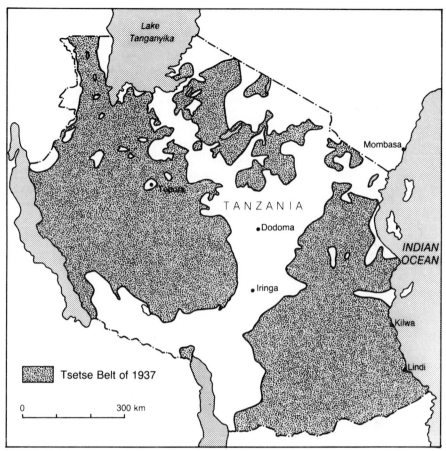

Figure 6.9 (*continued*)   (b) The tsetse belts in Tanzania (Tanganika), 1937 (from Kjekshus 1977).

bushland and thicket replaced what had been savanna grassland. Tsetse fly became established in wide areas as bushland grew in extent. This pest helped to prevent the livestock and savanna grasses from becoming re-established (Fig. 6.9).

The East African savanna differs from that in much of the rest of Africa in that the area is less densely peopled than the West African savanna and has a greater area devoted to game reserves than most other parts of the continent. Recent government policies are another factor creating differences in East African savannas. Within East Africa there are different priorities and emphasis between Kenya with its important private and government ranches, Tanzania with its apparently large unused areas and Ujama villages, and Uganda where small farms occupy much of the savanna area. National as well as ecologic issues are important in the problems involved.

237

THE DEVELOPMENT ISSUES

Several main development issues were identified earlier in this case study. They relate to trade-offs and conflicts in the use of land and water, inappropriate patterns and levels of use, and constraints in the physical environment which delimit use. A basic condition underlying these issues is change. Change in East Africa in general has involved dramatic changes in the numbers of people, changes in styles of living, imposed colonial governments, and now change through the political and economic patterns of independence. The growth in numbers of people has affected the savanna area less than some other areas and has had a greater impact in Kenya than in the other countries. In Kenya the savanna areas are partly located on the margins of the more humid uplands. As population numbers have increased on the uplands there has been an outward movement into the drier savanna areas. This, coupled with the natural increase of numbers in the savanna, has created a potentially difficult imbalance between resources and people. In Tanzania and Uganda the savanna areas have experienced growth in numbers of people and animals, but locally this has not yet had a severe impact on the land resource. But the other changes have had just as much of an impact on the savanna as on other parts of the area.

Conflicts of land use   Although a large part of the East African land area is savanna, conflicts in land use result in major environmental and developmental problems. In different parts of the area the conflicts involve the use of land for: (a) traditional grazing; (b) modern ranches; (c) irrigation; (d) game parks; and (e) agriculture.

Allocation of large areas to game parks has been an important part of the promotion of the tourist industry, a major foreign exchange earner; furthermore, it has helped in providing large area habitats where the world heritage of savanna animals can be preserved. But several kinds of problems have arisen. First, animal populations in some park areas have grown beyond the local carrying capacity and destruction of vegetation and soils has become a problem. Elephant numbers in the Amboseli (Kenya) game park and wildebeeste in Masai Mara (Kenya) and Serengeti (Tanzania) game parks are examples. When elephant numbers increase, their effect on vegetation is dramatic as the large animals regularly uproot or otherwise damage trees up to 10 m high in their attempt to reach succulent leaves. Even when elephant numbers remain constant, their impact on the vegetation is immense as their grazing territory has decreased because of human activity and trees no longer have enough time to regenerate themselves. It is analogous to the situation that results when periods of fallow decrease in farming systems.

Second, local people have been denied the use of land that was previously theirs. This has either caused them to poach in the game parks or has increased land pressures on the margins of the parks. Third, the parks are in most cases only a part of the habitat of most animals, seasonally or otherwise. Many animals move out of the park areas and cause damage to the nearby farms and crops.

In general, the East African governments have been far-sighted in their allocation of game park reservations, but there·has been a cost for the peoples of

Table 6.7 Land–use conflicts.

	Traditional grazing	Modern ranches	Game parks	Agriculture	Irrigation
traditional grazing		Masai, Kenya	Masai, Tanzania	Masai, Kenya (bottom lands)	
modern ranches	Masai, Kenya		southern Kenya near Nairobi		
game parks agriculture	Masai, Tanzania Kijado, Kenya, Kitui, Kenya, central Uganda	near Nairobi		near parks of Uganda	Mwea, Kenya, Kilimanjaro, Tanzania, Mbeya, Tanzania
irrigation				Mwea, Kenya, Kilimanjaro, Mbeya, Tanzania	

the areas concerned and political pressure from them to reduce that cost by reducing or otherwise modifying game areas. Table 6.7 sets out the major patterns of conflict in land use and the zones of their most major impact.

Pressure on grazing resources   One consequence of competition for land in the savanna resulting from expansion of agricultural lands is the concentration of grazing economies into smaller areas than formerly. A good part of the grazing land in East Africa is found in the semi-arid and arid areas of Kenya and Uganda but, as indicated earlier, grazing is a common land use in the savanna. In Uganda about 70,500 km^2 of savanna is, or could be, used for grazing, in Tanzania maybe 80,000 km^2 fall into this category, whereas in Kenya about 112,000 km^2 qualify. These figures rightly suggest that huge areas are available but, as analyzed earlier, large parts are designated for game reserves, other areas are tsetse infested, and still others are used for agriculture.

In this century, the reduction in land available for grazing has been accompanied by great increases in animal numbers. It is estimated that in 1900 there were 3 million cattle in East Africa; now it is estimated there are 25 million. What is not clear is how many there were before the rinderpest epidemic. Besides cattle, there are more than 12 million sheep and goats, though some of these and a proportion of the cattle live outside the savanna zone. It is a reasonable estimate that 10–12 million cattle and 6–8 million sheep and goats live in the savanna zone as defined for this case study.

There is clear evidence of decreasing land availability and increasing animal numbers as a general pattern. It is not so clear what is the full extent of the environmental impact of these changes. There are relatively few detailed and focused studies. Dunne (1977) in southern Kenya carried out a reconnaisance analysis of Kajiado district, which is partly in the savanna zone. He concluded that as a whole the effects of an animal grazing were not as bad as had been postulated. There were probably too many animals to ensure the continued maintenance of the range, but the process of deterioration seemed slow and capable of being reversed. On the other hand, he did identify specific areas and types of areas where there was a significant deterioration and a real danger of irreversible degradation. In his judgement, the problem could not best be dealt with by general destocking, a course that is so often recommended. General destocking is difficult to implement because cattle ownership varies, some people having herds of tens or hundreds of animals and others having only 2–6 head of livestock. Thus, any decrease in cattle could result in large numbers of inhabitants not being able to make a livelihood. In the Kajiado situation, Dunne recommends that controlled grazing with particular care in the use of vulnerable areas would solve most of the problem.

Rapp *et al.* (1972), in a study of the Dodoma region and other parts of Tanzania, found significant problems in land productivity, sediment yields and reservoir sedimentation which seem to result from the intensity of land use and the numbers of cattle in particular. In fact, the erosion in this area was encouraged by a reliable water supply (dam reservoir) that was part of a development project. Because of the reliable water supply, more cattle were brought into the area by their owners. This resulted in overgrazing the limited grasses in the area. Now the project is in peril and inhabitants are worse off, since a large part of the soil resource is destroyed for future generations.

In general it is probably correct to conclude that the current levels of animal stocking on the currently available land, and using the present pattern of land use, have resulted in a general degradation of the soils and vegetation of the area. There are a number of localities in the savanna where this process has resulted in serious long-term changes in the nature of the resource base.

Excessive use of wood and charcoal It has long been tradition for the peoples of the savanna to use the woody part of the ecosystem for a variety of purposes. Wood is needed for house construction, particularly 10–20 cm diameter logs for sideposts and small logs for roofs and intervening support. Cut thornbush is also used extensively for protecting agricultural plots from animals and for boundary enclosures to protect domestic animals from wild animals. But the most extensive use of wood is for fuel. Dried wood is burned directly for cooking, for heat on cold nights, or to produce smoke and fire to keep bugs, insects, and animals away. Vast quantities of wood are transformed into charcoal by a process which dissipates 20–60 percent of the heating value of the original material but produces a lighter, smaller product which is much more easily transported.

Several factors have been at work in the savanna areas of East Africa that reduce the quantity of wood available. In some areas, especially in Kenya, land registration has reduced access of people to woodlands and resulted in increasing pressure on the remaining public areas. In most places increasing numbers of people have contributed to this end, and in many places the growth of urban areas has created a demand for wood and charcoal which has been met by the heavy localized woodcutting around the larger towns. Lastly, in Kenya in particular there was a period in the late 1970s when export of charcoal to Saudi Arabia became a very lucrative enterprise. This has now been officially banned.

It is clear that a number of pressures have meant that each of these trends has increased in intensity in the last decade. Population growth, increasing unemployment, urban growth, and export opportunities all combine to emphasize the pattern of change.

The result is hard to quantify but easier to document through illustrative example. Large areas of the savanna and drier parts of Kenya were stripped of sizeable tree growth by charcoal exporters. The area around Tabora in Tanzania has lost its woody vegetation to meet the needs of tobacco curing (1 ha of tobacco needs 1 ha of woodland per year for curing). More generally, as people and agriculture expand into savanna areas, woody growth rapidly decreases under the demands of the new situation.

The local impact of these general trends is very varied. In parts of Tanzania the savanna zone is dominated by thick woody growth; in other parts of Tanzania, and more generally in Kenya and Uganda, there are areas where the availability of wood for local energy and construction is very low. Costs of wood and charcoal increase steadily and the pressure on local peoples grows likewise. In a similar way, the pressure on the environment in these locations grows steadily, in some places critically.

The reduction of woody plants is also resulting in a soil erosion and/or soil

241

deterioration as the surface is exposed to rainsplash and crusts tend to form on the bare ground. This, along with the poorer soil, limits the development of new tree growth. The resulting change in vegetation in turn affects the water resources of the area. A greater portion of rainfall flows over the land, reducing soil moisture. In addition, the greater overland flow moves more sediment into the streams. Behind the agricultural dams built in the area, sediment has increased and the capacity of the reservoirs has been reduced. This means that in many areas there is no longer sufficient water to carry through the whole dry season. A decrease in the economic potential of the area has thus resulted from the interaction between vegetation, soil, water, and human activities.

The impact of inappropriate development projects   Many of the environment and development issues of East Africa are those caused by changes in the traditional agriculture and livelihood systems; others are the result of development activities. Although the focus of many discussions of this issue has been upon recent impacts, the importance of development has been a factor for a long time.

One early example of the kind of problem involved is from Dodoma in central Tanzania. In this region, the construction of the railway in the early part of the century and the setting up of a wood-fired power station in the town resulted in major deforestation of the surrounding area. The current pattern of this area's soil degradation and rapid sedimentation is usually blamed on current farming practices. But the beginning of the problem probably dates back to the beginning of woodcutting for fuel and power.

Two more modern development activities serve to illustrate the type of problems involved. First, in the Masai area of Kenya new developments have disrupted traditional patterns of land and water use. The Masai in Kenya traditionally use a strategy where their normal grazing areas are the rolling plains of south Kenya. In years of average rainfall these grasslands provide an adequate range for the herd, though in the drier parts of the year use is made of wetter bottom lands. These same bottom lands are vital reserves which are held back to be used extensively in dry years as well as in the dry parts of the year. However, in the last decade, much of this land has been taken over for small farms or is incorporated into ranches often run on modern lines by expatriate or Kenyan farmers. This removal of an important component of the Masai system by modern farming greatly undermines the basis of their traditional system and increases the likelihood of overgrazing and steady degradation of their dry season pasture. It also makes the area very vulnerable when there is a series of dry years.

Low levels of agricultural productivity   At several points in this chapter the problem of low agricultural production from savanna lands is discussed. East Africa is no exception to the general pattern, and is no exception either to the paucity of detailed data on this issue.

At the national level, it is clear that per hectare production of most crops is at best stagnant, and there is some evidence of a slight general decline. Within the East African national framework, the savanna areas of Kenya and Tanzania appear to have the greatest problems in this respect, with apparent decline in general production offset by some local examples of improved land management and productivity. For example, the tobacco areas around Tabora are definitely producing more maize per hectare in response to closely supervised extension efforts in the tobacco–maize farming agricultural system in the area. However, other parts of the area are being degraded by the removal of vegetation to cure tobacco. In Machakos, Kenya, some middle-sized farms (20–80 ha) are adapting a well-balanced package of inputs which increase yields. The Katumani maize hybrids have greatly helped yields in some areas. Yet these farms appear to be counterbalanced by areas of poorly managed much smaller farms with little scope or capital available for modern inputs and, as a result, continue low levels of production. An important issue for the future is to get a better idea of the balance between these two trends and the specific human and physical factors involved.

Conclusion

In East Africa the savanna area is a very major part of the total resource base. It is an ecosystem which is occupied in very different ways in different parts of the area and which does in fact have different kinds of potential, especially in its relation to other ecosystems. The major problems of the savanna ecosystem constitute most of the major problems of East Africa resource management, and effective approaches to them will be vital to the area. The problems of levels of agricultural productivity, patterns of land-use change, supplies of wood and charcoal, and the continual viability of the game parks are central to the development of the countries concerned. Although, in respect to other parts of Africa, East Africa is well known, we still know far from enough to treat these environmental and developmental problems adequately.

7 The highlands

Introduction

No single criterion exists for determining when an area within Africa falls in the highland category. One arbitrary guideline delimits Africa into "high" Africa and "low" Africa, using 1000 m above sea level as the boundary between these two categories (Fig. 1.4). Included within the "high" Africa category are a diverse set of lands with little in common except altitude. They include nonvolcanic mountain ranges, such as the Atlas Mountains in Morocco; old crystalline land surfaces with the highest points being rock inselbergs, such as the Guinea Highlands; high volcanic plateaus deeply dissected by stream erosion, such as the Ethiopian Plateau; and isolated mountains, such as Kilimanjaro and Mount Kenya. The largest part of the land within the "high" Africa category consists of plateaus and lands of relatively moderate relief over large areas, such as the Serengeti "Plains" (Fig. 7.1).

Another criterion, previously used, restricted the term "highlands" to those tropical high plateau surfaces that attracted European settlement. The best examples of such areas are the Kenya Highlands, which were often referred to as the "White Highlands" before independence, and the relatively level highlands

Figure 7.1 The Serengeti plains near the Tanzanian and Kenyan border.

244

of Zimbabwe. Although the first criterion of "high" Africa and "low" Africa is too general and includes such a diversity of lands as to preclude generalization, the latter is too restrictive and today, owing to migration and resettlement and changing political economic circumstances, it is irrelevant.

A recent World Meteorological Organization (WMO) publication (Brown & Cochemé 1973) limits highlands to areas over 1500 m based on agroclimatologic criteria. For the purposes of this chapter, we shall utilize their boundaries. In addition, we shall limit our discussion to highlands that are critical in the economic development of the country. The highlands meeting these two standards are located within eastern and central Africa and include lands in Ethiopia, Kenya, Tanzania, and Uganda, as well as a very large percentage of the countries of Rwanda and Burundi (Fig. 7.2). Other highlands in Zimbabwe and Malawi meet these criteria of elevation and economic importance; however, these latter two areas are discussed in the next chapter within the context of southern Africa since their economic and environmental relations differ from the eastern and central African highlands due to political factors.

The highlands of eastern and central Africa

In Ethiopia approximately 50 million hectares are above 1500 m; this results in a little more than 40 percent of the country being classified as highland. On these lands, approximately 60 percent of the population lives. It is the main agricultural area, and all historical capitals, as well as Addis Ababa, have been situated in the highlands west of the Ethiopian Rift Valley.

In Kenya about 11 million hectares are highland. Nairobi, the largest city as well as the government, industrial, and business center of the country, is a highland city. Farms in the highlands account by value for about 70 percent of the Kenyan export crops as well as a very significant proportion of the agricultural production oriented to the domestic market.

Nineteen million hectares are classified as highland in Tanzania. The highland clusters in the northeast, including Mount Meru, Kilimanjaro, the Pare Mountains, and the Usambara Mountains, are economically the most important highland areas in the country. The Southern Highlands, both because of their remoteness from the Dar es Salaam market and, until recently, their poor transportation linkages with other parts of the nation, do not contribute to the national economy to the same degree as the northern clusters despite the fact that they are moderately populated. But the existence of coal, limestone, and iron ore in the extreme south near Lake Malawi, along with improvements in the railroad systems connecting this area to other important Tanzanian areas, means that the Southern Highlands are a potential area for development and are becoming of increasing importance in the national context.

Uganda has 3 million hectares of highland. The Mount Elgon area just east of Mbale, the Ugandan portion of the continuation of the western Kenyan Highlands, is an important coffee area. The Kigezi area along the Rwandan border is one of the most densely populated agricultural areas in East Africa. On this highland, terracing has permitted the utilization of steep lands for agricul-

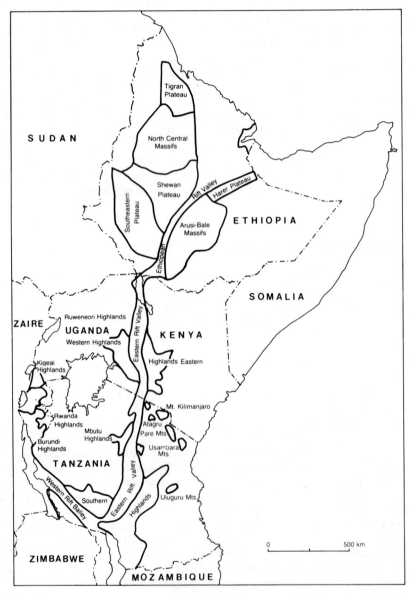

Figure 7.2 The major topogaphic units of Ethiopia, Kenya, Tanzania, Rwanda, and Burundi.

tural purposes. The Ruwenzori Plateau in the extreme western portion of the country is important economically for its tea production.

With only 26,338 km^2 of land, Rwanda has over 50 percent of its land within the highlands. About 1.5 million hectares are highland, and this is the area where the overwhelming majority of the 6 million inhabitants live. The economy of Rwanda is largely rural with about 90 percent of the working population engaged in agriculture. Its major export crop, coffee, and the majority of its food production for local consumption are grown on the highlands. The lands at lower elevations within Rwanda are drier and are not nearly as potentially productive as the highlands. Also, a national wildlife park (L'Akagara) occupies a significant proportion of these lower lands, and they are thus removed from the agricultural and livestock sectors. However, the area of the park need not remain what it is today. Recently the area of wildlife grazing was reduced and malaria controlled to permit colonization of a portion of these lower lands for resettlement of former highland residents. This was necessitated because of the high population pressure existing throughout the Rwandan Highlands, especially in the northern portion of the country.

Burundi (27,834 km^2), slightly larger than Rwanda, also has slightly over 50 percent of its land classified as highland. The approximate 1.5 million hectares of Burundian Highland overall is not as rugged in relief as the hilly Rwandan terrain. Over 50 percent of Burundi's highlands fall within its central plateau, an area with elevations between 1500 and 2000 m. In the extreme western portion of the plateau, the plateau drops rapidly down to Lake Tanganyika (about 775 m), providing the greatest local relief in the country. Average population densities range from over 350 to 100 per km^2 in the Rwandan and Burundi highlands. Over 98 percent of the female population and 88 percent of the male population are engaged in agriculture. The two countries of Rwanda and Burundi, though small in area, are the most densely populated nations in Africa. The majority of their populations live in the highlands. Given the population pressure on the land in some areas of these countries, the land resources are under heavy stress. This attribute is common in a large proportion of other African highland areas.

The highland areas of eastern and central Africa are generally areas of high population, steep slopes, and sufficient precipitation for agricultural activities. These highland areas, when farmed or overgrazed, are especially prone to environmental problems. Their physical characteristics of high potential geomorphic energy, resulting from high elevations and moderate-to-steep slopes along with moderate precipitation, make most highland areas environmentally fragile. In most of the countries the highlands are the most productive areas both potentially and in practice. The maintenance of good environmental conditions is thus critical for national development strategies. The highlands are often areas of reliable rains, good soils, no major malaria habitats, and minimal insect problems compared to lowland tropical areas. They are places where many mid-latitude agricultural crops can grow. In addition, as these highland areas are the source and the primary contributors of water for the Nile system, the economics of Sudan and Egypt are to a degree linked to the environmental conditions of the eastern and central African highland areas.

Characteristics of highland environments

Climate

The climate of most highland areas is usually related to the climate of the surrounding lowland in seasonal characteristics. This is particularly true for the annual temperature cycle and the times of occurrence of the wet and dry seasons. But both absolute temperature and precipitation change markedly with height above sea level. Average temperatures decrease about 6.5° per 1000 m. Conversely, precipitation generally increases with elevation up to heights of between 2800 and 4000 m. Above these elevations, owing to the decrease in atmospheric water vapor, precipitation begins to decrease.

Precipitation

Figure 7.3 shows the generalized precipitation patterns for Ethiopia, and eastern and central Africa. In Rwanda the areas of higher precipitation (greater than 1600 mm) occur in the northeast in the Ruhengeri area where the Volcanoes National Park (Karisimbi, 4507 m) is situated and along the north–south mountain zone just east of Lake Kivu. Both of these areas are the highest zones in the country. In Burundi this pattern continues southward decreasing rapidly south of Mount Heha (2670 m) where the land decreases in elevation. A small island of high precipitation in the south-central portion of the country occurs over the Kibimi Highlands, which exceed 2500 m (Fig. 7.3b). The same general pattern of high rainfall associated with highlands is reflected in Figure 7.3c for the three East African countries. A second area of high precipitation resulting from local lake–land wind systems is also noted along the shores of Lake Victoria. A comparison between Figures 7.2 and 7.3c shows that higher rainfall occurs in the highlands of Ethiopia too. An average annual rainfall of over 2000 mm occurs on the southwestern plateau in the vicinity of Ghecha. Everywhere on the plateau of Ethiopia average precipitation is over 1400 mm per year. But in dry years, such as 1984, the rainfall can be significantly less. The lower-elevation portions of the country are considerably drier.

The exact patterns of precipitation reflect not only elevation but also the interactions between wind and pressure systems, topographic orientation, and moisture sources. The pattern of rainfall in the vicinity of Mount Kenya illustrates many of the relationships between highlands and precipitation (Fig. 7.4). The relationship between wind systems, elevation, and topographic orientation is evident from this figure. The southeastern slopes of Mount Kenya, beginning near Embu, show an increase in precipitation of about 2 mm/m of altitude between 1400 and 2000 m (5000–7150 ft). At approximately 2800 m (9000 ft), precipitation begins to decrease until at the summit only about 850 mm (33 in) of rain (or snow) falls. The rôle of topographic orientation, that is the exposure of the land to the moisture-bearing winds, is clear. The southeastern portion of the mountain (windward side) at an equal elevation receives more rain than other exposures. The minimum occurs on the northwestern slopes (leeward side). Elevation for elevation along Kilimanjaro the same relationship holds true. The southeast receives more rain than the northwest. The critical rôle of highlands in Kenya is reflected in Table 7.1. Only 15

248

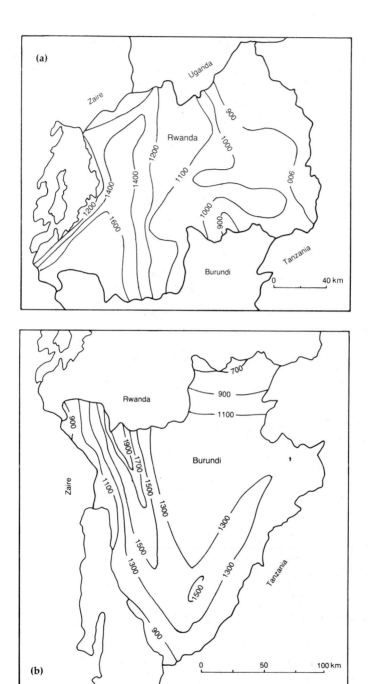

Figure 7.3 Average annual precipitation (mm) patterns: (a) Rwanda (from Prioul & Sirven 1981); (b) Burundi. (Modified from Lasserre & Menault 1979). (*Continued*)

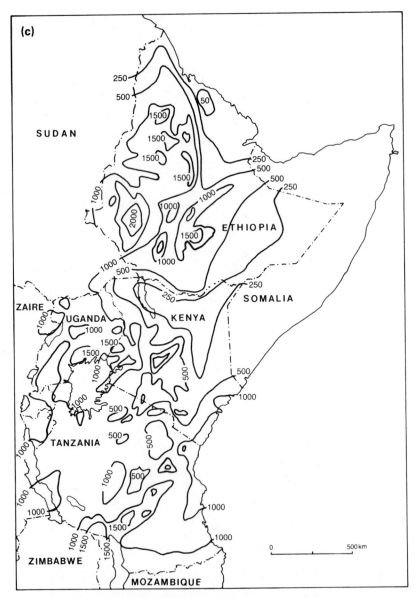

Figure 7.3 (*continued*)   (c) East Africa (from Griffiths 1972).

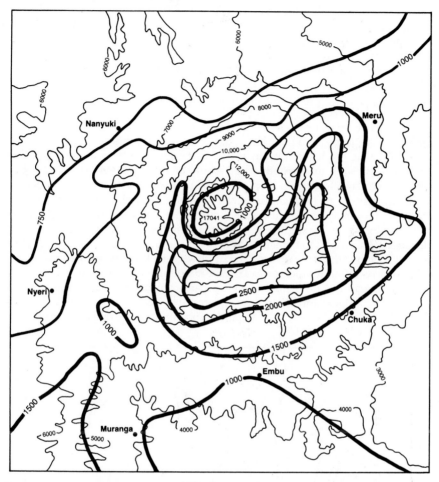

Figure 7.4 Average annual precipitation in the Mount Kenya area. Maximum rainfall occurs in the south and west of the summit on the windward slopes relative to the monsoon winds. (Modified from Cochemé 1973.)

Table 7.1 Percentage of land receiving selective amounts of annual precipitation in four out of five years.

Rainfall (mm)	Kenya	Tanzania	Uganda	East Africa
<500	72	16	12	35
500–750	13	33	10	20
750–1250	12	47	72	41
>1250	3	4	6	4

percent of the nation's total area receives over 750 mm of rain in 4 out of 5 years, and most of this area is highland. The lowlands in Rwanda, Burundi, and Ethiopia likewise are dry compared to their highland counterparts. The drier lowlands in all of these countries are not as important in contributing to the national economies or in supporting large populations.

Temperature

Figure 7.5a for Rwanda reflects the impact of elevation on temperature. The highest lands, just east of Lake Kivu, have annual temperatures slightly less than 15°C, whereas the lower terrain to the east is about 6°C warmer. The same pattern holds true in Burundi (Fig. 7.5b). In Kenya a comparison between Mombasa (50 m), having an average annual temperature of 26.5°C, and Nairobi (1800 m), having an 18°C annual mean temperature, reflects the altitude aspect affecting temperatures. Additional factors affect temperatures. The eastern Kenyan Highlands are slightly warmer than the western Highlands at the same elevations; this has been explained as being due to the greater cloud cover in the west. Likewise, the Ruwenzori Plateau in western Uganda is often misty, and the cooler resulting temperatures are favorable for tea cultivation.

In the equatorial highlands of eastern and central Africa the mean annual temperature range is small, just as in equatorial lowlands. For example, it is only about 2°C in the Kigezi area of Uganda. In southern Tanzania it is about 6°C,

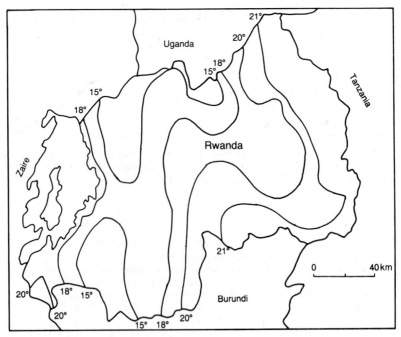

Figure 7.5 (a) Average annual temperatures, Rwanda. (Modified from Prioul & Sirven 1981.) (*Continued*)

252

whereas in Ethiopia at Addis Ababa it is 5°C. Because of the tropical location and elevation of the African highlands, mild temperatures exist throughout the whole year. This permits the raising of grazing stock such as dairy cattle and crops such as wheat, maize, and barley found in the middle latitudes. Of course different varieties often need to be introduced to respond to the different diurnal patterns of sunlight and temperature ranges experienced in the tropical highlands compared to those in the middle latitudes.

Evapotranspiration: moisture surplus and deficit in highlands

One of the most important aspects of the climatic environment related to potential development is the availability of water. Moisture availability in a specific area, when not considering exogenous sources, is a result of the surplus of precipitation over evaporation and transpiration. As defined by the WMO, potential evaporation is the amount of water evaporated from an open water

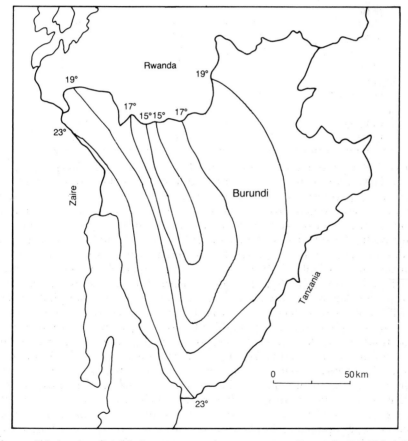

Figure 7.5 *(continued)* (b) Average annual temperatures, Burundi. (Modified from Lasserre & Menault 1979.)

253

Table 7.2 Annual potential evapotranspiration in Ethiopia, Kenya, Tanzania, and Rwanda.

Location	Altitude (m)	Precipitation (mm)	Potential evapotranspiration (mm)
Ethiopia			
Addis Ababa	2390	1071	1289
Asmara	2325	542	1573
Jimma	1676	1483	1259
Kenya			
Eldoret	2287	1005	1418
Equator	2762	1222	1388
Kericho	1982	1837	1211
Kiambu	1738	888	1387
Nairobi	1661	830	1295
Tanzania			
Loliondo	2134	896	1349
Mbeya	1736	883	1306
Njombe	1900	1155	1078
Sao Hill	1981	936	1231
Uganda			
Fort Portal	1539	1508	1356
Rwanda			
Robona	1706	1171	1392
Rwerere	2312	1166	1239

surface. Transpiration is the loss of water through plant pores. Evapotranspiration is the sum of the water evaporated from the soil and transpired by plants. Potential evapotranspiration is the maximum quantity of moisture that can be lost to the atmosphere from an area having complete plant cover and an unlimited supply of soil moisture. Actual evapotranspiration is the amount of water lost by the soil–plant system under existing meteorological, plant, and soil conditions. The figures presented for potential evapotranspiration for some highland areas (Table 7.2) use the Penman method explained in most climatological texts. Briefly, the Penman method utilizes temperature, vapor pressure, insolation, and elevation to estimate potential evapotranspiration. The annual amounts of potential evapotranspiration are relatively moderate and uniform throughout the African highlands. For comparison, in eastern Africa, at locations near sea level, potential evapotranspiration values of over 2200 mm are common. Because the highland locations have lower potential evapotranspiration, a highland area with a precipitation value equal to that of a lowland area in the same latitudinal zone will be more humid. Given that most African highlands also have greater precipitation than their lowland counterparts, the importance of highlands as water-source areas as well as agricultural areas in the economic development of the countries is clearly evident. This is emphasized by the relatively dry nature of much of the remaining portions of the countries with highlands.

254

One additional aspect of the cooler temperatures found in African highland climates that is an advantage agriculturally compared to the warmer lowlands concerns the generally prevailing lower potential evaporation in these areas. In the lowlands the potential evaporation is very high during the warmest seasons. The potential evapotranspiration, though lower in the highlands, is still high. Potential evapotranspiration is important in terms of agricultural yields since it represents the evaporation from the atmosphere required for a plant to maintain its proper internal temperature. When it is very high, as in some of the lowlands, even if sufficient water moisture exists in the soil, often there is evidence of wilting by mid-afternoon because the plants cannot conduct water from the soil to the leaves fast enough. This lowers the crop yield. In the hot and dry environments found throughout the lower lands in Africa, agricultural yields are constrained for many crops, even if sufficient water exists for irrigation, due to the limited moisture flow from the roots to the leaves. In the highlands, with their cooler temperatures and their lower potential evapotranspiration rates, wilting does not occur if sufficient moisture exists. Agricultural yields are thus not lowered by wilting if there is enough moisture in the soils. Additionally, plants have lower respiration rates at night in the highlands than in their tropical lowland counterparts due to the lower evening temperatures. This increases the net productivity of highland plants.

As illustrated in Table 7.2, most stations in the highlands have less annual precipitation than potential evapotranspiration. A comparison of mean monthly evapotranspiration with mean monthly rains gives an estimate of the extent to which sufficient precipitation occurs to allow plant growth not to be hindered by moisture shortages. Table 7.3 presents such data for Addis Ababa. During the four months when a moisture surplus exists, a large percentage of the surplus moisture is stored in the soil. It can be inferred that on average Addis Ababa has a good five-month growing season (June through October), with the additional month resulting from the plants' utilizing the soil moisture surplus stored

Table 7.3 Mean annual water balance: Addis Ababa.

	Evapotranspiration (mm)	Rain (mm)	Water deficit (mm)	Water surplus (mm)
January	107	23	84	–
February	105	25	80	–
March	129	55	74	–
April	125	81	44	–
May	123	56	67	–
June	102	113	–	11
July	83	258	–	175
August	87	260	–	173
September	95	161	–	66
October	120	28	92	–
November	109	2	107	–
December	104	9	95	–
Year	1289	1071	643	425

during the rainy season. The duration of the periods in which rainfall exceeds potential evapotranspiration is one of the best indices of an area's agricultural potential. The magnitude of the deficits are an indication of the amount of water needed for irrigation to extend the growing season. The matching of the duration of crops' growth cycles to that of an area's period of water availability is an important strategy for increasing agricultural output.

Hydrology

Matching the specific precipitation patterns of tropical highland areas to their potential evapotranspiration patterns not only gives an indication of the time and duration of the growing season but can also be used to approximate the hydrologic flow characteristics of local streams found in the areas. The mean monthly precipitation distribution for Kabgayi is presented in Figure 7.6. For Kabgayi (located in the heart of the Central Plateau of Rwanda) the average annual precipitation is between 1000 and 1100 mm. The annual potential evapotranspiration is approximately 1350 mm whereas the estimated actual evapotranspiration is 815 mm. The reason the actual evapotranspiration is less than the potential evapotranspiration is that during the dry season, when evapotranspiration is high, very little moisture exists. Thus little evapotranspiration occurs. A hydrograph of the River Nyabarongo, a tributary of the Akagera River, reflects the precipitation–evapotranspiration relationship in the Central Plateau in this area (Fig. 7.6). The discharge of the river represents the surplus of precipitation over actual evapotranspiration. The amount of stream runoff in a stream basin, along with its annual pattern, is largely the balance between precipitation and evapotranspiration. The fact that the hydrograph varies less than the precipitation pattern reflects to a large degree the amount of moisture surplus that infiltrates into the soil and enters the water table. This water, which flows as groundwater, emerges into the river system at a slower rate than the surface water runoff, due to the low velocity of groundwater. It is the groundwater flow that permits a river to have water in it continuously throughout the dry season.

The balance between evaporation and precipitation is one of the critical factors that determine the flow characteristics of streams and lakes. Lake Tanganyika's hydrologic characteristics reflect some of the interactions between evaporation and precipitation in the highlands of Rwanda and Burundi, the major watershed for the lake. The slight discharge from the lake illustrates that although the highlands are a good moisture area for agriculture this is not due to a large annual surplus of moisture. It is a result of the precipitation being concentrated in two seasons of moisture that permit two growing seasons in these countries. The dry periods between these wet seasons are characterized by dusty conditions. The dust results from the decrease in plant cover during these periods that permits the winds to remove some of the finer soil components from the exposed bare ground. If the same amount of precipitation was evenly distributed throughout the year, both Rwanda and Burundi would have a lower agricultural potential, due to the lack of moisture surplus.

A number of streams flow into the lake, but the major tributary of the lake is the Ruzizi; its source is Lake Kivu. The outlet of Lake Tanganyika is the Lukuga

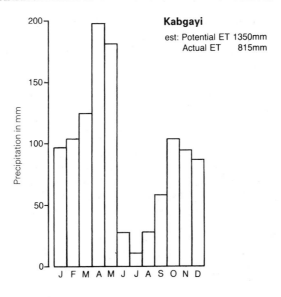

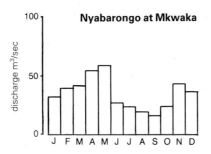

Figure 7.6 Annual precipitation pattern for Kabgayi in central Rwanda and hydrograph for the Nyabarongo River at Mkwaka in central Rwanda.

River at Kalémie (Albertville), Zaire, which is one of the sources of the Zaire River. In many years the outlet has only intermittent discharges. This is a result of a rough balance between the evaporation from the lake, the precipitation directly falling on the surface, and the inflow from the tributaries. This balance results from the approximate equality between annual precipitation and evapotranspiration for this portion of the highlands. In fact to ensure some outflow during some months in most years, at Kalémie in 1878 the outlet was artificially lowered.

Today the annual fluctuation of the lake is about 1 m. The lake rise reflects the flow régime of the local rivers. Beginning in December and ending in March, the lake gradually rises. This reflects the precipitation surplus in the watersheds of Lakes Kivu and Tanganyika during the period, as well as the time required for the water to flow through the system. The evaporation from the lake is at a maximum in September (167 mm) and a minimum in February (124 mm). The total annual evaporation from the lake is about 1700 mm.

Along with the evaporation and precipitation balances, the nature of the soil and underlying rocks, the vegetation cover, and the steepness of the land are other factors affecting the hydrology of surface waters. In the highlands, because of the elevation and steepness of the lands, a high potential for rapid surface water runoff exists when the vegetation cover is reduced.

The natural vegetation cover for most of the eastern and central highlands was forest cover. Under this type of cover, the canopy of forests intercepts rainfall and provides a temporary storage in the form of water droplets adhering to the leaves, branches, and trunks of the trees. Further temporary storage is provided by the pore spaces in the organic litter on the forest floor resulting from leaf-fall and the existence of pores in the soil due to the roots. This temporary storage dampens out the peaks of the storms and the rain water flows to the stream channels in a relatively regulated flow. Pereira (1971) reviewed the importance of managing ground cover to regulate the water flows in highland areas. His work was based on a controlled experiment near Kericho, Kenya, in the moist highlands overlooking Lake Victoria. The immediate effect of forest clearing in this area was a fourfold increase in the peak discharges of streams after rain events. By implementing major soil conservation procedures, including contour planting, planting grasses and other cover crops, it was possible to establish a tea plantation and minimize these peak discharges resulting from vegetation alteration. By the time the mature tea plantation was established, the total water yield and dry-season flows were approximately what they were under natural forest conditions. However, the stormflow peaks, although small, were double those existing under natural conditions.

Tea is one of the best crop covers in the cooler portions of the highlands if forests are cleared for agricultural activities. Annual crops with lower crop cover will always result in greater peak flows, in part due to the fact that they give lower ground cover and have lower water needs than forests. Even the better crops such as tea or heavily mulched coffee result in greater peak flows. Thus, when land clearing occurs in the highlands, under optimal conditions reservoir storage needs to be built to minimize the impact of the increase in peak flows during rain events. In actuality, tree clearing in most highland areas is occurring without any controls. This results in greater peak flows, greater raindrop impact on the soils, and lower storage, since the rainfall peaks are not dampened by the vegetation cover. The lower infiltration reduces stream flows during the drier seasons; the greater surface water flows increase soil erosion, which further reduces the groundwater storage potential. The net effect of forest clearing, because of the interaction of all the variables in the high elevation and steep slope environments found throughout the highlands, is a more extreme hydrologic cycle which lowers the water available for use. The greater runoff and higher peak flows during the rainy seasons mean that streams have lower flows during the drier periods; at times they can completely dry up. Prior to tree clearing, they were permanent streams. The greater runoff increases erosion and thus lowers the potential of the soils. It also will silt up reservoirs. Today, in many areas of the highlands, water is becoming an ever scarcer commodity during drier periods.

Rural population in the highlands

In Africa , the areas of densest population are in the Nile Valley, coastal areas, and the highlands. Regarding the highlands, this generalization is true not only for the lands discussed in this chapter but also for the plateaus and mountains of Cameroon, Nigeria, Atakora (Ghana and Togo), Moshi (Burkina Faso), Malawi, and Zimbabwe. In most African areas, agricultural activities produce food crops for local consumption. In most highland areas, although the majority of the area is also under cultivation with locally consumed food crops, the highlands generally produce the major export crops of the various countries.

In all six of the eastern and central countries the highlands are occupied by larger populations and population densities are relatively high in the highlands. For many years the better lands within the highland areas have been occupied and farmed. With ever-increasing population, the movement of people has been to steeper land which has either been planted with tree crops or left in forest. The greater population pressures in many places result today in land use that is severely stressing the environment as annual crops are substituted for trees; in many places soil erosion is becoming a major problem. Perhaps in no other country is the importance of the highlands as dominant as in Rwanda.

Approximately 90 percent of Rwanda's population is either directly or indirectly engaged in agriculture, with the overwhelming majority living in the highland portion of the country. A 1983 estimate of its population density on its agricultural lands is 390 per km^2; this is slightly higher than India, four times greater than Zaire, and eight times greater than Tanzania. Just over 40 percent of all land in Rwanda is under cultivation; slightly less than 40 percent comprises either lakes, parks, swamps, or urban areas. The remainder is grazing land (13 percent) and forest (7 percent). Thus only very little of the land remains unutilized.

Illustrative of population pressures in many of the highland areas of Africa are some recent figures that describe some of the Rwandan farm characteristics (Clay 1983). The average farm size in Rwanda is 1.14 ha. Almost all farms in Rwanda are fragmented. That is, the parcels of land under the ownership of individual farmers are separated from each other. The average farm is made up of five parcels; the average parcel size is only 22.8 ares*. In many parts of the country the arable lands are completely occupied so that the surplus population has to settle in new areas that are often more marginal environmentally. These lands are usually at lower elevations and are therefore drier. Given the small size of the farms and the amount of crops required to satisfy the nutritional requirements of the family as well as the social and economic requirements (bananas grown for beer production and coffee), livestock are only found on a quarter of the farms throughout Rwanda.
quarter of the farms throughout Rwanda.

As the average population for the country as a whole is 205 per km^2, little available land remains within the nation to absorb any population increase. The highlands provide better agricultural lands than the lower lands. In fact only small numbers of people can be resettled on the lower lands and still achieve a viable agricultural existence. Historically, Rwandans migrated either to areas in Zaire or

---

* 1 equals 1/100 of a hectare

Uganda. However, for a number of complex reasons most Rwandans do not want to leave the country. Recently migrants that had lived in Uganda for three generations were forced to flee to Rwanda as refugees, adding additional pressure to the economy. Most have filtered back into Uganda. Unlike some of the larger countries, the landlocked country of Rwanda, which is already densely populated, cannot absorb its rural population in any urban area.

The population pressures existing in Rwanda are also found in the Kenyan Highlands. The conditions in Kenya's highlands illustrates some of the interactions that are set in motion between rural and urban areas in the larger countries as lands for agricultural expansion diminish. Following independence, numerous large estates in the highlands became the focus of resettlement plans for some of Kenya's rural population. But over three-quarters of the large-scale farms were transferred intact to Kenyans with sufficient means to buy them (Odingo 1971). This included many individuals in government service. "By the late 1960s (only) some 35,000 families had been settled as smallholders in the former Scheduled Areas." (Porter 1979.) The fact is that today little land is available to absorb the rapid population growth existing in rural areas unless land is to be farmed more intensely on the larger tracts. Estimates of Kenya's population growth range from 3.5 to over 4 percent per year. Under existing conditions, the highland farms are not able to employ many more individuals than those already actively working the lands. The Kenyan rural landscape is an area of under-employment and a major source of outmigration to the urban areas. Nairobi, a city of less than 120,000 in 1948, had grown to 509,000 in 1970, 825,000 or more in 1980, and it is estimated that by the year 2000 its population will be over 2 million. The majority of this growth is a result of rural-to-urban movement with a large percentage coming from the highland areas. Some of the results of this rural-to-urban migration are discussed in Chapter 9.

River basins and some impacts of development

A watershed or river basin is the geographic area that collects and discharges its surface waters through a single river outlet. In many development projects it serves as the basic planning unit, largely because of the numerous economic activities directly or indirectly dependent on water. The physical properties of the river basin, such as vegetation cover, steepness, and geology, along with the climatic properties of the area, largely determine the characteristics of the water resource. The highland watersheds with their greater precipitation, generally moderate-to-steep river gradients, relatively narrow valley bottoms, and steep or moderate valley sides possess many of the favorable conditions conducive to dam construction. Many highland river basins in Africa thus represent a major natural resource for the development of these areas as well as surrounding lower lands.

The major demands, both present and future, for water use and control in the highlands include: potable water supplies, hydroelectric power generation, and irrigation. These demands do not arise solely from the population living in the highlands; lower lands to which either the water or energy can be transported for consumption are often the catalysts for increasing water utilization within the highlands. For example, to meet current and future needs for both potable water and energy of the Nairobi area, some dam construction and water diversions on both the upper Tana and Athi Rivers already exist, and others are being planned. Most of the discharges of these rivers result from precipitation in the eastern Kenyan Highlands around Mount Kenya and the Aberdares Mountains. Hydroelectric power generation is proposed in many plans for highland areas as one means of helping the countries to lower their petroleum imports.

Proposed sites range from on the Ruzizi River (Zaire, Rwanda, Burundi) to the Abay (Blue Nile, Ethiopia). In addition to power needs, irrigation waters are required to increase agricultural production both in the highlands and in the surrounding lowlands to help meet the needs of the growing total population, including those of the increasing urban population.

Watershed deterioration appears to be accelerating throughout many of the African highlands, and this threatens their positive potential contribution to economic development in the various countries. The very properties that contribute to a high energy potential in highland river basins, ample precipitation and steep slopes, contribute to environmental fragility. Immediate conservation strategies are required to maintain their resource potential. The principal direct causes of river basin degradation include:

(a) Deforestation for conversion to agriculture and grazing, or for fuelwoods.
(b) Accelerated soil erosion of uplands due to poor land use and management. This includes the use of inappropriate crops and poor cultivation techniques.
(c) Overgrazing and/or burning.
(d) Road construction and other construction activities.

Probably deforestation and the conversion of steep uplands to either agricultural or livestock uses are the major factors. To support the areas with growing populations, existing arable land is often used beyond its capacity under current agricultural systems. New arable land in most highland areas of Africa is gained by the expansion of cultivation into forest areas and onto steep slopes, often greater than 30°. This continuing development leads to increased soil erosion, causing reduction in crop yields and in certain places the abandonment of fields. The cutting of forests at an ever-increasing rate is not only removing a crucial renewable resource for use as timber, poles, firewood, charcoal, and pulp, but is resulting in a change in the hydrologic conditions of the affected river basins.

Forest areas usually have a veneer of leaf litter and shrubs covering the soil. As previously discussed, this cover, along with the trees themselves, lowers the impact of the raindrops on the soil as well as partially absorbing the precipitation. As the veneer disappears with forest clearing, during the rainy seasons the surface runoff both increases and is more rapid. This creates higher river discharges and often causes an acceleration in river erosion. Conversely, as less water has infiltrated into the ground during the rainy seasons, in the dry seasons the lower groundwater flows result in there being less water in springs and rivers. Many previously small permanent streams therefore become intermittent during the dry seasons (Fig. 7.7).

Similarly the increases in pollution that result from the higher sediment load have a detrimental effect on the riverbed. The higher sediment load leads to higher sedimentation rates in favorable depositional locations such as along valley bottoms, lakes, and reservoirs. The greater extreme in river discharges between rainy and dry seasons requires that larger storage capacities be provided in dam projects to ensure that there is a sufficient water supply to meet demand. But the increased sediment yield from the cleared slopes and the resulting higher river sediment loads increase sedimentation in the reservoirs. Many dam projects have not met their planned expectations because of the lower storage capacities behind the dams due to accelerated soil erosion.

In Kenya during the colonial period the government authorities understood the need to practice conservation in the highland areas. Soil conservation rules were laid down and strongly enforced. However, little emphasis was placed on explaining the need for, and the benefits of, the soil conservation practices to the Africans. Conservation was in fact viewed as a coercive policy by African farmers. The result was that during the first ten years after independence conservation practices declined. For example, in Kenya more terraces were destroyed than built during this period. In addition, another factor contributing to the erosional problems of the highlands was the opening up of large areas to African small farmers. The resettlement of Africans on some of the former lands of European farmers who had chosen to leave Kenya changed the nature of many farmlands from large mechanized operations to small-scale farming. These new farmers had little agricultural knowledge and little capital to invest. Many of the conservation practices utilized on the larger farms were impractical for the small farmers since the practices took much land out of cultivation. With farm size decreasing from hundreds of hectares to often less than 10 ha, many of the previous conservation practices were impractical, even though the stigma associated with the colonial authorities no longer existed. Also, crop substitutions took place that required other conservation practices than those previously used. Of particular importance is the fact that the area under maize cultivation increased. Maize not only requires a high fertility for large yields, it offers poor

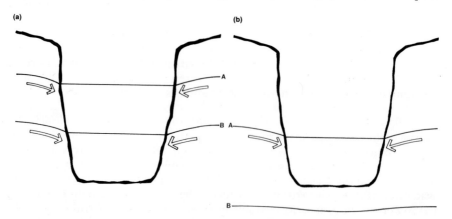

Figure 7.7 Hypothetical cross-sections of river channels: (a) before forest clearing; (b) after forest clearing. In (a) groundwater recharge permits stream flow during both wet (A) and dry (B) seasons. In (b) the water table is below the stream channel during the dry season (B) as rates of infiltration are lower during the rainy season. Thus the channel only contains water from overland flow during the dry season.

Figure 7.8   Maize growing on recently cleared steep slopes in Central Province, Kenya.

protection to the soil from direct raindrop impact even when it is mature, let alone when it has just been planted. Soil erosion usually is high under maize cultivation unless strong conservation practices are followed. The problem is exacerbated when maize is grown on steep slopes, as is often the case in the highland areas (Fig. 7.8) (Table 7.4). By 1966, 35,000 families were settled in the Kenyan Highlands on land formerly farmed by less than 4000 families (Odingo 1971). As a result, in most areas of the highlands new conservation strategies had to be devised to replace those that had evolved under former political and economic conditions.

Conservation practices within highland river basins

Conservation practices in the highlands antedate the arrival of Europeans to Africa. For example, in south and southwest Ethiopia the Konso terrace culture is believed to be of ancient origin (Westphal 1975). The practice of terracing was clearly more widespread in Ethiopia in past years as numerous remains exist throughout the area. In this area of Ethiopia the terrace serves a dual function, namely to encourage soil conservation and to facilitate irrigation. The Konso terrace requires a high labor input to construct, as terraces are separated from each other by stone walls anywhere from 20 cm to 6 m thick (Westphal). The steeper the land, the higher the stone wall. Irrigation is facilitated by the terrace in areas where water is available, since the gentle slope of the terrace permits more water to infiltrate into the soil.

263

Table 7.4 Soil loss, Kiambu District: first rainy season, 1982.

Field location	Slope (degrees)	Major crop	Terraced	Soil loss (ton/ha)
Kiambaa	3	coffee	yes	<1.0
	18	coffee	yes	1.6
	22	coffee	yes	1.1
Kikuyu	20	cabbage	yes	3.9
	11	cabbage	yes	1.2
	12	maize	no	39.6
Lari	45	potatoes	no	25.8
	20	mixed vegetables	no	10.3
	20	pyrethrum	no	7.8
	15	maize	no	11.5
	20	mixed vegetables	no	6.2
	16	mixed vegetables	yes	9.7
Limuru	14	plums	no	1.1
	11	pears	no	<1.0
	15	pears	no	1.5
Githunguri	3	tomatoes	no	<1.0
	10	bananas	no	5.3
	11	coffee	no	<1.0
	4	maize	no	16.5
	6	new coffee	no	13.1
Gatundu	20	maize	yes	57.4
	20	maize	yes	24.7
	9	mixed vegetables	no	11.2
	12	coffee	yes	4.1
Thika	9	beans	yes	22.9
	9	beans	yes	11.4
	10	chick-peas	yes	6.5

Today in many rural highland areas the need to control soil erosion is of primary concern. But shortages in skilled labor, machinery, and capital require strategies that place minimal demands for these needs if the soil control practices are to be widely accepted. In addition, the shortage of land requires that conservation practices do not remove lands from crop production. Beginning in the 1930s, the introduction of wattle as a commercial crop was a marked success both as a cash crop and a method of reafforesting the hill slopes and improving soil fertility in many areas of the Kenyan Highlands. But since the 1970s, with less land available for each family, due to population growth, wattle trees have been cut down and replaced by either food crops or tea in many areas to meet immediate economic needs (Fig. 7.9). Thus this past economic and conservation practice is no longer viable. Today the four major methods used for controlling soil erosion in the highlands are: terraces, agroforestry, mulches, and intercropping.

Figure 7.9 Land being cleared of wattle trees on steep slopes for annual crops in Central Province, Kenya.

Terraces

One method of terrace construction that has been accepted by farmers in Kenya utilizes soil erosion to help in the building of bench terraces. This minimizes the amount of labor required in the construction of the terrace. Locally it is known as the *Fanya Juu* method. Grass strips are planted in one or two rows along the terrace line. Below the grass line, a channel about 0.5 m wide and 1 m deep is dug. This material forms a ridge, and this is where the grass is planted (Fig. 7.10). Runoff from the upper field deposits soil on the ridge and in time a bench terrace evolves. The farmer must continue to keep the channel clear, but to a large degree the grass strip filters out a large percentage of the eroded soil. The grass can be cut and used either as fodder or as a mulch. The *Fanya Juu* method has been accepted in many parts of the central and eastern provinces in Kenya. A

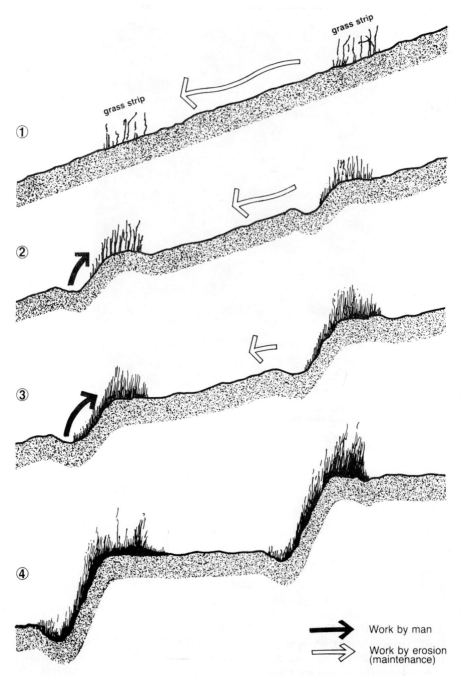

Figure 7.10 Development of grass strips into bench terraces. (Modified from Wenner 1980.)

similar method, using solely grass strips without channel digging on slopes of ten degrees, resulted in a set of terraces in only five years in an FAO experiment in Gikongoro, Rwanda. The advantage of this type of terrace is that it requires minimal capital and labor and little land is lost from production.

Agroforestry

It is widely agreed that soil erosion is very sensitive to the type and density of ground cover. Current land-use practices are commonly associated with the radical change of natural vegetation. In the highlands, the change generally has been from forest to crop cover, associated with agricultural or grazing systems. With a few exceptions, such as wattle, tree crops have rarely been cultivated. The changes in ground cover almost always result in higher soil losses, and in places the changes are extreme enough to result in land degradation. Agroforestry is considered by many to be a viable method of meeting both the crop and fuel requirements of developing countries while conserving the soil resource.

In this discussion, agroforestry is defined as a sustainable land-use system involving more or less intimate associations between conventional agriculture and horticultural crops, trees and shrubs, all on the same unit of land (Huxley 1981). In the highlands, as well as other environmental settings in Africa, it is evident that the necessity for food and fuel has resulted in rural inhabitants adopting land utilization practices that have generally led to the degradation of the ecosystem. There is evidence to suggest that forest trees and agricultural crops can be grown together without a deterioration in the site yet still meet the economic needs of the people.

In Kenya a study of the *shamba* system of agroforestry, in which young trees are planted among agricultural crops by small farmers, indicated that: (1) the planted pine trees (*Pinus radiata*) and cypress trees (*Cupressus macrocarpa*) have roughly the same water demands as the indigenous bamboo forests (*Arundinaria alpina*) however, the planted softwoods meet fuel needs better than the bamboos); (2) vegetables planted between the young trees can produce food for a number of years before the shade of the trees prevents vegetable growth. During the period of early tree growth, the *shamba* system successfully avoided both significant soil erosion and loss of permanent stream flows (Mongi & Huxley 1979). However, much research needs to be undertaken before the practice of agroforestry as a conservation strategy can be widely utilized. The correct mixes of food crops and tree crops to meet the demands of the multitude of different environments found throughout the highlands and at the same time to meet the food, fuel, and economic demands of the farmers need to be established.

Mulches

The use of mulches as a conservation device appears to be one of the best methods of soil conservation in the highlands. A mulch is any organic material spread directly over the ground. In the African highlands some common mulching materials include banana leaves, maize stocks, coffee branches, and grasses. Mulches curtail soil erosion in much the same manner as the shrub layer and leaf matter do in forest areas. The mulch protects the soil from the direct impact of the raindrops, increases infiltration, and reduces surface evaporation. In some recent investigations in the Kiambu and Muranga districts in Kenya, mulching was clearly identified as an effective conservation strategy (Lewis 1984). The Rwandan government recognizes the importance of mulching in erosion control as it requires it on all fields cultivated in coffee, the major export crop of the country. Unfortunately, in Rwanda most other fields are not mulched. This is a result of a combination of variables including competition for the mulch materials by livestock, shortage of mulch materials, and the amount of additional labor required for mulching. The lack of widespread mulching is unfortunate as it is a very good erosion control mechanism. Figure 7.11 illustrates the effectiveness of mulches in reducing soil loss. The mulch factor in the graph is the ratio of soil loss with mulch to a corresponding loss without mulch. As the percentage of the ground covered by a mulch increases there is a rapid decrease in the soil loss, as indicated by the very low values of the mulch factor when over 80 percent of the ground is covered by a mulch. When terracing and heavy mulching (95 percent ground cover) were combined in Kiambu District, Kenya (Lewis 1982), coffee growing on a 22° slope produced only 1.1 tons of soil loss per hectare during the long rainy season. This is almost an insignificant loss and no agricultural problems will result from losses of this magnitude in this area.

Unlike in warmer areas in the tropics, the cooler temperatures in the highlands help to prevent rapid breakdown of the mulches by bacterial and other organic activities. Thus the use of mulches can be a very valuable conservation technique in many highland settings.

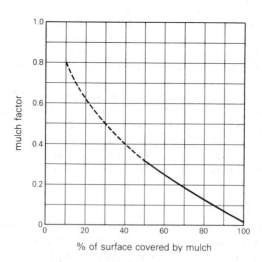

Figure 7.11 Effect of plant residue mulch on soil loss: mulch factor is the ratio of soil loss with mulch to corresponding loss without mulch (from Wischmeier & Smith 1978).

Intercropping

Although not purely a conservation technique, intercropping is a useful soil conservation practice. On most small farms in the highlands, especially for the noncash crops, usually two or more crops are interplanted in a single field. Some typical examples of crop mixes are: bananas with beans, beans with maize, and sorghum with sweet potato. When this intercropping includes a ground crop such as sweet potato with a tall crop such as sorghum, which gives slight protection to the soil, soil loss can be reduced to an acceptable level, permitting sufficient harvests of the erosion-prone crop (sorghum). Intercropping appears to reduce soil loss by preventing the direct impact of raindrops on bare soil. Therefore planting two or more crops at the same time in one field during the early part of the growing season is rather ineffective since the soil is exposed to direct rain for some weeks until the ground crop becomes dense enough to protect the soil. Intercroppping is most effective when it allows a ground cover to exist at the start of the rainy season. A crop such as sweet potato can be planted at different periods of the year, not solely at the start of the rainy season.

Besides the soil conservation benefits, another favorable aspect of inter-cropping is that plant disease and insect problems can be reduced by keeping the environment from being too favorable for a single disease or pest by reducing the concentration of single crops. Also, some legumes, such as certain varieties of beans or leucaena, can improve the fertility of the soil; furthermore, they can help to increase the yields of the crops with which they are interplanted.

As in other areas of Africa, in the highlands there is no single practice that is always best for reducing soil erosion. On steep slopes, if they must be farmed, terracing is often a useful conservation strategy because it reduces the slope angle in the areas where the crops are planted. This reduces both the velocity of the water flowing over the soil and as the absolute quantity of the water because the infiltration of rainwater is increased. These two changes normally reduce the potential for soil erosion. However, on some steep slopes, especially those underlain with a weak subsurface material such as a marl, the terrace could accelerate land degradation. With the increase of water infiltrating into the soil the upper portion of the ground could become saturated. When the groundwater reaches the marl layer, which is relatively impermeable, the friction of the upper portion of the ground at the interface with the marl could become reduced to such a low value that the whole slope might fail (Fig. 7.12). As lands are being cleared of forest and converted to crops on steep slopes this type of massive land degradation is likely to increase. This type of slope failure has already been recorded in Kiambu District, Kenya, which is under tea cultivation. Before any conservation practice is introduced, information on the general environmental setting needs to be examined in order to determine what the best practices might be.

The classification of lands according to their soil, climatic, topographic, and agricultural potential is one approach that might help planners to develop rational use of rural lands in order to meet food and energy requirements without damaging the land resource. Taking a portion of the Kenyan Highlands as an example, the agroclimatologic zones around Mount Kenya will be used to illustrate one approach to obtaining information of use in determining the

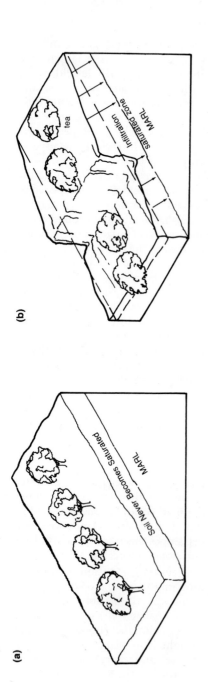

(a)

Soil Never Becomes Saturated

MARL

(b)

tea

Infiltration

saturated zone

MARL

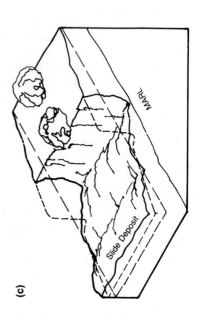

(c)

Slide Deposit

MARL

(d)

Figure 7.12 Slope failure, even with terracing, due to land clearing on a steep slope in Central Province, Kenya. (a) Under forest cover; (b) terraced and planted with tea; (c) failure of slope; (d) photograph of the area.

appropriate utilization of lands. One important purpose of the agroclimatologic approach is to provide a tool for assessing which areas are environmentally suitable for various land use alternatives.

Agroclimatologic zones: a Kenyan Highland example

When classifying lands into agroclimatologic units to determine the suitability of areas for crops or grazing, soil information, landform properties (steepness and stability), major aspects of climate that affect plant growth (precipitation–evaporation balance and temperature), and site conditions, such as soil moisture storage, need to be taken into account. The approach used in Kenya was to develop the soil and agroclimatologic properties at a small scale (1 : 1,000,000) (Sombroek *et al*. 1982) and then incorporate the site-specific properties at a larger scale (1 : 50,000) to develop the agro-ecologic zones for specific areas (Jaetzold & Schmidt 1983).

Soil properties

In the Kenyan Soil Survey's Exploratory Soil Map the general landform properties (Table 7.5), the geologic parent material having the greatest influence on the local soils (Table 7.6) and the soil classification (Table 7.7) based on the UNESCO/FAO 1974 classification are presented. From the general landform properties some basic attributes of an area's slope and drainage characteristics are inferred. The landform properties delimited on the map permit a first approximation of the erosional potential. These properties include the general steepness and the drainage properties of the lands. In areas where the possibility of erosion is high, the government needs to enforce conservation practices strongly. For example, areas with slopes in excess of 30 percent have a high erosional potential. This information alone conveys that, due to the steepness of the area, if the area is to be cultivated conservation practices are required. In Kenya and in many other areas in the African highlands, slopes in excess of 30 percent are cultivated. Steep lands are increasingly being cleared of trees and cultivated in annual crops. In addition, the M category in Table 7.5 indicates that the potential for mechanization would be low owing to the steepness of the terrain. In contrast, lands in the A category (Table 7.5) would be level but at the same time susceptible to frequent flooding. Here mechanization would be possible, but the type of land use in the area must be such that flooding would not cause critical drainage to the crops. Likewise, the equipment used in farming must not damage engineering works such as drainage ditches which are required when flooding occurs.

GEOLOGIC PARENT MATERIALS

The geologic information presented (Table 7.6), in conjunction with the landform data, permits an approximation of the erosional potential, permeability properties, and fertility of the soils. For example, soils derived from

Table 7.5 Key to landforms.

Code	Landform
M	mountains and major scarps
H	hills and minor scarps
L	plateaus and high-level structural plains
Lu	plateau–upper-level upland transitions
R	volcanic footridges
F	footslopes
FY	footslopes and piedmont plains, undifferentiated
Y	piedmont plains
U	uplands
Uu	upper-level uplands
Uh	upper middle-level uplands
Um	lower middle-level uplands
Ul	lower-level uplands
Ux	uplands, undifferentiated levels
Uc	coastal uplands
Up	upland–high-level plain transitional lands
P	plains
Pn	nondissected erosional plains
Pd	dissected erosional plains
Ps	sedimentary plains
Psh	higher-level sedimentary plain ("red sand" plain)
Psm	middle-level sedimentary plains ("enclosed" plains and sealing loam plain)
Psl	lower-level sedimentary plain ("grey clay" plain)
Psx	sedimentary plains of undifferentiated levels
Pv	volcanic plains
Pch	higher-level coastal plain
Pcl	lower-level coastal plain
Pt	sedimentary plains of upper river terraces
Pf	sedimentary plains of large alluvial fans
Pf1	older fans
Pf2	younger fans
A	floodplains
B	bottomlands
S	lava flows
T	swamps
V	minor valleys
W	badlands

quartzites (Q) are likely to have a moderate-to-high erosion potential and will not be particularly fertile since the weathering products of quartzites generally result in these soil characteristics. Conversely, soils derived from basic igneous material, including volcanic rocks (B), will often be resistant to erosion and quite fertile. The influence of the parent material on soils is likely to be higher in the highlands than in most other areas of Africa, due both to the relative youth of the area and the steepness of the slopes. Together these two factors result in the soil having relatively direct links with the parent material.

Table 7.6 Key to geologic material.

Code	Geology
B	basic and ultrabasic igneous rocks (basalts, etc.)
B+	as in B, but with volcanic ash admixture
BP	as in B, but with influence of volcanic ash predominant
D	mudstones, claystones
F	gneisses rich in ferromagnesian minerals, hornblende gneisses
G	granites, granodiorites
G+	as in G, but with volcanic ash admixture
GF	biotite–hornblende granites
GF+	as in GF, but with volcanic ash admixture
GP	as in G, but with influence of volcanic ash admixture
GR	complex of G and R
I	intermediate igneous rocks (syenites, etc.)
I+	as in I, but with volcanic ash admixture
K	siltstones
KT	complex of K and T
N+	as in N, but with volcanic ash admixture
O	Plio-Pleistocene bay sediments
P	pyroclastic rocks
Q	quartzites
R	quartz–feldspar gneisses
S	sandstones, grits, arkoses
T	shales
U	undifferentiated Basement System rocks (predominantly gneisses)
U+	as in U, but with volcanic ash predominant
UP	as in U, but with influence of volcanic ash predominant
V	undifferentiated or various igneous (volcanic) rocks
W	maris
X	undifferentiated or various rocks
X+	as in X, but with volcanic ash admixture
Y	acid igneous rocks (rhyolite, aplite)
Y+	as in Y, but with volcanic ash admixture

Note: If the source of alluvial sediments and bottomlands is known (e.g. basalts), then the code for this rock is used; otherwise the code A applies.

SOIL CLASSIFICATION UNITS

As the UNESCO/FAO soil classification (Table 7.7) utilizes diagnostic soil horizons which have specific properties, it is possible to infer a range of soil properties according to the specific soil unit that occurs in each area. For example, if an area's soils are classified as lithosols (i), the soils are very shallow. In Kenya this means that the soil is never more than 25 cm deep and that there is a layer of rock at the base of the soil. Thus only plants with shallow root systems can survive in the area. Also, because of the extremely shallow nature of the soil, great care must be taken to minimize erosion. Nitisols (m) on the other hand are generally well drained, quite deep (3–6 m), friable, and fertile. Therefore they

Table 7.7 UNESCO/FAO soil classification, 1974.

a	acrisols	gm	mollic	nt	ando-humic
ac	chromic	gv	vertic	nv	verto-eutric
ag	glyeic			nv	verto-mollic
ah	humic	h	phaeozems		
ai	ferralo-chromic	hg	gleyic	o	histosols
ai	ferralo-ferric	hh	haplic	od	dystric
ai	ferralo-orthic	hn	nito-luvic		
ao	orthic	ho	ortho-luvic	q	arenosols
ap	plinthic	hr	chromo-luvic	qa	albic
at	ando-humic	ht	ando-haplic	qc	cambic
		ht	ando-luvic	qf	ferralic
b	cambisols	hv	verto-luvic	qk	calcaro-cambic
bc	chromic			ql	luvic
bd	dystric	j	fluvisols		
be	eutric	jc	calcaric	r	regosols
bf	ferralic	je	eutric	rc	calcaric
bg	gleyic	jt	thionic	rd	dystric
bh	humic			re	eutric
bk	calcic	l	luvisols	rt	ando-calcaric
bn	nito-chromic	la	albic		
bt	ando-chromic	lc	chromic	t	andosols
bt	ando-eutric	lf	ferric	th	humic
bv	vertic	lg	gleyic	tm	mollic
		li	ferralo-chromic	tv	vitric
f	ferralsols	li	ferralo-ferric		
fa	acric	li	ferralo-orthic	u	rankers
fh	humic	lk	calcic		
fn	nito-humic	ln	nito-chromic	v	vertisols
fn	nito-rhodic	ln	nito-ferric	vc	chromic
fo	orthic	lo	orthic	vp	pellic
fr	rhodic	lv	vertic		
fx	xanthic			w	planosols
		n	nitisols	wd	dystric
g	gleysols	nd	dystric	we	eutric
gc	calcaric	ne	eutric	wh	humic
gd	dystric	nh	humic	ws	solodic
gh	humic	nm	mollic	wv	verto-eutric

are very favorable for most types of agriculture. Figure 7.13 presents some data for the vicinity of Mount Kenya from the Kenyan Exploratory Soil Map. From the summit of Mount Kenya in the southeasterly direction toward the Thiba River along the line on the figure, the area is classified as M9, M2, R1, R2, L1, and Um20. According to the Kenya Survey's classification these areas have the following characteristics:

M9 Slopes over 30 percent: shallow soils derived from recent lavas; ice can be found in the soil.

M2 Slopes over 30 percent: generally shallow, well-drained soils, but in places moderately deep; derived from igneous rocks.

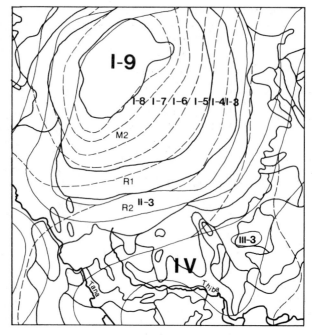

Figure 7.13 Agro-climatic classification for the area surrounding Mount Kenya (from Sombrock *et al.* 1982).

R1   Undulating to hilly volcanic footridge: well-drained, extremely deep fertile soil.

R2   Almost the same as R1 except there are friable clays in the soil.

L1   A flat to undulating plateau area: slopes usually less than 8 percent; well-drained, very deep soils with very friable clay.

Um 20 Soils found on middle uplands (1000–2000 m above sea level): derived from biotite gneisses, well drained and moderate to deep.

This soil information, along with the following agroclimatologic properties, should be integrated when decisions concerning rural land use are made for this highland area.

AGROCLIMATOLOGIC PROPERTIES

The purpose of the agroclimatologic component is to determine the climatic properties of an area in order to suggest what areas are climatically suitable for specific crops or grazing. The critical factors examined in Kenya are moisture availability and temperature.

Moisture availability zones The moisture availability zones for Kenya (Table 7.8) are based on the ratio of measured average annual rainfall to the calculated average annual evaporation (E_0). Empirically derived, the equation utilized for the Kenyan Highlands is $E = 2422 - 0.358h$ m, where h is the

Table 7.8 Boundary criteria for moisture availability zones.

Zone	$r:E_0$ ratio	$r:E_0$ ratio (%)	Climatic designation
I	>0.8	>80	humid
II	0.65–0.80	65–80	subhumid
III	0.50–0.65	50–65	semi-humid
IV	0.40–0.50	40–50	semi-humid to semi-arid
V	0.25–0.40	25–40	semi-humid
VI	0.15–0.25	15–25	arid
VII	<0.15	>15	very arid

Note: r = average annual rainfall; E_0 = average annual potential evaporation.

elevation above sea level. In this equation the annual evaporation is assumed to be a direct function of altitude. Higher elevations will have lower evaporation as they have cooler temperatures.

Potential evapotranspiration is considered to be 80 percent of the estimated potential evaporation, since water evaporates at a higher rate from an open pan than from vegetation and the soil. Therefore an area having a rainfall evaporation rate of 80 percent or greater is assumed to have 100 percent ($80/0.8 = 100$) or 365 full moisture days during the year. This would permit crop growth without any need for irrigation during any portion of the year. However, crops that need a dry season would do poorly in this type of setting. A location having an $r:E_0$ ratio of 45 (zone IV) is assumed to have 56.25 percent full moisture days in a one-year period ($45/0.8 = 56.25$) or 205 days (365×0.5625) of full moisture. This would approximate the length of the growing season in zone IV. Because precipitation patterns in the Kenyan Highlands are such that in over 50 percent of the years less than the average annual rainfall is received, if a location has an $r:E_0$ ratio of 56.25, the implication is that generally over half of the years will have full moisture days of less than 205 days. A full moisture day is defined as a 24-hour period with sufficient moisture for maximum plant growth. One disadvantage of using annual precipitation data for determining the moisture availability zones is that rainfall patterns in Kenya are complex. In some areas bimodal and trimodal rainfall régimes exist. Nevertheless, this classification provides useful first approximations for land planners, and it makes use of data that are widely available. For crops found in Kenya, Table 7.9 lists the moisture requirements of the plants. The solid lines represent good moisture conditions for the crops; the broken lines represent suboptimal (too wet or too dry) conditions. The whole moisture range for each crop is indicated by the arrowheads.

Temperature zones and crop choice Just as moisture availability restricts the choice of crops, so do the temperature properties of an area. The average annual temperatures within Kenya are also calculated using an equation that relates temperature to elevation. It has been found by the East African Meteorological Department that annual average temperature (Celsius) = 30.2 − 0.00650h m. Temperature boundaries for the agroclimatologic zones of

277

Table 7.9 Moisture range of crops, types of animal production, and types of forestry species in Kenya.

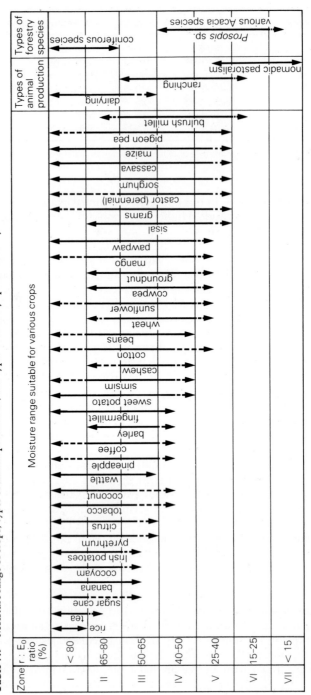

Zone	r : E₀ ratio (%)
I	< 80
II	65–80
III	50–65
IV	40–50
V	25–40
VI	15–25
VII	< 15

Moisture range suitable for various crops: rice, tea, sugar cane, banana, cocoyam, Irish potatoes, pyrethrum, citrus, tobacco, coconut, wattle, pineapple, coffee, barley, fingermillet, sweet potato, simsim, cashew, cotton, beans, wheat, sunflower, cowpea, groundnut, mango, pawpaw, sisal, grams, castor (perennial), sorghum, cassava, maize, pigeon pea, bulrush millet.

Types of animal production: dairying, ranching, nomadic pastoralism.

Types of forestry species: coniferous species, Prosopis sp., various Acacia species.

Table 7.10 Boundary criteria for temperature zones.

Zone	Altitude (ft)	Mean annual temperature (°C)	Climatic designation
9	>10,000	<10	cold to very cold
8	9,000–10,000	10–12	very cool
7	8,000–9,000	12–14	cool
6	7,000–8,000	14–16	fairly cool
5	6,000–7,000	16–18	cool temperate
4	5,000–6,000	18–20	warm temperate
3	4,000–5,000	20–22	fairly warm
2	3,000–4,000	22–24	warm
1	0–3,000	24–30	fairly hot to very hot

Kenya (Table 7.10) are based on this formula. Crops for the temperature ranges of the nine zones in Kenya are presented in Table 7.11.

Ten agroclimatologic zones (Fig. 7.13) are found from the vicinity of Mount Kenya to the Thiba River. These are: I-9, I-8, I-7, I-6, I-5, I-4, I-3, II-3, III-3, IV-4. The Roman number delimits the moisture zone (Table 7.8) whereas the Arabic number indicates the temperature zone (Table 7.10). By considering the moisture and temperature requirements of crops (Tables 7.9 & 7.11), the range of crops that might be favorably grown in an area can be determined. For example, in zone I-5, citrus, wattle, sweet potato, sorghum, maize, pyrethrum, and Irish potatoes are possibilities. However, this range of crops is restricted by the land and soil conditions also delimited on Figure 7.13. In the example, the soils all fall within the M2 category. This is a steep area with relatively shallow and well-drained soils. Crops such as sorghum and maize would probably be a poor choice since they do not protect the soil. Given the steepness of the area, soil erosion could be a problem if they were grown. A tree crop such as wattle would appear to be environmentally a better selection. However, there would have to be an economic benefit for the landowners to plant these trees. Other possibilities might be pasture, pine trees, or pyrethrum. Pyrethrum would require an extraction plant somewhere in the vicinity. Most likely the environmental conditions required for pyrethrum would not areally be large enough in this area to support such a plant. Thus it would be a poor choice.

One method of synthesizing primary environmental information is by using the soil and agroclimatic information presented in Figure 7.13. This information format permits land-use planners to make basic decisions concerning the rational use of the land resource from an ecological perspective. The broad patterns delimited at such a small scale should be reduced to a more site-specific form before specific recommendations are put into operation. The agro-ecologic zones (Jaetzold & Schmidt 1983) represent such a reduction. Not only is the information at a larger scale (1:50,000 vs 1:1,000,000), but additional information on the length of the growing season, the natural fertility of the soil, and crop selection is provided. In some of the highland areas, because of the steepness of the lands, the final decision on the best use of the land from an environmental perspective requires on-site evaluation.

Table 7.11 Altitude and temperature range of selected crops in Kenya.

Range of various crops (after Acland 1971)

Temp. zone									
9	8	7	6	5	4	3	2	1	

Crops shown: barley, pyrethrum, Irish potatoes, wheat, wattle, sunflower, maize, sorghum, finger millet, sweet potatoes, tea, pineapple, castor, beans, Arabica coffee, citrus, cocoyam, bananas, sisal, tobacco, pigeon pea, mango, simsim, sugar cane, groundnut, cowpea, cassava, Robusta coffee, cotton, rice, bulrush millet, coconut, pawpaw, cashew

General conclusions

In most highland areas of eastern and central Africa, population growth is causing continuous increases in environmental stress. In particular, both the soil and water resources generally are decreasing in quality. With land clearing on ever more marginal lands in the highlands, erosion is increasing in areal extent. This results in increases in the sediment in rivers originating on the highlands. The highlands are the major watershed for the Nile and for a whole set of small river systems flowing into the Indian Ocean. As a result, the impact of the degradation of these resources is felt beyond the highlands. Higher sediment yields result in increases in sedimentation rates behind dams. This acceleration in sedimentation shortens the potential life of these dams and makes them not economical. It thus reduces the likelihood of new dams being built.

In the highlands themselves, river flow characteristics are being altered. The net result of land clearing is that an ever greater proportion of rainfall fails to infiltrate the soil and instead flows overland directly into the stream systems. As a result, the high flows are becoming larger and the low flows smaller, due to the decrease of groundwater flows into the river channels. This increases the scarcity of water during the dry seasons. In addition, the greater runoff increases the intensity of erosion.

Since the highlands are an area of high population as well as the critical zone in most of eastern and central Africa for the production of large quantities of agricultural commodities, it is crucial to preserve the water and soil resources of these lands. First, if they continue to decline this will increase the population pressures in other areas, particularly the urban ones. This will happen because the highlands will not be able to support the existing populations directly from agriculture because yields will decrease. Second, food production will stagnate, and this will affect the economies of the countries involved. Third, because the highlands are the major watershed for a significant area within Africa, the impacts of the decline in resources will impose a direct financial burden on many of the lands and countries beyond the highlands.

8 Extratropical and southern Africa

Definitions and purpose of this chapter

Africa and South America are generally perceived as the most tropical of continents. In general this perception approximates reality. However, both in Africa and South America important parts of the continent lie beyond the tropics and/or are essentially extratropical in the characteristics of their physical environment. In this chapter we examine the environmental issues of these zones, in both northern and southern Africa.

The areas we are concerned with are easily divided into two meaningful groupings: the northern zone, made up of the Mediterranean fringe of Africa; and a less readily circumscribed southern zone, which we will define to include the general area of the Republic of South Africa and the contiguous territories of Botswana, Namibia, Zimbabwe, and Mozambique. Our discussion of the northern zone focuses particularly on the issues and problems of the Mediterranean climate areas, but it also includes the Atlas Mountains and the most densely occupied areas of Morocco, Algeria, Tunisia, Libya, and Egypt. Large parts of each of these countries are deserts, and there is some overlap with discussion topics in Chapter 5. But in this chapter dryland topics are examined only if they are clearly relevant to the coastal and mountain zones.

The southern zone is defined to include a large area that physically lies within the tropics, but needs to be treated here as a unit because of the close economic and political linkages between the countries (Fig. 8.1). Some of the areas within Botswana, Namibia, and Zimbabwe covered in this chapter could fall in the context of the discussion of dry zones (savanna). To avoid overlaps, the issues treated here are those dominating the southern African region rather than those relating to dryland ecologies of various kinds; some overlap is, however, inevitable.

The Mediterranean area

Figure 8.1 outlines the region under discussion. It is one of the most populated regions in Africa, with over 90 percent of the population of the five countries living in these nontropical portions. These countries account for a population of over 103 million. It has been estimated that in 1984 the population of these countries living in the extratropical zone was 90 million. This zone is the most urbanized part of Africa. Major cities in the region include Cairo, 9,500,000, Alexandria, 2,500,000, Port Said, 400,000, Benghazi, 500,000, Tripoli, 350,000, Tunis, 750,000, Algiers, 2,500,000, Oran, 600,000, Rabat, 700,000, and Casa-

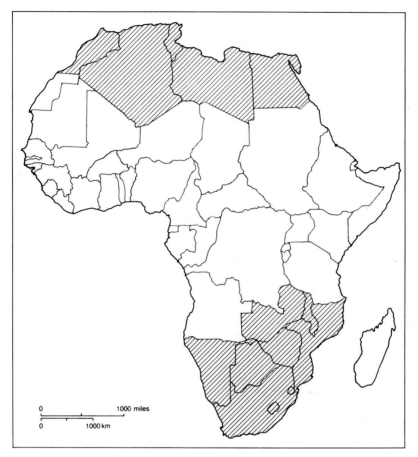

Figure 8.1 The areas discussed in this chapter.

blanca, 1,900,000. Around 50 percent of the population of the five northern countries lives in urban areas, and this percentage is increasing rapidly (Table 8.1).

Urbanization usually reflects trade and industry, though this is not always the case in tropical Africa. It is no surprise to find that this zone is, as it has been for centuries, a focus for trade and manufacture. The great trading ports of the Mediterranean have existed for over 3000 years, and they continue with this

Table 8.1 Percentage of population in urban areas, 1980.

Algeria	44	Libya	52
Tunisia	52	Egypt	45
Morocco	41		

Table 8.2 Mineral and manufactured products: North Africa.

	Minerals	Products
Egypt	oil, phosphates, kaolin	textiles, chemicals, steel, cement, fertilizer
Libya	oil, gas	oil, textiles, shoes
Tunisia	phosphates, iron	food processing, textiles, clothing
Algeria	oil, iron, zinc, phosphates	wine, oil, steel, textiles
Morocco	phosphates, cobalt, oil	carpets, clothing, plastics, fertilizers, leather

function. Industry also has been long established, but the products are now a mixture of traditional and modern. Oil and gas, iron and steel in Algeria, and textile and other light industry in Egypt are juxtaposed with traditional crafts and tourism in all five countries. Table 8.2 provides an indication of the range of mineral and manufactured products for the region.

Yet the region is typically African in that a significant proportion of its people still obtain their living directly from the land. Nomadic herders still maintain this livelihood in the interior, whereas coastal regions produce the typical Mediterranean climatic zone products of wheat, fruits, and olives, as well as cotton, dates, wines, and livestock.

Physically, the region is quite varied. The western part is dominated by the ranges of the Atlas Mountains, which emphasize the sharp gradients from the coast inland and create a sequence of bioclimatic zones. There is a rapid change from the interior arid areas to the semi-arid–humid coastal zone.

History of Mediterranean environmental change

The environment in the Mediterranean has undergone a great deal of change over the last few thousand years, partly in response to climate and sea-level fluctuation and partly as a result of the continuance of intense human occupance over this period. Much of the major climate and sea-level change occurred before the last 3000 years and leaves its impact on the environment mainly in the form of relict soils and landforms. Human occupance has had a continuing environmental effect, which is recorded in the historical and archaeological records.

For example, in Grecian and Roman times, 2000–2500 years ago, the northern African shores were a granary for the civilizations on the northern shores of the Mediterranean. Roman remains at Carthage show that this was an important outpost of the Empire and that a sophisticated system of aqueducts and water-supply links existed in an area which no longer appears able to support such a network. For long it was assumed that the change from a wheat-growing area with good water to a very dry location was the result of climatic change. Currently, it is judged that environmental degradation, mainly due to cultivation methods that caused soil erosion and silting of the water supply reservoirs, were the primary causes.

The sequence of influences in the western part of the region from the

284

Carthaginians, Greeks, Romans, Arabs, French, and finally independent status, has brought a succession of changes in the environment. In the eastern part of the area, including Egypt and Libya, there has been a similar long occupance, though the environmental changes may not have been so great in this drier area until the last 100 years. In this last century, however, major changes have occurred with the growth of population and the change in economic systems, especially in Egypt. One such change was the cutting of the Suez Canal, which, as well as bringing a new focus to Egypt as a crossroads and routeway, allowed for the first time a mingling of the Red Sea and Mediterranean fauna, if only on a limited scale.

More far-reaching have been the major changes brought about by the pattern of utilization of the Nile River. Starting with a dam at Aswan in the late 19th century, engineers have sequentially brought the river under total control. This control is now such that *no* water from this huge river reaches the sea without first being utilized in some form. The High Dam at Aswan, which blocks all flow beyond that point, also blocks silt discharge into lower Egypt. As water and sediment flow to the Delta have diminished, profound changes in many aspects of the area have occurred, including new river-bank erosion, delta-shoreline retreat, and changes in the distribution and intensity of diseases in the irrigated part of the country.

But, in the whole region of North Africa, the most profound changes in the environment may have been those due to urbanization and industrialization. The supply of pollutants to the coast and the spread of urban-related diseases has been one result.

Current environmental problems of the Mediterranean area

Current environmental problems in the region include:

(a) coastal pollution and control and offshore resource management;
(b) urban and industrial pollution involving air, water and land pollution, and the spread of disease;
(c) environmental problems related to agriculture, including irrigated and dryland agriculture.
(d) mineral extraction and related transport issues.

Those issues related to pastoral activities are primarily dealt with in Chapter 5.

COASTAL POLLUTION AND COASTAL AND OFFSHORE RESOURCE MANAGEMENT

The Mediterranean coast of North Africa is the southern shore of the Mediterranean Sea. The coastal problems of northern Africa are in part the problems of the Mediterranean Basin.

The Mediterranean Sea, though linked with the Atlantic through the Strait of Gibraltar and with the Red Sea through the Suez Canal, is in most respects an inland sea. It has a very low tidal range and comparatively few large rivers discharge into it. Of those rivers, the flow of the Nile, the largest, is almost completely halted. The Mediterranean Basin's water balance is negative in that greater evaporation occurs than precipitation and inflow of fresh waters from rivers. As a result, inflows of waters from the Atlantic are required to maintain its level.

The Mediterranean Basin is surrounded by countries with strong industrial bases. There is a widely distributed tourist industry and the Mediterranean Sea itself is one of the world's most important shipping highways. In addition, a dense, heavily urbanized population surrounds its shores. The industries include the heavy shipbuilding and port facilities at Marseilles and Malta, the oil and steel industries of Algeria, oil facilities in Libya, and the diverse industries of Cairo, Port Said, Naples, Tel Aviv, Athens, and the many other Mediterranean cities. This very large industrial complex is a major source of pollutants, and a large part of the pollution ends up in the Mediterranean Sea. Table 8.3 lists the major cities of the basin and their populations.

Table 8.3 Urban population around the Mediterranean in thousands (1977 estimates).

Malaga	450
Valencia	1,070
Barcelona	3,700
Marseilles	1,150
Genoa	930
Rome	3,400
Naples	2,115
Palermo	710
Venice	460
Trieste	270
Athens	2,700
Thessaloniki	700
Istanbul	3,400
Izmir	900
Beirut	1,100
Haifa	250
Tel Aviv	1,400
Port Said	360
Cairo	7,000
Alexandria	2,500
Benghazi	450
Tripoli	280
Tunis	750
Algiers	2,000
Oran	550
Total	38,595

Source: UN *Demographic yearbook.*

Note: North African cities total 13,490,000 – 35 percent of total.

286

Table 8.4 Estimated input of contaminants to the Mediterranean.

Contaminant (tonnes/yr)	Domestic	Agricultural	Industrial	Rivers	Total
BOD	500,000	100,000	100,000	1,800,000	3,300,000
COD	1,100,000	1,600,000	2,400,000	3,500,000	8,600,000
phosphorus	22,000	30,000	5,000	300,000	360,000
nitrogen	110,000	65,000	25,000	800,000	1,000,000
mercury[a]	0.8	—	7	120	130
lead	200	—	1,400	3,200	4,800
chromium	250	—	950	1,600	2,800
zinc	1,900	—	5,000	18,000	25,000
others[b]					

Notes
[a] The estimate of industrial mercury is based on insufficient data and therefore is unreliable. The value for mercury in domestic discharges is almost certainly too low.
[b] Estimated inputs of other substances include 60,000 tonnes of detergents, 12,000 tonnes of phenols, 350 million tonnes of total suspended solids, and 90 tonnes of organochlorine pesticides.

Of the almost 40 million people in these twenty-five urban areas, over 35 percent live in North Africa. This large urban population surrounding the Mediterranean produces a large discharge of urban waste, which, although much has been undergoing treatment in recent years, has for many centuries ended up in the Mediterranean in its raw state. Table 8.4 lists the resultant input of contaminants into the sea.

The tourist industry has paradoxically been focused on the Mediterranean because of the area's good climate and natural conditions. But it too has contributed considerably to the added pollution of the area. The tourist industry is heavily concentrated on coastal and marine areas and has a disproportionate impact on these delicately balanced ecosystems. Also, of course, the pollution of beach and marine areas in the longer run has a negative impact on the tourist industry. Last, the heavy commercial traffic through the Mediterranean and the confined nature of the basin means that marine pollution is, and has been, quite high relative to other marine areas.

Eighteen nation states abut onto the Mediterranean, so problems of coastal and marine resource use necessarily involve many different decision makers. As a result of the need to achieve this coordination, all but one of the states (Albania) joined in cooperation with the EEC and the UNEP and other UN agencies to assess the extent of the problem and to cooperate on remedies (Boxer 1978).

Although the Mediterranean is relatively well known, the impact of the heavy metals, toxic substances, oil, and other material ejected into the sea is not clearly known. Because the Mediterranean is divided into different basins, has a diverse climate, is complicated hydrologically and has inadequately charted circulation patterns, it is hard to estimate cause and response scientifically. In the section that follows, we concentrate on the North African coast and the issues that most directly affect this coastline.

Figure 8.2 (Boxer 1978) indicates that although 35 percent of the urban population of the Mediterranean Basin live on the North African coast, there is a lower than average discharge of industrial and chemical waters and domestic sewage into the sea from Africa. This reflects Africa's lower industrial development relative to Europe, though there is a high localized level of oil and petroleum hydrocarbon pollution. In the few years since Figure 8.2 was drafted, there has been a significant increase in the latter, accompanied by a steady growth in other types of discharge onto the North African coast. As industrial and extractive mineral development has increased, so has the need for improved environmental management of the coastal area. One important factor for Tunisia and Morocco, and to a lesser degree Egypt and Algeria, has been the importance of the tourist industry. The North African countries have, however, all been a part of the planning process for Mediterranean coastal and marine management – the first of its kind on this scale. The first four activities of the EEC and UNEP were:

(a) improved monitoring and assessment;
(b) drafting of compatible legal protocols;
(c) financing of ameliorative and protective measures on a pilot basis; and
(d) coordination of training, equipment and standards for nearly 100 laboratories in 15 countries.

Specific activities so far undertaken include:

(a) studies of the degree of oil and petroleum hydrocarbon pollution;
(b) metals, DDT, and chlorinated hydrocarbon in marine organisms;
(c) biochemical cycling of pollutants;
(d) establishment and maintenance of protected zones; and
(e) effects of agricultural and industrial wastes on rivers discharging into the Mediterranean.

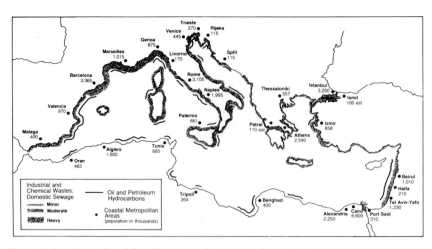

Figure 8.2 Generalized distribution and severity of pollutants in Mediterranean coastal waters (from Boxer 1978, Figure 1, p. 586, copyright © 1978 by AAAS).

288

The construction of a plan for the monitoring and rehabilitation of the Mediterranean Basin took a major diplomatic and scientific effort. Through a growing understanding of the magnitude and nature of the problems, and the ramifications of doing nothing, all the Mediterranean bordering nations except-ing Albania, despite their very different perspectives and viewpoints, were able to agree in general to a coherent plan that attempts to arrest the growing environmental decay of the sea.

The Plan is unique in the extent to which governments, international agencies, and scientists have become involved; in the diversity of its scientific work; and in the contractual arrangements with laboratories in support of this work. It is realistic in scope and is tied to the region's future through governments' endorsement of the role of UNEP. (Boxer, 1978.)

Although this assessment still stands, the problems of the Mediterranean continue to grow, and the North African coastal problems have increased more rapidly than those of the European areas. The importance of cooperation has been accepted. The scale of the problem leaves a very large part of the work unfinished. The scale of this international effort and the complicated mix of activities needed to even initiate a program of coastal and marine resource management is a stern reminder of the long-term nature of the task.

URBAN AND INDUSTRIAL POLLUTION

Although most of the large cities of North Africa are coastal, a good part of the environmental and resource-use issues related to them do not directly affect the coastal zone. Some of these cities feature both the poverty of a Third World society and its attendant problems, as well as the pollution associated with a modernized society. Cairo, Alexandria, and Algiers combine to house well over 12 million people, and it is in these three large agglomerations that some of the worst problems occur.

Cairo: some details of environmental issues and problems   Cairo rep-resents a large part of the Egyptian population of Egypt's 40 million inhabitants. In 1984 over 9.5 million lived in Cairo, the largest city of Africa and the Middle East. It has grown rapidly both in absolute terms and in relation to other cities in Egypt. In 1950 its population was just over 2 million. It increased to 5 million in 1970 and added another 3.5 million in the 1970s. Between 1980 and 1984 its population is estimated to have grown by 1 million.

Today over 50 percent of the industrial enterprises of Egypt are found in Cairo and Alexandria, the majority in Cairo. A large part of the economy of the country is concentrated in this small area. Cairo with its 1984 population still had a transportation network, public health and other infrastructure facilities that were barely adequate for a city of 2 million. Population density in some areas of the city is around 2000 people per hectare, and squatting even on burial land is not uncommon. The environmental problems that result are not all adequately documented and quantified, but their nature is clear.

289

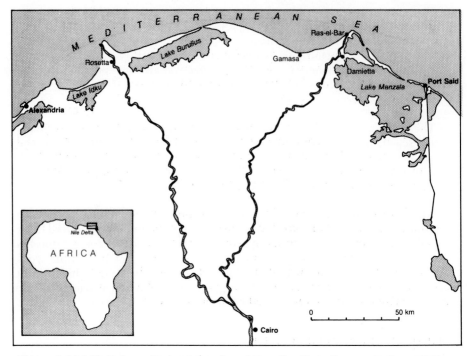

Figure 8.3 Nile Delta and Lakes Manzala and Borullus (from Farver & Milton 1972).

WATER POLLUTION

Although rural water in Egypt is polluted by salinity and agricultural chemicals, that is a relatively minor problem in relation to the massive pollution due to raw sewage and industrial effluent from the city. The Nile north of Cairo is severely polluted in a zone where a large part of the agricultural and middle-sized town population of Egypt lives. Lake Manzala (Fig. 8.3), the discharge point of a number of canals, is eutrophied. Coastal pollution from Cairo and Alexandria is one probable cause of a drop in fish catch both in the Nile and the immediate waters of the delta.

HEALTH AND DISEASE

Health hazards relevant to urban pollution are clearly identifiable; however, the statistical impact of these is not. Alexandria, with conditions like Cairo, has the sad distinction of having one of the highest urban infant mortality rates in the world. About a third of Cairo's population is currently served by modern sewage systems, and half the city's raw sewage is carried to the sea in open sewers. Dysentery is probably the largest single cause of death in the country, and typhoid, paratyphoid, and hepatitis are endemic. Against this critical set of health problems, problems of noise and air pollution, very real indeed in the city, seem less important. Yet chronic eye infections are a feature of both rural

290

and urban Egypt and are due in part to dust and other air pollutants. Other respiratory ailments are quite common.

It is not inappropriate that a good deal of government and donor attention is being given to urban problems in Cairo and Alexandria, but any such effort faces what appears now to be continuing rapid urban growth, at least over the next two decades. In summary, the most important problems related to these cities are:

(a) Disposal of human and industrial waste – resulting in

    (i)   health hazards for the adult population,
    (ii) high rates of infant mortality,
    (iii) poor aesthetic environment.

(b) Congested living conditions.
(c) Air and noise pollution from automobiles.
(d) Automobile and industrial accidents.

ENVIRONMENTAL PROBLEMS RELATED TO AGRICULTURE

Issues of dryland pastoral occupation have been dealt with extensively elsewhere in this book, so this section focuses primarily on the problems of rainfed and irrigated agriculture.

Rainfed agriculture in northern Africa is confined to the coastlands of the Mediterranean east of Libya and the Atlantic shores and to a few highland areas. It ranges from the vineyards, orange groves, and wheatfields of Algeria, Tunisia, and lowland Morocco to the small-scale subsistence wheat and maize cropping of those countries. Environmental problems are less severe in this zone than in most other parts of Africa, partly because of the high investment in export crop production and partly because of the characteristics of climate, soil, and topography in this coastal area. The steady winter rain and relatively low land gradient in many areas combine to make this a lower energy erosive environment than many parts of humid tropical Africa. The most important problems may be those of pesticide and insecticide use and, on small farms, the increasing intensity of land use forced by increasing numbers of people on a fixed land resource.

Irrigated agriculture is common throughout the whole region. It is the dominant pattern of cultivated land use in Egypt, and is becoming ever more important in Libya and other countries.

In Egypt most of the irrigated land is provided with water from the Nile; in Libya almost all irrigation is from groundwater and a few intermittent streams. In the other countries, irrigation comes from a combination of streams with sources in the highlands and groundwater. The source of the water and the scale and type of the irrigation are important elements in determining the resultant degree of success and sustainability of the irrigated farming.

Irrigation from the Nile Irrigation from the Nile has been the basis of Egyptian agriculture for many thousands of years. For most of that time, water was diverted from a silt sediment laden Nile in flood to the cultivated fields. The standing water on the fields deposited its nutrient-rich silt and fertilized as well

291

as watered the lands. The annual flooding of the lands resulted in low rates of salinization, and the silt deposits further helped to dilute any concentration of salts at or near the surface.

The traditional system did bring the attendant problems of bilharzia and malaria, but again the seasonal pattern helped to keep this from epidemic proportions. In the last 100 years and, most dramatically, in the last 25 years, the pattern of utilization has changed. By building dams, changes in the methods by which water is brought to the fields have been accompanied by increases in the area flooded and also by large additional numbers of people fed from the products of Egyptian agriculture. Now all Nile water is stored behind the High Dam at Aswan before it is used. This means that most of the silts, with their nutrients, are deposited on the floor of Lake Nasser, not on the fields. The demands for agricultural products to feed a population of 40 million has meant that existing lands are now being used more frequently for two or three crops a year, and that new lands are being brought under cultivation. The older lands, now flooded two or three times a year, have proved more susceptible to salinization, and the new lands have also proved to be vulnerable to this problem. The need for additional fertilizer to replace the missing nutrients, brought formerly in the silt, compounds the problem and also increases costs. The greater length of irrigation may also have increased the incidence of water-related diseases, though the data to back up this conclusion are not available. The Egyptian government, with assistance from donors, is beginning to tackle some of these problems and other environmental problems of disease control, but the task is likely to be long and complex.

Irrigation from groundwater In northern Egypt and in Libya, groundwater is the main source of irrigation. The prototype has been oasis gardens which for many years have created gardens in the desert at locations where subsurface water, reasonable soil, and human occupance have coincided. In those cases the lands under cultivation were usually quite small since water was obtained by human or animal power, and this somewhat limited the quantity available for irrigation.

Modern irrigation can of course tap deeper groundwater, and pumps move larger water volumes over short periods. Quite large parts of the northern Sahara do have a coherent groundwater table, and today this is only tapped in some localities. Pump irrigation of the type used in Colorado and California is becoming more common, especially in Libya. Isolated green spots are being created in the desert. In some cases this appears to have been a good investment of the petro dollars and has been helpful in diversifying the Libyan economy.

This is especially the case where active recharge of the aquifer is taking place from desert-stream floods or from the intermittent flows of many north coast rivers during the humid winter months. Further south, where the groundwater is more likely to be fossil, this may not be the case. Already in some areas pumping has resulted in a rapid lowering of the water table and an accompanying increase in the salinity of the water.

Carbon-14 dates on some water samples have yielded dates of 35,000 years or older, and the indications are that this groundwater is residual from former periods of colder and more humid climate. In both Libya and Egypt, use of such fossil water can only be a short-time resource and could result in the salinization of some soils of good potential in these dry areas.

Further west, in Algeria and Morocco, most of the irrigation near the coast or in the higher irrigated areas is derived from either surface or subsurface water from contemporary rivers on the highlands, largely resulting from the winter rains or snows. Of all the irrigation types in North Africa this area has the fewest supply problems, although in areas where upland deforestation is widespread increased variability in the seasonal flows and uncertainty in supply is a result. The problems that occur in this area are more connected with the management of water on the farms, particularly as regards drainage, than with the water supply. In these areas the efforts are now oriented toward soil erosion control and encouraging infiltration of rainfall.

Extratropical southern Africa

For the purpose of this analysis, we are treating the Republic of South Africa and the countries which economically have linkages with it, Namibia, Botswana, Zimbabwe, Lesotho, Mozambique, Malawi, and Swaziland, as the unit of study (Fig. 8.4). Although this group includes territory that falls within the tropical zone, the common pattern of problems and history provides the unity for the area, and the economic linkages with the Republic remain important for most of this zone.

Environmentally, the region ranges from the humid coasts of Mozambique, the cool upland plateaus of the Republic, and the Mediterranean-type climate of the southwestern tip of the continent to the very dry desert lands of Botswana and Namibia. For much of Africa the environmental regions provide the best framework through which to analyze major resource-use issues. But in southern Africa the pattern of land use imposed by the history of the area is equally important. The history of white occupance has resulted in a stark differentiation of land use in many places within a similar environmental setting. In Zimbabwe

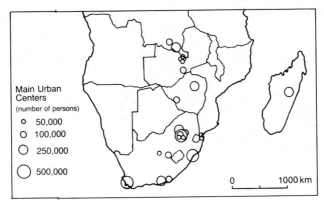

Figure 8.4   Countries and urban areas in southern Africa. (Modified from Hance 1975.)

293

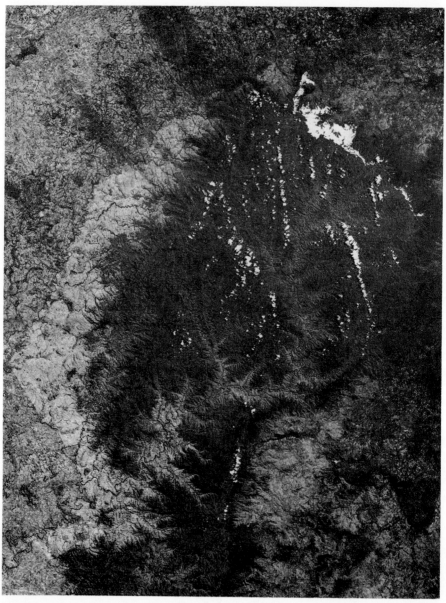

Figure 8.5 Landsat image of the Lesotho/South African border showing the poorer vegetation cover in Lesotho.

there are less than 150,000 Whites, most of whom live in urban areas, and around 7 million Blacks, the majority of whom live off the land. Yet white farmers own and occupy about half of the agricultural land, whereas black farmers occupy the remaining half. The obvious discrepancy is further emphasized by the fact that the black farmers are generally situated on the poorer agricultural lands.

Lesotho occupies primarily hilly, less fertile land in a part of the region that is, overall, good agriculturally. Over three-quarters of the country has steep hill slopes which should not be farmed because of their high erosional potential. The soils on these slopes are generally both infertile and thin. Even on the remaining arable land at least 10 percent has been destroyed by gully erosion, the result of the combination of dense rural population, low investment, and poor management practices. A Landsat image of the boundary area between Lesotho and the Republic of South Africa shows the boundary as though it were a natural geologic feature of the Earth (Fig. 8.5). The main reason for the abrupt landscape change is that the differences in population density and types of land use on the two different sides have greatly altered the vegetation cover. In Lesotho high densities are accompanied by low levels of agricultural investment per hectare of land per year.

This same effect of dense population, low investment, and poorer management practices is reflected in the land status between the newly established Black Homelands and the surrounding terrain of the Republic. These Black Homelands exist solely as a result of the political policy of separate development, one of the overriding philosophies of the current South African government. Almost no other sovereign governments recognize their existence. Nevertheless, their existence as the internal policy of the government encourages the environmental contrasts between the Homelands and the Republic areas. Because of the enforced limitation of the movement of people within the national boundaries, population densities remain high in the areas, and this density of occupance contributes to the stress placed on the water and land resources. The Homelands of the Republic of South Africa are located in a horseshoe-like discontinuous ring around the northwestern segment of the country (Fig. 8.6). This area has generally good rainfall conditions and moderately fertile soils, but the density of occupance on these lands and the low levels of technology and investment has meant low levels of productivity.

Population densities vary greatly in this area. Botswana and Namibia have very low densities of settlement because all of their territory is arid or semi-arid and arable agriculture is only possible in a small part of each country. Malawi, Swaziland, and Lesotho reflect the high densities typical of Black settlement in southern Africa, though they do not approach the densities in the humid areas of Rwanda and Burundi. Both the Republic of South Africa and Zimbabwe, with intermediate densities, reflect the different pattern of Black and White occupancy in those countries. Mozambique falls into a different environmental setting and has a density which hides the great variety in this large country.

Mozambique is a country as large as Texas. It extends north–south over 1800 km and thus is cut across by several climatic zones. Rainfall is greatest in the north and is concentrated between October and March; further south the southern summer rainfall pattern is shorter, and the totals are less. Further diversity arises as an extensive coastal lowland is replaced in the inland direction

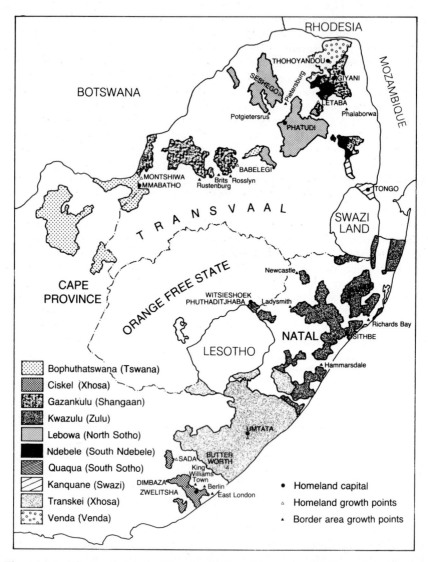

Figure 8.6 The South African Homelands (from Department of Bantu Administration and Development 1975).

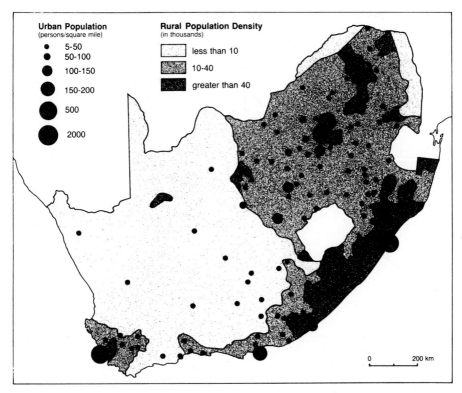

Figure 8.7 Population distribution and population density in the Republic of South Africa (from Board *et al.* 1970).

by low plateaus and highlands, rising first to 1000 m and then to isolated highlands as much as 2100 m high.

The humid areas in Mozambique and the highlands of Zimbabwe and Malawi are separated by subhumid areas in the lower elevation areas of Zimbabwe and the northern part of the Republic. The southern and eastern pastures of the Republic are favored by cooler temperatures and winter rainfall, whereas large parts of Namibia and Botswana are arid and semi-arid. A large part of the Republic of South Africa falls into the semi-arid zone with pastoral or ranching systems predominant in terms of land use.

An important part of the South African settlement is related to industry and mining and is concentrated in or near major urban agglomerations (Fig. 8.7). Table 8.5 lists the major urban centers. The small size of the capital cities of many of the African states is indicative of their low level of industrial development. The number of large cities in Zimbabwe and the Republic is indicative of the high level of industrial economy of those two countries.

Mining is an important economic activity in both countries, with diamonds, copper, coal, nickel, chrome, and uranium all being important. Diamonds and coal are also important in Botswana.

Table 8.5 Urban areas in
southern Africa.

	Population
Pretoria	715,000
Cape Town	820,000
Port Elizabeth	480,000
Johannesburg	900,000
Durban	930,000
Soweto	1,500,000
Maseru	20,500
Maputo	400,000
Harare	710,000
Bulawayo	420,000
Windhoek	53,000
Gaborone	45,000
Beira	132,000
Lilongwe	84,000
Mbabane	18,400

Given this distribution of settlement and economic activity, the rest of this section is organized around the themes of agriculture and land use, urban problems, the mining environment, and dry lands.

Agriculture and land use

The uneven distribution of land in southern Africa has already been emphasized. After some more detailed discussion of South Africa, we examine Zimbabwe as a case study on the effect of such uneven land distribution.

THE REPUBLIC OF SOUTH AFRICA

The pattern of rural land use in the Republic of South Africa reflects a political economy as well as a set of environmental circumstances. By African standards the country is highly urbanized. Still, some 13 percent of the Whites, 26 percent of the Coloreds, 13 percent of East Indians, and 67 percent of Blacks live and work in rural areas. Figure 8.7 illustrates the density of population throughout the country. The dry west has about five persons per square kilometer; the southeast has over 20. However, these average densities hide much local variability. Africans, who make up 72 percent of the population, have been allocated under the Homelands policy only 13 percent of the Republic's total land area. Most of these Homeland areas are relatively humid, but they are areas of relatively infertile soils which were reduced in potential productivity by widespread erosion even prior to the establishment of the Homelands policy. "In general, these homelands remain poor, overpopulated, lacking in resources and unable to provide the range and wealth of economic opportunities available outside their borders." (Williams 1981b.)

298

In contrast, the agricultural scene in the Republic, varied as it is from the sugar cane areas of Natal, the wheat and citrus zones of the Cape, and the maize and wheat farming of the high Veld, is generally a scene of modern farming enterprises without great problems of investment capital, shortage of land, or available technology. The rural land-use pattern of South Africa needs truly to be explained by both political and environmental factors.

In some respects Lesotho, although long an independent country, has similar problems to some of the Homelands. It is a country without a range of resource conditions, with severely overtaxed land and water resources, and with an economy that does not easily permit increased per hectare investment in these resources. Swaziland has a much better and more varied resource base, including tourism. It has a greater diversity of economy, generally allowing for more investment in resource use.

ZIMBABWE

The case of Zimbabwe is chosen partly because it is a well-defined portion of Southern Africa where the problem of land and resource allocation is well articulated, and partly because there is a good and available literature on the area. The analysis presented draws heavily on the work of Stocking and Elwell (1973), Stocking (1972, 1978), Elwell (1980), and Whitlow (1980a,b).

Walker (1975) set out the basic land situation in the early 1970s. Fifteen million hectares (38 percent of the country) were reserved for European farming, of which 700,000 ha (less than 5 percent) were cultivated; 16.28 million hectares (41.5 percent of the country) were designated as Tribal Trust Lands (TTL), of which 9–11 percent were cultivated. These were the farming areas for black Rhodesians, allocated by the former Rhodesian government. Estimates suggest that, although there was ample opportunity for at least a threefold expansion of arable cultivation in European farmlands, there was little if any available arable land for expansion in the TTL (Walker 1975). The analysis of TTL conditions shows that 3 million people cultivated 1.8 million hectares of land at a ratio of 0.6 ha per person, whereas the 12.25 million hectares available for grazing supported near the maximum number of animals the land could sustain (Walker 1975). Walker's projections for the next ten years (1975–85) estimate a decrease in land available per person to 0.36 ha. From all indications this is the current picture, which is little affected by some resettlement on farms formerly owned by Whites but complicated by the influx of refugees from Mozambique in the east.

The following 1979 data (*The Economist* 1984) illustrate the relation between production and the three legal categories of farmland found in Zimbabwe. Approximately 1 percent of the 714,852 farms are commercial farms, almost all owned by Whites or large companies; another 1 percent are purchase area farms, which Blacks can own freehold; the remaining 98 percent are TTL farms (now known as "communal areas"). With 45 percent of the farmland in 1979, 77 percent of the commercial crops by value came from the commercial farms, 2 percent from the purchase area farms, and only 21 percent from the TTL farms. The low productivity on the TTL farms for many of the farmers results in malnutrition and poverty, resulting in large numbers of these farmers migrating into the urban areas. In addition the low income produced on the TTL farms

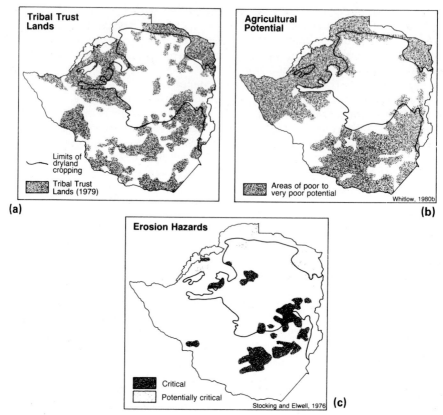

Figure 8.8 Environmental constraints on agricultural development in the tribal trust land areas of Zimbabwe: (a) Tribal trust lands and dryland cropping limits; (b) agricultural potential; (c) erosion hazards (from Whitlow 1980b).

prevents enough capital being raised, and thus the farmers cannot make large investments on the land. Environmental conditions on the TTL generally are degrading as a result. It is interesting to note that production has grown rapidly in areas of former "white" farmland which have, since independence, been subdivided for "black" small farmers. In 1983–4, during a period when much of the country was suffering from drought, production from "white" farms was at average levels, but production from the new "black" small farmers was twice previous levels of that land. Large maize surpluses for sale to the rest of the country come from the new intense production.

Whitlow (1980b) examines some of the environmental contexts of TTL. Figure 8.8, adapted from Whitlow (1980b) illustrates the major issues. Figure 8.8 shows that nearly three-quarters of the TTL are located in the drier parts of the country (zones IV and V of a five-part classification of Zimbabwian land, with zones I and II being the most well watered and productive). Figure 8.8b expands this climatic parameter into general agricultural potential, and again the

300

major part of the TTL is in areas of poor or very poor agriculture potential. Sixty percent of the TTL were located in these areas. Figure 8.8c illustrates the degree of the erosion hazard, the zones with the highest hazard being found in the TTL. "In contrast just over 25 per cent of the general land (in the country as a whole) is of marginal value and nearly 50 per cent of areas were classified as having good to very good potential." (Whitlow 1980b.)

Whitlow further uses an index of sustainable land productivity to give some measure of the degree of intensity of use of the TTL. While we may disagree with the details of his "carrying capacity" approach, the resultant analysis gives a good index of the relative intensity of "overuse" of the land. Figure 8.9 (Whitlow 1980b) and Table 8.6 illustrate the nature of the problem. The two sets of illustrations demonstrate the situation precisely. Stocking and Ewell (1973) provide the next piece of analysis in Table 8.7, where they set out the physical and human parameters associated with erosion. It is clear that the combination of mid-to-low rainfall, moderate-to-steep slopes, and the TTL settlement combine to create the three highest levels of erosion risk and actual erosion.

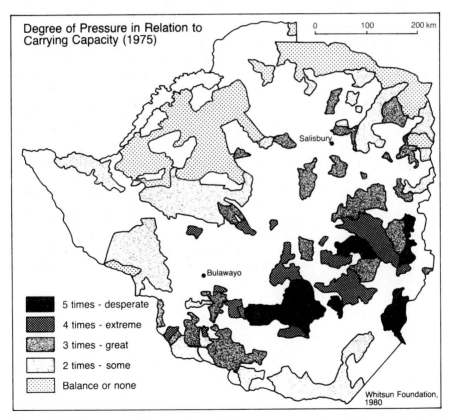

Figure 8.9 Human and livestock population pressure in the tribal trust lands of Zimbabwe (from Whitlow 1980b).

301

Table 8.6 Degree of population pressure in relation to carrying capacity.

Class	Proportion of TTL (%)
balanced or none	32.7
2 times optimum use, some pressure	29.8
3 times optimum use, great pressure	12.9
4 times optimum use, extreme pressure	11.7
5 times optimum use, desperate	12.9

Stocking (1972) further reviews some of the data in the field. He examines the extent of gully erosion in different land-tenure systems and, not surprisingly, finds that the sample of the TTL and other African farming areas has a greater frequency and magnitude of gullying than that of the Sabi-European sample area in a similar climatic zone. In fact, the gullying in the Sabi area appears to be associated most directly with areas of dense African land use within the broader European zone. He points out that this pattern has more to do with density of settlement and funds available for investment in land than any other factor.

The conclusion from these studies is quite clear: a very uneven pattern of land allocation within the country, flowing only from a hundred year history, has resulted in a situation where by far the largest number of farmers (Blacks) are restricted to land of moderate-to-low potential. The resulting pattern of land use necessarily leads to accelerated erosion – at least in some areas – and to impoverishment of the resource base. The rest of the land, which is under much higher investment levels and much lower density of use, is in better environmental shape. The economic and political difficulties and the resources problem which the pattern involves are well known. In both Zimbabwe and the Republic of South Africa most economic and political pressure for change is centered around the issue of equal access to resources and to opportunities to use the land and water resources in particular. Zimbabwe, now of course under Black rule, is struggling with the complex issues of independence, of maintaining the economy and yet creating greater equity in resource allocation. South Africa is experiencing some of the repercussions of its policies. The outlook in both cases is far from certain.

Urban problems

The urban population in southern Africa is a much higher percentage of the total population than in most of the rest of Africa. In the Republic of South Africa over 50 percent of the population are urban and about 85 percent of the non-African population live in towns.

The large cities include Johannesburg, the center of the Rand urban and mining area. This comprises the largest urban agglomeration in Africa south of the Sahara. It includes service and major industrial sectors within its economy, as well as mining. Vereeniging, Vanderbigl Park, and Sasolberg are old heavy

Table 8.7 The categories of erosion.

Category	Erosivity (J mm/m²/h)	Cover (mm of rainfall) and basal cover estimated (%)	Slope (degrees)	Erodibility	Human occupation
low I	below 5,000	above 1,000 / 7–10	0–2	ortho-ferralitic regosols para-ferralitic	extensive European ranching national parks or unreserved
below average II	5,000–7,000	800–1,000 / 5–8	2–4		most European farms
average III	7,000–9,000	600–800 / 3–6	4–6	fersiallitic	low-density TTL (below 5 p. p. km²) and APAs
above average IV	9,000–11,000	400–600 / 1–4	6–8	siallitic vertisols lithosols	moderately settled TTL (5–30 p. p. km²)
high V	above 11,000	below 400 / 0–2	above 8	noncalcic hydromorphic sodic	densely settled TTL (above 30 p. p. km²)

Source: Stocking and Elwell (1973).

Notes
Cover, erodibility, and human occupation are only tentative and cannot as yet be expressed on a firm quantitative basis.
p.p. km² = persons per square kilometer.

industrial towns; Cape Town and Durban are the major ports, with associated tourist and other industries.

Some of the more general problems of South African urban areas will be dealt with in Chapter 10; in this section we look especially at the separate development of cities especially characteristic of southern Africa, where racial integration is unlawful in the Republic or was previously discouraged, as in Zimbabwe.

The juxtaposition between Johannesburg and Soweto serve to illustrate the nature of the problem dramatically. Soweto is probably the largest urban area in South Africa. About 1.5 million Africans live less than an hour's drive from Johannesburg where most of them work but where most are not allowed to live. The one road leading to the area provides potential for easy control and even now homeowners can only lease, not own, the land in the area. Soweto is not all a slum. Many of the houses are of good quality, but the pattern of social services and professional services is absurdly low for this population. In some official contexts this city does not exist. It has been the scene of bloody rioting and major civil disorder. It is a major urban area largely without an official right to be there.

This contrasts in some ways with cities outside the Republic where the problems of African living are those of rapidly growing urban areas with poor facilities around the cores of European-style settlements. The African townships around Harare and Bulawayo have the problem of sanitation and health so common to "bidonvillles" everywhere. These are dealt with directly in the next chapter.

Mining landscapes

The mining output of southern Africa is summarized in Table 8.8. In Zimbabwe, the Republic of South Africa, Botswana, and Swaziland mineral production is an important part of the economy.

Figure 8.10 illustrates the distribution of the main mining areas in southern Africa. They are concentrated in South Africa, Zimbabwe, Namibia, and Botswana; in particular, the major gold-producing area around and south of Johannesburg, the coal fields around Vereeniging and Withbank, and the Botswana coalfields are important locations. There is no significant production in Lesotho and Malawi and only localized production in Mozambique. Namibia has some uranium mining.

Table 8.8 Mineral production in southern Africa.

Botswana	copper, coal, nickel, diamonds
Lesotho	none
Malawi	none
Mozambique	coal, tantalite, copper, iron, bauxite
Namibia	diamonds, copper, lead, zinc, uranium
Republic of South Africa	gold, diamonds, antimony, platinum, nickel, coal, manganese
Swaziland	asbestos, coal, iron
Zimbabwe	asbestos, copper, iron, coal, chrome

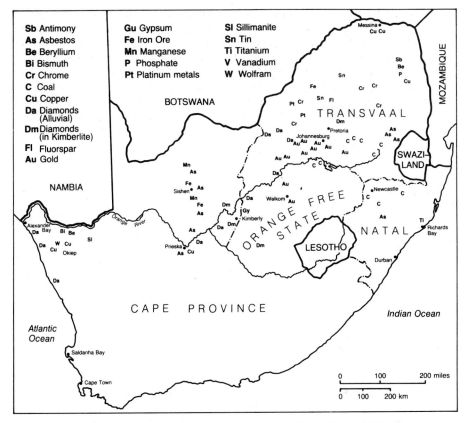

Figure 8.10 Mining areas in southern Africa (from Hance 1975).

Some of the physical impacts of mining on the landscape are readily visible on the surface of South Africa. The familiar man-made landscapes of debris from the coal mines and generally smaller waste heaps from the other minerals rise above the plateau surface of the mines. The rapid runoff from these waste areas clogs streams with coarse sediment and in some areas deposits the waste on agricultural land, ruining it.

Some of the other impacts of the mining industry are less readily observed but affect the human condition in southern Africa even more widely. Among these less visible impacts are the local air and environment pollution due to dust, local wastes, and fumes. A totally different effect of mining on the landscape is the removal of able-bodied males from many areas. All of the manual mine labor in southern Africa is traditionally recruited from the areas of South Africa where Blacks live and from the neighboring states of Botswana, Malawi, Mozambique, Lesotho, and Swaziland. This labor, almost entirely male, is retained on short-term contracts that permit only the worker to take up residence at the mines. Male mineworkers leave their homes and farms to fulfill their contracts, sometimes but by no means always remitting funds to their families and then returning after a year or two with a few consumer goods and a small amount of cash. Restrictions by the independent countries and the spread of mechanization have reduced the flow, but for 50 or more years the economy and pattern of living for a large part of southern Africa has been greatly influenced by this labor pattern. The full impact of this process is not well documented, but, like the apartheid policy, it has had the effect of tying the economy of much of the region to the mining operation in ways that have not encouraged other more widespread development. On the other hand it can be argued that migrant labor has brought cash income and a certain kind of prosperity to a wide part of the region.

The drylands

Although the general environmental problems of drylands in Africa have been dealt with in other chapters, the particular nature of drylands in southern Africa deserves a brief special mention. It is clear that the drylands of Botswana, Namibia, Zimbabwe, and the Republic of South Africa suffer from the same problems of drought as similar areas in the rest of Africa. In 1983–4 these areas were in the throes of a major drought. This reduced crop production drastically and has led to increasing wind and water erosion over much of the area. During these drought periods the plant cover is consumed below a rapid recovery level. When it does rain the bare soil is easily eroded; when it is dry and high winds exist, the clays and silts in the soil are removed under wind erosion.

In comparison with areas in the Sahel and in eastern Africa, there are indications that the deterioration of the semi-arid environment is not nearly as great. Also, the degradation of the land is a more recent phenomenon in southern Africa. Comparisons between ecosystems in the southwest African desert, one of the driest areas of the world, and the Sahel suggest a greater diversity of species and a less degraded ecosystem than in the north. Gritzner (1981) points out that this may well be due to the 2000–3000 years of major interference with the ecosystem by man in the western Sahel, compared with a few hundred years of intense interference in the southwest.

However, there are strong signs that parts of the area are, quite apart from the drought, becoming much more stressed. The reduction of this stress is a very important priority for the governments concerned, and Botswana in particular has taken the lead in experimental approaches to dealing with problems of drought and land degradation.

The physical environments of southern Africa are quite diverse and of themselves present important management problems and opportunities. However, many of these issues have been overshadowed by the impact on resource use of the political and racial problems of the area. The most fundamental and pervasive of these, from the point of view of resource management, is the issue of land and resource distribution. The allocation of resources and the parallel availability of funds to improve the productivity of resources together makes a sharp and generally destructive impact on the environment. Similarly, in the mining economy the physical problems of resource use are compounded by the far-reaching human problems involved.

306

As evident from a brief discussion of drylands, the degree of degradation of ecosystems is not so great as in some other parts of Africa, and *if* in some way the fundamental problem of access to resources were dealt with, there would be room for some optimism. It is unfortunate that the current prospects for a real change in access to resources are slight.

9 Water: a scarce resource

Introduction

The climatic feature of most significance for development in Africa is rainfall. Previous discussion (Chs. 5 & 6) has illustrated the fact that most areas of Africa have moisture deficits for a portion of the year, and vast areas (e.g. the Sahara) have moisture deficits throughout the whole year. Compounding the problem of water availability is the nature of the underlying rocks found in Africa (Ch. 1). Given that the basement rocks found within most of Africa are impermeable, most of the continent has but modest groundwater resources. As a result of these climatic and geologic characteristics, water availability is a crucial issue in resource development. In this chapter we examine the primary characteristics of Africa's surface waters – its lakes, rivers, and wetlands.

Precipitation and water-balance patterns

Some of the meteorologic records throughout the continent do not give a true picture of the climatologic situation, since some of the observation stations are located at atypical sites. For example, Marsabit in northern Kenya is built on a hill encircled by scrubland. It is relatively humid compared to its surroundings, and climatological data gathered here are not representative of the area as a whole. Given that the drier zones in northern Kenya have few weather stations, data from Marsabit will bias the moisture situation if its atypical location is not accounted for when these data are extrapolated to surrounding areas.

Similarly, rainfall averages need to be used with caution since in many areas the variability of rainfall from year to year is great. This large variability is normal for semi-arid and arid areas when compared to rainfall patterns in humid areas. Unfortunately, in recent years large parts of Africa have been experiencing less than average rainfall. Drought has become widespread in many parts of Africa recently because of a combination of factors, including this shortfall in precipitation; the geologic conditions that limit the utilization of groundwater; the poor existing infrastructure in most areas including water storage facilities, poor farming practices, and overgrazing. In the remainder of this chapter, the distribution of water in Africa will be examined. Some of the discussion will consist of brief reviews of information already presented in previous chapters, but in the main we will be concerned with providing new background information to illustrate the characteristics of the surface-water resource throughout Africa.

Figure 1.1 is a first approximation to a description of the water-balance conditions throughout Africa. The areas with values of less than 1 have a moisture surplus throughout the year, areas having values of between 1 and 2 have seasonal wet and dry periods, and areas having values greater than 2 overall are dry. The humid areas (values <1), which together equal less than 20 percent of the whole of Africa, are the major source areas of the larger African rivers. Within the dry areas (values >2) permanent bodies of water are rare, and where they are found the water has flowed from sources outside these dry zones. In most cases in Africa, the sources of these waters are in foreign countries; thus these important water resources require international cooperation in their management. This fact complicates their use in development projects. About 52 percent of Africa's total landmass has no permanent streams. A large proportion of these areas are zones of internal drainage. The shortage of water in these areas is a major impediment to development. When you add the lands that have seasonal water deficiencies (values between 1 and 2), over 80 percent of the continent experiences a shortfall in the water needed to meet agricultural, urban, and industrial demands at least during one portion of the year.

The water resources found in a specific location depend upon the local relationship between rainfall and evapotranspiration, as well as the water transfers via groundwater and surface water (lakes, rivers) flows. As discussed in previous chapters, the most distinguishing climatic attribute in Africa is the temporal balance between precipitation and evaporation. Only in the few highland areas and the extreme north and south of the continent is temperature a primary climatic determinant. In areas with a long positive water balance, such as the Zaire River Basin (Fig. 9.1), lakes or permanent rivers are a common landscape feature; obviously in the areas where evaporation is in excess of precipitation for most of the year surface waters are generally nonexistent or short in duration (hours to days). When a permanent lake or river is found in these dry areas, such as Lakes Chad and Turkana or the lower Tana River, it is because the upper reaches of the basins are humid. However, the natural transfer of water from humid areas to drier areas is not a widespread phenomenon in Africa. Most of Africa's larger rivers flow away from those areas that need water. Of Africa's major rivers, only the Nile and the Orange flow through desert and arid lands in their middle and lower courses. The lower Niger and Zaire both flow away from dry Africa and empty into the ocean in some of the more humid areas of the continent.

Clearly there are numerous smaller rivers that do flow from more humid areas into drier climates. The Juba and Shebelli in Somalia, the Tana and Galana in Kenya, and the Curoca in Angola are examples of rivers that have their sources in highlands and their mouths on the coasts in arid environments. But because of their moderate discharges their potential in supplying water to the down-stream drier areas is limited. Already water diversions are occurring, and additional ones are proposed in the Tana and Galana river systems to meet the increasing water demands for highland agriculture and urban supply for Nairobi. This places additional limits on the waters potentially available in some of the drier areas in Kenya. Some of these smaller rivers have the characteristic that their sources are in one country, their mouths in another. The greatest percentage of the discharge in both the Juba and Shebelli rivers originate in Ethiopia; thus for Somalia to be ensured of a guaranteed flow to meet its needs an international agreement with Ethiopia is required. Given the political re-lations between these two countries, this is an unlikely probability in the near future.

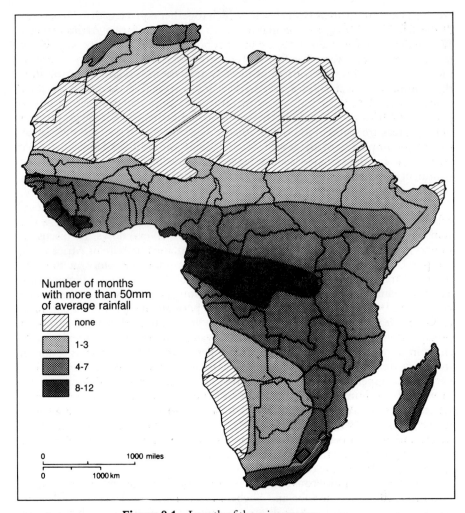

Figure 9.1 Length of the rainy season.

A final problem associated with the use of the moderate-size rivers to meet water demands in arid areas is that their flow has large ranges from year to year. Because they are small, in drier years little water is available for use. The Curoca, which has its sources on the Huila Plateau, has a small catchment. Therefore, if sufficient precipitation does not occur in this single area, the flow of the Curoca will be small. Thus, unlike larger rivers, the smaller rivers have both a smaller discharge and a less consistent baseflow from year to year. Both of these attributes make them less reliable as a water supply for development projects.

Figure 9.1 illustrates that over 50 percent of the continent experiences rainfall in a period of three months. In fact, over 66 percent of Africa has more than half of its rainfall during a three-month period or less. This concentration of precipitation into a few months results in widespread extreme river régimes throughout a large proportion of the continent. This makes it both difficult and costly to utilize the waters from most African rivers. The general case for most African areas is to have short periods of water surplus followed by long intervals of water shortage. Because of the seasonal distribution of rainfall, most of the land is out of balance with regard to water needs and water supply during most of the year; periods of large water surpluses, sometimes marked by floods, are often followed by periods of large moisture deficits, during which rivers dry up or have very low discharges. To have sufficient water available during the dry periods, if economic development is to increase, requires major construction and management of water storage facilities to capture even a small percentage of the water surplus from the brief wet periods. For some countries, such as Mauritania and Namibia, because their national territory is almost completely arid and semi-arid even these options do not exist. The extreme limitation of water resources in the African countries that are completely in semi-arid and arid climates greatly restricts most development options because of the paramount importance of water for most economic activities.

The sub-Saharan area

Regarding the scarcity of the water resource, perhaps the most widely analyzed and publicized region is sub-Saharan Africa, an area stretching the whole width of the continent between 11°N and 20°N. In the 20th century three major droughts 1908–14, 1940s, and 1968–73 have been documented. In addition there is good evidence that the 1968–73 drought has essentially continued into the 1980s (Nicholson 1983). The persistence of extreme rainfall deficits throughout the 1970s and mid-80s appears to be the result of natural events and possibly the existence of a biogeophysical feedback mechanism. Charney (1975) suggests that the persistence of the drought in this area of Africa is partially a result of changes in the landscape resulting from human activities. He suggests that vegetation removal in the Sahel, both through drought (natural) and desertification (human, e.g. overgrazing), will increase the surface albedo (the reflecting capability of the surface). This increases the radiant energy lost to space, thus increasing air subsidence. Since sinking air currents suppress rainfall, the dry period continues and even spreads areally. Other climatologists have developed mathematical models that support the hypothesis that human activities have contributed to the persistence of the drought in sub-Saharan Africa. Nicholson (1983) summarizes these models and concludes that when agriculture and pastoralism are extended into marginal areas during wet years the environmental damage that occurs during a subsequent drought is accelerated and intensified.

This conclusion appears to have been substantiated in a recent analysis made by the Club du Sahel (1983). This report concludes that in the Sahel, as from the early 1980s, food production is rising less than population, meat exports are dropping, food imports (cereals which provide about two-thirds of the calories consumed by the Sahelians) into the area are increasing, deforestation and desertification are advancing, and urban migration is increasing.

The water shortage in this area requires new initiatives if the region is to remain as a viable food-producing zone in the future. A need exists to develop a system to replace the existing production systems, which remain very vulnerable to climatic conditions. The new systems need to be geared to production that is possible during dry years. During periods of increased rainfall, as during the 1950s, agricultural and pastoral expansion must be limited so as to prevent land degradation from occurring when the rainfall returns to a lower, more frequently expected amount.

From year to year, variability in rainfall is expected in semi-arid areas such as the Sahel. Care must be taken not to consider the wet years to be the norm, since when the drier years return the environment must be maintained. Given the possibility of a biogeophysical feedback in the sub-Saharan area, groundcover needs to be maximized to increase the probability of rains in the area.

River characteristics

Three factors, relief, tectonics, and precipitation, determine the primary flow characteristics of African rivers. The vegetation within the river basins modifies these discharges by its water demands, which reduce the amount of precipitation available for flow. The broad warping of the continent by tectonic forces results in a typical pattern of relief that is characterized by broad shallow basins separated by divides of mountains and plateaux. In some areas (e.g. eastern Zaire), the divides between the shallow basins, especially where the warping is of recent geologic history, are imperceptible. In these areas the divides are marked by swamps, and the river courses result in a pattern of marshy lakes, as opposed to the common image of a discrete river channel. The Sudd in the Nile system, the lower portion of the Kagera, and the inland delta on the Niger are illustrative of the effects of warping and very slight gradients on river flows. A second characteristic of many African rivers resulting from geologic factors is the widespread existence of rapids in their systems. The Zaire is navigable upstream from the ocean for only 130 km before its channel is marked by a series of major rapids. Additionally many of its major tributaries throughout the system have their courses interrupted by rapids. The Nile has six major cataracts and the middle Niger is divided into two sections by rapids. The general result of the interaction between hydrology and geology in Africa is that few rivers have the potential for development as major transport routes.

Almost all river discharges in Africa are directly determined by precipitation, since most are fed solely by rainwater. Only in Morocco does snowmelt represent a significant component in river discharge patterns. Except in some mountainous areas, only in the narrow zone along portions of the equator does rainfall not exhibit a strong seasonal pattern. Since rainfall patterns are the primary factor in determining the discharge régime of African rivers, most rivers have strong seasonal patterns on the continent. The Zaire, which straddles the equator and drains floodwaters alternately from north and south as the wet season changes, is an exception to this generalization. It has a relatively stable discharge with a flow régime characterized by slow rises and falls in its discharge. But the vast majority of African rivers fall within the flood category. That is, their water levels rise and fall sharply. Some, like the Senegal, have a number of short, sharp spates during a single annual cycle. For river basins that are completely within a single wet–dry climatic régime, during the rainy seasons the discharges are high, whereas during the dry seasons they often become almost completely dry. For example, many of the Limpopo River's tributaries reflect this strong direct climatic control as they are intermittent, flowing only during and immediately after the rainy season. Because of the small discharges that occur in most African rivers during the drier periods, many of the river sections that are classified as navigable are only navigable during a small part of the year. The combination of rapids in many African rivers, along with the generally highly variable discharges during the annual cycle, results in very few rivers on the whole continent serving as important transportation routes.

The relationship between vegetation and river flows is strong for the smaller river basins in many parts of the continent. With the rapid change in vegetation cover that is occurring during the 20th century, the flow characteristics of many African rivers are being altered toward more extreme flow régimes. Vegetation affects stream flows both by the amount of moisture it requires for its growth and by its interception of rainfall. Generally, trees consume more water than any other vegetation cover, with broadleaf trees transpiring more moisture than conifers. Grasses and permanent crops, such as tea and coffee, are intermediate in terms of their moisture consumption, whereas annual crops usually consume the least amount of moisture during a yearly cycle. Likewise, trees overall intercept the greatest amount of rainfall, grasses and permanent crops are intermediate, and annual crops usually result in the lowest amounts. The net result of the changing vegetation pattern in Africa, as land is cleared for either food or energy, is to increase the percentage of rainfall entering the river systems (lower water demands); at the same time the rainfall enters the river systems faster, due both to lower interception and infiltration into the soil. Together these two changes result in a larger percentage of the rainfall flowing overland directly into river channels. As a result, the river régimes in many places in Africa are becoming more extreme and more directly in phase with the climate. Streams that were perennial under natural conditions have become intermittent as forests have been cleared, since the greater runoff results in lower ground-water recharge. One effect of the lower recharge during the wet season is a lower water table during the dry seasons. This reduces the groundwater inflows into river channels, which are the major source of water for streams during the dry periods. The result is that the water resource has deteriorated and is becoming ever more costly to manage. Welcomme (1976) states that 99 percent of Africa's rivers are very small, and short in length. Altogether, 90 percent of Africa's total river lengths are in these small streams. These small streams are those most affected by the changes in vegetation cover. In the remainder of this section three river systems will be examined to illustrate some of the diversity of river systems in Africa.

The Niger system

The Niger River Basin is within eight countries; Benin, Cameroon, Guinea, Ivory Coast, Mali, Niger, Nigeria, and Burkina Faso (Fig. 9.2). Its total basin area is approximately 1,500,000 km^2, discharging 180 billion m^3 of water in an

313

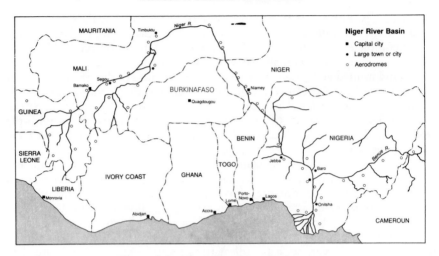

Figure 9.2 The Niger River Basin.

average year. A schematic representation of the Niger and its important tributaries is presented in Figure 9.3.

The Niger is often divided into three parts: the upper, the middle, and the lower sections. The upper river begins in highlands in humid areas and the channels are situated in narrow valleys with moderately steep slopes. The middle section begins when the waters spread out on a large floodplain at the edge of the Sahara. The middle section is marked by seasonal flooding and a decrease in discharge in the downstream direction, due to the dry climatic conditions of this section. The lower section is marked by a well-defined course and flows largely through savanna and more humid lands beginning near the Nigerian/Niger border. The climate in this section becomes ever more humid in the downstream direction. As a result, the discharge of the Niger increases in the downstream direction. The whole Benue River system, the major tributary of the Niger (which has a larger discharge than the Niger at its confluence), is considered to be in this lower section.

Two major headwater systems are found in the upper section. The stream system designated as the Niger has its source at an altitude of 800 m and a distance of 250 km from the Atlantic in the Futa Jallon Highlands. This is a high-rainfall forested area along the Guinea/Sierra Leone border. A short distance upstream from Bamako this portion of the upper Niger leaves the forest and descends in a series of rapids for about 60 km. The other major upper Niger tributary system, the River Bani, begins in the humid northern highlands of the Ivory Coast and flows into the Niger at Mopti. During the Late Pleistocene an additional source of the Niger flowed southward from the Ahaggar Mountains in the Tilemsi and Azouak rivers. Both of these systems today are almost extinct. These two systems, as well as the other relic channels found in the Sahel and Sahara, make almost no contribution to the Niger's hydrology during most years. Nevertheless, when rains do occur in these dry areas the runoff flows toward these relic channels and infiltrates into the dry channel beds. This

314

permits some vegetation to grow in these "dry" channels as the plant roots can tap the ground moisture, which is closer to the surface in these zones.

The middle Niger flows in a very flat terrain, which has a dry climate. The area is often described as a zone of inland deltas, swamps, and lakes. It stretches from Markala to near Timbuktu. The land gradient in this area is very slight (0.005 percent) and large areas lie below the flood levels of the Bani and Niger. During wet years, about 80,000 km^2 of land are flooded in this section. It is estimated

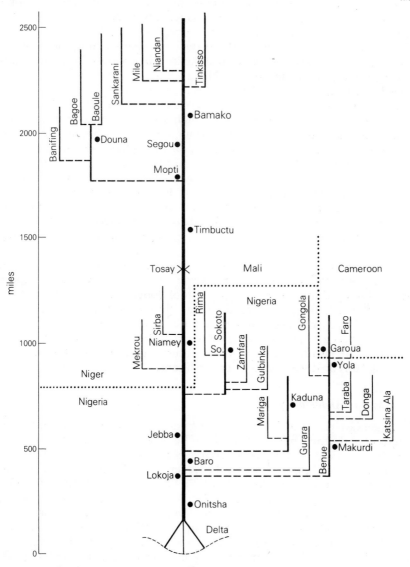

Figure 9.3 The main tributaries of the Niger River and their distance upstream from the mouth of the river.

that the evaporation loss from these shallow waters in this Sahelian climate is equivalent to about 2500 mm of precipitation. This is reflected in the decrease of the average annual discharge (1457 m³/s) of the Niger between Koulikouro, which is upstream from the Bani, and the average annual discharge (1065 m³/s) at Timbuktu, which is downstream from the Bani–Niger confluence. This decrease in discharge in the downstream direction reflects the dry nature of the middle Niger section. By the time the Niger reaches Niamey, the mean flow is down to 1000 m³/s. The Niger continues to decrease in size until the Sokoto River joins the Niger about 500 km downstream from Niamey. This is the first permanent tributary entering the Niger in over 1300 km.

The lower Niger's hydrology reflects the increasingly humid conditions that are encountered in the downstream direction. In contrast to the decreasing discharges in the middle section, the Niger's flow once again begins to increase in the downstream direction. This flow is increased greatly at the confluence of the Benue with the Niger. For the waters that enter the Niger system in the upstream section, it takes approximately eight to nine months for them to reach the sea. In some years during extreme drought in the Sahelian area of the basin (middle section), little water originating in the uplands reaches the sea. In contrast to the middle Niger, the lower Niger has a well-defined course. During periods of high water its flows are relatively restricted to a narrow floodplain, in marked contrast to the general widespread flooding conditions found in the middle section. This has permitted a major dam, the Kainji, to be built near Bussa in Nigeria. In addition, two other dams are planned on the lower Niger, one near Jebba on the Niger and another on the Kaduna River in the Shiroro Gorge.

When it was built, the Kainji power station was intended to meet electrical power needs in western Nigeria. However, because of lower than expected flows in the upper and middle Niger, it took longer than expected to fill the reservoir. In addition, a lower discharge than expected into the lake has prevented the power plant from generating its planned capacity. Both of these shortfalls reflect a general fact about African hydrology. For almost all rivers, the records are insufficient to permit an accurate prediction of flow and of the effects of dams on downstream river conditions.

The Kagera (Akagera) system

The Kagera River, the major river flowing into Lake Victoria, contributes about 25 percent of the total inflow into the lake. Because of this significant magnitude of discharge, it is considered as the source of the White Nile. This is especially true in Rwanda and Burundi where the Kagera's sources are found. The basin's 59,800 km² is situated in four countries (Table 9.1); however, the major proportion of its waters originate in the Western Highlands of Rwanda and Burundi along the Nile–Zaire river basin divide. Water balance measurements indicate that over 85 percent of the discharge of the Kagera Basin is generated in Rwanda and Burundi. The largest water source of the Kagera is the Nyabarongo River in Rwanda. This tributary's catchment area is about 16,000 km². The sources of the Nyabarongo, in western Rwanda, are about 300 km upstream from where the river enters Lake Rweru on the Burundi/Rwanda border. The

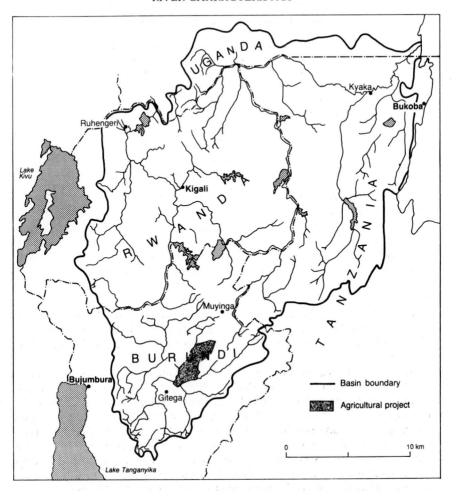

Figure 9.4 The Kagera River Basin (from Kagera Basin Organization).

Ruvubu River in Burundi and its tributary, the Luvironza, are the other major water sources in the Kagera Basin. Together they drain about 12,300 km². The Ruvubu flows for about 350 km before it joins the Kagera 2 km upstream from the gorge of Rusumo Falls.

Above Kigali on the Nyabarongo and upstream of Mumwendo Ferry on the Ruvubu the runoff coefficients, the ratio of runoff to precipitation, are high (0.3). This reflects the steep terrain and small forest cover found in these areas. Downstream from these two locations the slopes decrease, the valley floors become more gentle and wider, and the bottom lands often become occupied by swamps or lakes. The major exception to these characteristics is the gorge of Rusumo Falls where the Kagera drops 30 m in a distance less than 1 km. The result of these terrain changes is that the runoff coefficients below Mumwendo

Table 9.1 Location and extent of the Kagera Basin.

Country	Total area (km^2)	Kagera Basin (%)
Tanzania	20,000	35
Rwanda	19,900	33
Burundi	13,300	22
Uganda	5,800	10
Total	59,800	100

Ferry and Kigali decrease to 0.15 or less. Downstream from these two locations precipitation also begins to decrease. The combined effects of lower runoff, lower precipitation, and increased evapotranspiration from the swamps and lakes are a decrease in the seasonal flow and only a moderate increase in river discharges beyond these two reference points. Below Rusumo Falls, the valley widens again and the gradient decreases. For the next 230 km it flows through a series of lakes and papyrus swamps until its junction with the Kagitumba River at the Rwanda, Tanzania, and Uganda boundary. Below Rusumo Falls, the evapotranspiration is about equal to the precipitation in the basin. The only increase in discharge in this lower area of the Kagera Basin results from the flows of the Kagitumba (Rwanda, Uganda), Mwisa (Tanzania), and Ngono (Tanzania) rivers.

Long-term discharge records do not exist for most of the Kagera Basin. In Rwanda, systematic observations did not begin until 1963. Using the available data, the median annual flow at Kigali is 225 m^3/s, at Kanzenze 258 m^3/s, and at Rusumo 390 m^3/s. At Kyaka in Tanzania, only 60 km from its outlet in Lake Victoria, the mean annual discharge has decreased to 184 m^3/s. The decrease in the downstream discharge below Rusumo reflects the high evapotranspiration losses resulting from its flow through the swamps. The impact of the swamps on the discharge of the lower Kagera is also reflected in the régime of the river. The ratio between the maximum recorded flow at Kyaka (540 m^3/s) and its minimum flow (103 m^3/s) is five. This indicates that the lower Kagera is naturally a well-regulated river. The swamps store water during high-flow periods and release water during low-flow periods. The lakes found throughout central and eastern Rwanda – which are all within the Kagera Basin – give the whole river system a very regulated flow. At the four Rwandan recording stations in the Kagera Basin, the difference between the high and low mean monthly discharges is less than three. This low value reflects the regulated flow in the system (Table 9.2). As evident from the low range of flows experienced throughout the Kagera system, flooding generally is not a major problem within the basin.

The portion of the basin immediately up and downstream from Rusumo Falls is one of the lowest populated areas in Rwanda and Burundi. It is an area of generally poor soils as well as a relatively dry area. However, because of the need to open up new lands in response to the population pressures in the other areas of the country, it has become an area of new settlement. One possible strategy

Table 9.2 Range of annual flows in the Kagera Basin.

Location	High mean monthly flow (m^3/s)	Low mean monthly flow (m^3/s)
Nyabarongo-Mwaka	55 (May)	25 (September)
Nyabarongo-Kigili	117 (May)	48 (August)
Nyabarongo-Kanzenze	165 (May)	59 (September)
Kagera-Rusumo Falls	305 (May)	130 (October)

for agricultural development in this area is to irrigate the better lands. Generally these are the lands at the lower elevations. For irrigation to be economically viable in this area, there is a need for inexpensive energy, as pumping of water will be necessary. A dam situated at Rusumo Falls has been proposed to provide this power. Tanzania is particularly interested in the dam, as western Tanzania is extremely power poor.

If the dam is built, the water diversions will have three obvious impacts on the environmental situation in eastern Africa. It will lower the inflow into Lake Victoria, flood some of the existing wetlands, and place increased land pressure on L'Akagara National Park in the northeast of Rwanda. Already, for the new settlements in eastern Rwanda, wildlife has been removed from the area and the area of the park has been reduced. Yet, given the poverty of the area, it is likely that the project will be undertaken. The probability is high since dam construction is generally a favored activity for many international aid agencies. The Kagera River Basin Commission created to facilitate international cooperation in this area has already initiated studies on dam building in the Kagera Basin.

The Juba River Basin

The most humid areas in Somalia receive an annual average rainfall of only slightly more than 500 mm. It is one of the African countries in which the total national territory is either semi-arid or arid. With these pervasive dry conditions, it is not surprising that only two permanent rivers, the Juba and the Shebelli, are found in the whole nation. Both of these rivers have their headwaters in the Ethiopian Highlands. In Somalia, the discharges in both rivers decrease downstream, reflecting the dry environments through which they flow. From a technical viewpoint, the Shebelli River is part of the Juba system. However, since only on rare occasions does the lower Shebelli flow into the Juba, it is usually treated as a separate river system. If proposed increases in water use for irrigation are implemented, then the flows of the Shebelli into the Juba will become even less frequent as more and more water is consumed for agriculture.

The total area of the Juba Basin is about 180,000 km^2. Its source is in the Mendebo Mountains in Ethiopia. None of the catchment area in Somalia contributes any significant flow to the river. During its entire 650 km length in Somalia, the river continuously loses water through infiltration and evaporation. The result is that the Juba River's discharge decreases along its entire course

319

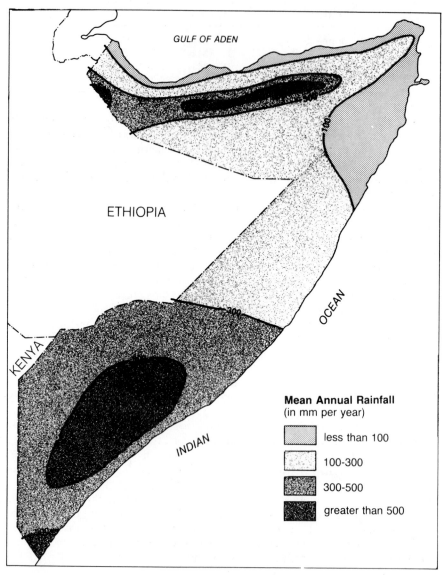

GULF OF ADEN

ETHIOPIA

KENYA

INDIAN

OCEAN

Mean Annual Rainfall
(in mm per year)

less than 100

100-300

300-500

greater than 500

Figure 9.5   Average annual precipitation in Somalia (from Berry *et al.* 1980).

in Somalia. During some months in dry years, it completely dries up. The 1974 discharge data at Lugh Ganana, located near the Ethiopian border, illustrate this phenomenon. Although streamflow data began to be recorded for the Juba in 1965, no actual measurements have been made for discharges greater than 300 m³/s. All values above this magnitude are extrapolated and could be significantly in error. In addition, it is only at Lugh Ganana that the annual flow has been determined. At this location its average annual flow is 6.1 billion m³. The minimum annual flow measured is 3.5, and the maximum annual flow measured is 8.5 billion m³. The lack of a good data base makes it very difficult to develop a rational plan for the utilization of the Juba's waters. This is further compounded by the fact that all of the Juba's waters originate in Ethiopia and no agreement on the allocation of its waters exists between these two countries. Fortunately for Somalia, the Juba Valley in Ethiopia is narrow, with little potential for irrigation. This should ensure for Somalia that the majority of the Juba's discharge will remain available for use.

Rainfall in dry climates usually has a high variability. Precipitation patterns in the Juba Basin illustrates the typical erratic nature of rainfall in arid areas. Tremendous variations occur areally and temporally. This is reflected in the wide range of discharges that occur on the river from year to year. Table 9.3 illustrates the wide range of monthly discharges that occurred in 1972 and 1974 at Lugh Ganana.

According to a 1981 World Bank report, enough water exists in Somalia to meet its needs for agricultural development. However, because of irregular flows in its rivers, it is necessary to regulate the river discharges through the building of reservoirs and irrigation works if the agricultural utility of the existing waters is to increase. For Somali's water resources to meet the nation's needs, a major improvement in the physical and human infrastructures is required. At present, about 12,000 ha are irrigated in the Juba Basin. This irrigation exists without any regulation of the river's flow. Given the wide range of discharges (Table 9.3), shortages occur during dry periods and low water flows. Conversely, during floods there is too much water and the irrigated lands are damaged. In addition, the surplus water during the periods of high flows is not stored for use during the low-water periods. Most of the Juba's waters during high flows are lost to the Indian Ocean. Today a very low water-use efficiency exists throughout the Juba Basin. This is a major contributing factor to the low agricultural productivity of the area.

Table 9.3 Streamflow (m³/s) in Juba River, Somalia: Lugh Ganana Station.

Jan.	Feb.	Mar.	Apr.	May	June	July	Aug.	Sept.	Oct.	Nov.	Dec.
1972											
52	49	54	113	307	217	219	256	230	329	411	136
1974											
1	0	0	16	80	183	161	227	381	230	169	21

Source: Ministry of Agriculture.

A major dam at Bardera is planned. It will increase the areal potential for irrigated lands. Through regulation of the river's waters, at least an additional 73,000 ha could be brought into useful production, and existing irrigated lands would become more productive. However, because of the very poor data base, care will be required if the water resources are to be used rationally. Given the aridity of the area, salinization of the lands could easily occur if they are not properly managed. Likewise, because of the wide range in annual discharges, especially when drought conditions occur, enough water might not be available for all of the irrigated lands during dry years. Policies will need to be formulated to develop a strategy for allocating water during these dry periods. To develop this policy, a better hydrologic data base, and effective water management for the lower basin, must be developed.

From the three river systems just examined, the diversity of fluvial conditions on the continent becomes clear. In the Niger system, even though all the stream segments experience strong seasonal flows, the three major sections have different flow and catchment characteristics requiring different strategies to maintain the environment and at the same time permit development to occur. In contrast, the range in the annual flow is relatively small throughout the whole Kagera system. The major development needs in the basin are for irrigated waters and electrical power in the lower portion. In the future this portion of the basin is likely to be an area for dam construction. Because of the presence of numerous lakes within the river basin, sedimentation will probably not be a major problem. But the flooding of bottom lands, the decrease of inflow into Lake Victoria, and increased land pressures on a large game reserve have the potential for making important environmental impacts in this area of east-central Africa. The Juba system illustrates the need for major investments in the infrastructure of the area. For agricultural development, a large increase in the water-use efficiency of the river is required. Because of the large variability of annual discharge in this system, future plans for the area carry the risk of being inadequate during the dry years. Sedimentation problems, water supply, and salinization are some possible environmental problems that could result if development strategies are based on the Juba's discharge during the wetter years.

African lakes

Of the ten largest freshwater lakes in the world, three are within Africa. Lake Victoria (69,500 km^2), Lake Tanganyika (32,900 km^2), and Lake Malawi (29,600 km^2) are the second, sixth, and ninth largest lakes respectively. Besides these three, there are numerous other freshwater lakes scattered throughout the area. The greatest concentration of these lakes is within the rift system of eastern Africa. In the drier portions of the continent, a number of brackish lakes are found. Of these, Lakes Turkana and Chad are the largest. With the beginning of major dam construction in the 1950s, numerous artificial lakes, including Cabora Bassa (Mozambique), Kafue (Zambia), Kainji (Nigeria), Kariba (Zambia-Zimbabwe), Kossou (Ivory Coast), Nasser (Egypt), and Volta (Ghana) have appeared on the African landscape (Table 9.4). The primary purpose of these dams is hydroelectric power generation, although Lake Nasser

322

is an exception. This lake's main purpose is to increase the area under irrigation, although power production is a very important secondary objective. In the following sections we will describe the basic attributes of some important lakes within Africa to illustrate the different environmental settings in which the lakes are situated.

Lake Victoria

Lake Victoria is clearly in a humid area since its main source of water is from direct rainfall on its surface. Nevertheless, because of its large width-to-depth ratio and equatorial location, it loses over 80 percent of its river inflows and precipitation falling on the lake to evaporation. The lake is situated at an elevation of approximately 1150 m in a shallow basin between the eastern Rift Valley (e.g. Lakes Turkana and Naivasha) and the western Rift Valley (e.g. Lakes Mobutu Sese Seko, Edward, Kivu, Tanganyika) (Fig. 9.6). Because of the geologically recent tectonic activity that has upwarped the western portion of the Lake Victoria Basin, many of the tributaries entering the western portion of the lake exhibit topographic properties that indicate their flow direction has been reversed. The rivers Kafu, Katonga, and Kagera have along their courses swampy areas from which their waters flow in two different directions (Fig. 9.6). Waters from the Kagera and Katonga flow into both Lakes Victoria and Edward; the Kafu flows into Lakes Victoria and Mobutu Sese Seko. The swampy shoreline is another manifestation of this recent upwarping. Out of Lake Victoria's total area (69,500 km^2), there are 3000 km^2 of swamp along its edges. For its large magnitude, it is a relatively shallow lake, having a maximum depth of only 80 m. Although the average annual surface level fluctuation is only 65 cm, since the 1960s the lake level has been about 1 m higher than its average level since 1900. This higher level must reflect a prevailing regional characteristic in east-central Africa as lakes as far away as Kivu and Tanganyika are reported to have had an increase in their levels too.

Another contributing factor to its current lake level is the building of the Owen Falls Dam in 1954 at the lake's outlet, the source of the White Nile. This dam, which produces hydroelectric power and is located in Uganda, also increased Egypt's ability to regulate the flow of the White Nile. Egypt contributed to the cost of building the dam and, by international agreement, was given the right to determine Lake Victoria's discharge within a range of flows.

The fishing industry, long in existence before colonization, is an important source of food supply for the area. Many species, both endemic and nonendemic, are now found in its waters. One type of fish species, the potamodromous (river-ascending), moves into the lake's tributary rivers for breeding during the rainy season when the rivers are flowing at a high discharge. Any diversion of river waters for upstream irrigation, such as proposed in the Kagera Basin, could upset the life cycle of these types of fish and should be considered in the management of the development project.

In the 1920s, after gill nets were introduced, fishing efficiency increased as traditional fishing techniques declined. With the increase in the annual catch, overfishing resulted, and the endemic species of tilapia drastically decreased. In

323

Figure 9.6 The Lake Victoria watershed. Recent upwarping has resulted in very flat lying areas along the western boundary. In many places this boundary is occupied by swamps which sometimes drain toward Lake Victoria and at other times drain toward either Lake Edward or Mobutu Sese Seko. The direction of flow depends on the prevailing winds. ———, Western watershed of Victoria Basin; ← → swamp divide, site of river reversal. (Modified from Beadle 1974.)

the 1950s nonendemic tilapias were both introduced and escaped from nearby ponds into the lake. These nonendemic species helped to increase the fish yield of the lake, but overfishing in the shallow, sheltered areas of the lake, which are important breeding areas, once again lowered fish production. The introduction of the Nile Perch, a large predator fish, originally by accident and then by design, has also been implicated as a factor in the decline of fish yields in Lake Victoria. With the important links between the hydrology of the Victoria Basin, the ecology of the lake, and the economies of the bordering peoples, care must be taken in development plans that affect the complex relations found in the area.

324

Lakes Kivu and Tanganyika

The Lake Kivu and Tanganyika basins, situated within the western Rift Valley, are the easternmost portion of the Zaire Basin in east-central Africa (Fig. 9.7). Within 30 km of the eastern shore of Lake Kivu, the streams flow toward Lake Victoria and the Nile. Until the Late Pleistocene, the majority of the area within the Kivu Basin drained toward the north via the Rutshuru River into Lake Edward. With the eruptions of the Virunga volcanoes (Fig. 9.8), the northward drainage was blocked, the Rift Valley bottom flooded, and Lake Kivu was created. When the rising waters of the newly formed Lake Kivu reached the elevation of some older lava flows, just south of Cyangugu, they spilled over this low point and gradually created a gorge and the Penzi waterfalls. With the formation of this new outlet, the drainage of the area was reversed and these

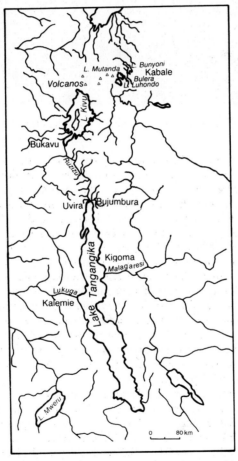

Figure 9.7 The Lake Kivu and Tanganyika watersheds: one of the sources of the Zaire River is the Lukaga River, the outlet of Lake Tanganyika near Kalemie. (Modified from Beadle 1974.)

325

Figure 9.8   The Virunga volcanoes along the Rwanda, Uganda. and Zaire borders.

waters became the major headwaters of the Ruzizi River, one of the two permanent streams entering Lake Tanganyika. During its flow from Lake Kivu to Tanganyika the Ruzizi descends from 1460 m at Cyangugu to 773 m at its mouth near Bujumbura. This drop of almost 700 m in a distance of less than 100 km, along with its relatively constant discharge and confined valley, make the Ruzizi River an excellent hydroelectric power setting. Today, with the construction of power plants along the river, Burundi, Rwanda, and Zaire obtain important electrical power from the Ruzizi.

Lake Kivu's shoreline reflects its recent drowning. Numerous bays dot the shoreline, giving the appearance of a ria coastline. In addition, the steep slopes that border most of the lake give it a very picturesque setting. Before Zaire's independence the lake was a tourist area for Europeans working in the Belgian Congo. Due to the large exodus of expatriates from Zaire, the area's relative inaccessibility, and the high cost of reaching it, today tourism is minor, in spite of its being one of the most beautiful areas in Africa with the additional advantage of a delightful climate.

In spite of the bays, which give large areas of sheltered waters, the fishing potential of Lake Kivu is very restricted. This is a result of the hydrologic conditions found within the lake. The lake is quite deep, reaching a depth of 478 m in its northern portion. Studies to date indicate that all circulation in Lake Kivu is restricted to the upper 70 m. Below this depth, the lake's waters are both saline and free of oxygen. With its steep shoreline, the waters near most of the shore quickly attain depths of 200 m or more. The result is that only about 12 percent of the lake's bottom is in contact with oxygenated water. Because of the

326

close proximity of the shore with deep water, most organic matter entering the lake settles into oxygen-free areas and is lost as a food supply for fish. This results in Lake Kivu having a very low potential for productivity in regard to fauna. The net effect is that fishing is of only minor economic importance, and its potential for fishing is very limited.

Although the lake has a minimal potential for the economic development of fisheries, its lake bottom in the northern portion near Goma (Zaire) and Gisenyi (Rwanda) is known to have methane deposits beneath it. A pilot gas plant using these deposits has been built in Gisenyi. However, until an economic agreement can be reached between Rwanda and Zaire regarding royalties, this resource's potential cannot be ascertained, let alone developed.

Lake Tanganyika is the second largest lake in Africa and the second deepest lake in the world, after Baykal in the USSR. It occupies the floor of the western Rift Valley and attains a depth of 1470 m only 4 km east of its shoreline near Moba (Zaire). A second deep portion of the lake, 1310 m, is near the western shore across from Kigoma (Tanzania). Unlike Kivu, Tanganyika's origin dates back over a million years. But with the release of Lake Kivu's waters into Tanganyika there is evidence that the lake's surface rose approximately 200 m. Today the lake is about 650 km long and 40–70 km wide.

As the shorelines of the lake are the eastern and western escarpments of the Rift Valley, they are very steep along most of the lake's periphery. Only the shores near Bujumbura, Mpulungu, and Kalemie have moderate gradients. A result of this topographic setting is that few locations along the lake are readily accessible. This is reflected in the paucity of settlements along the lake. Given the small number of settlements along both Kivu and Tanganyika, neither of the lakes are used as major transport routes, even though they are both navigable.

As mentioned previously (Ch. 7), Lake Tanganyika's water inflows are almost in balance with the evaporation loss from its surface. The outflow of the lake into the Lukuga River is not continuous, but it is clearly sufficient to prevent the lake's waters from becoming too saline. In fact, Tanganyika is less saline than Kivu. Because of this, during the dry season, when the Ruzizi's discharge is largely from Kivu, the inflowing water tends to sink beneath the water of Lake Tanganyika. During the wet season, when a large component of the Ruzizi's discharge is from flows originating below Kivu, the waters are less saline and mix with the lake's surface waters. The Malagarasi River is the only other permanent water source entering Lake Tanganyika (Fig. 9.7). Most of the other rivers discharging into the lake are small streams that flow as torrents into the lake basin in response to the thunderstorms that develop along the escarpments.

The waters of Lake Tanganyika support a far larger fish population than those of Lake Kivu, even though it is deeper and also has a narrow fringe of shallow waters. The explanation for this is that a completely different circulation pattern exists in this lake. Unlike Kivu, which has no circulation below depths of 70 m, in Lake Tanganyika, because of strong seasonal winds, water is mixed within the lake's upper 200 m between April and September. The mixing not only transports oxygen from the surface waters to greater depths, it also brings nutrients from the lower waters up toward the surface. The result is that Lake Tanganyika's waters can support a far richer fauna population than those of Lake Kivu. One consequence of this is that on Lake Tanganyika commercial fishing has developed into an important economic activity. This occurred because a market for fresh fish is readily accessible at Bujumbura, and a large market for dried fish exists in the nearby copper-mining area in northern Zambia.

Lake Chad

The lake occupies the center of a structural shallow geologic basin that drains an area of about 2,500,000 km^2. Being an area of internal drainage, the lake has no outlet. Because of the general aridity of the basin, only two rivers, the Chari and its tributary, the Logone, supply approximately 95 percent of the inflows into the lake (Fig. 9.9). No significant inflows originate to the north and east of the

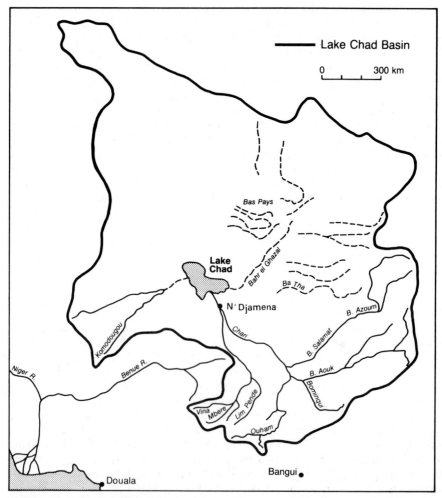

Figure 9.9 The Lake Chad Basin. Most of the area within the watershed does not contribute any flow to the lake due to its aridity. Under the current climatic regime, only the southeastern portion of the basin contributes significant flows into the lake.

328

lake as the little drainage that exists in these areas flows away from the Chad depression. Precipitation on the northern portion of the lake is estimated to average about 200 mm/yr, whereas on the southern margins the average precipitation is no more than 500 mm/yr. Because of both the tropical and arid location of the lake, evaporation losses from the waters are estimated to be about 2000 mm/yr (Beadle 1974).

Topographically, the lake is situated in a vast open plain which has very gentle gradients. These characteristics produce a very shallow lake. Maximum depths in the northern portion of the lake are generally between 4 and 7 m; in the southern portion, maximum depths are generally between 2 and 5 m. As is common with all shallow lakes in arid areas, the areal extent fluctuates greatly from season to season and year to year, depending on climatic conditions at the sources of the inflowing rivers. During the last 100 years the lake has shown a trend toward contraction. On average its size ranges between 10,500 and 26,000 km^2 during an annual period. In the 1950s and early 1960s a generally wet period existed and the lake expanded significantly above its average. Since this period, as the rains have decreased, Lake Chad has gradually become smaller. From 1984 its size has continued to decrease (Fig. 9.10). However, this trend could shift abruptly since in any given year the inflows into the lake could be greater than its total volume. Size fluctuation is a characteristic of Lake Chad, as well as of most lakes found in the Sahara and Sahel.

Given the high aridity of the Lake Chad vicinity as well as the lack of outlet, it would be expected that the lake's waters would be quite saline. Interestingly, the salinity of the lake is less than the salinities of the East African rift lakes such as Edward, Kivu, Mobutu Sese Seko, and Tanganyika, which are situated in more humid areas. This must be due to the outflows of the lake's waters in groundwater. Measurements of the groundwater leaving the lake indicate that it is about 10 times more saline than the waters of the Chari and Logone rivers. These groundwater flows prevent the gradual accumulation of salts in the lake.

Lake Chad has two critical economic functions. First, its fish production is a very important food supply for the area. Second, its waters are used for irrigation to increase the agricultural production of the area. Given the gentle gradient of the Chad Basin, the margins of the lake, especially in the south, are vast swamps covering thousands of square kilometers. During the high-water periods of the Chari and Logone, the swamps spread and become a huge breeding area for the lake's fauna. As the discharges of these rivers drop during the dry season, the swamps begin to contract and the fish migrate back into the main channels of the rivers. Traps set into the rivers are very efficient under these conditions. Fishing in the open lake usually is done with gill nets.

For agriculture, the lake's rôle is critical, given the aridity of the surrounding area. Especially along the eastern shore of the lake, where thousands of sand-dune islands exist, polders have been built and irrigation is an important component of the local agriculture. Unfortunately, salinization of the soil is beginning to limit the agricultural potential of the area. New management strategies for these irrigated lands need to be introduced if the area is to remain in production over the long term.

As examples of the diversity of African lakes, the properties of Chad, Kivu, and Tanganyika demonstrate that lakes are an important resource within

Africa. Because of lower oxygen content due to warmer waters and different annual circulation patterns, most tropical lakes are not as productive as mid-latitude lakes. Generally, however, tropical lakes are still important local food sources. There are a number of locational factors limiting the rôle of most large African lakes in the economic developments of the surrounding lands. Many of the African lakes border more than one country. This political factor requires international cooperation if their use is to be maximized. Many lake basin authorities exist such as the Niger, Chad, and Victoria Commissions. In reality, few strategies have been implemented by these authorities. An additional locational factor is that many of the lakes are situated in regions that are remote from the economic centers of the nations. For example the majority of the East African rift lakes are relatively inaccessible. This limits their rôles in becoming important transportation systems as well as areas of large investments. The health aspect is another factor limiting economic development in

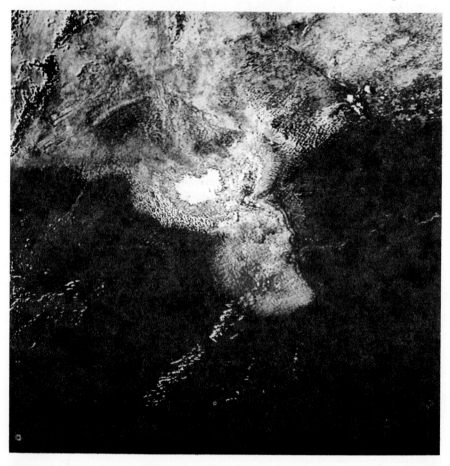

Figure 9.10 Landsat image of Lake Chad. As the image was taken during a dry period, the lake surface has been drastically reduced in area.

some lacustrine areas. Various waterborne diseases associated with lake environments have already been discussed (Ch. 5). Because of all of the factors presented in this section, African lakes generally have not been a major consideration in most national development plans.

Artificial lakes

Major dam construction for Africa began with the series of dams built to regulate the Nile's flow. These include the Sennar, Roseires, and Jebel Aulyia reservoirs. Since 1958, with the building of the Kariba (Table 9.4), the size of some of the reservoirs has exceeded some of the largest natural lakes. Many other dams, smaller than those listed in the Table, have been built throughout the continent.

The primary catalyst for dam construction in Africa, in theory, has been economic development. Almost all dams built were part of a development project associated with either hydroelectric power generation or irrigation. Dams and irrigation systems alter the fluvial relationships that existed with the environmental setting before the dam was built. Large areas of valley bottoms are flooded, removing some of the best agricultural lands from production. Also, major changes often occur in the erosional and deposition patterns of the affected river system. The lake behind the dam creates a new higher base level and water table in the immediate upstream areas. In addition, new wetlands form along the lake's margins. These changes usually result in new areas of deposition within the wetlands and the reservoir. Downstream from the dam, waterflow and sediment supply are often greatly reduced, and this can increase erosion.

It is illustrative of some of these changes that when the Kariba Dam was built over 50,000 inhabitants had to be resettled from the flooded areas. The Volta Lake, which resulted from the Akosombo Dam, inundated 3 percent of Ghana. As the lake's elevation fluctuates during an annual period, approximately 7200 km^2 of mud flats are created along its margins during low lake levels. With the trapping of a large percentage of the Volta's sediment in the lake, the growth of the river's delta has been restricted. In addition, fauna and flora are altered because of changes in the hydrologic régime of the rivers. Clearly, dam construction sets in motion a whole set of environmental changes. Because of their complexity they are usually not completely included in the cost benefits of the development scheme or are overlooked because of political considerations. This more often than not results in dam projects not meeting expectations.

An examination of the effects of dam construction on the diversity of settings found within Africa is beyond the scope of this book. However, to illustrate some of the environmental impacts of dam construction in detail, we shall examine a small development project in Tanzania undertaken in the Kisongo River Basin. Located in northern Tanzania near Arusha (Fig. 9.11), the Kisongo is situated in a semi-arid area about 1415 m above sea level. The climate makes the area marginal for rainfed agriculture. The area was settled in the 1950s; before that it had been part of a grazing system of nomadic peoples.

In response to the increased water supply resulting from the construction of the reservoir, the new pastoral agriculturalists who settled in the area increased the

Table 9.4 Characteristics of major artificial lakes in Africa.

Name of dam	Date	Hydropower capacity	Volume (km³)	Area (km²)	People resettled	Estimated annual fish production (tons)
Akosombo (Volta)	1964	768	165	8,730	88,000	40,000
Kariba	1958	800	147	5,000	57,000	2,000
Cabora–Bassa	1974	2,000	70	3,700	–	–
Kainji	1968	960	12	1,280	50,000	10,000
Aswan High (Nasser)	1964	107	132	5,000	120,000	10,000
Kossou	1971	175	30	1,600	100,000	13,500
Kafue	1970	500	–	3,100	–	–

Source: Symoens *et al.* (1981).

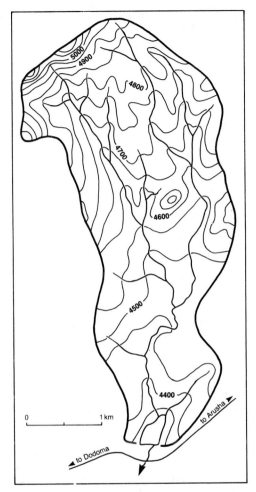

Figure 9.11 Contour map of the Kisongo River Basin: the contour interval is 50 ft (15.3 m) and the map is based on the 1 : 50,000 Tanzania series (from Murray-Rust 1972).

Table 9.5 Carrying capacity and actual grazing stock in the Kisongo Basin.

area of basin	9.3 km²
general elevation	1130–1590 m
estimated safe[a] carrying capacity for the catchment	actual catchment stock, 1971
95–460 stock units	500 cattle + 700 sheep and goats = 700 stock units

Note
[a] Safe means the number of stock that can use the area without overgrazing and erosion.

Table 9.6 Erosion and sediment data: Kisongo Basin.

Year	Reservoir volume (m³)	% Original volume	Gullies Linear (m³)	Gullies Dendritic (m³)	Gullies Sheetwash (m³)	Total
1959	121,000	100.0	n.a.	n.a.	n.a.	
1969	83,600	69.1	4,170	2,990	30,240	=37,400
1971	71,700	59.6	n.a.	n.a.	n.a.	

number of livestock. Two different sets of erosional landscapes and related deposition patterns developed in response to the dam construction and the effects of the dam on vegetation and land use. One set of erosional features is directly related to overgrazing (Table 9.5) and is typified by the occurrence of gullies forming a dendritic drainage pattern. Other erosional features, related to the movements of livestock as they are herded toward the water supply, developed into linear gullies. The deposition of the eroded materials from these gullies and the widespread sheetwash from the areas of degraded grass cover occurs in the lower portion of the basins and the reservoir itself. Table 9.6 shows the record of rapid reservoir infilling resulting from the overgrazing and the gullies.

Approximately 800 mm of water annually evaporates from the open water surface in the Kisongo area. The storage capacity of the reservoir must be large enough to absorb this water loss and also to supply the livestock through the dry season. Stock needs are estimated at 12,000 m³ of water. Table 9.7 indicates that since 1976 the reservoir has not been able to meet its proposed goal of supplying sufficient water to the local area. In fact, in this area the net effect of the dam construction has been to lower the land-resource potential. The attempt to modify the natural system for man's benefit has resulted in unforeseen effects throughout the whole river basin. The problem of dry-season water for the cattle has not been solved, and the agricultural and grazing potential of the area is now less than it was before the dam was built. This is due to the accelerated erosion that resulted from the short-lived greater water supply provided by the reservoir during its first few years.

Table 9.7 Storage and water needs for Kisongo Reservoir.

Year	Capacity at full level (m³)	Volume lost to evaporation in 5-month dry season (m³)	Volume required for stock and human consumption (m³)	Total volume required (m³)	Surplus storage (m³)
1960	121,000	43,000	12,000	55,000	66,000
1969	83,000	37,600	12,000	49,600	34,000
1971	71,700	37,200	12,000	49,200	22,500
1975	47,900	35,900	12,000	47,900	none
1979	24,300	35,900	12,000	47,900	−23,600

The previous example should not be extrapolated to other dam sites within Africa. It is only meant to illustrate that where dams are built a large range of human and physical interactions are set in motion that need to be considered prior to construction in order to minimize environmental problems and maximize development.

Swamps

The total area occupied by swamps within Africa is estimated to be between 300,000 and 350,000 km^2. The major swamps are all located in areas of low relief (Table 9.8); this property results in the swamps having a high ratio of surface area to water depth. Because of the tropical setting of Africa, all of the swamp areas have high evapotranspiration rates which result in high water losses. The decrease in the Kagera's mean annual discharge between the Rusumo Falls (390 m^3/s) and Kyaka (184 m^3/s) (previously discussed in this chapter) is partially a result of the high evapotranspiration losses occurring in the swamps that parallel the river. As another example, Balek (1977) estimates that 60 percent of the inflows into the Bangweulu Swamp in Zambia are lost by evapotranspiration.

Another important hydrologic function of swamps is that they regulate the flow régime of rivers passing through them. During periods of high water, the swamps expand, acting as reservoirs; during periods of low flows, the swamps contract as water is released into the river channels. The magnitude of floods downstream from large swamps is thus greatly reduced; conversely, the discharges during low flows are augmented by swamps. Within the Zaire River Basin, including its numerous tributaries, is found the largest total area of swamps on the continent. These swamps, along with its equatorial location, contribute to the river's relatively consistent régime.

Besides the hydrologic impacts of swamps, of great importance are the multitude of ecological habitats that swamps create. The Okavango Swamp (Botswana) is famous for its diverse wildlife; and the Sudd (Sudan) not only

Table 9.8 The ten largest swamps in Africa.

	Name	Location	River	Area (km^2)
1.	The Sudd	Sudan	White Nile	100,000
2.	Middle Zaire River swamps	Zaire	Zaire	40,500
3.	Lake Chad swamps	Chad	Chari-Logone	38,000
4.	Lake Mweru swamps	Zambia-Zaire	Luapula-Mofwe	33,000
5.	Bahr Balamat	Chad	Chari	27,000
6.	Okavango	Botswana	Okavango-Botletle	26,800
7.	Upper Lualaba	Zaire	Lualaba	26,000
8.	Kyoga	Uganda	Victoria Nile	22,000
9.	Bangweulu	Zambia	Chambeshi	15,875
10.	Lotagipi	Sudan-Kenya	Tarach	13,000

supports a diverse wildlife, but during the dry season when its margins retreat the grasses growing in these transition zones provide crucial pasture lands for the pastoral people living in the area. All swamp areas in Africa have abundant game living in and near them. The swamps located along the margins of dry areas, such as the Lake Chad swamps, provide water crucial for a host of wildlife.

The draining of wetlands, because of their flat topography, has long been an established strategy for increasing agricultural lands. Perhaps the most dramatic examples of this in the world are the Netherlands and a significant percentage of farmlands in the American Midwest. These two areas have some of the most productive farms in the world. Without artificial drainage neither area would have such high agricultural yields. Today, with the need to increase both water availability and food production, pressure is mounting in some parts of Africa to begin large-scale drainage projects. The wetlands are a major area of conflict between environmentalists and land developers. The following examination of the Jonglei development project for the Sudd elucidates many of the environmental pressures on wetlands in Africa that result from development projects.

The Sudd and Jonglei Drainage Project

The Sudd, in southern Sudan, is a vast swamp area covering about 100,000 km^2 (Fig. 9.12). Upon entering the Sudd, the Nile slowly flows for about 350 km in a vast network of anastomotic river channels. A dense plant cover of papyrus and mats of floating vegetation are found in the channels throughout the whole area. Because of the vegetation and the spreading of the river's waters, navigation in this portion of the Nile is greatly restricted. Because of the Sudd's location in a dry climatic area, high evaporation losses occur. The primary purposes of the Jonglei Canal are to increase the water flow of the Nile by reducing evaporation losses in the Sudd and to improve navigation and the road transport in this area of southern Sudan.

Egypt's water supply is almost entirely dependent on the Nile's waters. In the early 1900s the Nile provided on a daily basis an average of 25 m^3 of water per person. By 1975, it had dropped to 4 m^3. In the near future it is estimated that only 3 m^3 of water will be available. The extra water made available by the Aswan High Dam will soon be fully used. Egypt needs more water to irrigate more lands to feed its ever-growing population. The 1959 Nile Waters Agreement allocated to the Sudan 18.5 billion m^3 of water per year. By 1984 the Sudan was almost utilizing its total available water. Planned irrigation projects will require approximately an additional 8 billion m^3 of water. If these projects are to be implemented, new water must become available. The only obvious source for both countries is the Nile.

The Jonglei Canal was begun in June 1978 to divert about 25 percent of the White Nile's water from the Sudd. When it is completed, it will divert these waters east to the Sudd from Bor to Hilet Doleeb in a canal 350 km long, 4 m deep and varying in width between 50 and 100 m. This will permit 20 million m^3 of water to flow through the canal in a 24-hour period. Eventually, in a second phase after the canal is completed, the project envisions the building of dams at the outlets of Lake Mobutu Sese Seko and Lake Kioga, as well as

336

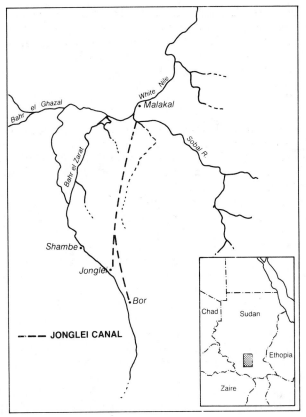

Figure 9.12 Map of the Jonglei project, Sudan (from Omu 1978).

modifying the Owens Falls Dam. These changes are being proposed to further regulate the Nile's waters and increase the water available to northern Sudan and Egypt by 4.3 billion m³/yr.*

Studies evaluating the likely impacts of the water diversion around the Sudd conclude that changes in the temperatures and humidity in those areas of the Sudd that are altered by the diversion will probably occur, but no major climatic changes are expected. Fish catches will decrease, cattle will increase, and game will decrease. But, since 75 percent of the Nile's waters will continue to flow through the Sudd, the ecosystems existing will probably continue to exist. The major environmental impacts are unlikely to result directly from the canal and its water diversion. They will probably occur through development projects made possible by the additional water. The increase in irrigated lands and new cattle lands will clearly have environmental impacts. However, if the dams on the lakes are ever actually built in the second phase of the project, then direct

---

* This project has currently been abandoned because of disruption caused by the north–south conflicts in Sudan.

major environmental impacts are likely. The water demands of Egypt and northern Sudan will probably continue to increase in the future. The Jonglei Canal will meet their needs in the immediate future by reducing evaporation losses and thus increasing the lower Nile's discharge.

Summary

An overview of the surface-water resources in Africa has been presented in this chapter. Two categories of developmental constraints exist: physical and economic–political. As a whole the continent's development is severely constrained because of the large areal extent of its drylands. Additionally many physical attributes of its rivers contribute to development problems. Among the most important are: the paucity of navigable rivers from the coasts into the interior – many river sections that are classified as navigable are only navigable for a portion of the year; few rivers flow from humid areas toward drier areas; and the extreme seasonal flow régime of most streams means that when water is in short supply for economic activities the rivers are at low flows.

African lakes also present some difficulties for their use in economic development. Because most of the larger lakes border more than one country, international cooperation is a prerequisite if their potential is to be maximized. In addition, many of the lakes are distant from the commercial regions of the countries. Because of their tropical location, resulting in warmer waters and no seasonal circulation due to temperature changes, the lakes have lower oxygen levels than middle- and higher-latitude waters. The lack of seasonal circulation in the deeper lakes results in stratification of the lakes' water. This results in anoxic conditions in the lower layers of the deeper lakes such as Kivu and Tanganyika. The deficit of oxygen in the lakes limits their potential productivity for food supply. Also, as many of the lakes' waters are moderately saline, this increases environmental problems when their waters are used for irrigation. Finally, many waterborne diseases are prevalent in lacustrine, riverine, and wetland environments.

Swamps in Africa are important in dampening the extremes between high and low river discharges. They also provide important land reserves and habitats for larger numbers of wildlife. To integrate these areas into the contemporary economies of the national governments, pressures exist in many nations of Africa to drain these wetlands to provide new lands for agricultural and pastoral activities. In the future the conflicts between environment and development in Africa's wetlands will almost certainly increase.

10 Urban and industrial growth

Some of the most important issues related to urban and industrial growth in Africa are discussed in this chapter. Although this involves a modest overlap with topics covered in previous chapters, these issues are vitally important for Africa now and will continue to be so in the future. In this chapter we only begin to outline the main themes and problems. Urban and industrial growth over much of the continent are relatively recent phenomena, so that the environmental implications, although clear enough to people living in any particular area, are not as well charted and documented as some other aspects.

In some areas in Africa, particularly in the north, urban growth stems from deep historical roots, but in others it is a product of the events of the last hundred years and in many cases of only the last two decades. Because of the close relationship between urban growth and general population growth, we shall consider urban growth first in the general population context and next in terms of its economic and political history. We shall then proceed to examine the environmental and resource issues in general and in respect to some case studies.

General population growth in Africa

As reviewed in Chapter 3, Africa's population appears to have grown slowly from the 1600s to around 1900 (Table 10.1). During that period of 250 years, the population only grew by 33 percent. In the next 50 years it grew by over two-thirds and in the next 30 years (1950–80) the population more than doubled.

Table 10.1 Population growth in Africa and the world, 1650–2000.

Year	African population (millions)	World population (millions)
1650	100	543
1750	106	791
1800	107	978
1850	111	1260
1900	133	1630
1930	164	2069
1950	222	2513
1971	354	3706
2000	865	6920

Source: Modified from Monsted and Walji (1978).

Projections for the next twenty years (1980 to the year 2000) show a further near doubling of the population. It is interesting to note, however, that, even in the year 2000, Africa will have a much smaller share of the world population than it had in 1650 (12 percent compared with 18 percent in 1650); but the periods of rapid growth in Africa appear to be occurring later than in most parts of the world and at present it appears that they will also continue longer than elsewhere.

Urban population growth in Africa

Some of the oldest towns in the world are found in Africa, mostly in North Africa; yet some of the most rapid new growth in towns and the world is to be found in Africa. The Mediterranean coastal towns in Morocco, Algeria, Tunisia, and Egypt have urban histories of over 3000 years. In this area the urban population has long comprised a significant percentage of national population totals. Urban centers also have long histories in the savanna areas of West Africa (Yoruba towns in Nigeria) and South Africa, but for much of Africa significant urban agglomeration is a comparatively recent phenomenon. The year 1960 (about the time of independence for much of tropical Africa) is a good benchmark date against which to measure change. In 1960 less than 20 percent of the people of tropical Africa lived in towns, and most of these towns were small (less than 50,000 population). At the same time almost 30 percent of North African people and nearly half of the population of the Republic of South Africa lived in towns.

Table 10.2 outlines the rapid pattern of change over the next twenty years from 1960 to 1980. Total urban population more than doubled with major changes in the proportion of the population living in urban settlements in all areas. The greatest relative increases, which started from low levels, occurred in central and eastern Africa. In 1980 there was less diversity in the proportion of urban population in tropical Africa than earlier. In 1980 there were more than 63 million people in towns outside North Africa, and in sub-Saharan Africa about 20 percent of the population was urban. That percentage continues to grow steadily. In North Africa the percentage of urban population is growing rapidly: by 1980 it was over a third, and by the year 2000 it will approach 50 percent. By 1985 the Republic of South Africa and Egypt's populations were over 50 percent urban.

Table 10.3 provides some comparative data for urbanization in terms of size of urban centers in 1970 and 1980. Although there is growth in almost every category, there is a rapid increase in the size of cities and in the size of the largest cities in particular. The largest urban centers are generally still found outside the tropical zone, but urban growth continues at a rapid pace throughout many parts of Africa. In Nigeria, Zaire, Kenya, Ethiopia, Ivory Coast, and Tanzania urban populations over or close to 1 million already exist. In nontropical Africa, Casablanca in Morocco grew from 20,000 in 1900 to 500,000 in 1946 and is 1.6 million today. Algiers grew equally rapidly to its present 2.3 million, and smaller Tunis now approaches 1 million in population. But the largest North African city is the huge Cairo metropolitan area with an estimated population of

340

Table 10.2 Growth of urban population of tropical Africa, 1965–80.

Subregion	1965 A	1965 B	1970 A	1970 B	1975 A	1975 B	1980 A	1980 B
West Africa	12,425,000	12.8	15,710,000	14.2	21,075,000	16.5	30,500,000	21.0
central Africa	2,855,000	9.8	3,695,000	11.1	4,690,000	12.7	6,550,000	10.0
East Africa	5,455,000	6.2	7,010,000	7.3	8,990,000	8.4	12,400,000	11.0
southern Africa	7,815,000	21.3	9,490,000	23.1	11,445,000	24.7	14,300,000	27.0
totals	28,550,000		35,905,000		46,200,000		63,750,000	

Sources: Economic Commission for Africa (1975). Modified from Udo (1982).

Notes
A = total population in towns of 20,000 or more.
B = urban population as percentage of total population.

Table 10.3 Urbanization in tropical Africa by size of cities in 1970.

Subregion	20,000–50,000			50,001–100,000			100,001–500,000			Over 500,000		
	A	B	C	A	B	C	A	B	C	A	B	C
West Africa	79	2.32	17.29	33	2.37	18.05	30	5.81	43.61	4	2.77	21.05
central Africa	34	0.99	16.13	16	0.97	16.13	14	2.65	45.70	1	1.32	22.04
East Africa (including Ethiopia)	36	1.16	20.00	14	0.83	16.00	13	2.68	42.33	2	1.31	21.67
southern Africa	35	1.14	15.71	8	0.65	8.80	12	2.63	37.15	3	2.64	38.34
Africa south of the Sahara	184	5.61	17.50	71	4.81	15.00	69	13.77	42.30	10	8.04	25.20

Source: Economic Commission for Africa (1975).

Notes
A = number of urban centres.
B = urban population in millions.
C = urban population in size category as percentage of total urban population.

8–9 million. In South Africa, Cape Town (1.2 million), Durban (620,000), Port Elizabeth (450,000), and Johannesburg (2 million) are the largest centers.

Whereas in 1960 these North African and South African cities dwarfed those of tropical Africa, this is now no longer the case. Lagos is probably home to a population of well over 3 and perhaps 4 million, Khartoum's "three town" population is 2 million, Addis Ababa's population is 1.5 million, Kinshasa's over 2 million, and even cities like Nairobi, Dar es Salaam, Dakar, Abidjan and many more exceed or approach the 1 million mark.

In summary, urban growth for most of Africa is recent, rapid, and likely to continue. The past two decades have seen very rapid growth of major cities; the next decade or so will probably continue to feature such growth, though there will also be strong growth in many of the smaller cities.

Industrial growth

Although urban growth appears to be associated most strongly with the surge in general population growth, it has also been accompanied by a general increase in industrial and commercial activity in Africa. Table 10.4 provides a summary of the percentage of GDP in industry for African countries. The North African countries have long had a substantial industrial sector which, however, has grown considerably, in pace with urban growth. This is particularly true in Egypt and Algeria. In Egypt a wide range of processing and service industries has grown up in Cairo and Alexandria – mostly relatively small-scale and very diverse. In contrast, Algeria has attempted to build an integrated modern industrial base on iron, coal and steel, and petrochemical industries and has complemented this with consumer-oriented products, such as shoes. The Republic of South Africa has had a wide range of industry for a long period, including heavy industry such as steel, industries centered on mining activities such as diamonds and gold, and a wide range of manufacturing industries to produce consumer goods both for the domestic and export markets.

The percentage of GDP in industry for most African countries is low, but it is growing steadily, as most countries have sought to improve their industrial base since independence. Zimbabwe, South Africa, and Nigeria have strong mining and industrial sectors, but most African countries have had agriculture as their main economic lifeline and are only now building an industrial base. However, in nearly all cases that industrial sector is preferentially located in the major city or cities of the country. In the cities of Africa in the third quarter of the 20th century, the growth of industry and the growth of population in urban centers reinforce each other to focus a major change element in a small segment of space and time.

The growth of cities in Africa has been a function of several different variables. First, as general population growth has speeded up, some rural areas have become very crowded in comparison with their historical conditions; land for farming has become scarce, especially good land; and many potential farmers have felt it necessary to move elsewhere, some to other rural areas, many to the towns and cities.

Table 10.4 Industry as a percentage of gross
domestic product in African countries.

Countries	1979
Low-income semi-arid	
Chad	11
Somalia	11[a]
Mali	11
Burkina Faso (Upper Volta)	20
Gambia	9
Niger	32
Mauritania	33
Low-income other	
Ethiopia	15
Guinea–Bissau	9
Burundi	15
Malawi	20
Rwanda	21
Benin	12
Mozambique	16
Sierre Leone	23
Tanzania	13
Zaire	24
Guinea	26
Central African Republic	18
Madagascar	20
Uganda	7
Lesotho	15
Togo	23
Sudan	13
Middle-income oil importers	
Kenya	21
Ghana	21
Senegal	24
Zimbabwe	39
Liberia	26
Zambia	41
Cameroon	16
Swaziland	—
Botswana	30
Mauritius	28
Ivory Coast	23
Middle-income oil exporters	
Angola	23
Congo	36
Nigeria	45
Gabon	65
Middle-income oil exporters, North Africa	
Morocco	16[b]
Tunisia	35[b]
Algeria	57[b]
Libya	72[b]
Egypt	35[b]

Sources: World Bank (1978, 145, 1981, 145, 1982, 120).

Notes
[a] Figure is for 1978.
[b] Figure is for 1980.

Second, as education has become available to more and more children, many who leave school think themselves potentially qualified for jobs in the urban sector, and they choose to leave rural areas in search of prosperity in the towns.

Third, as industries began to develop in independent countries, work opportunities arose in the towns and people moved from rural to urban areas to take advantage of these. Equally important to industrial growth has been the excessive expansion of jobs in the public sector. In many cities this sector of employment has grown far more than the industrial one.

Fourth, it has been the policy of many governments to orient their investments to the urban sector at the expense of the rural one. Infrastructure improvements such as electricity are concentrated in the urban areas. This permits a higher standard of living in the urban areas. Also, it gives the rural areas a disadvantage compared to the urban areas for the location of new industry, which requires power, transportation, and other infrastructure support. Likewise, the artificial setting of food prices to minimize food costs for the urban areas has meant that farmers are not able to sell their crops at a reasonable profit in many countries. This has accelerated internal migration to the cities and has made it necessary for food to be imported. The lack of investment in the agricultural sector has resulted in agriculture becoming less efficient since independence in many countries. Both Nigeria and Ghana are classic examples of this phenomenon. Cameroon, recognizing the disadvantages of investment in rural areas, has had a different policy. In contrast to its Nigerian neighbor, it has invested its oil revenues in its agricultural sector, and therefore urban growth and the outmigration from rural to urban areas has been minimized.

Last, the existence of towns as service centers for health, for education, for government, and for entertainment has helped to attract people to urban areas. To complement these immigration flows, the urban population continues to grow at about the same rate as the population in general.

The immigration streams so typical of Africa in the last 20 years (with some extending back much further) are depicted in Figure 10.1. In eastern and southern Africa the original movements were from rural areas throughout the whole region to the mining areas and cities of South Africa. In the last two decades this movement has been supplemented by large internal rural–urban migration within Zimbabwe, Malawi, Tanzania, Kenya, and Zambia. In West Africa the dominant movement has been and continues to be from the rural areas of the interior to the coast. A similar pattern is clearly displayed for North Africa.

Another pattern not shown on the map is of the movement of Africans to Europe and the Middle East. Very large numbers of West and North Africans currently reside and work on a more or less temporary basis in Europe. Equally large numbers of Egyptians, Sudanese, and Somalis live and work temporarily in the Arab countries of the Gulf States.

These overseas migration patterns, together with the internal ones, result in flows of goods, resources, and ideas back to the cities and countryside of Africa; but they also create a shortage of skilled individuals in some sectors of the African countries, especially those where Arabic is spoken (e.g. Sudan). Skilled individuals earn significantly more income in the Gulf States and Saudi Arabia, and access to these countries is easily provided.

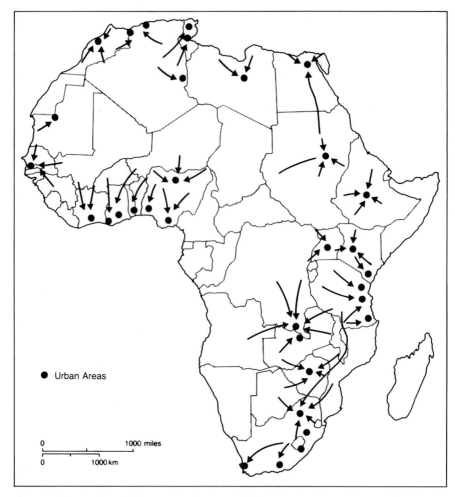

Figure 10.1 Internal migration of population within Africa: the dominant movement is from the interior toward the coast (from Pritchard 1979b).

Distribution and classification of cities

In discussing cities and towns, many different characteristics can be used to describe and classify them. Of the various systems used, the most important for our discussion are: size, location, function, and dominant cultural heritage.

Size

Size appears to be a most important factor. When cities become very large, in many (but not all) cases there seems to be a very different relationship between

346

a city and its resource environment both internally within the city and externally. This change occurs when the population surpasses a point between 150,000 and 400,000. Large cities of over 400,000 inhabitants need a large catchment area for their resources; smaller towns and cities need much less complicated networks.

The rate of urban growth in Africa is increasing. In 1960 there were only 21 cities in sub-Saharan Africa with more than 100,000 people and only one over 1 million. In 1970 there were 85 over 100,000 and only three over 1 million, whereas in 1980 there were about 160 over 100,000 and 17 over 1 million. More significantly perhaps, the number of cities over 400,000 in tropical Africa rose from zero in 1930 to more than 25 in 1980. During the decade of the 1970s, the number of cities exceeding this size range doubled.

As the populations of cities increase to larger size categories in Africa, a number of changes appear to take place in the relationship between the cities and the environment. Among the most significant are internal city issues of waste disposal, food production within the city, pollution and transport, and external issues of food supply, energy supply, and water supply.

With the very rapid increase in size of many African urban centers, along with the general shortcoming of limited capital, there is no way that modern city services and infrastructures can keep pace with the growth. In many of the small African cities there is enough land available for considerable production of food within the city or on the margins. In larger cities there is a tendency for this to be more difficult. Land is in short supply and further away, and houses soon tend to occupy spare space. The margins of the city often become squatter settlements with only limited opportunities for food production.

As a result, as cities increase in size external resource relationships change. In small and middle-sized towns, food, energy, and water supplies are usually provided from local resources. In larger cities these relationships all change. Cities need to develop longer supply lines, and this changing pattern of food supply has a varied impact on surrounding areas, sometimes stimulating production generally and production of fruit and vegetables in particular, sometimes resulting in an overdependence of the cities on imported foods because the needed new systems do not develop. The pricing of local foodstuffs, their control by government, and the high costs of transport of foodstuffs from the hinterlands of many African cities are all factors contributing to the dependence on imported foodstuffs. Another factor is that many cities in Africa developed not out of the growth of their region but in response to colonial needs. They did not evolve from a productive local agricultural base.

Modern waste-disposal systems are expensive to construct, and most large African cities have sewage disposal systems designed for populations at least 50 percent smaller than the current size of the towns. Sewage treatment plants are similarly overstrained. Most cities are not served by modern disposal systems for either solid or liquid wastes. Consequently there is much local pollution. Traditional systems which work well in the dispersed settlement pattern of the countryside do not work well in the congested urban and peri-urban areas.

Alongside these problems are those of modern technology. Many of the larger African cities have a large number of automobiles. The municipal and national governments find it hard to legislate and enforce emission controls. Air and noise pollution is, therefore, a major and growing urban problem.

Urban energy demands on the surrounding environment have so far been almost universally destructive to the environment. As cities grow, the wood and charcoal demands grow proportionately, and the economics of transporting these commodities often result in stress being placed on woody reserves in the immediate vicinity of the city. Ibadan in Nigeria, Ouagadougu in Burkina Faso, and Dar es Salaam in Tanzania, all situated in very different ecological settings, have problems of land degradation around them, largely resulting from the removal of woody plants from their countryside.

The provision of a water supply for growing African cities is also another major problem of resource use. White *et al.* (1962) have shown that the poor in African cities pay the highest price for water of all consumers, in part a reflection of the difficulty of finding water on the margin of the city. Water is either from local supplies such as wells or small streams, with consequent dangers of pollution and disease, or from piped urban water which has usually been brought in from a distant location. Few African cities have been able to provide low-cost piped water to a majority of their population.

Large cities each have their own particular relationship with their environs. The pattern of problems outlined above is a common one in large African cities in a variety of ecological and economic settings.

Location

African cities have varied origins. In tropical Africa many cities were initiated during the colonial period, and their location reflects the needs and priorities of that time. Many are ports which linked the colonial territories with the metropolis. Mogadishu, Mombasa, Dar es Salaam, Beira, Dakar, Abidjan, and Kinshasa are but a few examples. Others such as Nairobi, Khartoum, Kampala, are colonial establishments located as centers of government or transportation networks. Even in extratropical Africa external links are important in city location. In North Africa and in the Republic of South Africa, most cities are ports – the main exception being the mining centers of the Republic.

The importance of the colonial period and of external links in city location has meant that in Africa, more perhaps than in other parts of the world, cities have not grown up in relation to their immediate rural and economic environment but in relation to alien government priorities. This has perhaps in some cases skewed the pattern of growth of urban areas and resulted in problems of access and linkage. As cities have grown up around the coasts, problems of coastal pollution have a special significance.

Function

Most African cities have multiple functions – like cities everywhere. The original function of a disproportionate number of cities compared with other parts of the world was that of a government center. For example, all of the main cities of Kenya and Tanzania had administration, national or regional, as an important part of their initial purpose. The trading center function was the other main initiating purpose of urban growth. Trading encompassed a range of activities from local market distribution to large transhipments of goods to

348

ports. Later the rôle of service center, or industrial center, began to be important for most towns and cities. Modern industry is a comparatively new function for many African cities. Some industry was started during the colonial period in tropical Africa, usually set aside in "industrial areas" as designated parts of the city. But the major industrial growth occurred in most cases after independence with newly independent governments wanting to diversify the national economy and large multinational companies wanting to export it. The normal pattern was to contain much of the new industry within confined segments of the city. Assembly, textiles, soaps, drinks, and small-scale production were the main types of manufacturing. The pattern was different in extratropical Africa. In North Africa in cities such as Cairo and Algiers a range of manufacturing activities are spread over the city, as opposed to a localized industrial sector development within the urban area. In the Republic of South Africa many towns grew up as mining centers, as did some of the urban areas in Zaire, Zambia, and Zimbabwe. The growth of industry has taken place without consideration of the impact on the quality of the urban environment. It was as if by designating an area "industrial" the government felt that they had disposed of the problem of pollution and industrial waste disposal. Nothing could be further from the case. The growth of industry in the last two decades particularly has contributed greatly to the overloading of water supply and disposal systems and has resulted in very intense, if localized, land, water, and air pollution. In some cases, as in the Khartoum North industrial area, almost all industrial waste is disposed of on the land surface in the area nearby. In Khartoum most of the rest finds its way into the Nile.

An additional function in many towns has been experienced in the post-independence period. In general, the rapid growth of education and medical center facilities was concentrated in one or two cities. As national governments have established expanded educational systems, schools at all levels have multiplied, and universities have been established. Most of the higher educational institutions and medical centers have been located in the large towns, especially in or near the capital. Both of these activities contribute to the character and functioning of the city, but they may also be an important factor in contributing to the rapid growth of towns and cities in Africa.

Most large African cities, and many small ones too combine all or most of these various functions. Cairo, Nairobi, Kinshasa, Lagos, Algiers, and Khartoum are examples of cities where all of these activities are found within their political boundaries. Mombasa and Tanga are primary ports and industrial towns; Lusaka and Harare are government centers; and Dodoma in Tanzania is being redesigned almost solely as a center of government.

Dominant cultural heritage

The dominant origin of most African cities results from processes established during the colonial period, including governmental, export, and mission sites. But African urban life has existed for much longer than the colonial period, and even the more recently founded cities owe much of their character to the cultural heritage of Africa, not the imposed patterns of colonists.

At least four different cultural traditions can be distinguished in African cities:

349

the Moslem, West African, colonial, and East African. This is the place to discuss only some of the environmental and resource implications of those traditions, not the traditions themselves.

The Moslem cultural tradition is concentrated in North Africa but also extends significantly along much of the East African coast. Towns have long been a characteristic of Moslem communities, and there is still a tendency, if possible, to develop urban arrangements that permit the traditional style of housing having an enclosed courtyard and a comparatively low urban population density. This, as in the case of Khartoum and Mogadishu, results in widely dispersed cities with a very high per capita cost of providing the necessary amenities – water, sewage, light and power, and public transport. In other areas a new, more crowded, but still secluded urban tradition has appeared. Algiers and Cairo are examples where the notion of an inner courtyard has been retained even in crowded areas, though the inner space may be small or may even hardly exist at all. Nevertheless, the houses are organized in the traditional fashion, with domestic activities centered on a central open space shielded from the public. Thus the noise and air pollution concentrated in the streets are somewhat offset by the relative tranquillity of the inner space.

In West Africa, two traditional urban settlement patterns exist: the Youba and the Sahel or Sudan Muslim. In this area, savanna cities and empires of the 16th and 17th centuries were clearly established prior to the colonial period (Fig. 10.2). Some of the patterns of these traditional "urban" areas create a host of problems in the modern context. In the Youba towns, such as Ibadan, the historical town nucleus is surrounded by crowded single-storey dwellings arranged in patterns based on family units which do not allow easy distribution of blocks or streets. The buildings are arranged more in the pattern of rural homesteads with groups of houses around a square or in a rough half-moon around a well. These basic units are very functional at the individual house level but do not fit well together in an urban matrix. It is an especially difficult problem to bring vital services to these traditional urban areas due to the problem of limited access. In the family units it was the custom to bury family members within each single family compound. Because of both the congestion of these areas, where paths of access are too narrow for motor vehicles, and the occurrence of sacred grounds, it is difficult to provide modern public services to these areas. For example, it is impossible to bring modern sanitary conditions into the areas through such services as rubbish collection. Likewise, it is difficult to provide safety functions such as fire protection.

The colonial tradition in African cities is the antithesis of traditional African patterns. Cities were often planned to reflect the pattern of the times. Areas were set aside for government buildings and for well-spaced quarters for the higher civil servants. Special areas were designated for other groups such as Asian and African communities. Also land use was often segregated, keeping industrial and other functional groups, such as government, in separate areas of the urban zone.

East Africa "swahili"-type urban development is centered around the expendable swahili-type house with its wood and daub construction. Although the house types are different, the arrangements are very similar to those in West Africa. Again, housing is arranged in groups located around wells or markets,

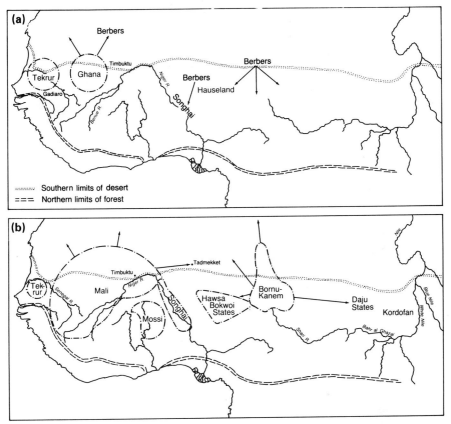

Figure 10.2 (a) Areas of power in the western Sudan, 11th century: showing the major urban centers in Ghana and Mali during this period. (b) Areas of power in Sudanese states in the middle of the 14th century (from Page 1978).

or in social groups and not along streets. Typically the housing unit includes a garden area maybe 20 m square, and there is considerable food production in these urban areas.

A matrix of size, locating functions and cultural heritage, may be used to define a good part of the variation of the many different African urban areas. It cannot be enough to distinguish the diversity of combinations to be found in Africa. The following brief descriptions and analyses of different African cities serve to illustrate the points made in the past section. Khartoum, Lagos, Kigali, and Nairobi are used here to provide an indication of the range and variety of African urban conditions and resource-use problems.

KHARTOUM: AN URBAN PROFILE

Table 10.5 illustrates the growth of Khartoum over the past 60 years. Population during this period increased from 48,000 to over 1,802,299. Figure 5.10

351

Table 10.5 Population of greater Khartoum, Sudan, 1924–83.

	1924	1955–6	1973			1983		
			Males	Females	Both sexes	Males	Females	Both sexes
Khartoum		93,000	189,196	144,710	333,906	265,021	211,197	476,218
Khartoum North		120,000	85,930	65,079	150,959	189,236	151,910	341,146
Omdurman		48,000	161,958	137,441	299,399	288,721	337,566	526,287
total Greater Khartoum	48,000	261,000	437,084	347,210	784,294	742,978	600,673	1,343,651
total Khartoum Province			598,486	497,131	1,095,617	982,179	820,120	1,802,299

Sources:
For 1973: Democratic Republic of the Sudan, Second Population Census of the Sudan (unpublished).
For 1983: Democratic Republic of the Sudan, Third Population Census of the Sudan, Preliminary Results (unpublished).

Notes
The Department of Statistics, Democratic Republic of the Sudan, assumes that in both censuses there was a 5 percent undernumeration. This was not added to the above figures.
Total population of the Sudan was thought to have been just under 15 million in 1973 and in 1987 was about 21.6 million (including the 5 percent undernumeration).

illustrates the spatial growth of the Khartoum metropolitan area that has been required to absorb this population increase. The original city in the metropolitan area was Omdurman.

Khartoum or, more precisely, the three cities of Khartoum, Omdurman, and Khartoum North which together comprise greater Khartoum illustrate many of the themes generalized in the first part of this chapter. Omdurman is an indigenous city built mainly of single-storey brick or mud-daubed dwellings; large parts of the city do not have paved streets and its margins have always been the site of informal camel, sheep, and goat markets. Its brown houses and courtyards merge almost imperceptibly with the desert around it. Omdurman is a traditional African city of Arab origin; its population has grown steadily, which has resulted in large areal expansion because its buildings are almost all single storied.

Khartoum North is a new planned urban development essentially of the post World War II period. It was initially to include some modern residential and agricultural areas, but the largest amount of the land was set aside as the industrial area for the three-town complex. Almost all the "large-scale" industries established in the 1950–80s in greater Khartoum were situated here. A wide range of enterprises is located in the city, including a brewery and a distillery (both since closed for religious or political reasons), textile industries, soap manufacturing, metal goods production, vehicle assembly, and a range of chemical and plastic enterprises. The area within and around the industrial area is heavily polluted with liquid and solid waste. This is a greater problem today as urban growth has greatly increased the residential population of Khartoum North. The flat terrain of the city compounds the problem of drainage for the efficient removal of both industrial and residential waste from the area.

Khartoum city itself was the British colonial town designed to be the center of government and education for the nation. Its center was along the Nile River. Here were located the palace, the government offices, the university, and the more modern stores and offices. Through the early 1950s, houses and even stores were usually only one or two stories high. Since then the town has expanded southward away from the river. It now extends up to 20 km from the Nile in a Los Angeles-type sprawl, without the services or individual automobile ownership which a city of this size needs.

The three towns, epitomized by their origin, served different functions and had different characteristics. There was the traditional town with its markets, the government center of colonial origin, and the industrial center of the country.

In the last two decades of independence these separate functions have become more blurred but remain essentially intact. All three centers have expanded dramatically, but Khartoum has grown physically more than the others, now stretching in successive blocks for up to 20 km from the original city center. Like Khartoum, Omdurman and Khartoum North have grown and also diversified their functions, but not as rapidly as the old colonial city.

The resource and environmental problems of the Khartoum complex reflect this origin and growth, as well as some special geomorphologic characteristics of the site. As the agriculturally productive environment immediately adjacent to Khartoum is limited to the irrigated lands along the Nile margins, the impact

353

of urban growth on resource use in surrounding areas has been great in recent years. Since 1960 the zone of wood exploitation for charcoal has moved more than 300 km southward (Fig. 10.3) and is continuously moving further from the capital. Pasture lands for grazing have undergone heavier use and land degradation has intensified, especially west of the city, because of the limited land resource and increasing numbers of livestock. Much of the area surrounding Omdurman today is bare waste ground whereas formerly it was a mixture of shrubs and sparse grasses.

Khartoum has therefore greatly increased its impact on the surrounding environment, in fact causing some considerable desertification as it has grown in the last two or three decades. Domestic water supply has not been a major issue because of the proximity of the Nile and its associated groundwater, though distribution problems do occur. The supply of energy for the modern as well as the traditional sector is a problem. The growth of the city has been accompanied by an even greater increase in demand for electricity, most of which is supplied by a grid from hydropower stations on the Blue Nile. New higher levels of energy demands, rapid siltation in reservoirs, and inadequate maintenance of the system result in very major energy shortages in the urban area.

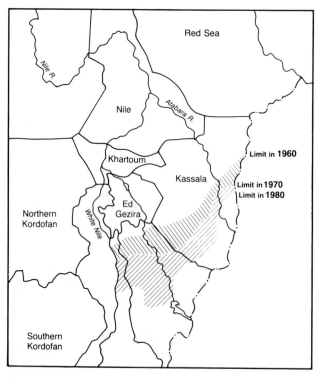

Figure 10.3 Increasing distance from Khartoum needed to supply the metropolitan area with its wood (energy) needs 1960–80. (Modified from Berry 1983.)

Internally the greatly enlarged city has new problems of transportation and pollution (air, water, and land), and there are new health risks associated with growth. The number of motor vehicles in the three towns has increased tenfold since 1965, and air and noise pollution has grown at a similar rate. The growth of industry has not been accompanied by environmental and other safeguards, and the Khartoum North industrial area is surrounded by, and partly located on, a wasteland of chemical waste, discarded metal, and air pollutants – its most obvious characteristic to the casual visitor.

Most importantly, the problem of waste disposal in the city, combined with the spread of the mosquito, has created new health hazards. Malaria, which was rare 20 years ago, is now a common disease. This is because there is now ample standing water associated with urban functions. Under natural conditions, in such an arid area as the location of Khartoum malaria would be extremely limited. In addition gastrointestinal diseases are a common cause of death, and many other diseases also are due to poor sanitary controls. The problem is perhaps symbolized by a 7 m mound of garbage recently located in the street outside the palace. However, it has been pointed out (Whitney 1982) that the waste material dispersed throughout the city provides a major source of food for a large population of goats, which in turn provide much needed milk. It may not be all as bad as the Western eye would see it.

LAGOS

Because of its increasing importance during the colonial and independence periods in Nigeria, Lagos grew rapidly. It was a small town with a population of barely 5000 in 1880, but by 1964 it was the first city in West Africa to reach a population greater than 1 million. Currently its population is likely to be in excess of 3.5 million and there is no indication that this increasing population trend is changing. From a physical perspective the location of Lagos has presented numerous problems, as it evolved from a relatively insignificant urban area to one of the paramount metropolitan areas of Africa.

The name Lagos, which is derived from the Portuguese word for lakes, gives some indication of the city's environmental situation. A large proportion of historical and modern-day Lagos is situated on islands and former mangrove lands cut by lagoons, and many parts of the city are susceptible to flooding (Fig. 10.4). Both oral tradition and contemporary records indicate that drylands have been lost to the receding coastline and through the changing water level of the lagoons. This attests to the accelerated erosion that has resulted both from land clearing for harbor works and other construction that removes the protective mangrove vegetation and from the mining of sands from the beaches for construction.

By the 1850s a small European quarter was established near the coast in an area that had been used by the local people for refuse disposal (Aderibigbe 1975). The coastal location of this European settlement indicates the importance of maritime trade during the early period. However, the poor drainage of this location and its close proximity to mangrove made it an unhealthy place to live: Both the location of the settlement and the types of housing the settlers built – some of which were prefabricated in England with little regard for the heat and humidity of the area – resulted in a high loss of life among the British settlers

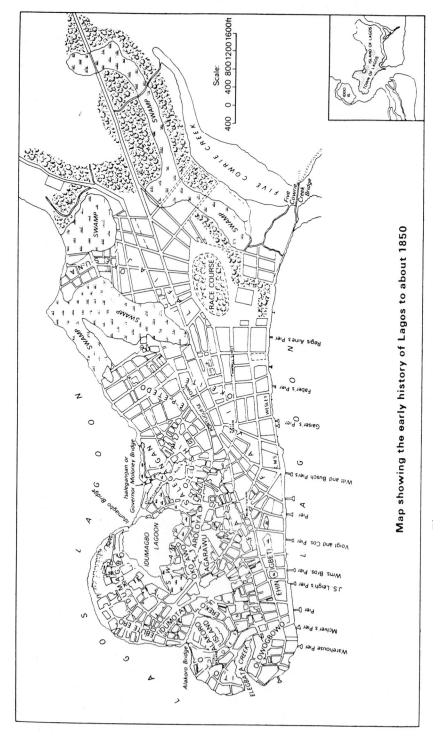

Figure 10.4 Lagos around 1850 (from Aderibigbe 1975).

(Burton 1963). Nevertheless, the high value placed on land fronting on the ocean by the Europeans began a "struggle for the possession of land in this formerly despised area of the town. This struggle for land fronting the sea was to find its highest expression in the latter-day scramble on the part of eminent Nigerians for land on Victoria Island which was, in the time past, the haunt of humble and itinerant fisherman." (Aderibigbe 1975.) Today Victoria Island is one of the choicest residential areas for the Nigerian elite and the international community.

According to Sada and Adefolalu (1975), until 1901 Lagos town only included the western portion of Lagos Island, an area of 4 km^2. Its estimated population was almost 42,000. Today the city's official area is 69 km^2, including both mainland and island portions (Fig. 10.5). The growth of Lagos has required continuous land and drainage of swampy lands and clearing of mangroves. Because the area is flat and low-lying, flooding remains a problem throughout large areas of the city during periods of heavy rains. The presence of numerous lagoons, wetlands, and creeks interspersed throughout the city also restricts access from one section of the city to another. The transportation of both people and goods is funneled toward the few bridges and main roads that link the various parts of the city with the country. Traffic regularly becomes congested at these hubs. The physical setting of Lagos has limited and increased the costs of development. It is clearly one important factor that contributes to the difficult living conditions (e.g. congestion) found within the city.

As late as the early 1950s, about 65 percent of the city's population was on Lagos Island. Today over 75 percent of the population is found in mainland Lagos, which stretches from Apapa to Agege beyond the international airport at Ikeja (Fig. 10.5). In some African cities, for example Khartoum and Nairobi, urban growth has been much less restricted by physical settings. This results usually in the spread of the modern cities over large areas in almost all directions from their historical centers. However, in Lagos growth is almost completely unidirectional toward the north. This is due to the extreme physical constraints of the city setting. Toward the south is the ocean, toward the east a large lagoon, and toward the west are numerous creeks and poorly drained lands. Thus it is only toward the north, where the majority of well-drained lands are found, that Lagos is growing. Lagos' overland connections with the rest of Nigeria, including both rail and road, are also restricted to this same zone. This concentration of transportation, housing, and employment, primarily limited to the north–south axis, has contributed to the infamous congestion of the metropolitan area.

Historically, when the primary foci for the Portuguese and British of Lagos were overseas, as during the slave trading and British colonial periods, the restricted access to the interior was not a prime problem. However, Lagos has evolved into the nation's major manufacturing, governmental, port, and business center; the concentration of these activities in such a restricted physical setting illustrates the relatively poor spatial location of Lagos for an independent Nigeria vis-à-vis the rest of the nation. This is in contrast to its good spatial location for a colonial Nigeria when its economic focus was toward Britain. The city's physical setting, along with its rapid population growth, has set into motion a host of environmental problems.

With Nigeria's post-independence economic policy favoring urban-industrial

357

development at the expense of rural-agricultural growth, rural-to-urban migration became a major factor during the late 1960s. With the concentration of industries (excluding those dependent on raw materials such as oil) and commerce in Lagos, an overwhelming proportion of this migration centered on the capital. The provision of housing and public services could not keep up with the huge population inflow and high natural growth rate. Shanty areas, such as the one in Mushin, mushroomed and are continuing to grow. These areas lack

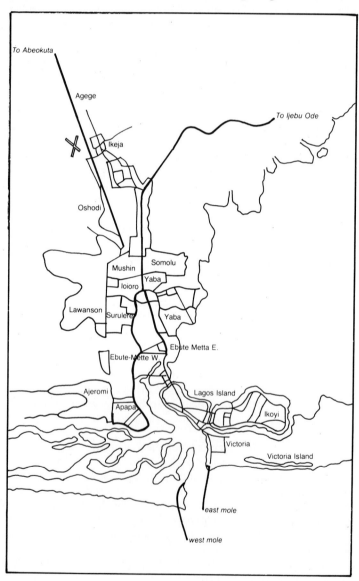

Figure 10.5   Metropolitan area of Lagos, 1980. (Modified from Aderibigbe 1975.)

adequate sewage and water supplies with resulting health problems for the inhabitants. Furthermore, the concentration of population and the flat terrain make it difficult to rectify the situation. The daily movements of Lagos's inhabitants from their residential to employment areas, as well as the movement of goods from the manufacturing plants to other areas within the country in the confined area of Lagos, are contributing factors that result in the city's massive congestion. Additionally, the city's inadequate transportation system exacerbates traffic problems.

Recognizing the dominant position of Lagos within Nigeria as well as the need to decrease its rate of growth, the government of Lagos State moved its capital to Ikeja from Lagos Island in 1976 (Fig. 10.5). However, today Ikeja is exceedingly congested too with its proximity to the international airport, industrial growth, population growth, and expansion of the Lagos metropolitan area beyond it to the north. The benefits of the state capital move are thus not obvious. In addition, the federal government has decided to move the federal capital north to Abuja in central Nigeria. This decision is an attempt to counter some of the historical advantages that have resulted in the excessive growth of Lagos. However, due to a host of problems, the move has been delayed and Lagos remains the political, business, and manufacturing center of the nation despite its physical constraints. The problems of housing, sewage, flooding, water supply, transportation, and overpopulation remain to be solved.

KIGALI

In clear contrast to Lagos, Kigali became a city only after Rwandan independence. In 1916 Kigali's population was between 600 and 700, by 1945 it had tripled in size to 2000, and at independence (1962) it had grown to 5000. Prior to independence when Rwanda and Burundi (Ruanda-Urundi) were administered first by the Germans (1896–1916) and then the Belgians (1916–62), Bujumbura (Usumbura) in Burundi was the primary administrative city for both countries. At independence, Bujumbura's population was under 25,000. Butare (Astrida), located in the extreme southern portion of Rwanda, about 35 km from the Burundi border, was the largest Rwandan city during most of the German and Belgian colonial periods. In 1959, near the end of the colonial period, all urban centers in Rwanda had populations of less than 3500. Less than 2 percent of the country's total population lived in these urban centers, which ranged in size from 80 to 3500 inhabitants (Atlas du Rwanda 1981).

At independence, Kigali became the nation's capital and began to grow rapidly. By 1970 its population had increased to 54,200, in 1978 it was 88,600 (Census Summary Report 1982), and its estimated population in 1985 was between 120,000 and 130,000. Even with this growth it is still a small city. Most of the population growth in the city has been the result of migration into the area. According to the 1978 Census summary, 3 percent of Kigali's current growth is due to the difference between the birth and death rates.

Average population density within the town limit is 1000 hab/km^2 (Fig. 10.6). This is quite low for an urban area and contrasts greatly with Lagos where values would be 10 to 40 times greater. This relatively low urban population density is partially the result of government policy and partly due to the topographic

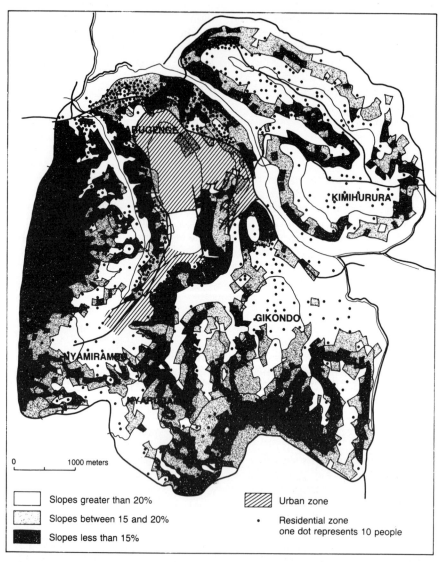

	Slopes greater than 20%		Urban zone
	Slopes between 15 and 20%	•	Residential zone one dot represents 10 people
	Slopes less than 15%		

Figure 10.6 The steep terrain found within the city limits of Kigali. Housing (the dots) is concentrated on lands with a slope of less than 15 percent. With the new location of government ministries in the Kimihurura area, housing is likely to increase in the northeastern portion of the town (from Prioul & Sirven 1981).

setting of the city. One of the government's policies has been to limit migration into urban areas by allowing in only those who have guaranteed employment. Thus it is unlike many African cities where, typically, large numbers of rural people enter the city in search of employment. Employment opportunities within the city remain quite limited. In tertiary occupations, including government, business, and house employment, 33,000 positions existed in 1978. In second-level occupations, including traditional artisan industry and modern industry, only 8500 positions existed in 1978 (Atlas du Rwanda 1981). For several reasons future growth in employment will probably remain low. First, because of the relatively inaccessible location of Rwanda, transport costs for imports and exports are high. This is one factor that results in the high costs of Rwandan goods. The result is that the manufacturing industry in Kigali is solely oriented to the small domestic market. Second, because the domestic market is small, the potential for industrial growth is low. Thus both the government policy and the limited employment opportunities in the city have prevented large rural-to-urban migration into Kigali. One result is that Kigali has avoided the development of large shanty areas common in many African capitals.

The extreme hilly nature of the town's setting is also a contributing factor in preventing the development of a densely populated urbanization. Level land is in short supply in Kigali (Fig. 10.7). The steeper slopes are both costly and difficult to develop for urban use. As a result much open land remains within the city and is put into food production by the city dwellers (Fig. 10.7). This production meets a significant proportion of the food demands of the urban

Figure 10.7 Crops being grown within the Kigali urban area.

homeowners. Interestingly, to prevent malaria from becoming a major health problem it is illegal to grow bananas, the staple food of the country, in the built-up areas of Kigali. Banana leaves can collect a small amount of rain which might become a breeding area for mosquitos. In reality, bananas are grown in the city, but at a far lower density than in the countryside. One important negative environmental factor that has resulted from the urban growth in this hilly setting is erosion. Accelerated soil erosion throughout the whole city is a major problem as more and more of the landscape becomes urbanized. Many streets within the city are still unpaved. During the intense rains common in the area large amounts of soil and dirt are removed from the slope and road surfaces. This material is transported to the valley bottoms and the Nyabugogo River. As would be expected, flooding is frequent on the valley bottoms, but most of these lands are not built-up and minimal problems result from the flooding. Because of both the physical setting and the lack of congestion within the city limits, Kigali's environmental situation is better than most African capitals, even though the country is one of Africa's poorest and most densely populated nations.

NAIROBI

Nairobi, capital of Kenya, is an example of a colonial city that grew into the major urban center of an independent country (Fig. 10.8). The town first became established just before the turn of the century as the first terminus of the Uganda–Mombasa railway. Prior to that Nairobi was nonexistent as an urban center. The railway was conceived as linking the coast with Uganda to help the British protect the Nile (Egypt). The railway was built largely by labor imported from India. The early Nairobi, like its modern-day counterpart, had three main ethnic groups: Africans, "Asians", and Europeans. The town rapidly became an important trading center and the social and government focus of European settlement in the highlands to the north and west. Located at the margins of the moist highlands but on the edge of the drier sweeping plains, it was a natural transition point for many different activities.

Nairobi grew steadily through the century but in the 1950s was still a modest-sized town of about 200,000 people. It was then a settlement with a large, dominantly Asian-owned trading center, a small European-owned business center, a government area, and significantly segregated suburbs. The Europeans, with their 1–2 acre gardens, were on the cooler western slopes; the Asians were on the inner margins of the city; and the Africans were in more crowded dwellings on the east and north.

Since independence Nairobi has developed several new functions or emphasized earlier rôles. It has become the capital of Kenya, this development, as in many African capitals, necessitating the establishment of many diplomatic missions and embassies. Nairobi has also become an international center housing the United Nations Environmental Program (UNEP – the first UN major establishment in a developing country) and Habitat (another UN agency). It is a major center for international conferences and seminars and a headquarters for a number of African research and educational programs.

These developments have been accompanied by the great expansion of the tourist industry. Tourists flocking to Nairobi often start or end their visits with

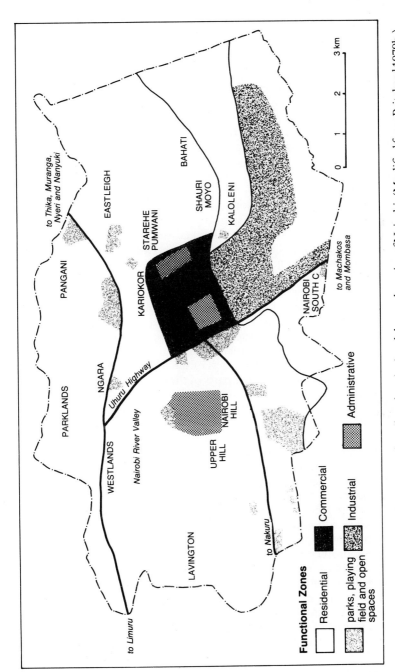

Figure 10.8 The historical center (near the railroad station) and the modern city of Nairobi. (Modified from Pritchard 1979b.)

game park tours. Some of them are in transit to the attractive East African coast. All of these developments were linked with Nairobi having the main airport in Eastern Africa with good connections across the continent and overseas. In response to this phase of change, Nairobi has become in part a town of modern hotels, modern luxurious stores, and a center of sophistication within Africa.

Other trends have also been operative. Nairobi has grown as the industrial center of Kenya, though in the most recent decade new industry is also being located in other Kenyan towns. However, the automobile and other major industries are located within or near Nairobi. The industrial center located on the drier, flatter east margin of the city now stretches over several square kilometers and is occupied by vehicle assembly plants, a tire manufacturer, textile and soap industries, small metal goods factories, canning plants, and a host of other agricultural and consumer-oriented activities.

Nairobi has become the focus for education with two large and expanding universities and many high schools and colleges. Kenya's modern medicine is centered in Nairobi and services the rest of the country and many of the surrounding countries. Most of the national trading organizations and other government parastatal bodies have their headquarters in Nairobi. Government has grown rapidly and employs thousands of civil servants and many more as drivers, messengers, and the like.

The result is a city which has grown rapidly since independence in 1963. Government estimates predict that the growth will continue and Nairobi will approach 2 million inhabitants early in the 21st century. Today the city retains its broad segregated pattern, though income rather than race provides the basis for differentiation. It is a city of strong contrasts. The western suburbs remain as elegant as any in the world, and parts of the downtown area fit the model of modern urban development. Other parts of the city are more modest. Some are characterized by one- or two-story stores, still mostly occupied by business men and women of Asian origin; others are crowded, unorganized and unhealthy squatter settlements, some without light or water supply.

The government has attempted to improve the housing situation through the building of numerous government-financed housing estates in the eastern and southern portion of the city. Attempts have been made to improve the slum conditions existing in the Mathare valley, and low cost housing was built in Dandora. However, the plain fact is that too many people are moving into the Nairobi area, and housing conditions for the vast majority of these recent immigrants are substandard. In the years ahead, all indications are that the housing problem will become worse.

The urban problems of Nairobi reflect its history and its environmental setting. Located as it is on the margin of the highlands, there is no obvious circle of resource devastation around the city as in many other African situations. However, the wood and charcoal demands of the city are huge and have grown substantially. Studies of several different locations within 150 km of Nairobi indicate the impact of this trade on both supply and prices.

The internal problems of Nairobi are a combination of old and modern urban ailments. Despite its hosting UNEP and despite a strong national concern with the environment, it has been difficult to generate effective and enforceable laws on industrial pollution. Air, water, and land pollution are all major problems in the metropolitan area. Everywhere there is an air and noise pollution problem as the large truck, bus, and car population generates unregulated noise, smoke, and particulate matter. Traffic accidents, often tragic, are an all too common feature of the city and its surrounding areas. Crime is a major and growing problem and the security industry is one of the fastest growing in town. As in many African cities, the combination of the best the world can offer and living conditions for some which are among the worst in the world is hard to manage. Nairobi manages the problem better than most.

Summary and conclusions

In this chapter, in addressing the resource management and environmental issues associated with urban areas in Africa, we have identified the problems resulting from rapid growth as being the most important. Urban areas, especially capital cities, are growing at unprecedented rates. More and more cities are passing the size thresholds that require major investment in the infrastructure if environmental problems are to be minimized. African cities in different environmental settings appear to experience new levels of intensity of environmental and resource problems when they become much larger than 400,000 population. Because urban areas tend to be politically and economically sensitive, they have usually received preferential treatment in the allocation of national resources. There is a real danger that urban areas will continue to get much more than their fair share of development funds, and this will lead to relative neglect of rural areas and further escalation in urban growth rates. The problem is that even with inflated levels of urban spending urban environmental and resource problems are not getting priority attention; furthermore, sufficient funds could not be made available even if they were given such priority. It is salutary to remember that a plan drawn up for the development of Dar es Salaam some years ago appeared to need the expenditure of almost all the national development budget for its fulfillment.

Solutions to the problem of African cities will not come by massive injections of new capital to reproduce western levels of urban living. The funds just are not there. Therefore improvements will have to be built upon better management of existing resources, innovative ways of slowing urban growth, and imaginative local answers to improving life in poor urban areas. As cities will continue to grow, this array of problems needs much more attention from governments and researchers alike.

11   Minerals, industry, and the environment

Introduction

The accelerating consumption of resources by industrialized societies and the modern sectors of developing countries has resulted in widespread environmental pollution problems. At the 1972 UN Conference on the Human Environment, held in Stockholm, the view of the developed nations was that the demands for energy, nonmetallic and metallic minerals, and food could threaten their population's health, damage ecosystems important to their quality of life, as well as modifying the global environment over time at a great cost to humanity.

The developing nations of Africa viewed the environment from a different perspective. In Africa energy and resource consumption was not high, and industrial pollution was generally nonexistent or localized. With widespread poverty, short life expectancy, and inadequate shelter, most African governments, like other Third World nations, dismissed environmental concern as the business of the rich countries. In fact, environmental concerns could delay economic development by increasing costs (UNEP 1978). Pragmatically, most African governments have always accepted the philosophy of industrializing first, using the cheapest and fastest approaches and correcting for the pollution afterwards. Because of the limited resources available, in reality little pollution control has been implemented in Africa, despite the fact that pollution is a real problem today, affecting health and long-term economic development in many areas.

This strategy of industrialization with minimal attention paid to pollution is similar to the approach used in Europe and North America during the development of their modern economies. But two significant differences exist today. First, many waste products produced in modern industries have greater toxicity and are more stable than the pollution produced during the early stages of the industrial revolution. Second, modern plants produce pollution in sufficient quantity potentially to overwhelm the affected natural systems. These two differences have the potential to cause irreversible environmental damage.

The Global 2000 Report to the President of the USA (1980) documents numerous environmental problems in the less developed nations, most of which are pertinent for Africa. In the water domain, pollution from persistent pesticides in irrigation canals, lakes, and rivers affects health and wildlife; as urban population grows and industry expands heavily polluted waters from sewage and industrial wastes are widespread in rivers and coastal areas below many African cities (Ch. 10). For example, former mangrove swamps near Lagos, and coastal areas, such as near Dar es Salaam, are less productive today due to the delivery of pollutants into these habitats. Impacts on the atmosphere are likewise common in the rapidly growing urban areas. With the rapid increase in the number of motor vehicles and the concentration of industry in only one or two cities in most African countries, urban areas such as Cairo and Nairobi expose their inhabitants to ever-increasing air pollution.

It is evident to most individuals that have traveled or lived in Africa that environmental problems are growing throughout the continent as populations grow and cities, industry, agriculture, livestock, and forestry continue to expand. Because of the economic and political constraints that exist in most African countries, these problems are likely not to disappear in the future. However, in response to the issues raised in the Stockholm conference, the United States and most European countries support environmental appraisals of bilateral assistance projects (United States Secretary of State Advisory Committee on the 1972 UN Conference on the Human Environment 1972). These appraisals are part of many development schemes and in theory attempt to identify and minimize potential negative environmental impacts by incorporating corrective measures in the projects prior to inception. In practice, for most organizations, excluding specific conservation societies such as the World Wildlife Fund, it has been unrealistic to give the environmental concerns a high priority relative to other pressing needs. Thus, in spite of a multitude of policy pronouncements in both the public and private domains, the status of the environment is of a relatively low priority in most areas of the continent. Many effects of development on the environment have already been presented in previous chapters. In the remainder of this chapter some of the consequences of mining and industrial activities on the environment are explored.

Minerals, mining, and the environment

Mineral mining and processing have a wide range of environmental impacts including the land, water, atmospheric, and socioeconomic domain. Direct results of mining and drilling include surface disturbance and waste disposal on the land and in the air and water. In many mining operations a considerable quantity of material needs to be moved in order to extract the desired mineral. For example, in Botswana at the Orapa Mine only about 0.89 carats of diamonds are found per ton of ground. The large amount of tailings associated with many mining operations is the source of significant water and air pollution. As another example, coal tailings are acidic and water running off these deposits into streams will kill most organisms; tailings that are dry often result in excessive dust. Additionally, the processing operations associated with many mining operations are another source of significant pollution. Copper smelters emit large quantities of sulphur oxides, contributing widely to the problems of acid rain and respiratory diseases for the individuals living immediately downwind from the smoke stacks.

Within Africa, broad categories of energy fuels (petroleum, coal), metallic and nonmetallic minerals are found. In the African context the production of these resources more often than not results in significant pollution. To curtail the pollution would require large investments of capital, which would reduce the amount of income generated from these economic activities. Mining companies have little incentive to control pollution since it would lower their profitability. The pressure must come from the host government, which often is not in a strong position (politically or technically) to require pollution controls. In a number of African countries, income generated from mining operations is the largest source of government revenue. Any reduction in this income will have significant immediate consequences, some of which would probably be political. The costs associated with environmental protection are clearly a major reason why minimal environmental controls are found at most mining operations on the continent.

Extensive deposits of a large variety of minerals are found throughout Africa (Fig. 11.1). Table 11.1 lists the major mineral producers for selected metals. Of

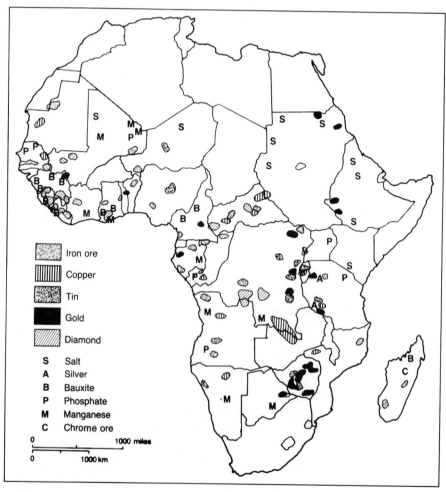

Figure 11.1 Distribution of minerals in Africa (from Hance 1975, Udo 1982).

Table 11.1 Major African metallic mineral producers in 1981.

Metallic mineral	Share of world production (percentage)
bauxite	Guinea (15)
chromite	South Africa (33), Zimbabwe (6), Madagascar (1)
cobalt	Zaire (45), Zambia (8), Morocco (2)
copper	Zambia (6), Zaire (6), South Africa (3)
gold	South Africa (53)
iron ore	South Africa (5), Liberia (5)
manganese ore	South Africa (24), Gabon (9)
uranium	South Africa (15), Niger (10), Nambia (9)

Source: Africa south of the Sahara, 1984–5.

particular interest to the world is that a host of critical minerals are concentrated in southern Africa in Shaba Province (Zaire), South Africa, and Zimbabwe, including 86 percent of the world's reserves of platinum group metals, 53 percent of manganese, 64 percent of vanadium, 95 percent of chromium, and 52 percent of cobalt. Each of these deposits potentially can result in a host of environmental problems during their extraction. To examine these problems in detail is beyond the scope of this section. However, to illustrate some of the environmental problems associated with mining, two case studies will be used. The first examines copper production in Zambia; the second looks at gravel quarrying in one location in Nigeria.

Copper production and environmental impacts in Zambia

The dominant position of the copper industry in the Zambian economy is reflected by the following information: approximately 30 percent of its gross domestic product comes from copper production; from 50 to 60 percent of total government revenues and over 90 percent of its foreign exchange are derived from copper; cobalt, gold, lead, selenium, and silver (all by-products of the copper mining) contribute additionally; only 14 percent of paid employment is directly associated with copper mining in Zambia; to feed the miners and associated urban population connected with the mineral economy requires approximately 30,000 laborers working on approximately 700 large farms; and finally, the drop in the world price for copper in the 1970s was a contributing factor in the stagnation of the Zambian economy.

The Zambian Copperbelt is situated in northern central Zambia along the border of Shaba Province (Fig. 11.2). Although mining only began in the area in 1921, today over 90 percent of the country's urban centers are found in this 50 × 145 km area, which is mostly within the Kafue River Basin. Since wages are significantly higher in mine-related activities than in agricultural activities, the Copperbelt mines attracted thousands of men from throughout the country, some from as far away as Malawi, Tanzania, and Mozambique. This draining of young men to work in mine-related activities resulted in some villages having as many as 60 percent of its male workforce absent at any given time.

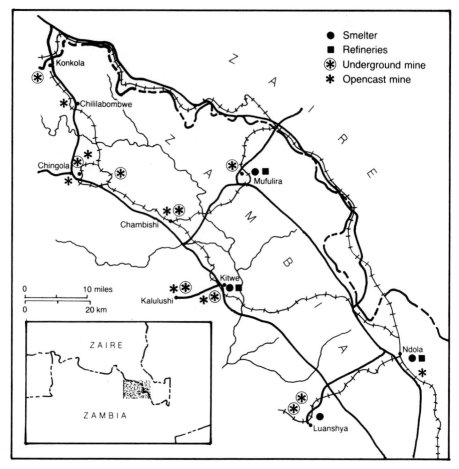

Figure 11.2 Location of the Copperbelt (Kitwe to the Zaire border), Zambia (from Johnson & Roder 1979).

Some environmental ramifications of this temporary migration were that the traditional shifting agricultural techniques practiced in large areas throughout the surrounding regions became disrupted. Lands could not be cleared and planted because of the large rural shortage of labor. This resulted in a decrease in the use of fallowing. Agricultural yields decreased and soil erosion increased. In the Zambesi Valley in western Zambia, the physical infrastructure required to continue practicing an irrigated farming system fell into disrepair because of the labor shortage. This too resulted in decreasing agricultural outputs, soil erosion, and the economic decline of the zone compared to the mining area (Van Horn, 1977).

Until 1957, when electricity was imported from the Congo (Zaire), the large labor requirements in the Copperbelt were not for mining itself, which always has been heavily dependent on machinery, but for the clearing of forests to supply firewood to the thermal power stations of the Copperbelt. The environmental effects of the forests clearfelled in the area affected the water balance of the upper Kafue River Basin.

The Kafue River enters the Copperbelt near Chililabombwe (Fig. 11.2). The area upstream from this town (5000 km^2) is a forest reserve, and settlement here is restricted. As a result, this portion of the basin remains largely under natural conditions. Downstream from Chililabombwe, major environmental changes have occurred since the 1930s. These changes are a result of the direct and indirect impacts of copper mining. Important direct impacts of the mining operations are land-surface changes, including huge open pits and tailings; air pollution from the copper- and lead-refining operations; and water contamination, also associated with the refining processes. Some indirect impacts are the rapid growth of the urban population in the line-of-rail towns from Luanshya to Konkola, with the majority of the new urban dwellers living in dense squatter compounds consisting of shanties constructed of mud bricks, tin, and wood scraps; the draining of the countryside of its young inhabitants and its ramifications on existing farming systems; the establishment of large farming operations along the line of rail from Lusaka northward to supply food to the growing urban and mine-working populations; and the massive tree cutting to provide fuel for energy production needed by the mines.

It is estimated that in the mining and metallurgical operations about 0.4 m^3 of wood was used for every ton of copper produced. Until 1957, when electricity began to be imported from Zaire, tree cutting in the upper Kafue Basin was continuously increasing and expanding into new areas to meet the increasing energy demands in the Copperbelt (Table 11.2). The effect on the hydrologic régime of the river resulting from the decrease in tree cover is difficult to assess as little hydrologic data were collected prior to the 1960s, by which time tree cutting was decreasing and afforestation programs were being established.

Table 11.3 compares precipitation and runoff for the headwaters area (above Chililabombwe) with that of the Copperbelt from 1959 to 1964. Since both areas

Table 11.2 Area of forest clearfelled in the Copperbelt.

Year	Area (ha)	Year	Area (ha)
1947	5,790	1956	8,756
1948	5,930	1957	1,613
1949	9,074	1958	1,750
1950	9,667	1959	1,493
1951	13,590	1960	2,873
1952	11,929	1961	1,778
1953	10,017	1962	2,504
1954	12,070	1963	2,494
1955	15,031	1964	2,498

Source: UNDP (1966).

371

Table 11.3   Rainfall and runoff for the Kafue
headwaters and the Copperbelt.

	Headwaters region (5000 km)	Copperbelt (6530 km^2)
Rainfall (mm)		
1959–60	1275	1354
1960–1	1491	1295
1961–2	1636	1694
1962–3	1344	1466
1963–4	1074	1115
total	6820	6924
average	1364	1385
Runoff (mm)		
1959–60	139.7	160.0
1960–1	203.2	203.2
1961–2	419.1	467.4
1962–3	350.5	439.4
1963–4	175.3	254.0
total	1287.8	1524.0
average	257.6	304.8

Source: UNDP (1966).

had similar rainfall and the relief is greater in the headwaters area, the greater average annual runoff (304.8 mm vs. 257.6 mm) for the Copperbelt is probably a result of the difference in groundcover (natural forest vs. mining, farming, and partially cleared forests) between the two areas. The UNDP/FAO 1966 report on the Kafue River Basin estimates that runoff increases due to clear cutting of timber are equivalent to 467 mm from the 673 km^2 cleared of timber during the 1959–60 to 1963–4 periods. During the earlier periods, when tree cutting was more extensive and afforestation less so, changes in the hydrologic régime of the river must have been greater.

Some specific environmental problems resulting from copper mining documented by Seidman (1976) include the partial collapse of the mine at Mulfulira that resulted from the piling of excessive waste materials over the excavated areas. At the Chingola mine, midway between Chililabombwe and Chambishi, each day thousands of liters of water are pumped out of the mine directly into the Kafue River. Today, most mining is being done in open pits. The vast holes being created by these operations are permanently scarring the landscape and removing it from productive use in the future.

To summarize all of the environmental impacts of copper mining in Zambia would require a scale of documentation that does not exist. But it is clear that since the start of mining numerous significant changes have occurred. Some of the demographic and physical environmental alterations have been presented. Clearly a wide range of contemporary environmental problems that exist in

Zambia are a result of the dominance of copper in the nation's economy. The final example illustrates the complexity of linkages between environment, development, and copper in this area of Africa.

In the 19th century vast areas of Zambia were reported to have large herds of cattle. With the outbreak of rinderpest, about 1890, in these areas, many of the cattle died. In the 1920s, before cattle numbers could attain their prior size, the areas lost a significant percentage of their manpower to provide labor for mining and related activities. The shortage of manpower and the decrease in cattle permitted an extensive cover of undergrowth bush to become established in these former grazing areas. One result was that the tsetse fly expanded into these areas, making the former grazing lands now marginal for cattle. The neglect of these lands at the expense of expanding the mining sector permitted vegetation changes to alter the environmental health situation. This lowered the economic activity in these areas. To develop these lands today it is necessary to reverse the set of complex interactions set in motion by the outbreak of rinderpest and then exacerbated by the establishment of the Copperbelt economy.

Gravel quarrying and some environmental impacts

Gravel is not a mineral in that it has neither a specific crystal structure nor chemical composition. Its composition is determined from the rock type from which it is derived. Its rôle in African economies and development plans also differs from minerals in that gravels are mined in almost all cases for domestic, not foreign, markets. Additionally, most African gravel operations are small in size, use primarily manual labor, and are staffed and managed by local inhabitants. Yet gravel is a critical raw material needed in almost all modern construction including roads, bridges, large office buildings, and houses. Because a major component determining the price for gravel is the cost of transportation, almost every region within a country has its own local gravel source. Consequently the environmental impacts of gravel quarrying are widespread, though usually they are of a lower magnitude than those associated with large mineral mines.

Unlike northern Europe and North America where large gravel deposits exist from glacial deposits, the major African sources of gravel are river alluvium or quarried rocks. Generally, no legal constraints control the removal of gravels and, where they do exist, they are usually not strongly enforced. The result is that most gravel operations throughout the continent result in a variety of environmental problems. Probably because most gravel enterprises are run as small local businesses, many on an *ad hoc* basis, few data are published regarding this industry. This probably explains why in the African context there is a paucity of references to this critical raw material in journals and books.

Typical of many highland areas in Africa, there are numerous small quarries in the Central Province of Kenya. These quarries supply materials for local building and are widely dispersed throughout zones with steep slopes. Wherever they exist, due to the disruption of surface material, soil erosion is widespread (Lewis 1982). These small, one- or two-person operations are a source of high local sediment production. In some instances they cause localized slope failures.

Most quarry operations are not on hillslopes but are (1) situated along rivers

373

in zones where gravels can be removed from the riverbed and riverbank materials, and (2) are in areas where the subsoil materials have heavy concentrations of gravels. In most cases these are former alluvial deposits. Ekpenyong (1984) documents the effects of gravel quarrying in one such setting. Situated in Nigeria's Cross River State (near Calabar), his study area is located where the tropical rainforest has been changed by cultivation into a vegetation cover of secondary bush and wild oil palm. This is the typical land cover for this portion of eastern Nigeria. Formerly the livelihood of the inhabitants was subsistence farming supplemented with small cash payments derived from inmigrants who quarried for gravel along the riverbanks and riverbeds. Today this traditional pattern has undergone large modifications.

With the end of the Nigerian civil war, there was an increase in the demand for gravel to repair or rebuild the damage to buildings and public works in eastern Nigeria. At the same time, there were additional demands for gravel to build the new development projects being funded from Nigeria's petroleum-derived revenues. As a result, the price for gravel increased by a factor of six and gravel quarrying became a profitable venture for the local inhabitants. Farmers left their fields, and gravel quarrying spread throughout the community lands. Farming now became the supplementary activity for many of the inhabitants.

Today much of the agricultural land in the area has been ruined by the quarrying. This reduction in arable land limits the system of shifting cultivation still practiced in the area. One result is the decrease in the length of fallow. This decrease is resulting in the exhaustion of the soils. Crop yields are dropping. Yet, if quarrying continues at the current rate, the gravel deposits will become exhausted in 10 to 15 years and no further income will come from this source. Meanwhile the land is being destroyed.

The reduction in locally grown foodstuffs requires many inhabitants to purchase an increasing amount of food. Cash employment is now a necessity for these people. When the gravel is exhausted, much of the farmland will be ruined and many inhabitants will have to leave the area. They are likely to move to urban areas. With the current halt in most government projects because of Nigeria's balance of payments problems, the demand for gravel has slackened. The decrease in local foodstuffs, along with the lower income, is already creating hardship in the area.

The long-term degradation of the physical environment from quarrying limits the future agricultural options and opportunities in this rural area of Nigeria. This is another example of short-term benefits resulting in a deterioration of the environmental situation. As a result, development options become more constrained, and the long-term viability of the area becomes questionable.

Industries and the environment

Industrial development affects the environment in three major ways. First, waste materials almost always are a by-product of manufacturing. Their release into waters, air, or landfills has the potential to alter the existing conditions in any of these three domains. Second, the location of the industries themselves and the requisite site preparation often results in morphological changes of the land that modify drainage. Included in this category are the infrastructural changes, such as road building, that are required for industrialization. Third, because of the needed infrastructure, government contacts, labor pool and market, most industries are concentrated in a single urban area within each country. In Africa, excluding those heavy industries which are usually dependent on a natural resource, the overwhelming majority of manufacturing industries are located in the capital. Thus industrialization contributes to the acceleration of urban growth and the environmental impacts discussed in the previous chapter.

Documented data regarding direct environmental impacts of African industry are even scarcer than those related to mining activities. In Africa, most investigators interested in the links between the environment and industry are required to collect their own data or rely on visual observations since few governmental agencies collect data specifically related to environmental issues. Where national ministries of the environment are established, they are almost without exception understaffed and weak. They are thus of little use in providing documentation of the environmental situation in their countries.

According to a recent International Labor Organization report (1983), each year 25,000 deaths result from occupational accidents in Africa's modern sector. Additionally, the report estimates that serious but nonfatal accidents exceed 1 million per year. The probability of having an occupational accident in Africa is three to five times greater than in an industrialized country. This is particularly striking, given that modern-sector industries are more closely regulated than other enterprises. Although most of these injuries or deaths are the direct result of accidents with machinery and for the purposes of this book not considered environmental, the high incidence is indicative of the generally lax attitudes toward aspects of the manufacturing process not directly related to product outputs. The same report also stresses that inadequate regulations or enforcement result in large quantities of atmospheric pollutants and effluents being released by modern-sector industries. These waste products clearly alter the physical environment.

In many modern factories and plants, during the construction phase inadequate funding is provided for the installation of filters and waste-disposal appliances. Where adequate precautions have been taken, all too often inadequate maintenance results in improperly treated waste materials going directly into the air, rivers, lakes, and oceans. Likewise, it is only on rare occasions that the environmental setting for a proposed industry is considered as a critical input in determining industrial location. For example, in the development plans for an integrated steel industry in Nigeria, neither economic nor environmental factors were of primary concern in determining the locational setting of the mills. A crucial factor determining plant location was the government's policy of economic decentralization, intending to unite the federation's diverse areas. The steel plant constructed at Aladja (near Warri) is in a swamp and mangrove setting within the delta region. Its products have to be shipped overland to the rolling mills at Ajaokuta. Because of the high production costs, which result in a finished product twice the world price, the Nigerian government must subsidize its steel industry. Environmental considerations would further increase the costs. Both the modifications that affected the

375

environment during the construction phase and the continuing alterations associated with the manufacturing process, including the release of wastewaters into the Niger and smoke into the atmosphere, are of minor importance in the context of Nigerian economic development.

Udo (1982) divides African industry into seven categories. Of these, textiles and footwear, chemicals and pharmaceuticals, metals and light industry, and heavy industry have important environmental linkages. The manufacture of footwear, involving leather, often results in water pollution due to the lack of water treatment during the tanning of the hides. The release of tanneries' untreated wastewaters into river systems is a widespread phenomenon on the continent. The tannic acid released in the rivers, especially during dry periods when the acid cannot be sufficiently diluted, kills most aquatic life in the affected reaches of the river and restricts the use of the rivers' waters downstream from the pollution sources.

In most of Africa, because of the large amounts of capital, advanced technology, and large markets required for the establishment of integrated chemical plants, most countries have opted for the development of import-substitution chemical industries. These plants import the basic raw chemicals and then manufacture paints, insecticides, pharmaceutical products, and a host of other products specifically needed in the local economies. Since these plants require transport facilities, power, and skilled labor supply, they are almost always located in urban centers.

Many of the environmental effects of these industries are identical to those associated with tanning. Additionally, in the Third World many chemicals deemed too dangerous to be used in the industrialized countries, where the raw materials are produced, are formulated in local factories and then sold for local distribution. This is particularly true in the agricultural sector, where many chemicals are used as fertilizers, pesticides, and herbicides. The crops, the water, and the agricultural workers, both because of the chemicals and the improper handling of them, can become poisoned (Hill 1983). However, it should be noted that the negative environmental effects of these industries are partially countered by the benefits accruing from the activities of these companies. Increased food supply, lower costs, greater availability of medicines, the reduction of disease-causing insects, and increased employment are some important benefits of these industries. When the chemical and pharmaceutical products are properly used, they can contribute to improving both development and the environment.

The metals and light engineering category includes the factories that fabricate steel drums, corrugated iron sheets, storage tanks, nails and similar products, as well as assembly plants including electronics such as television and motor vehicles. Most of the industries in this category require imported materials in their finished product and a large market. Proximity to government facilitates the paperwork required to obtain the import licences needed for imports; the largest markets are usually around the nation's capital. The result is that most fabricating and engineering industries are in a country's dominant urban center, the capital. Thus industries in this category also contribute to the environmental impacts of large urban growth.

376

Summary

Industrialization is having important environmental consequences throughout the continent. The air, the land, and the water, as well as the people themselves, are being exposed to a wide range of new environmental conditions. These conditions will probably continue unabated as most national policies are oriented toward industrial development. But it must be remembered that Africa remains the least industrialized continent. Its per capita consumption of energy and its industrial rate of growth is the lowest among the inhabited continents. This includes its use of hydroelectric and fossil fuel energy, the growth in motor vehicles, and the production and consumption per capita of chemicals (UNEP 1982). From a global perspective, African industrialization results in a low level of pollution. But its industrialization is extremely uneven and concentrated in the areas of greatest population density, the large urban areas. Additionally, because of a multitude of factors, pollution control is not a major priority throughout the continent. The result is that the inhabitants of Africa, especially in the urban areas, will be exposed to ever-increasing pollution. The relationships between the environment, industrialization, and development need to be documented and understood within the African context in order to ensure the future potential for growth on the continent.

12 Environment and development in Africa: a review and prospect

Introduction

In this book we have unashamedly taken an environmental and resource management perspective of the African continent. We adopted this viewpoint firstly because the fundamentals of African development are at least partly rooted in the characteristics of the resource base and secondly because these fundamentals are often ignored or at least misstated. There are clearly complex factors at work in the conditioning of any particular country or continent to its current economic and social situations. We have tried to introduce some of these factors but have clearly not presented a total view of development issues in Africa. Rather, we have tried to contribute a resource management perspective to the pressing development problems of the continent.

In this chapter we seek to summarize some of the major issues that have surfaced in the process of outlining the problems reviewed in the past eleven chapters. In addition, we try to go a little further and present a perspective on some of the current trends and to share some views and hopes for the future.

The general characteristics of the African environment

Africa has three distinctive features which help to create special circumstances in relation to the issues of environment and resource management. The first is the basic geologic and geomorphologic history, the second is the distinctive climatic environment, and the third is the history of climate and environment change.

Africa is an old continent. It achieved its basic form over 200 million years ago when a major breakup of a southern hemisphere land block occurred. Since that time the continent has changed its location on the Earth's surface through motions associated with plate tectonics, but not as much as India, Australia, and South America, the other southern landmasses. Tectonically, Africa overall has been exceedingly stable. Recent mountain building and volcanism has been localized and relatively minor. The northwestern part has been affected by shallow submergence under a pre-Mediterranean sea and by mountain-building processes resulting in the Atlas Mountains; a major rift valley has developed along almost its entire length in its eastern portion with some volcanic activity. But the largest proportion of the landmass has remained overall stable with minor broad regional uplifting and subsidence being the major tectonic activity on the continent. Along with Australia, Africa generally reflects the landscape properties of old, relatively stable land surfaces.

The dominant tectonic activity of downwarping and faulting of the crust has helped create numbers of large river basins, inland lakes, and alluvial depressions on the continent. Former lake floors and river alluvium are the main locations of "new" soils on the African continent. Elsewhere most of the soils are "old", in the sense that they are developed on land surfaces that have been in existence for many millions of years. Many are old too in the sense that they are underlain by deep layers of weathered rock, and soil-forming processes have gone on for so long that many soluble elements and minerals have been largely removed from the system. The soils of the continent bear special characteristics, some of which are due to their tropical genesis and others of which are due more to their long development on very old land surfaces. This is in great contrast to the situation in Western Europe and a large percentage of North America, where in the last few tens of thousands of years soils are forming on newly created glacial and glacio-alluvial debris.

Climatically Africa can be distinguished as one of the driest of continents. About 50 percent of the continental surface has a rainfall deficit season of sufficient magnitude to restrict agriculture and make the area arid or semi-arid. Over 20 percent of this dryland area is classified as arid. Surplus rainfall is generated only from a small part of the continent. The Zaire Basin, mountains and highlands in northwest, eastern, and central Africa, extreme southern Africa, and the uplands and coastal areas of West Africa make up the bulk of water surplus territory. From these areas rivers typically flow through drier zones enroute to the sea, holding out for many people the tantalizing prospect of watering drylands to create greater prosperity.

For much of the continent, however, rainfall variability is the biggest problem in agriculture and utilization of water resources. Rainfall régimes in all but the year-round wet areas produce a highly variable pattern of precipitation from year to year and, within years, from place to place.

Over historical and prehistorical time there have been very important changes in climate, especially as reflected in rainfall amounts. Sometimes these have current beneficial effects in that relic alluvial soils formed in earlier wetter climates may have good potential for agricultural development, providing water can be supplied to the land. The Sudan Gezira is one such area.

However, the pattern of change of climate has had "hard-to-define" impacts on the vegetation. Rainfall change has been most important in the arid, semi-arid, and savanna zones, and in each of these zones there is a tendency for vegetation complexes formed in wetter periods to be able to maintain their characteristics in drier episodes under natural conditions. However, once these ecosystems are modified or stressed, they tend to revert to a lower status more appropriate to the current drier pattern of rainfall.

In the humid rainforest areas an important characteristic of the ecosystem is that a large proportion of the nutrients are held within the thick layers of the living biomass and, additionally, the vegetation complex is able to create its own microclimate. If the vegetation is removed, there are two resultant problems: firstly the nutrients are in danger of being worked out of the system and secondly the near-ground climate is changed dramatically.

People thus have important impacts on the status of vegetation in Africa, as everywhere, and it is important to remember that in large parts of Africa this impact has been occurring for very long periods of time. The rôle of fire in the development of the grassland and savanna vegetation is still a matter of discussion, and the varying rôle of different invasive groups in Mauritania over several thousand years is well documented.

The physical environment in Africa is varied and it is hard to make useful generalizations that fit this huge area. The most important generalizations we find are:

(a) The geomorphologic and geologic history of the continent is distinctive, creating a setting for soil development which is not replicated elsewhere.
(b) The soils of the continent combine characteristics related to the tropical setting and features related to the great age of the land surface. Nevertheless, some much younger and generally more nutrient-rich soils are found, especially in the volcanic highlands.
(c) The climate is predominantly one of high temperatures, and most areas have water deficiencies during some part of the year.
(d) Rainfall, the key climatologic parameter, is highly variable in time and space in the semi-arid areas. In recent years rainfall has been below average in many of these dry areas.
(e) Climatic variation over historical and prehistorical time has been an important factor in current soil and vegetation patterns.
(f) The influence of people on vegetation and soils is profound. In particular, forested areas have declined, with grasslands expanding into the former forested areas. On the drier margins of the grasslands, overgrazing in many places is resulting in the expansion of desert lands.

Historical patterns of resource use

The record of the precolonial period in Africa is far from complete, but the information we have suggests that for large parts of the continent there was at this period a reasonable adjustment between people and environment. This adjustment, then as now, broke down in periods of prolonged drought or in the face of long periods of war and pestilence. The balance in terms of food products seems to have been maintained by a low-input–low-output system which avoided major risks. Farming systems were usually on a small scale and involved a degree of shifting cultivation. North Africa was much more in contact with the Mediterranean Basin and life there followed a pattern that was much more integrated with Europe.

In Africa south of the Sahara major changes occurred with the beginning of European interest in this portion of the continent. First there was a massive population dislocation due to the slave traffic. Second, the partitioning of the continent into spheres of economic interest initiated a reorientation of economic activities resulting from important political constraints imposed on the environmental situation. These external constraints began in the west and the extreme south, then spread to the eastern and central parts of Africa. During the 19th and

380

20th centuries the colonial division of Africa brought about many different disruptions in normal life patterns. Among the most important were:

(a)   the division into many, often small, territories, frequently with boundaries cutting across cultural groups;
(b)   change of trade patterns with a dominant interior-to-coast pattern imposed by the colonial powers;
(c)   development of export crops;
(d)   alienation of the best land in some parts of Africa, especially in South Africa, Zimbabwe, Kenya, Tanzania, and Zambia;
(e)   development of towns and transport structure which reinforced the trade interior–external orientations; and
(f)   the beginning of a period of population growth and urban growth which was especially rapid from the 1950s onward.

The relatively short colonial period was critical in the emergence of nation states in Africa, particularly south of the Sahara. It appears to have created rigidities which will continue for a long, long time.

Independence of the nation states, which occurred dominantly in the 1950s and 1960s, served at least initially to emphasize the colonial boundaries. The more than sixty nation states in Africa vary greatly in size but, from a resource management point of view, very few have the optimal size or configuration to manage their natural resources readily. In addition, the independent nations inherited political boundaries from the colonial era, making it extremely difficult for many of the countries to develop a viable economy. Due to the lack of environmental diversity found within many of the nations, some countries, such as Burkina Faso, are almost completely comprised of arid and semi-arid lands. Much national resource management in Africa, especially water management, is dependent on international cooperation. This need is unfortunate and difficult to accomplish in a continent of small states, most of which are still working on problems of national identity and internal control.

Special issues related to ecologic zones in Africa

In this section we summarize Chapters 4 through 8 which analyze the environmental and resource management issues of the rainforest, the drylands, the savanna, and highlands, and the extratropical areas of Africa.

Rainforest

Rainforest is becoming a rarity in Africa. The major exception is in the Zaire Basin where large areas of rainforest exist and appear currently to be only threatened at the margins. In West Africa the spread of agriculture and the growth of population in the southern parts of the region has reduced rainforest to about 10 percent of its former condition. The change of forest lands in West Africa has until recently been a sequential process, and the transfer from forest to cultivation has largely been achieved without widespread immediate deterioration of the land. This is also true of some areas of highland Kenya and Tanzania, where natural forest has been rapidly replaced by perennial tea and coffee bushes. Under these circumstances there are changes in hydrology and a consequent loss of soil, but under these new "tree" crops an equilibrium is rapidly obtained that maintains the soil and does not alter the major hydrologic patterns. However, total annual stream flow often increases due to the lower evaporation and transpiration from the new vegetation cover.

The sequence is quite different when rainforest is replaced by maize or other annual crops on slopes and on rolling terrain. In these circumstances nutrients are quickly washed out of the soil and the soil itself is subject to rapid removal. In all circumstances the switch from a multispecies, multilayered vegetation system to the monoculture of agriculture is a difficult one to make. All too often the result has been the creation of a degraded area having little economic use after a short number of years. The recovery of the land in most rainforest areas is a long-term process.

Problems have occurred in a number of formerly rainforested areas as population densities increase. The agricultural areas of southern Ivory Coast and the upland cultivated areas of Kenya and Tanzania are all now producing many times more sediment through soil loss than in earlier years. This high rate of absolute loss of soil is a fact; what is not so clear is the impact of these losses on the productivity of these very productive soils. Current studies suggest that their continued high productivity over a long period of time is in question, unless remedial measures are undertaken.

It is clear that the greatly increased yield of material from these areas has already had an impact on sediment load in streams and rivers and on the effectiveness of water control and development projects downstream. In Kenya, the Tana River irrigation and hydropower developments are being compromised, partially by the higher than expected sediment loads; for similar reasons, the Kashm el Gerba Dam and irrigation project and the Roseires hydropower and irrigation dam in Sudan are both much below expected efficiency.

The dry lands

Africa is dominantly a dry continent and "drylands" – arid and semi-arid lands as we define them – occupy about half the total land area. This excludes the remaining large area of seasonally dry (savanna) lands which are dealt with in the next section. As well as their large extent, drylands are an important feature of more than 25 African countries, including most of the poorest. Scarcity and variability of rainfall are the most important limiting development features of the drylands. Agriculture, when it is found in these areas, is almost always based on the need to obtain additional water supplies beyond the local precipitation. Rainfall in the African drylands varies considerably from year to year and, within each year, from place to place. It is also variable in sequences of years, a sequence of generally wetter years being followed by a run of drier years.

Both traditional and modern systems of livelihood attempt to accommodate the uneven influx of this most important resource. More traditional systems tended to adapt by utilizing nomadic or semi-nomadic lifestyles and by a flexibility of movement north and south. Even so, there are records of devastating losses of human and animal life in historical times.

In this century, and particularly in the last two or three decades, a number of factors have encouraged settlement rather than mobility. Among these factors are government preferences for a settled population for reasons of security, education, and social service. As a result, the growth of agriculture along the margins of the wetter dry areas is being pushed into ever drier lands to accommodate growing numbers of people. This is removing some of the best lands from the grazing systems. A result is decreasing potential productivity for pastoral activities in many areas. This is due to the removal of some of the diverse environmental settings that nomadic peoples have traditionally utilized during the annual fluctuations in the moisture supply. In most of Africa the economic possibilities are becoming more restrictive due to these political and environmental changes. This movement of agriculture into drier areas has required the establishment of new water sources, including wells and reservoirs around which people tend to settle.

There is evidence to show that over a long period of time the dry areas have undergone a steady and progressive reduction in the diversity of wild plants and animals and that ecosystems are generally degraded. This underlying process appears to have been speeded up in the last 30 years and has been made dramatically more apparent by the sequence of dry years in the early 1970s and again in the early 1980s. Desertification of drylands has become an important focus of international attention and is regarded as one of the very important global problems of our time. The areas of its greatest impact are the semi-arid lands of Africa. The degradation of this ecosystem is one important element that is contributing to the difficulty of achieving economic growth in these areas. The areal growth of this land devastation further taxes the limited land resources in these countries. This further restricts the options available for economic change.

Both traditional and modern forms of irrigation have been a strategy to improve production and reliability of production in the dry areas. Traditional forms are typically small scale, in oases or along rivers – for instance along the banks of the Nile and Niger. The traditional flood irrigation of Egypt was of course much larger in scale.

Modern irrigation includes the large-scale projects in Egypt and central Sudan, the Office du Niger in former French West Africa, and the more recent activity on the Senegal and Niger Rivers. A good part of large-scale irrigation has been devoted to export crops rather than food staples, so irrigation has not yet had a major direct impact on food security for domestic consumption. In addition, indifferent management of irrigation projects and difficult environmental circumstances have resulted in problems of salinization and lowered productivity. Also problems of disease associated with new zones of humid conditions within the dry lands have resulted.

In summary, the dry lands of Africa are large enough and have enough potential to constitute a very important area of food production. But at present they are a focus of concern for their present degraded condition, their decreasing productivity, and for the future well-being of the people and countries in which they are located.

Savanna: the wet–dry lands

Another large part of the continent (approximately 25 percent) constitutes the savannas. This is a wide transition zone between the rainforest and the dry lands. Natural vegetation is typically a mixture of grassland and scattered trees. On the drier margins the grasses are shorter and trees and shrubs are largely restricted to the river valley bottoms. On the wetter margins grasses are taller and woodland occupies a larger percentage of the land surface. The dry season in the savannas ranges from three months to more than seven, and rainfall totals are always 750 mm or greater.

It is somewhat difficult to generalize about the broad range of conditions found in these areas, but some generalizations are possible. First, all parts of the savanna zone have a significant period (three months or more) when there are moisture deficiencies. Along the drier margins of the savanna, in the drier years the savanna can fall within the semi-arid category, a soil-moisture deficit for the whole year can exist, and agricultural yields plunge. Under severe drought conditions the entire harvest can be lost.

In most parts of the savanna the dry period is so long that there is little or no moisture in the soil at the beginning of the rainy season, which is the beginning of the growing season for crops. This makes the incidence of the first rains and the spacing of individual storms at the beginning of the rainy reason as important, if not more so, than the total amount of annual precipitation. Likewise, as the growing season for the crops is usually longer than the rainy season the retention of soil moisture, for which nondegraded soils are required, is critical for successful harvests. Thus savanna areas as a whole are high-risk areas for rainfed agriculture. This has made savanna areas prime zones for water development projects, all of which have attempted to ameliorate the variability in the annual water supply.

The savanna areas have been the major zones for the extension of agriculture in the last three decades, and the recurrent seasonal problems outlined above, together with year-to-year variations in rainfall, are major obstacles to sustained levels of agricultural production from these zones.

The savanna region of Africa, as defined by its typical vegetation complex, has changed significantly over the last three to four decades. Clearing of forest on the wetter margins of the savanna has resulted in an extension of the grass-dominated vegetation complex in that direction, whereas desertification on the drier margins of the savanna has reduced its extent there. The savanna area as the habitat for wild game has also been significantly reduced in Africa. Although many African countries, particularly in eastern and southern Africa, have made major efforts to establish and maintain game parks, game outside the parks has been very much reduced by the spread of people and agriculture. Savanna game are becoming a rarity in West Africa and even in East Africa outside the established parks. However, other characteristics of the natural ecosystem still have a major impact on both small and large-scale farmers. Birds such as the quela-quela, which flock in millions, insects such as locusts and grasshoppers, animals such as wild pigs and monkeys, are all great destroyers of crops and farmers consider them a menace at least equal to drought.

The savanna areas are the location of major water-control projects in Africa, partly for hydropower, partly for water supply to urban areas, and sometimes for irrigation. As in the drylands man-made lakes are beneficial for specific economic activities, but they have created new habitats for disease and pests which can introduce new health problems into the areas. The Kariba and the Volta dams are good examples of both kinds of impacts.

The highlands

Some of the characteristics of the highlands have been discussed in connection with tropical forests, but a summary of their functions may be useful here. Although relatively small in area, the highlands are key components of Africa's natural systems. They are important areas of water surplus and constitute a large part of the flows of most eastern and southern African rivers. They are areas of good soils and support the most dense rural populations of the continent; they are now also areas which are under stress because of the greatly increased pressure of people on the land. They are important agriculturally both for food and export crops.

These key areas are especially important in eastern and central Africa. Kenya, Tanzania, Uganda, Ethiopia, Zimbabwe, Rwanda, Burundi, and Malawi are among the countries that depend heavily on the resources and production of these upland areas. The importance of the highlands of these and other countries emphasizes the concern for their continued productivity. These are key areas which require careful assessment and where the relationship of people to resources must be improved to ensure continued productivity.

Extratropical

Extratropical Africa is typified more by the environmental problems of "the modern world" than by those of the rest of Africa. The main exception to this is in the Black Homeland areas of South Africa, in Lesotho and in parts of Swaziland where unequal land allocation, overcrowded conditions, and lack of political power have combined to create widespread soil erosion and general resource degradation.

In southern Africa generally, mining is an important part of the economy of most countries. The resource and environmental problems of mining are generally understood and certainly result in land and water pollution, as well as locational air pollution and health hazards for the miners. Africans understand the negative effects of mining on the environment. Yet it is difficult in many cases to require mining corporations to invest in environmental safeguards. Recent low prices for many metals have greatly reduced revenue from some mining operations. If the necessary investment for environmental controls were required, many operations would cease to be profitable and would close. Given that the revenues from mining operations are often a very significant source of "hard" currency for many countries, environmental considerations are secondary to the short-term economic realities.

Additionally, mining in southern Africa has had a widespread impact on the economy and family livelihood patterns over a very wide area. Young men have for many decades migrated to engage in wage labor in the mines, typically leaving less able individuals to manage agriculture. Although it is true that in

385

many places women have traditionally provided much of the labor in rural areas, the removal of a significant percentage of the male population has clearly resulted in environmental problems. Home remittances in some cases have helped investment in the land and national economy but do not by any means always seem to have done so. The net impact of this major dislocation is difficult to judge. The abandonment of agricultural lands through labor shortages caused by the exodus of men to work in the mines in some instances has permitted brush vegetation to re-establish itself. The expansion of the tsetse fly into these former agricultural lands today limits their economic utility. Conversely, agriculture has needed to expand to meet the food demands of the urban mining areas. In areas where this expansion has occurred on marginal lands, the soil and water resources are generally deteriorating.

Urban Africa

In northern Africa urban growth and the concentration of industries along its periphery is resulting in a host of environmental problems. Pollution of the Nile and the Mediterranean, as well as more localized health and sanitation problems, are major issues. Throughout all of Africa, urban growth has become a major resource management focus in the last two decades. Towns all over the continent have typically grown at 7–8 percent a year and many appear to have passed important thresholds. With the increased and increasing number of cities of over 400,000 population, both the impact of the city on the surrounding countryside and the internal resource management within the city have grown greatly in importance.

Cities have typically had a negative effect on their surroundings because of their need of traditional energy sources (wood and charcoal) beyond the means of the local area to produce; they have in some cases had positive effects in stimulating agricultural production. But for political reasons the common case in most of Africa has been to subsidize food costs for urban areas. Generally this results in low prevailing food prices, which is good for the urban population. Yet a result of this policy is that agriculture is not very profitable, and large numbers of the rural population emigrate into urban areas in search of better economic opportunities. As a result, the increased demand for foodstuffs for urban areas is often satisfied by food imports, not by increased domestic food production. The low profitability of food growing is one reason why little investment is made in agriculture. This is clearly one important factor contributing to environmental deterioration in rural areas.

Internally public works have been unable to keep up with the rapid urban growth. Water and sanitation services are not able to meet minimal standards in the majority of urban areas. Cities are typically split between small areas with modern facilities and much larger areas with inadequate and deteriorating services. The rapid growth of many urban areas, along with the shortage of capital for investment in basic urban infrastructure, is resulting in a growing proportion of African cities being comprised of slums. Even though medical facilities are more accessible in urban compared to rural areas, the poor living conditions in the slums to a large degree offset the advantages of greater accessibility.

Water systems

The rivers of Africa provide the key to many of the continent's resource opportunities and also provide a clue to many of the continent's problems. Most river systems in Africa, as befits an old warped continental surface, are organized in large basins. The Nile, the longest river in the world, is dwarfed in discharge by the Zaire. The Niger, Zambesi, Senegal, Rufiji, are just a few of the other major fluvial systems. Because these rivers have large discharges and also experience sharp drops in gradient, rapids or waterfalls are common in most African river systems. Thus many of the streams have a high potential for hydropower development. But, conversely, they generally are not navigable in many portions. This has hindered many African rivers from developing into important transportation systems. Many African rivers are fed from relatively small water surplus areas and traverse drier water-deficit areas. These waterways have a considerable potential for irrigation. Sometimes, but not always, the riverine areas possess the best soils throughout Africa for irrigation.

The problems of river development are partially a function of scale. The perennial African rivers are generally large and most development projects on them are necessarily large scale. As the rivers are also long, they are international and long-term exploitation is only achieved effectively through international cooperation. Most countries have only one major river system; the development of that system can absorb most of the national attention. The Volta in Ghana, the Nile in Sudan and Egypt, and the Senegal in Senegal have tended to become the focus of development. The Nile is an example of a river system whose water is almost totally allocated for development, and disputes over relative allocations between countries are likely to occur. In river systems, the potential for pollution and unwise development is high and has a considerable future cost. The lakes of Africa are probably a potential resource but have not yet been adequately assessed and utilized.

The key to long-range African development lies heavily with the right mix of rainfall, agriculture, and supporting development from the present water systems. To define that right mix has so far proven hard.

Trends in African development

The theme of this book has been the resource situation in Africa in the light of the dominant patterns of change in the continent. This century and particularly the last three decades have been times of dramatic change and it is not possible to summarize all aspects of those transformations. Among the more important from the point of view of resources and resource utilization are the following:

- the growth and political changes, particularly those creating the colonial situation and the emergence in the 1950s and 1960s of independent states;
- the growth of export economies and their impact on food production;

- the growth in numbers of people, especially since the 1960s;
- the change in distribution of people, especially in high potential areas, in urbanized areas, and in marginal lands;
- the current development era with large sums of development aid often expended in large projects and for nonproductive purposes;
- the growth of cities and of industry;
- the spread of education and social and health services; and
- the spread and the curtailment (political) of communication.

The list could go on, but even at this point it provides some backdrop to a summary discussion of the most important resource development and environment issues that have emerged.

Critical development and environment issues for Africa

Food production

Can Africa feed itself? Why does it not do so? Is environment part of the problem? Africa is the only continent where per capita food production has dropped consistently in the past two decades. This fact is viewed by many as one of the most disturbing of continental trends and many different reasons have been put forward to explain it.

From the resource and environmental viewpoint alone it is a complicated question. Crop production experiments in northern Nigeria have shown that under controlled circumstances grain production per hectare in Africa can be as high as most places on Earth. However, Porter (1979) has shown that the basic productivity of maize in East Africa varies considerably from coastal areas (low) to mid altitudes (high) depending on the day and night energy balance in those areas. Some African soils are very fertile – especially those on volcanic uplands – and are capable of high levels of crop production. Others in alluvial basins have good potential but are subject to flooding or are very difficult to work. However, generally the red and yellow soils which cover much of the moist areas and the sandy soils which are found over large areas in drier Africa are not very fertile and even under modern farming technology are hard to work.

Moisture availability, especially at the beginning and end of the rainy season, is almost everywhere a problem and the unreliability of that moisture adds another dimension.

Once the crops are growing the problem of pests and diseases comes into focus. It is clear that the savanna and dry areas of Africa have a wide spectrum of pests, animals, and insects that can dramatically reduce yield.

Environment in Africa can in places be very conducive to food production, but over wide areas any productive activity has a special mixture of risks and problems. It is clear that many of these can in the long run be overcome but that at present the prevailing social, economic, and political conditions are not conducive to this happening easily. The current pattern of weather and climate greatly compounded the underlying trends and has served to highlight many basic problems. Lands tend to be overstressed during drier periods since the lack of surpluses requires needs to be met from each growing season. Most plans are based on the climates remaining stable or being more humid than recent conditions. A result of this has been that there have been shortfalls in expectations. More and more marginal lands are being brought under cultivation in an attempt to meet these shortfalls. Also deforestation has become a widespread phenomenon. One result is that land deterioration is a problem in dry areas and may be a less visible but a growing problem in moist uplands. Generally the tendency has been to focus on soil erosion, not on the underlying factors that have caused practices to result in accelerated erosion. There are millions of hectares of semi-arid land in Africa and, although these are of low potential productivity, there is, in many areas, room for the replacement of existing deteriorating cultivated lands with others of similar low quality. However, this substitution would be costly in terms of human, economic, and environment factors. In the long term the "mining" of the land resource in these areas will limit future options.

Of greater immediate concern is the problem of land deterioration in the more highly productive parts of Africa. These areas are much smaller, but they produce a very high percentage of most nations' food and export crops. A drop in their productivity through environmental degradation is hard to replace since most high-potential areas are already under cultivation. Once land degradation occurs in these areas it is difficult and costly to reverse.

The summary answer to the question of why Africa is having difficulty in feeding itself is a combination of:

(a) uncertainty of rainfall;
(b) a relatively small percentage of high-quality soils;
(c) a high level of insect and animal pests; and
(d) localized pressure on soil resources.

All of these points are important contributory factors to the problem of food production in Africa. But they are far from being the only factors. Issues of management, poverty, government investment, and political stability and effectiveness of aid programs are among the many other factors contributing to Africa's food production patterns.

Energy and environment

Most of the energy needs for the majority of the people in Africa are still met by the use of traditional fuels, especially wood and charcoal. As urban areas grow rapidly, electricity becomes an additional energy source for many people, used first only for lighting, then for cooking, and later for refrigeration and air-conditioning. As economies become more integrated and transport networks are set up, petroleum products become important factors in the energy equation.

Modern energy resources in Africa include petroleum, coal, and hydropower. The first two have been found in only a few areas on the continent and geologic conditions indicate that the potential for most areas is very limited. Petroleum products for most African countries are imported. Coal has a limited use outside the Republic of South Africa and in most areas is imported. Hydropower has a much wider potential. The physical nature of many African river basins provides good widespread opportunities for hydro-development. Rivers tend to develop single arteries and have steep gradients on many localized segments of their courses.

Potential hydro-energy is there, and quite often the sites are available for development. The Cabora Bassa Dam in Mozambique, the Akosonbo Dam in Ghana, the Roseires Dam in Sudan, the Manantali Dam in Mali, the Kafue Dam in Zambia, and the Jinga hydropower project at the Lake Victoria source of the Nile are all examples of electricity generation. Much more hydroelectric power potential exists in Africa, especially in the Zaire Basin.

But economic and environmental problems need to be solved before projects are begun. The nature of many of the river systems encourage – some would say necessitate – large dams, large projects, and large outputs of hydropower. One difficulty has been to find economic uses for the large output of power and to encourage the auxiliary investment needed to use the resource. Another problem has been the changes brought by such large projects to the people and environment of the area. A third problem has been the economic justification of large-scale hydro-development.

The change from potential to developed hydropower and the presumed eventual spread of modern power resources through much of rural Africa in the short term is beyond the capabilities of most African nations. For the rest of this century it seems likely that most rural and many urban people will continue to use wood and charcoal resources for heating and cooking. This fact gives rise to justifiable concern, especially around towns and cities and in the more densely peopled dry rural areas. The concerns are centered around the fact that the demand for wood and charcoal in these locations is growing much faster than the supply can grow and that existing market mechanisms do not seem to be working well in addressing the problem. Particularly around towns and cities the environmental impact of the problem has been obvious, intense, and not easily reversed in the short run. Costs of fuel have risen dramatically both in monetary terms and in environmental terms. But, because fuel reflects a basic necessity and its use is relatively inelastic, poor people have had to allot more of their time and money to obtain this basic need. This "other energy crisis" is *the* crisis for most rural African people and the problem will probably worsen in the near future.

Water and development

Figure 1.1 shows that most of Africa is arid or semi-arid. Water surplus areas outside the Zaire Basin comprise relatively small parts of the continent. In the chapters that deal with the drylands and savannas the climatic background to Africa's dryness is explained. For much of the continent the rainy season is shorter than the growing season, and the uncertainty of the pattern and amount of rainfall in any season is high.

In Chapters 9 and 11 we outline the nature of the river systems and water bodies of the continent and point out that in many parts of Africa a small water surplus area generates most of the water flow in the major rivers. This water then flows through water-deficit zones on the way to the ocean.

The Nile is a good example of this water-balance arrangement and illustrates a typical development response. A variety of mechanisms ranging from ancient technologies such as the *shaduf* to modern dam and irrigation canal distribution systems have been used to provide water to drylands. The Sudan and Egypt depend absolutely on these systems for a very significant part of their economy and food supplies.

Water is obviously a critical component in the economic life of most Africans and most African countries. The last few years have heightened our realization of the delicate "balance" between water availability and need as drought laid bare the fragile nature of many semi-arid and savanna production systems as they have evolved within the constraints of national policies of independent African nations.

No simple approach seems possible. Among the environmental concerns that are most pressing are:

(a) a better ability to predict climate and especially rainfall variation from year to year and from place to place;
(b) active development of crop varieties and animal husbandry systems appropriate to specific physical environments as well as the economic realities of the countries;
(c) a variety of approaches in using supplemental water for crops ranging from large-scale irrigation where appropriate, but also including much more prominently small-scale irrigation systems.

Improving health

Improved health is a very important component in the needs of most African people. Many of the diseases which are endemic are environment related. These range from the gastrointestinal diseases, the greatest killer of children in many areas, to malaria, schistosomiasis, and river blindness. Some health problems may be eased by the growth of numbers of people as habitats for the hosts are reduced. However, in most cases this is not so and in fact greater numbers of people in (and of) themselves create a network for the transmission of disease. Aids is a new and rapidly growing threat in Africa.

Among the most difficult of health environments are the rapidly growing urban areas where investment in modern water and sanitation systems cannot keep pace with city growth. There is an urgent need to look at alternative systems appropriate to the financial resources of the countries concerned. In both rural and urban areas, piped water into neighborhoods and villages has been seen as the single greatest breakthrough in moving to a new level of health. The sad situation is that this does not seem achievable for most African people in the near future.

Maintaining the resource base

Overriding all resource issues for Africa is the dilemma of two sometimes conflicting needs in the light of rapid population growth: the need for continued economic development and the need for maintaining the resource base. In many respects they ought not to be conflicting needs. In the long run the sustainability of economic development will depend on the maintenance and enhancement of the resource base. Hopefully it is only in the short run, but today, for most African cases, maintenance of the environment has been replaced by exploitation just to attempt to meet economic needs.

At the present time those parts of the resource base that are most vulnerable are:

(a) woody resources, especially in semi-arid and savanna areas;
(b) water resources in dry areas; and
(c) soil resources, especially in highland, savanna, and semi-arid locations.

Woodland resources are most threatened when areas of high demand for wood and charcoal are coincident with areas of low supply and slow plant growth potential. They are also threatened in areas of rapid agricultural expansion into tropical rainforest areas, such as in West Africa. As has been stated several times, even in this summary, wood resources around cities and towns are already obviously depleted. FAO and UNEP projections suggest that the problem will be widespread in dry areas by the end of this century if present trends are not arrested.

Water resources need to be maintained. In growing numbers of African water systems the ability to store and use water is hampered by the silt and other sediment contents of the water. Reservoirs quickly fill with sediment and within short periods hold less water than is needed. In addition, both large and small streams in some parts of the continent are now showing greater irregularity of flow, probably because removal of vegetation in the catchment has resulted in high immediate runoff and lower groundwater recharge. This change in the hydrologic cycle requires even greater storage facilities just to maintain present water availability. This, together with silt load problems, compounds the problem of improving the water resources for development.

In a few cases in Africa, water resources are close to being used to their maximum capacity and further allocation of water will need a reduction in some current uses. The Nile is a river where the main flow has become heavily allocated for use between Sudan and Egypt. Further needs have to be met by mechanisms for increasing flow, such as the draining of wetlands in the Sudd and control of the outflow from many of the Rift Valley lakes. Yet, end-water use from Lake Nasser and other dams is very inefficient and much water could be saved by improved management. The message for the future is, however, very clear. Water resources in most areas are finite; their use needs to be planned with a view to future as well as current benefits, and all aspects of use need integration and conservation. Pollution of water systems and water shortages are becoming important concerns in many parts of Africa.

Soil resources in Africa start off with generally modest levels of productivity, though some localities have a combination of soils and climate potentiality as productive as any in the world. Although it is difficult to generalize, the following three kinds of considerations appear to offer most concern in relation to problems of maintaining the soil resource base:

(a) areas of mechanized rainfed cultivation in semi-arid and savanna regions;
(b) areas of high potential soils in uplands; and

(c)   areas where grazing and agriculture compete for limited soil and water resources.

Under each of these circumstances there are documented cases of important deterioration in soil quality and in productivity. The rainfed agricultural lands of Sudan and the uplands of Ethiopia and along the Sahel/Savanna boundary in West Africa are examples of these three concerns.

The development of land-use systems that first arrest erosion and then restore the soil productivity in these areas is a critical issue for African agricultural and pastoral development.

Environment and development in Africa: the next two decades

What are the few vital trends in Africa over the next two decades and how will resource management be affected by those trends? The clearly defined and somewhat predictable trends are those concerning population. It is clear that population is very probably going to continue to increase steadily. It is also highly probable that urban growth will continue at rates above that of general population growth.

Climatic future trends are impossible to predict, but a certain scenario is for a continuing period of rainfall uncertainty in the drier parts of Africa. Even if mean annual rainfall totals increase, unless the soil and vegetation resources improve the dryland areas will have even greater difficulty in producing the food yields required to meet the needs of these areas.

Population growth will continue to exert pressure on existing and new agricultural land. There will continue to be dual pressures for food production and export growth. Great uncertainty exists concerning what will happen politically within most African countries. Clearly political stability is needed if economic development and environmental maintenance are to be coordinated. Mineral exports and industrial development will help some countries, but for the next two decades the soil and water resources and their products will provide the basis for most African economies.

Much of what will happen in the next two decades will depend on people and management, and the development of responses to problems. There are signs in Africa – by no means universal – that governments and donors are beginning to treat issues with the concern and certainty that they deserve. If this continues, there is hope that some of the very basic issues raised in this book may be addressed in some areas. The very seriousness of the problems of desertification, water management, wood and fuel supply, and soil resources may in itself be a factor in a new level of responsiveness. The best hope for the next two decades rests with the development of a new level of responsiveness. We need new levels of knowledge and understanding, we need more fact-finding and research, but most importantly we need new levels of individual governmental and institutional awareness. Unfortunately even the best scenario sees a period of continuing difficulty in issues of resource management in Africa.

References and bibliography

Acland, J. D. 1971. *East African crops*. Rome: FAO.

Adanson 1759. *A voyage to Senegal, the Isle of Gorre and the River Gambea*. London: Morse.

Aberibigbe, A. B. 1975. *Lagos – the development of an African city*. London: Longman.

Africa south of the Sahara 1984–85, Vol. 14. London: Europa Publications.

American Society of Agronomy 1982. *Soil erosion and conservation in the tropics*. Special Publication 43, American Society of Agronomy/Soil Science Society of America, Madison.

Anyadike, N. 1984. The white elephant of steel. *African Business* **68**, 45–8.

Balek, J. 1977. *Hydrology and water resources in tropical Africa*. Amsterdam: Elsevier.

Banda, H. K. 1971. My country's agriculture promise. *African Development* August, M6.

Beadle, L. C. 1974. *The inland waters of tropical Africa*. London: Longman.

Berggren, W. A. 1972. A Cenozoic time-scale: some implications for regional geology and paleobiography. *Lethaia* **5**, 195–215.

Berry, L. 1983. *East African country profile – Sudan*. Program for International Development, Clark University, Worcester, Mass.

Berry, L., T. Taurus and R. Ford 1980. *East African country profiles – Somalia*. Program for International Development, Clark University, Worcester, Mass.

Birot, P. 1966. *General physical geography*. London: Harrap.

de Blij, H. and E. Martin (eds) 1981). *African perspectives*. New York: Methuen.

Board, C., R. J. Davies and T. J. D. Fair 1970. *The structure of the South African space economy*. Regional Studies 4. Oxford: Pergamon.

Board of Trustees (IITA) 1975. *Annual report*. International Institute of Tropical Agricultural, Ibadan.

Boxer, B. 1978. Mediterranean action plan: an interim evaluation. *Science* **202**, 586.

Brown, L. H. and J. Cocheme 1973. *A study of the agro-climatology of the Highlands of Eastern Africa*. Technical note 125, World Meteorological Organization, Geneva.

Brunig, E. F. 1970. *Ecological studies in the Kerangas forests of Sarawak and Brunei*. Kuching: Borneo Literature Bureau.

Budyko, M. I. 1979. Climate aridity index. In *Desertification: its causes and consequences*, Secretariat, UN Conference on Desertification (ed.). Oxford: Pergamon.

Bureau National De Recensement 1982. *Recensement Génerál de la Population* (Census Summary Report), B. National de Recensement (Kigali).

Burton, R. 1863. *Wanderings in West Africa*. London.

Butzer, K. W. and C. L. Hanson 1968. *Desert and rivers in Nubia*. Madison: University of Wisconsin Press.

Butzer, K. W. 1974. Geological and ecological perspectives on the middle Pleistocene. *Quarternary Research* **4**, 136–48.

Carpenter, R. A. (ed.) 1983. *Natural systems for development*. New York: Macmillan.

Chambers, C. 1973. *Mwea: an irrigated rice settlement in Kenya*. Munich: Weltform.

Charney, J. G. 1975. Dynamics of deserts and drought in the Sahel. *Quarterly Journal of the Royal Meteorological Society* **101**, 193–202.

Chow, V. T. (ed.) 1964. *Handbook of applied hydrology*. New York: McGraw-Hill.

Clay, D. C. 1983. Resultats preliminaires de la phase pilote. *Enquête nationale (Rwanda) de l'Agriculture*. ISPC (US Bureau of Census), Washington, DC.

Club du Sahel 1983. *Drought control and development in the Sahel situation at the start of the*

1980s: overview and prospects. Paris: Organisation de Cooperation et de Developpement Economiques.

Cole, M. 1961. *South Africa*. New York: E. P. Dutton.

Consul General 1925. *Report by His Majesty's agent and consul general on the finance and administration of the Sudan*. London: HMSO.

Council on Environment Quality 1980. *The global 2000 report to the president*. Washington, DC: US Government Printing Office 1,2,3.

Curtin, P., S. Feierman, L. Thompson and J. Vansina 1978. *African history*. Boston: Little, Brown & Co.

Davidson, B. 1964. *The African past*. New York: Grosset & Dunlap.

Davidson, B. 1978. *Let freedom come*. Boston: Little, Brown & Co.

Department of Bantu Administration and Development 1975. *Map of South African Homelands*. Bureau for Economic Research and Bantu Development, Pretoria.

Department of Foreign Affairs (Transkei) 1976. *The Republic of Transkei*. Johannesburg: Chris van Rensburg.

Department of International Economic and Social Affairs 1978. *UN Demographic Yearbook, 1977*. New York: UN Press.

Department of International and Social Affairs 1979. *UN Demographic Yearbook 1977*. New York: UN Publishing Service.

Dietz, R. S. and J. C. Holden 1970. *The break-up of Pangaea in continents adrift-readings from scientific American*, J. T. Wilson (compiler). San Francisco: W. H. Freeman.

Downing, T. E. 1982. *Climate change, variability and drought in East Africa*. Publication No. 9. Worcester: Program for International Development, Clark University.

Doxiadis Associates 1964. Land use and water survey in Kordofan Province, Sudan. *Sudan Republic Bulletin* **N71**, 106–15.

Dunne, T. 1977. Studying patterns of soil erosion in Kenya. Soil conservation and management in developing countries. In *FAO soils bulletin*, **33**, 109–22. Rome: FAO.

Eckholm, E. P. 1976. *Losing Ground*. New York: W. W. Norton.

Economic Commission for Africa 1975. *Handbook for Africa 1975*. Addis Abada: ECA.

The Economist 1984. A survey of Zimbabwe, April 21, 15.

Environmental Development Action 1981. *Environment and development in Africa*. Oxford: Pergamon Press.

Ekpenyong, S. 1984. The effects of mining activities on a peasant community: a case study. *Development and Change* **15**, 251–71.

El-Swaify, S. A., E. W. Dangler and C. L. Armstrong 1983. *Soil erosion by water in the tropics*. Honolulu: Hitahr.

Elwell, H. A. 1980. *Design of safe rotational systems*. Harare: Department of Conservation and Extension.

FAO 1977. *Food production yearbook*, 31, Rome: FAO.

FAO 1980. *Food production yearbook*, 34, Rome: FAO.

FAO 1982. *Food production yearbook*, 36, Rome: FAO.

Farvar, M. T. and J. P. Milton (eds) 1972. *The careless technology*. Garden City, New York: The Natural History Press.

Gaitshell, A. 1959. *The Gezira: a story of development in the Sudan*. London: Faber & Faber.

Geiger, R. 1965. *The climate near the ground*. Cambridge, Mass.: Harvard University Press.

Glantz, M. H. (ed.) 1977. *Desertification*. Boulder, Colo.: Westview Press.

Government of Kenya 1979. *Republic of Kenya Statistical Digest*. Ministry of Economic Planning and Community Affairs, Nairobi.

Greenland, D. J. and R. Lal (eds) 1975. *Soil conservation and management in the humid tropics*. Chichester: Wiley.

Greenwald, S. 1968. Traditional farming and coconut schemes in the Tanga region. In *Smallholder farming and smallholder development in Tanzania*, H. Ruthenberg (ed). Munich: IFO Institut.

Griffiths, J. F. (ed.) 1972. *World survey of climates – Africa*, Vol. 10. Amsterdam: Elsevier.

Gritzner, G. 1981. *Environmental degradation in Mauritania – staff report*. Washington, DC: National Academy Press.

Grove, A. T. 1967. *Africa south of the Sahara*. Oxford: Oxford University Press.

Grove, A. T. 1978. *Africa*. Oxford: Oxford University Press.

Grove, A. T. 1981. *The climate of the Sahara in the period of historical records*. London: MENAS Press.

Guy, H. P. 1976. *Residential construction and sedimentation at Kensington, Md.* Miscellaneous Publication 970, Agricultural Research Service, Washington, DC.

Hallett, R. 1974. *Africa since 1875*. Ann Arbor, Mich.: University of Michigan Press.

Hance, W. A. 1975. *The geography of modern Africa*. New York: Columbia University Press.

Henning, D. and H. Flohm 1977. *Climate aridity index* (Budyko Ratio). Nairobi: UNEP.

Herbert, D. T. and N. B. Hijazi 1984. Urban deprivation in the developing world. *Third World Planning Review* **6**, 263–81.

Hill, R. D. 1983. Controlling the epidemic of hazardous chemicals and wastes. *Ambio* **12**, 86–90.

D'Hoore, J. L. 1954. *L'accumulation des sesquioxydes libres dans les sols tropicaux*. INEAC, Ser. Sc 62, 1–132.

D'Hoore, J. L. 1964. *Soil map of Africa*. Lagos: Commission de Co-operation Technique en Afrique au sud du sahara.

Hoy, D. R. (ed.) 1978. *Geography and development*. New York: Macmillan.

Huxley, P. A. 1981. *Agroforestry – developing a new research discipline*. Nairobi: ICRAF.

Ibrahim, A. M. 1975. The Jonglei development project 1975. *Sudan International* **1**, 46–9.

ILO (International Labor Organization) 1983. Conditions of work and the working environment. In *Sixth ILO African Regional Conference*. Report III, Tunis.

IUCN (International Union for Conservation of Nature and Natural Resources) 1981. *Conserving Africa's natural heritage*. Gland, Switzerland: CNPPA/IUCN.

Jackson, I. T. 1981. *Climate, water and agriculture in the tropics*. London: Longman.

Jaetzold, R. and H. Schmidt 1983. *Farm management handbook of Kenya*, vols I–V. Nairobi: Ministry of Agriculture.

Johnson, D. H. 1962. Rain in East Africa. *Quarterly Journal of the Royal Meteorological Society* **88**, 1–21.

Jones, W. I. and R. Egli 1984. *Farming systems in Africa: the great lakes highlands of Zaire, Rwanda, and Burundi*. Washington, DC: The World Bank.

Kagera Basin Organization/UNDP 1982. *Development programme of the Kagera Basin – final report*. Kigali: The Executive Secretariat of the KBO.

Kalms, J. M. 1975. Studies of cultivation techniques at Bouake, Ivory Coast. In *Soil conservation and management in the humid tropics*, D. J. Greenland and R. Lal (eds). Chichester: Wiley.

Kessa, M. 1972. Impact of River Schemes on the shoreline of the Nile Delta. In *The careless technology*, M. T. Farvar and J. P. Milton (eds). Garden City, Kans.: The Natural History Press.

King, L. C. 1967. *Morphology of the earth*. Edinburgh: Oliver & Boyd.

REFERENCES AND BIBLIOGRAPHY

Kjekshus, H. 1977. *Ecology control and economic development in East African history.* Berkeley: University of California Press.

Kraus, E. B. 1977. Subtropical droughts and cross equatorial energy transports. *Monthly Weather Review* **105**, 1009–18.

Lal, R. 1976. *Soil erosion problems on an Alfasol in western Nigeria and their control.* Monograph 1, IITA (International Institute of Tropical Agriculture), Ibadan.

Lasserre, G. and J. Menault, (eds) 1979. *Atlas du Burundi.* Paris: Ministere de la Coopération de la Republic Française.

Lewis, L. A. 1981. The movement of soil materials during a rainy season in western Nigeria. *Geoderma* **25**, 13–25.

Lewis, L. A. 1982. *Land degradation monitoring programme of the national environment and human settlements secretariat.* Program for International Development, Clark University, Worcester.

Lewis, L. A. 1984. *Progress report on assessing soil loss in Kiambu and Murang'a Districts in Kenya.* Program for International Development, Clark University, Worcester.

Linn, A. 1983. Saving the Mediterranean. In *Colliers yearbook*, 57–63. New York: Macmillan.

Maignien, R. 1958. Le cuirassement des sols en Afrique tropicale de l'Ouest. *Sols Afrique* **4**, 5–41.

Maddock, G. P. 1960. Stablecrops of Africa. *Geography Review* **V**, 523–40.

Man and Biosphere/UNESCO 1975. *The Sahel: ecological approaches to land use.* Paris: The UNESCO Press.

Mascarenhas, O. 1982. *River basin development in Eastern Africa.* Program for International Development, Clark University, Worcester.

McCauley, J. F., G. G. Schaber, C. S. Breed, M. J. Grolier, C. V. Haynes, B. Issawi, C. Elachi and R. Blom 1982. Subsurface valleys and geoarcheology of the Eastern Sahara revealed by shuttle radar. *Science* **218**, 1004–19.

Menault, J. (ed.) 1979. *Atlas du Burundi.* Bordeaux: Universite de Bordeaux.

Ministry of National Planning (Sudan) 1974–5. *Economic survey.* Khartoum: Ministry of National Planning.

Ministry of National Planning (Sudan) 1976–7. *Economic survey.* Khartoum: Ministry of National Planning.

Mongi, H. O. and P. A. Huxley (eds) 1979. *Soils research in agroforestry.* Nairobi: ICRAF.

Mohr, E. C. J., F. A. van Baren and J. van Schuylenborgh 1972. *Tropical soils.* The Hague: Mouton.

Monsted, M. and P. Walji 1978. *A Demographic analysis of East Africa – a sociological interpretation.* Uppsala: Institute of African Studies.

Morgan, W. T. W. 1969. *East Africa: its peoples and resources.* Nairobi, London, New York: Oxford University Press.

Morris, M. D. 1979. *Measuring the conditions of the world's poor.* Washington, DC: Overseas Development Council.

Murdock, G. P. 1960. Stable subsistence crops of Africa. *The Geographical Review* **50**, 523–40.

Murray-Rust, D. H. 1972. Soil erosion and reservoir sedimentation in a grazing area west of Arusha. *Geografiska Annaler* **54A**, 3–4.

National Research Council 1982. *Ecological aspects of development in the humid tropics.* Washington, DC: National Academy Press.

Nicholson, S. E. 1976. *A climatic chronology for Africa.* PhD thesis, University of Wisconsin, Madison.

397

Nicholson, S. E. 1978. Climatic variations in the Sahel and other African regions during the past five centuries. *Journal of Arid Environments* **1**, 3–24.

Nicholson, S. E. 1979. Revised rainfall series for the West African subtropics. *Monthly Weather Review* **107**, 620–3.

Nicholson, S. E. 1980. The nature of rainfall fluctuations in subtropical West Africa. *Monthly Weather Review* **108**, 473–87.

Nicholson, S. E. 1980. Sahara climates in historical times. In *The Sahara and the Nile*, M. A. J. Williams and H. Foure (eds). Rotterdam: A. A. Balkema.

Nicholson, S. E. 1981. Rainfall and atmospheric circulation during drought periods and wetter years in West Africa. *Monthly Weather Review* **109**, 2191–208.

Nicholson, S. E. 1983. Sub-Saharan rainfall in the years 1976–80: evidence of continued drought. *Monthly Weather Review* **111**, 1646–54.

Nicholson, S. E. and H. Flohn 1980. African environmental and climatic changes and the general atmospheric circulation – Late Pleistocene and Holocene. *Climatic Change* **2**, 313–48.

Nieuwolt, S. 1973. *Rainfall and evaporation in Tanzania*. BRALUP Research Paper No. 24, Bureau of Resource Assessment and Land Use Planning, Dar es Salaam.

Nieuwolt, S. 1977. *Tropical climatology*. Chichester: Wiley.

Nye, P. H. and D. J. Greenland 1960. *The soil under shifting cultivation*. Harpenden: Commonwealth Agricultural Bureaux.

Odingo, R. S. 1971. *The Kenya Highlands*. Nairobi: East African Publishing House.

Odingo, R. S. (ed.) 1975. *An African dam*. Ecological Bulletin 29, Swedish Natural Science Research Council, Stockholm.

Office of International Agriculture 1978. *Moisture conservation and utilization in low water rainfall areas of LDCs*. Corvallis: Oregon State University Press.

Oliver, R. and G. Mathew (eds) 1963. *History of East Africa*. Oxford: The Clarendon Press.

Omu, J. 1978. The Jonglei. *African Business* November, 14–15.

Organisation pour la Mise en Valeur du Fleuve Senegal 1975. *Assessment of environmental effects of proposed developments in the Senegal river basin*. Dakar: Societe Africaine d'Etudes Techniques.

Paden, J. N. and E. W. Soja (eds) 1970. *The African experience*, vol. 1: *Essays*. Evanston, Ill.: Northwestern University Press.

Page, J. D. 1978. *An Atlas of African History*. London: Edward Arnold.

Pereira, H. C. 1973. *Land use and water resources*. Cambridge: Cambridge University Press.

Porter, P. W. 1979. *Food and development in the semi-arid zone of East Africa*. Syracuse: Maxwell School of Citizenship and Public Affairs.

Pratt, D. J. and M. D. Gwynne 1977. *Rangeland management and ecology in East Africa*. London: Hodder & Stoughton.

Press, F. and R. Siever 1986. *Earth*, 4th edn. New York: W. H. Freeman.

Prioul, C. and P. Sirven (eds) 1981. *Atlas du Rwanda*. Paris: Ministere de la Coopération de la Republic Française.

Pritchard, J. M. 1979a. *Landform and landscape in Africa*. London: Edward Arnold.

Pritchard, J. M. 1979b. *Africa*. Burnt Mill, Essex: Longman.

Program for International Development 1980. *Trends and interrelationships in food, population, and energy in Eastern Africa*. Program for International Development, Clark University, Worcester.

Rapp, A., L. Berry and P. Temple (eds) 1972. *Studies of soil erosion and sedimentation in*

Tanzania. Dar es Salaam and Uppsala: BRALUP and Department of Physical Geography, University of Uppsala.

Richards, P. W. 1961. *Land, labour and diet in northern Rhodesia.* Oxford: Oxford University Press.

Richards, P. W. 1952. *The tropical rainforest.* Cambridge: Cambridge University Press.

Riquier, J. 1960. Les "lavaka" de Madagascar. *Bulletin Societé Géographic* **69**, 181–91.

Rodhe, H. and H. Virji 1976. Trends and periodicities in East African rainfall data. *Monthly Weather Review* **104**, 306–15.

Rougerie, G. 1961. Modelés et dynamiques de savene en Guinée orientale. *Etudes Africaines* **4**, 24–50.

Ruthenberg, H. 1971. *Farming systems in the tropics.* Oxford: The Clarendon Press.

Sada, P. O. and A. A. Adefolalu 1975. Urbanisation and problems of urban development. In *Lagos,* A. B. Aderibigbe (ed.). London: Longman.

Saunders, R. J. and J. J. Warford 1976. *Village water supply.* Baltimore, Md.: Johns Hopkins University Press.

Scientific American 1976. *Continents adrift and continents aground.* San Francisco: W. H. Freeman.

Secretariat of the Kagera Basin Organization 1979. *General background information on the planning for the development of the Kagera River Basin.* Kigali: Kagera Basin Organization.

Secretariat of the UN Conference on Desertification 1977. *Desertification: its causes and consequences.* Oxford: Pergamon.

Seidman, A. 1976. *The impact of copper production on environmental problems in Zambia* (mimeo).

Sharon, D. 1972. The spottiness of rainfall in a desert area. *Journal of hydrology* **17**, 161–76.

Simoons, F. J. 1960. *Northwest Ethiopia.* Madison: University of Wisconsin Press.

Smith, D. 1953. *Tree growth in Sudan.* Publication 3, Sudan Department of Forestry, Khartoum.

Sombrock, W. G., H. M. H. Braun and B. J. A. van Pouw 1982. *Exploratory soil map and agro-climatic zone map of Kenya.* Nairobi: Kenya Soil Survey.

Stock, R. F. 1976. *Cholera in Africa.* London: International African Institute.

Stocking, M. A. and H. A. Elwell 1973. Soil erosion hazard in Rhodesia. *Rhodesia Agricultural Journal* **70**, 93–101.

Stocking, M. A. 1978. Relationship of agricultural history and settlement to severe soil erosion in Rhodesia. *Zambezia* **6**, 129–45.

Symoens, J. J., M. Burgis and J. J. Gaudet (eds) 1981. *The ecology and utilization of African inland waters.* Nairobi: UNEP.

Tricart, J. 1972. *The landforms of the humid tropics, forests and savannas.* New York: St Martin's Press.

Udo, R. K. 1978. *A comprehensive geography of West Africa.* Ibadan: Heinemann Educational Books (Nigeria).

Udo, R. K. 1982. *The human geography of tropical Africa.* Ibadan: Heinemann Educational Books (Nigeria).

UN Conference on Desertification 1977. *Livelihood systems in dry areas.* New York: Pergamon.

UNDP (UN Development Program) 1966. *Multipurpose survey of the Kafue river basin.* Rome: FAO.

UNEP (UN Development Program) 1978. *Review of the areas of environment and development and environmental management,* UNEP Report 3, UNEP, Nairobi.

UNEP 1982. *The world environment: 1972–1982.* Dublin: UNEP.

UNESCO 1977. *Soil map of the world,* Vol. VI; *Africa.* Paris: UNESCO Press.

UNESCO 1978. *Tropical forest ecosystems*. Paris: UNESCO Press.

United States Secretary of State Advising Committee on the 1972 UN Conference on the Human Environment 1972. *Stockholm and beyond*. Washington, DC: US Government Printing Office.

Van Horn, L. 1977. The agricultural history of Barotseland, 1840–1974. In *The roots of rural poverty in central and southern Africa*, N. Parsons and R. Palmer (eds). Berkeley: University of California Press.

deVos, A. 1975. *Africa, the devastated continent?* The Hague: Dr. W. Junk bv Publishers.

Walker, B. H. 1975. Ecological constraints to growth in Rhodesia. *Rhodesia Science News* **9**, 3–5.

Waterbury, J. 1979. *Hydropolitics of the Nile valley*. Syracuse, NY: Syracuse University Press.

Webster, C. C. and P. N. Wilson 1980. *Agriculture in the tropics*, 2nd edn. New York: Longman.

Welcomme, R. L. 1976. Some general and theoretical considerations on the fish yields of African rivers. *Journal of Fish Biology* **8**, 351–64.

Wenner, L. G. 1980. *Soil conservation in Kenya*, 6th edn. Nairobi: Ministry of Agriculture.

Westphal, E. 1975. *Agricultural systems in Ethiopia*. Wageningen, The Netherlands: Center for Agricultural Publishing and Documentation.

White, G., D. Bradley and A. White 1962. *Drawers of water*. London: Oxford University Press.

Whitlow, J. R. 1980a. Agricultural potential in Zimbabwe. *Zimbabwe Agricultural Journal* **77**, 97–106.

Whitlow, J. R. 1980b. Environmental constraints and population pressures in the tribal areas of Zimbabwe. *Zimbabwe Agricultural Journal* **77**, 173–81.

Williams, M. A. J. and D. A. Adamson 1980. Late Quaternary depositional history of the Blue and White Nile rivers in central Sudan. In *The Sahara and the Nile*, M. A. J. Williams and H. Faure (eds). Rotterdam: A. A. Balkema.

Williams, M. A. J. and H. Faure (eds) 1980. *The Sahara and the Nile*. Rotterdam: A. A. Balkema.

Williams, M. A. J., J. O. Clark, D. A. Adamson and R. Gillespie 1975. Recent Quarternary record in central Sudan. *Bulletin ASEQUA (DAKAR)* **46**, 75–86.

Williams, O. 1981. Irrigation farming in the southeast lowveld of Zimbabwe. *Geography* **66**, 228–32.

Williams, O. 1981b. "South Africa" in *African Perspectives*, H. de Blij & E. Martin (eds). New York: Methuen, Inc.

Wischmeier, W. H. and D. D. Smith 1978. *Predicting rainfall erosion losses – a guide to conservation planning*. Washington, DC: United States Department of Agriculture.

World Bank 1978. *Accelerated development in sub-Saharan Africa: an agenda for action*. Washington, DC: World Bank.

World Bank 1981. *Accelerated development in sub-Saharan Africa: an agenda for action*. Washington, DC: World Bank.

World Bank 1982. *World development report 1985*. Washington, DC: World Bank.

World Bank 1985. *World development report 1985*. Washington, DC: World Bank.

Index